THE GREAT CELLISTS

THE GREAT CELLISTS

by

MARGARET CAMPBELL

Trafalgar Square Publishing
NORTH POMFRET, VERMONT

First published in the United States of America in 1989
by Trafalgar Square Publishing, North Pomfret, Vermont, 05053

First published in Great Britain 1988 by Victor Gollancz Ltd

© Margaret Campbell 1988

ISBN 0-943955-09-2

Library of Congress Catalog Card Number: 88-50782

Printed in Great Britain

Dedicated to the memory of
Helen Airoff-Dowling
Beloved friend and
constant source of
inspiration

ACKNOWLEDGEMENTS

MANY PEOPLE HAVE helped me in the writing of this book, but it would be impossible to name each one individually. I therefore offer my collective gratitude to all the musicians, writers and friends who have given of their time to grant me interviews, or who have loaned me documents. Each one has provided a piece to fit into the jig-saw that I hope presents a fair picture of the subject. They will, undoubtedly, recognize their individual contribution and know that I am indebted to them.

However, there are a few people who must be singled out for special mention. Armand d'Angour, Steven Isserlis and Sylvia Rotter who worked as honorary research assistants, Charles Beare for his valuable advice on master instruments, Nona Pyron for her generous provision of material regarding the early history of cello playing, Tomotada Soh for the background research in Japan, Keith Harvey for allowing me access to his archive recordings, Edmund Kurtz and Christopher Bunting for technical and general advice, much of which has been incorporated in the text, and the Violoncello Society of New York and Stephen Kates who ferreted out information on the other side of the Atlantic. In addition I would like to thank Anthea Baird of the Music Library at the University of London, Philip Robinson of the County Music Library, Welwyn Garden City, and the staff of the Public Library at Hemel Hempstead.

Finally I am grateful to my husband who has played second fiddle to this project for several years, and nonetheless encouraged me throughout.

Acknowledgement is made to the following publishers and copyright-holders for quoted material: Applebaum, Samuel and Sada, *The Way They Play*, Paganiniana, New Jersey 1973–1983; Brown, David, *Tchaikovsky: A Biographical and Critical Study Vol II: The Crisis Years (1874–78)*, Gollancz, London 1982; Burney, Charles, *A General History of Music* Vols I and II, Foulis, London 1935; Cowling, Elizabeth, *The Cello*, Batsford, London 1975; De'ak, Steven, *David Popper*, Paganiniana, New Jersey 1980; Fuchs, Carl, *Musical and Other Recollections*, Sherratt & Hughes, Manchester 1937; Gavoty, Bernard, *Pierre Fournier*, Kister, Geneva 1956, and *Antonio Janigro*, Kister, Geneva 1962; Ginsburg, Lev, *History of the Violoncello*,

Paganiniana, New Jersey 1983; Grove, *Dictionary of Music and Musicians*, 5th and 6th ed., Macmillan and St. Martin's Press, London and New York 1954 and 1980; Harrison, Beatrice, *The Cello and the Nightingale*, ed. Patricia Cleveland-Peck, Murray, London 1985; Itzkoff, Seymour W., *Emanuel Feuermann, Virtuoso*, University of Alabama Press, *c.*1979; Kahn, Albert E., *Joys and Sorrows*, Eel Pie, Chichester 1970; Kennedy, Michael, *Barbirolli*, MacGibbon & Kee, London 1971; Piatigorsky, G., *Cellist*, Da Capo, New York 1965; Pleeth, W., *The Cello*, ed. Nona Pyron, Macdonald, London 1982; Rothschild, Germaine de, *Luigi Boccherini: His Life and Work*, trans. Andreas Mayor, Oxford 1965; Shaw, G.B., writings, various, The Society of Authors on behalf of the Estate of George Bernard Shaw; *The Strad*, Novello, London 1898–1986; Temianka, Henri, *Facing the Music*, Alfred, California 1980; Tortelier, P. & Blum, D., *A Self-Portrait*, Heinemann, London 1984; Van der Straeten, A.E., *History of the Violoncello, the Viola da Gamba, their Precursors and Collateral Instruments*, Reeves, London 1914; Violoncello Society, *Newsletters*, New York, 1968–1984; Wordsworth, William (ed), *Jacqueline du Pré: Impressions*, Granada, London 1983.

M.C.

CONTENTS

Introduction   15

Prelude: The Tools of the Trade   21

I   The Birth of the Butterfly   29
Bononcini—Vandini—Linigke—Alborea—
Dall' Abaco—Cervetto

II   Berteau and the Duports   34
Berteau—Barrière—Corrette—Cupis—
Bréval—J. P. Duport—J. L. Duport

III   The French Influence   42
Janson—Baudiot—Levasseur—Lamarre—
Platel—Norblin—Franchomme—Delsart—
Vaslin

IV   The Forgotten Genius: Boccherini   48

V   Enter the English   55
Saunders—Johnson—Hallet—Crosdill—
Cervetto—Lindley

VI   Father of the German School: Romberg   61
Schlick—Romberg

VII   The Dresden School   66
Dotzauer—Kummer—Dreschler—Lee—
Schuberth—Cossman—Goltermann—
Grützmacher

VIII   The Dresden Influence   74
Klingenberg—Hausmann—Fitzenhagen—
Lebell—Hegar

IX   'Paganini of the Cello': Servais   78

X   Belgium and Holland   82
Chevillard—Franco-Mendes—Appy—Batta—
F. De Munck—E. De Munck—de Swert—van
Biene—Jacobs—Hollman—Mossel—
C. Hekking—A. Hekking—G. Hekking—
d'Archambeau—Maas

XI   'Czar of Cellists': Davidov   90

Wielhorsky—Davidov—Wierzbilowicz—
Brandoukov—Cherniavsky—Hambourg
XII   The Bohemian Touch   96
Neruda—I. H. Mara—J. B. Mara—Reicha—
Fiala—A. Kraft—N. Kraft—B. W. Stiastny—
J. Stiastny—J. N. Hüttner—J. Schmidt—
F. Hegenbarth—Wihan—Zelenka
XIII   'Sarasate of the Cello': Popper   104
XIV   'Grand Master of the Cello': Piatti   110
XV   The Twin Peaks: Klengel and Becker   116
Klengel—Becker—Grümmer—Fuchs—Diem—
Van der Straeten
XVI   The British Element   125
Libotton—Howell—Whitehouse—Stern—
Squire—Walenn—James—Barbirolli—Cameron
XVII   'Freedom with Order': Casals   133
XVIII   The European Vanguard   143
Herbert—Willeke—Britt—Rosanoff—
Bolognini—Eisenberg—Schoenfeld
XIX   Across the Atlantic: Salmond   153
Salmond—Saidenberg—Cole—Shulman
XX   'The Jewel in the Crown': Feuermann   160
XXI   The Last Great Romantic: Piatigorsky   169
XXII   The Unique View   175
Alexanian—Feder—Matz—Silva—Janigro
XXIII   Versatility par Excellence: Greenhouse and Rose 185
XXIV   The Italian Quartet   192
Cassadó—Mainardi—Baldovino—Aldulescu
XXV   Ladies on the Bass Line   200
Cristiani—Platteau—Eveline—Mukle—
Suggia—Harrison
XXVI   The French Tradition   210
Maréchal—Navarra—Fournier—Tortelier—
Gendron
XXVII   American by Choice   223
Scholz—Rejto—Starker
XXVIII   From Russia—with Talent   232

Garbousova—Nelsova

XXIX   The Japanese Phenomenon   241
        Saito—Inoue—Hirai—Tsutsumi—Yasuda—
        Iwasaki—Kanno—Fujiwara—Yamazaki

XXX   The British Heritage   252
        Reiss—Butler—Hooton—Pleeth

XXXI   The Continuing Line   261
        Dickson—Bunting—Fleming

XXXII   Russia—Home and Away   269
        Kurtz—Kubatsky—Kosolupov—Shafran—
        Gutman—Maisky

XXXIII The Russian Dynamo   281
        Rostropovich

XXXIV   The Art of the Necessary   290
        Wenzinger—Markevitch—Harnoncourt—
        Bylsma

XXXV   Scandinavia and Europe   297
        Bengtsson—Palm—Goritsky—Schiff

XXXVI   'Excellent is Enough'   302
        Parnas—Kates—Kirshbaum—Rosen—
        Walewska

XXXVII The Rose Line   312
        Harrell—Foster—Ma

XXXVIII The Sunset Touch: du Pré   321
        Coda   327
        Notes   331
        Selected Bibliography   337
        Chronology   340
        Index   343

ABBREVIATIONS

The following are used in the course of the book:

CEMA   Council for the Encouragement of Music and the Arts,
        (now ACGB).
ENSA   Entertainments National Services Association
ESTA   European String Teachers Association
GSMD   Guildhall School of Music & Drama
LPO   London Philharmonic Orchestra
LSO   London Symphony Orchestra
NBCSO   National Broadcasting Corporation Orchestra, NY,
        USA
NHKSO   Japanese Broadcasting Association
RAM   Royal Academy of Music
RCM   Royal College of Music
RPO   Royal Philharmonic Orchestra
VSNL   Violoncello Society of New York, *Newsletter*

LIST OF ILLUSTRATIONS

Following page 128

The cello played in horizontal position, from a fresco at Roccapietra near Varallo (*photo Nona Pyron*)

Family making music, by Jan Miense Molenaer, mid–17th century

'The Quartette Party', 18th century (*courtesy Beare and Son*)

Giacobo Basevi detto Cervetto (*courtesy Nona Pyron*)

J. L. Duport, from a drawing by J. Denon

Robert Lindley, from an original lithograph by Charles Baugniet (*courtesy Keith Harvey*)

Benjamin Hallet (*print from a painting by Thomas Jenkins*)

Alfredo Piatti

David Popper

Hugo Becker

Julius Klengel (*courtesy Edmund Kurtz*)

Carl Fuchs

1898: The young Casals in a string quartet led by Crickboom, with Galvez (vla) and Rocabrunna

The young Beatrice Harrison with Elgar (*courtesy Sylvia Cleveland-Peck*)

May Mukle (*courtesy Lyndon de Lecq Marguerie*)

Felix Salmond, caricature by Virginia Quarles Wendt (*courtesy of the artist*)

Diran Alexanian (*courtesy Edmund Kurtz*)

Following page 224

Beatrice Harrison with her dogs (*courtesy Sylvia Cleveland-Peck*)

Emanuel Feuermann with Franz Rupp (*courtesy Franz Rupp*)

Guilhermina Suggia (*courtesy Lyndon de Lecq Marguerie*)

André Navarra (*photo Gordon Clarke, Sydney*)

Thelma Reiss (*courtesy Thelma Reiss*)

Maurice Gendron (*photo Margaret Campbell*)

Gregor Piatigorsky (*courtesy Keith Harvey*)

Bolognini's cello (*courtesy Smithsonian Institution, photo No. 81–3367*)

Zara Nelsova (*photo Christian Stainer, courtesy Herbert Barrett Management*)

Hideo Saito (*photo Akira Kinoshita, courtesy Kajimoto Concert Management*)

Tsuyoshi Tsutsumi (*photo Akira Kinoshita, courtesy Kajimoto Concert Management*)

Janos Starker (*photo Margaret Campbell*)

William Pleeth

Lawrence Foster shortly before his death (*photo Fabian Bachrach*)

Mstislav Rostropovich (*courtesy Lyndon de Lecq Marguerie*)

Jacqueline du Pré with Sergio Peresson (*photo Adrian Siegal, courtesy Sergio Peresson*)

INTRODUCTION

IF THIS BOOK were true to its title, there would be only half a dozen names of real significance. It all depends how we define 'greatness'. Some are great because they dazzle by their virtuosity, others achieve greatness through innate musicianship. There are those who have made radical changes in the presentation of programmes, or in the instrument itself. The Belgian, François Servais, revolutionized cello playing in the late nineteenth century by the introduction of the end-pin or spike. Until this time the cellist held the instrument between his knees, with the weight resting on the calves. Servais invented the end-pin because he grew too fat to hold the instrument in the traditional fashion.

Then there are the great teachers, or teachers who have taught the great—an important contribution, not to be overlooked. Pablo Casals was a great cellist who would doubtless have continued to follow a highly successful performing career had not the political disaster in his own country prompted his decision to go into exile. In many ways the fact that he retreated from the limelight, and concentrated his energies on studying the capabilities of his instrument, was of even greater benefit to the musical world at large. After the inception of the festivals at Prades and later Puerto Rico, the world came to him.

If we can therefore take the term 'great' in a broad sense, so as to encompass the wide range of talent that, over the centuries, has contributed to the development of cello playing, we must include many musicians who play a smaller but nonetheless important part.

This is not only a book about the history of cello playing, but also about players as *people*. There have been many changes over the centuries in style, taste and in the instrument itself. Social conditions have had considerable influence on the lives of the musicians and we can trace their progress from being servants of the court or church to the freedom of the concert platform as we know it today. I believe that this is all reflected in the lives of the cellists themselves.

During my researches I have read a number of books, waded through a great deal of correspondence and consulted endless press reviews spanning three centuries. I have listened to hundreds of recordings and have attended as many concerts. One overriding conclusion I have reached is that the *raison d'être* of every cellist is the collection of J. S. Bach's Six Solo Suites. It is the cornerstone of the repertoire and many admit they could spend the rest of their lives studying and playing them. They are the works most often quoted in interviews.

I have also discovered some interesting sidelights. Throughout the centuries, cellists seem to beget cellists. In some families it is the chosen instrument for generation after generation, and to find virtuosity in both father and son is not uncommon. This is not true of violinists. The only example in the history of that instrument is David and Igor Oistrakh.

Generally speaking, cellists appear to be knowledgeable about almost every aspect of cello playing, and are also interested in many subjects outside music. There is a refreshing absence of the rivalry that occurs in so many other sections of the musical profession. Many cellists have been included in this book because their colleagues recommended me to hear them or listen to their records.

It would be interesting to investigate more fully the reasons for the brotherhood among cellists, but one is that the cello is the root of the harmonic structure. In a string quartet, a fine leader will receive the accolades, but he owes a great deal more to a first class cellist than is generally admitted. The cello's clarity in expression is vital because it controls the entire rhythmic balance.

Another aspect, irrespective of solo or orchestra playing, is that the cellist is always seated. The instrument is cradled by the body and is connected to the floor by its spike. In a sense, the cellist shares a partnership with the instrument that—apart from a few exceptions—discourages a *prima donna* approach.

The teacher-pupil relationship is as important as that of the great violinists, with the principles and style being handed down from one generation to another. In the case of the cellists it is more convoluted and therefore difficult to link to a main root. Since the various influences tend to flow from one country to another, there is, for the most part, no option but to treat them geographically.

Nevertheless, whatever their origins, the cellists have proved a fascinating body of people. There have been scholarly cellists, inebriates, gamblers and gourmets. Two of the 'great' were originally prize fighters. Whatever else may be said about the players of the 'bass' violin, they are never dull.

Piccotts End   Margaret Campbell
1987

THE GREAT CELLISTS

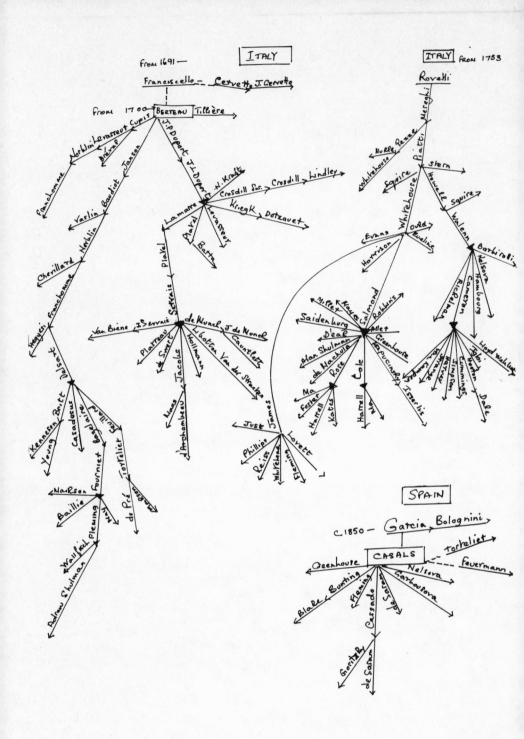

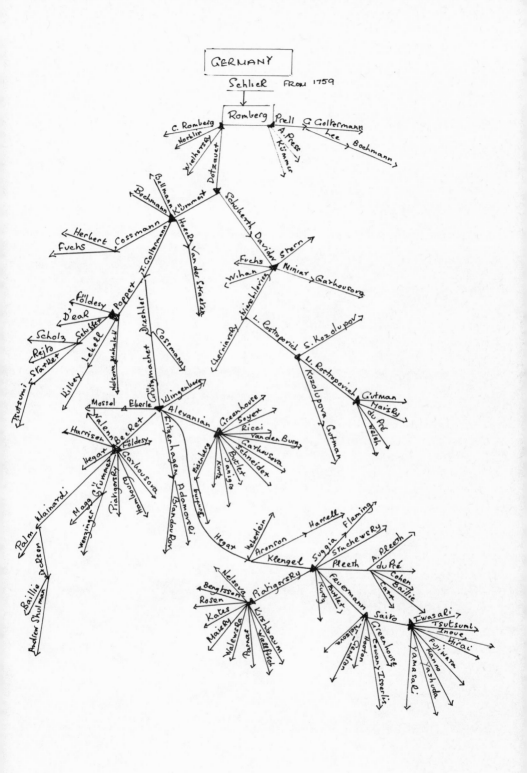

PRELUDE

The Tools of the Trade

THE HISTORY OF the earliest bowed stringed instruments is deeply rooted in folklore and legend. The first examples came from India and the Far East, and the most likely ancestor of the violin family is the three-stringed rebec brought to Spain from Arabia in the ninth century. From this time ancient paintings and sculptures provide evidence of further development.

Clearly, there have been two families of instruments, side by side, for many centuries; the fretted viols which are pear-shaped with sloping shoulders, and the unfretted violin—violin, viola and violoncello—designed on two overlapping circles. These differences can be seen in paintings where cello and viola da gamba are depicted side by side together with hybrid instruments combining the qualities of both families.

The violin, in archetypal form, was known in the late twelfth or early thirteenth century, whereas the 'bass' violin did not arrive until the fifteenth century. This late introduction of the cello stems from the 'sound ideal' in Western Europe in the Middle Ages which, until the fifteenth century, was high-pitched and nasal. Singing then resembled the sound we associate with Eastern music today. The instruments used to accompany them were designed with this sound in mind, so there was no call in music for the bass voice.

Around 1450, composers of the Flemish school began to use a lower and lower, vocal range. Bass parts appear for the first time in musical notation and, having achieved their own line, the need arose for bass instruments—hence the viola da gamba and the 'bass' violin. Both instruments coexisted for almost three centuries, and happily fulfilled their separate functions. The viola da gamba had an independent life as a solo instrument that went far beyond the life of the other viols, and enjoyed this status until the middle of the eighteenth century.

For generations there has been the mistaken idea that the cello is a descendent of the viola da gamba—a member of the viol family.

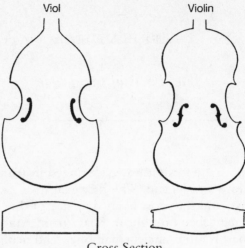

Cross Section

Fortunately few subscribe to this concept today, but in the past, most writers on the subject place too much emphasis on the influence of the gamba on the cello.

The early cello had three or four strings, usually tuned in fifths, whereas the viol had five or six strings tuned in fourths with a third between the middle strings. There are other structural differences which affect the sound of both instruments. The back and belly of the violin are distinctly arched whilst the viols have flat backs and only slightly curved bellies. The ribs of the violin tend to be narrower than those of the viol, and the sound-holes on the violin are *f*-shaped, whereas on the viol they are c-shaped; however you play a cello and a viola da gamba they will never sound the same.

By the beginning of the sixteenth century, bass violins were commonplace and came in roughly three sizes corresponding to the bass, baritone and tenor voices. These were held either on the ground, resting between the calves, or across the breast. For the instruments of the violin family, the bow was held in an overhand (palm-down) manner as is the violin-bow today. The viols, due to their Arabic influence, were bowed underhand (palm-up). In early terminology the violins were called 'viole da braccio' (arm viols) and the viols 'viola da gamba' (leg viols). As can be seen from the illustration facing p.128, the smaller 'viole da braccio' were held across the breast and the larger ones in an upright position. For instruments used in church processions, a small hole was bored in the centre of the back to which a cord or ribbon was attached, by which it was suspended from the player's neck and was held across his breast. This was probably the instrument which was called a 'viola da spalla'.

Not only did the bass instrument arrive late but it was also given many different names. The largest of the violin family was at first known as the 'violone', to which the Italians added the diminutive 'violoncino', so that by the 1640s we have the small violone called variously violoncino, violonzino, violonzelo, violoncelo and finally 'violoncello'. The shortened version, 'cello', in use today was quoted by C. P. E. Bach in 1765. In the north of Europe, the name 'violone' was also used for the largest member of the viol family, whilst 'bass violin'—except in Italy—remained popular well into the eighteenth century. In London, Walsh, the publishers, replaced the term 'bass-violin' with 'violoncello' in 1737.

The first known maker of the cello was Andrea Amati (*c.*1505–*c.*1577), founder of the Cremonese school of violin makers and of the dynasty that bore his name. The most historically famous of his cellos is the 'King' Amati, ordered by Pope Pius V and given to Charles IX for his Chapel. A magnificent instrument, it is painted and gilded with arms, devices and mottoes. It is thought to be one of eight basses (cellos) included in a total of 38 instruments ordered by the king from Amati. At the time of the Revolution in 1790, the 'King' Amati was said to have been in use at the court of Louis XVI. On 6/7 October the mob destroyed the whole set—24 violins (12 large and 12 small), 6 tenors (violas), and 8 basses (cellos). Three violins, a viola and the 'King' Amati were later recovered. During the Napoleonic era the instrument was owned by Jean Louis Duport, a member of Napoleon's Band, and the finest cellist of his day. Over the years it has suffered some damage but is still in a remarkable state of preservation. It has a rich and powerful sound and is basically the same as today's cellos but had to be reduced in size to suit modern requirements. Its present owner is the Belgian gambist, Wieland Kuijken.

The founder of the Brescian school of violin making, Gasparo da Salò (*c.*1540–1609) (real name Bertolotti, called da Salò after his birthplace on Lake Garda), certainly made some cellos but very few have survived. A fine example dated 1580 is in the possession of a British cellist, Vivian Couling.

Giovanni Paulo Maggini (1580–1632), da Salò's pupil, made a few fine cellos, both large and small models, all of which have the double purfling that is characteristic of the Brescian school.

Nicolò Amati (1596–1684), Andrea's grandson, brought the art of violin making to a very high level, and his cellos were greatly sought after. Alfredo Piatti owned one and several prominent players today favour the Amati sound. His instruments were all large models, but most have since been reduced in size.

It was Nicolò Amati's pupil, Antonio Stradivari (1644–1737), who brought the Cremonese school to a peak of achievement that was never surpassed. His instruments remain today objects of beauty, both visually and acoustically. In their book published in 1902, the Hill brothers estimated that before 1700 Stradivari made at least 30 cellos, of which 25 have been traced. These were exclusively of large size and all but one, the 'Castelbarco' dated 1697, have had their dimensions reduced.

At the turn of the century, Stradivari began to direct his inventiveness towards the problems of the cellist. Maggini and other Cremonese makers had made smaller instruments to meet the demands of the increasing number of virtuoso cellists. Stradivari's first concessions to this trend came in 1699/1700, but about 1707–10 he began making smaller cellos, and these have served as a model for almost every maker since the beginning of the last century. He made about twenty cellos in what is known as his 'Golden' period. They have an extraordinary quality of sound that carries through a hall even when played pianissimo, coupled with immediacy of response and swelling power.[1] In the last ten years of his life Stradivari made narrower cellos and, although excellent instruments, they are not to be compared with the 'Duport' and others of the same period. Many of today's famous cellists own these instruments, and they will be mentioned in the relevant chapters.

The Ruggieri and Rogeri families were all distinguished makers of cellos. Of the Bergonzi family only two are known. Giovanni Grancino, from Milan, made instruments with a powerful voice that sound well in large concert halls. Matteo Gofriller, who worked in Venice, is celebrated for cellos that are beautifully strong and resonant: both Casals and Feuermann played Gofrillers for many years. Domenico Montagnana (1690–1750), also from Venice, and a disciple of Stradivari, produced some big, strong-toned instruments which are particularly suitable for players with a large physique: Piatigorsky owned a Montagnana. Giovanni Battista Guadagnini (1711–86) worked in Cremona, Parma and Turin, and made some excellent cellos—not large but with a warm and sonorous voice. Francesco Pressenda (1777–1854), a pupil of Guadagnini, and

Giuseppe Antonio Rocca (1807–65), Pressenda's apprentice, produced some beautiful cellos.

The most famous name in the Austrian school is Jacob Stainer (*c.* 1617–83), whose instruments are distinguished by the high arching of their bellies, and scrolls carved in the shape of lion's heads. There was a time—around the late eighteenth century—when Stainer's instruments were considered superior to those of Stradivari. David Tecchler was another fine Tyrolean maker who settled in Rome and whose cellos were made in the new styles of Amati and Stainer.

William Forster (1739–1806), Thomas Dodd (1760–*c.* 1820) and John F. Lott (1775–1853), were British makers who have left some beautiful examples of their work to posterity.

In the nineteenth century the French school of violin making was highly regarded and its cellos possessed a remarkable resonance. Two of the first important makers were Nicolas Lupot (1758–1824) and Pierre Silvestre (1801–59). The best known, Jean-Baptiste Vuillaume (1798–1875), was a prolific copier. He also happened to be the most celebrated dealer in Paris. So convincing were his instruments that owners often mistook them for their originals. Paganini was said to have been taken in by Vuillaume's copy of his 'Cannon' Guarneri del Gesù violin. Other French makers of good cellos were Gand, Bernardel and Miremont.

Among the most outstanding contemporary makers of cellos are Francesco Bissolotti (b. Cremona 1929), his ex-pupil, Vanna Zambelli (b. Cremona 1953) and Carl Becker Jnr. of Chicago (b. 1919). Sergio Peresson (b. Udine, Italy 1913), now living in Philadelphia, made the fine, strong-toned cello that Jacqueline du Pré used for all her concerts and recordings during the last two years of her performing life. A young English maker who has produced some good cellos is Martin Bouette (b. 1951).

Finally, it would seem useful to look at the current phenomenal interest in authentic performance on original instruments. In recent years, the so-called 'Baroque' cello has come into its own with many accomplished players.

However, there seems to be some confusion as to what a 'Baroque' cello really is. To many, it is thought to be an ancient instrument which later gave way to the modern cello. This could not be farther from the truth. The cello *per se* has remained in the same form for over four centuries. The name 'Baroque' was given in the latter half of the present century to distinguish it from the modern cello. The cellos made by Stradivari, Amati and their

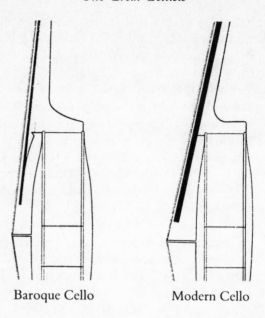

Baroque Cello   Modern Cello

contemporaries were, in fact, baroque instruments but their fittings
have been modified to meet the demands now placed upon them. In
other words they are 'set-up' differently. Nona Pyron's diagrams[2]
show how the two instruments are at variance. With the development of the piano in the late eighteenth century, and the consequent
search for a more brilliant and penetrating sound, string players had
to look for a way to increase volume if they were to compete in the
playing of chamber music. By the turn of the eighteenth century,
modifications were already taking place. The neck was canted back
and the bridge heightened, whilst the fingerboard was lengthened to
facilitate playing in the higher positions. The result was that a more
brilliant sound was obtained. When, in the twentieth century, metal
strings began to replace the normal gut (many cellists, today, still
use gut strings on *modern* instruments), the sound became even more
penetrating.

In the mid-eighteenth century there seemed to be a change of taste
in playing style that demanded a longer line, greater dynamic variety
and short springing strokes. It was natural that cellists should look
for new ways of achieving these effects. The Tourte bow, with its
curve in direct opposition to the bridge and greater tension of the
hair, could achieve all the subtlety and power that was required by
contemporary composers.

The perfection of the modern bow by François Tourte (1747–

1835) in the late eighteenth century, and its consequent influence on contemporary performance practice, cannot be overestimated. The early bow, which, for convenience, can be called 'Baroque', was not replaced overnight. Throughout the eighteenth century it appeared in various forms, from early to transition, until Tourte completely reversed its outward curve. In short, the early bow had less tension and responded to the shape of the bridge so that it almost caressed the strings, coaxing from them a gentle but rich sound. In baroque music, where articulation and light strokes were of the greatest importance, the outward-curved bow created just the right resonance.

These two factors, then, were the most significant influences on the instrument. There were others which also had a bearing on performing styles, but they will be dealt with chronologically and related to the cellists concerned.

CHAPTER I

The Birth of the Butterfly

MOST OF THE history books claim that the early cellists led fairly unexciting lives, employed purely in accompanying. Not until Boccherini in the eighteenth century were they supposed to have seen music approaching virtuoso quality. Certainly the cellist's main role was to provide the accompaniment for singers and instrumentalists, but it was an invaluable part of any musical performance. Cellists needed a greater knowledge of music than their soloist colleagues, often coming to the rescue of singers by filling in with skilful improvisation when memory lapses occurred. At such times they were invited to play 'short preludes and embellishments' but were advised to 'be modest therein, and use . . . ornamentations at the proper time and with taste'.[1] The method recommended by the Paris Conservatoire in 1804 points out that in order 'to accompany a recitative well one must have a perfect knowledge of harmony as well as of the violoncello'.[2]

In any case, it is unlikely that the cellist would have sat alongside his colleagues listening to virtuoso playing on the violin and viola da gamba, merely accepting the lesser role. The gamba, as we know, had always enjoyed a virtuoso repertoire: Simpson's 'Divisions on a Ground' (1667) is still considered difficult, even by modern standards.

Recent research has proved that long before the eighteenth century there were solo performers on the cello whose virtuoso facility matched that of their fellow musicians on the violin. The assumption that nothing exciting was written for the solo cellist before Boccherini, and therefore no soloists existed, is one of those recurring myths perpetuated by generations of plausible writers.

This misconception arises because, although the virtuoso repertoire for the violinist (by way of the sonata and related forms) had blossomed in the early seventeenth century, there was no similar provision for the cellist. From the late eighteenth century onwards it has therefore been assumed that the cello was a primitive instrument which could provide nothing better than the *basso continuo* line, until Boccherini, 'discovering its solo potential, transformed the caterpillar of the violin family into a butterfly'.[3]

Since cellists were considered 'bass' violinists, when a piece of violin music took their fancy they simply transposed it down, tackling it with the same dexterity as any contemporary violinist. It is therefore easier to understand why a cello repertoire never emerged and also why eighteenth-century cellists were conversant with the treble clef.

The first known reference to the violoncello in France is in Jambe de Fer's *Epitome Musicale* (1556), and the earliest mention of a cello performance in that country is in the orchestra of the Ballet Comique de la Reine in 1581. In the seventeenth century, the violin family of instruments were used in the 'Vingt-Quatre Violons du Roi' established by King Louis XIII, and, later, cellists played alongside gambists in Lully's orchestra at the French Court.

However, cello playing in the sixteenth and seventeenth centuries was dominated by Italy. It was around 1620 that the first generation of composers for the violin emerged in that country, coinciding with the development of the idiomatic technique for the instrument. Since the cello was the 'bass' violin it was part of that same development.

The first known piece of music written specifically for the cello is *Partite sopra diverse Sonate*, composed about 1650 by Giovanni Battista Vitali. It was never published, but some three decades later we have Domenico Gabrielli and others publishing sonatas and *ricercari* specifically for cello. By the early eighteenth century compositions for the solo instrument proliferated and the repertoire for violin and cello took on separate identities. Before the middle of the century, thousands of works had been written for the cello. It is arguable that never since has the cello been indulged by such a rich and diverse repertoire.

The first paid cellist we know of, is Petronio Francheschini (1650–81), employed by the Chapel of San Petronio in Bologna, who encouraged some of the first composers to write specifically for the instrument. He was one of the founders of the Accademia Filharmonica in that city. Also associated with the Chapel was Giuseppe Jacchini (*c.*1700), who wrote sonatas for cello with continuo. In addition to being of historical interest they are charming and quite acceptable to the modern cellist. His Op. 4, *Concerti per camera a 3 e 4 strumenti, con* *violoncello obbligato*, are generally considered to have been the first cello concertos.

But it was that inventive genius, Antonio Vivaldi, who gave us the first solo cello concertos. He wrote 27 in all, mostly for the young girls in his orchestra at the Ospedale Della Pietà in Venice, so they are not works of great difficulty. Nonetheless, they contain scale passages, arpeggios, string crossings, double stops and pedal notes. Vivaldi, in his Six Sonatas for cello, as always, knows how to use the voice of the instrument to its best advantage. The twelve sonatas of Benedetto Marcello (1686–1739) are also an important contribution to the cello repertoire. Although not a cellist himself, the great Venetian obviously understood the instrument. There is in these sonatas a hint of the way in which violin music was beginning to affect composition for the cello. These sonatas are inventive, and the development of passage-work is free, flowing and greatly in advance of anything up to that time. These were the first baroque sonatas to be published in modern times in the edition by Piatti in 1874.

Giovanni Bononcini (1670–1755), one of the earliest travelling virtuosos, was also a prolific composer for the instrument, and Johann Baptist Stuck, born in Florence of German parents in 1680, went to Paris at the beginning of the eighteenth century. He became a member of the private band of the Duke of Orleans, and, later, first cellist of the grand opera. It is said that it was he who introduced the cello to France.

Three decades later we have Antonio Vandini (*c.*1700–73), principal cellist at the Church of St Antonio in Padua, where his friend Tartini was first violin in the same orchestra. It was said that when Vandini played, he made his instrument 'speak'.

Johann Georg Linigke, a cellist in the Berlin Court Orchestra, was later employed in the orchestra at Köthen under J. S. Bach. It has been suggested that it was Linigke for whom Bach wrote the Six Solo Suites but there is no firm evidence for this assumption. Another German named Riedel was known in Russia, about 1727.

The first cellist to make a real impact on the public was the Neapolitan, Francesco Alborea (1691–1739), known universally as 'Franciscello' and described as the greatest cellist of the early years of the century. He was also the first virtuoso to make the art of the cello known in Eastern Europe. When Quantz, that accomplished flautist and court composer to Frederick the Great, heard him in Naples, he described him as 'outstanding' and 'incomparable'. The violinist, Franz Benda went to study with Franciscello in Vienna and adopted his style completely. Burney writes that Geminiani was present in Rome when Alessandro Scarlatti and Franciscello accompanied the singer Nicolini in one of Scarlatti's cantatas. It seems that Franciscello played so admirably that 'the company, being good catholics and living in a country where miraculous powers have not yet ceased, were firmly persuaded it was not Franchischelli [sic] who had played the violoncello but an angel that had descended and assumed his shape'.[4] Franciscello died in Vienna where he was employed as Chamber Virtuoso to Count Uhlenfeld.

Evaristo Dall'Abaco (1675–1742), from Verona, was a violinist, cellist and composer, and for some time chamber musician to the Elector Max Emanuel at Munich. His son, Joseph (Giuseppe) (1710–1805), born in Brussels, was one of the most outstanding players of his time. He travelled successfully all over Europe, and in Vienna created a stir by introducing a piece he himself had written for five cellos. His many other virtuoso pieces require a very advanced technique. Burney speaks highly of him and credits him with helping to popularize the cello in England. Another Italian, Giuseppe Dall'Oglio, born in Padua *c.*1700, was the younger brother of Domenico, the famous violinist. In 1735, the two brothers went to St Petersburg to become members of the Imperial chamber-music group where, as 'pillars of the orchestra', they stayed for 29 years.

Another Italian who travelled throughout Europe, astonishing audiences with his virtuoso performances, was Salvatore Lanzetti (1710–80). His staccato, both up and down bow, was said to be remarkable. He also wrote ten concertos and two sonatas for the instrument.

Giacobo Basevi Cervetto (1682–1783), born in Italy of Jewish parents, came to London in 1728 and set up as a dealer in musical instruments. Finding little profit in his chosen trade, he turned to perfecting his playing on the cello, and apparently achieved a high standard of performance. He was one of the first to promote interest in the cello in England, and, in 1739, Burney says of him: 'This worthy professor, who remained in England until the time of his death, at above a hundred, with Abaco, Lanzetti, Pasqualini and Caporale, about this time, brought the violoncello into favour, and made us nice judges of that instrument.'[5]

For many years Cervetto was solo cellist at Drury Lane when David Garrick was the darling of the London stage. A popular figure, he was constantly teased about his large nose. 'Play up, Nosey', was a frequent call from the gallery, which he took all in good part. He was also a born diplomat. Once when Garrick was playing Sir John Brute—the rapt audience drinking in every syllable uttered by their idol—Cervetto yawned so loudly that he had the entire house in fits of laughter. Garrick was highly offended, but Cervetto pleaded: 'I beg ten thousand pardons, but I always do so ven I am ver much please.'[6]

Eventually, Cervetto went into theatre management and became a very rich man. But he still continued to play the cello and took on a number of pupils, one of the most talented being his son, James, to whom he left £20,000, a considerable fortune at that time.

CHAPTER II

Berteau and the Duports

IN ITALY, THE cello had become so popular that by the middle of the seventeenth century it had ousted the viola da gamba. However, in northern Europe the gamba remained the favourite instrument, and in France the cello was regarded as a crude interloper. The best illustration of this is the famous diatribe by Hubert le Blanc against the entire violin family in his *Défense de la basse de viole contre les enterprises du violon et les prétentions du violoncelle* (1740):

> The violoncello, that until now has been looked upon as a miserable, hated, and pitiful wretch, whose lot was to starve to death for want of a free meal, now flatters itself that it will receive many caresses . . . It conjures up a bliss that will make it weep with tenderness.

The undisputed founder of the French school of cello playing was Martin Berteau (*c.*1700–71) from Valenciennes. He was a most important influence, not only for his own performances, but for his pupils, who were to become some of the most famous figures of the late eighteenth century: Jean Pierre Duport, Jean Baptiste Cupis, Tillière and Jean Baptiste Aimée Joseph Janson. They all inherited his powerful but sweet tone and imparted this quality to their pupils in turn.

Berteau began his career as a gambist but once heard the legendary Franciscello and immediately became attracted to the cello. From this time onwards he devoted himself to that instrument. An enormous success in the Paris salons, his charming personality and ready wit endeared him to the socialites. He would preface his playing with a droll request for 'rosin' which he needed in order to play well, whereupon a footman would bring him a flagon of wine and a glass on a silver salver. By all accounts he imbibed freely before commencing his recital, which no doubt prompted the remark that 'nobody can flatter himself at present on possessing more fire than Monsieur Berteau'.[1]

Beauty of tone and depth of expression would seem to have been his chief qualities. He developed and made extensive use of harmonics, which, at the time, were unusual for the cello. In 1739 he made his debut at a 'Concert Spirituel' in Paris, scoring a success with some of his own compositions. (The 'Concerts Spirituel' were founded in 1725 for the performance of sacred vocal music, but later their scope was widened to include secular instrumental works.)

It is interesting that Berteau continued to use the underhand hold of the bow, which he retained from his gamba playing days. More advanced in his fingering, he already employed a more modern system, as seen in the tutors written by his pupils, Cupis and Tillière. Berteau also used the thumb position in his performances. (The thumb position performs the function of a movable nut enabling the hand to play full scales across the strings similarly as in first position by means of a fixed nut using the open string.)

Little is known about the life of Berteau's compatriot and contemporary, Jean Barrière (c.1707–47), who came from a humble Bordelaise family and whose most important contribution to the development of cello playing in France is his composition. His first set of sonatas, published in 1733, shows an advance on its predecessors, and contains bravura passages that are a challenge even to modern performers. His later works are still more virtuosic. The example from his Sonata No. 4 in D major, shown on page 36, gives some idea of the very advanced technique required. When he died, the *Siècle de Louis XV* for that year notes, 'The famous Barrière, who died recently, possessed everything one could wish for from a violoncellist; nobody could equal his performance.'

One of the most versatile musicians of the eighteenth century was Michel Corrette, a virtuoso on the harpsichord, organ, cello and violin. He wrote instruction books on singing and on almost every instrument from the flute to the musette and hurdy-gurdy. In 1741 he published a cello tutor, *Méthode, théorique et pratique, pour apprendre en peu de temps le violoncelle dans sa perfection*. The importance of this tutor is that it was probably the first, and it throws considerable light on the early development of cello playing. He describes three different ways of holding the bow, and gives precise instructions on the thumb position, fingering, shifting and how to play double stops and arpeggios. He shows how to make the transition from the gamba to the cello and, obviously influenced by the older

The Great Cellists

Jean Barrière: from the Sonata in D (1733)

instrument, advocates the method of marking the fingerboard with frets in order to ensure perfect intonation.

Jean Baptiste Cupis, Le Jeune, born in Paris in 1741, received his first lessons from his father, François, a cellist in the Paris Opera Orchestra, and became a pupil of Berteau when he was eleven. Before he was twenty he was solo cellist at the Grand Opera in Paris and toured successfully throughout Italy and Germany. Cupis wrote a great deal of music for his instrument and an instruction book with a title running into some 85 words. Cupis's main claim to fame is that through his pupils, Levasseur and Bréval, he formed a link between Berteau and the ongoing French school of cello playing.

Jean Baptiste Bréval (1756–1825) is mainly remembered for his prolific *oeuvre* as a composer. He wrote seven concertos, numerous trios, duets and solos, many of which have been resuscitated in the present revival of baroque playing.[2]

One of Berteau's most important pupils was Jean Pierre Duport (1741–1818), usually called Duport l'aîné to distinguish him from his even more famous brother, Jean Louis. They were the sons of a Parisian dancing master and both showed early signs of musical talent. At twenty Jean Pierre made his début at a Concert Spirituel in Paris, the success of which led to an immediate appointment as a member of the Prince de Conti's private band. Subsequently he was engaged to play a solo every night for two weeks in the 'Concerts de la Quinzaine de Pâques'. The *Mercure de France* in April 1762, wrote:

In his hands the instrument is no longer recognizable; it speaks, expresses and renders everything with a charm greater than that thought to be exclusive to the violin. The vigour of his playing is always accentuated by the most exact precision in the performance of difficulties of which one can have no idea without a knowledge of the instrument. It appears to be unanimously agreed that this young man is the most singular phenomenon to have appeared in our salons.

In 1769 he relinquished his position with the Prince in order to travel, and during this time visited Spain and England. In London he played at the 'Professional Concerts' (under Lord Abingdon's management) at the Hanover Rooms in Hanover Square with the violinists Pierre Lahoussaye and Maddalena Lombardini Sirmen, both of whom were Tartini's pupils. The latter was the young girl

for whom Tartini wrote the famous letter on the 'Art of Bowing'
dated 1760.

Jean Pierre once had an amusing experience in his own country.
When visiting a small provincial town, he saw placards announcing
that he was to play that evening. Intrigued, he decided to attend the
concert *incognito*. News of his virtuoso reputation had travelled fast
and the room was packed with an eager and expectant audience. The
pseudo-Duport finally appeared and gave a very inferior performance. The audience started to fidget and murmur, but when they
became threatening, Duport could stand it no longer, and introduced
himself. The impostor, suitably ashamed, handed his instrument to
Duport who played to a spellbound audience for the remainder of
the evening. The pretender apologized profusely and handed Duport
the money he had dishonestly earned. But Duport threw it back
warning him never again to perpetrate such deceit.

In 1773 Duport went to Berlin where Frederick the Great engaged
him as chamber musician for the Royal Chapel and as solo cellist for
the Royal Opera. Duport was also tutor to the Crown Prince who
afterwards became Friedrich Wilhelm II. When the prince succeeded
to the throne in 1786, Duport was made director of Royal Chamber
Music, and henceforth played only at court concerts. During this
time he met both Mozart and Beethoven. The three Mozart String
Quartets, K.575, 589, and 590 (dedicated to the King), show
evidence of advanced cello technique, so presumably he had some
influence on the young composer. When Mozart was in Potsdam in
1789 he wrote a set of piano variations (K.573) on a minuet by
Duport. The two sonatas for piano and cello Op. 5 by Beethoven,
also dedicated to the monarch, show a similar influence. It is said
that the composer played them at court with Jean Pierre.

Jean Pierre's younger brother, Jean Louis Duport (1749–1819),
originally studied the violin, but due to his brother's phenomenal
success, turned to the cello, receiving his first lessons from Jean
Pierre. When he made his début at a Concert Spirituel on 2 February
1768, the *Mercure de France* wrote: 'His execution is brilliant and
astounding. His full tone is of great sweetness. Boldness and
certainty characterize his playing, and promise a great future for his
fine talent.'

In 1783 Jean Louis visited London where he played at the same
Professional Concerts in which his brother had taken part some
fifteen years earlier. Cramer's *Nachrichten* of that year tells us that he
surpassed Cervetto (the younger) in expression and style, although
his tone was not so powerful.

Jean Louis had been persuaded to visit London by his fellow student and close friend, John Crosdill, also a pupil of Duport l'aîné. They appeared together in many concerts and remained close friends throughout their lives. Once when Crosdill was to play a *concertante* with Viotti at the private apartment of Marie Antoinette, the great violinist did not arrive. Duport, who had been billed to play a sonata only, asked to see the violin part, read it through quickly and signalled for Crosdill to begin. It seems that he played it so beautifully that it appeared doubtful if Viotti could have done better on the smaller instrument. It is interesting that he had always taken Viotti as his model, and his playing bore many of that artist's characteristics, noticeably his flowing line and purity of tone. Viotti appeared many times in public with Duport, who consequently achieved the nickname, 'Viotti of the cello'.

When the French Revolution broke out, Jean Louis quickly joined his brother in Berlin. Here too, he was given an appointment in the Royal Chapel and stayed for seventeen years.

During the 1780s, Jean Louis visited Geneva where he met the writer, Voltaire, who knew very little about music. Surprised at the sweet tone that Jean Louis produced from such a large instrument, he exclaimed, 'Monsieur Duport, you will make me believe in miracles, when I see that you can turn an ox into a nightingale!'[3]

After various changes of residence, owing to invading armies and the demise of his royal patron, Duport returned to Paris and regained his popularity by a single concert performance. Paris was still unsettled, so Duport joined the Private Band of the ex-King Charles IV of Spain then living at Marseilles. In 1812, when the King went to Rome, Duport returned to Paris and embarked upon the most successful period of his career.

He was appointed professor at the Conservatoire, solo cellist to the Emperor and member of the Empress Marie Louise's chamber-music group. In this capacity he frequently performed in private concerts at the Tuileries. There is a famous story about one such 'Réunion intime' when Napoleon entered unexpectedly, booted and spurred as was his wont. After listening attentively for some time, he marched over to Duport, took the instrument from him and sat down straddling it between his legs. Making some show of imitating Duport, he demanded, 'How the devil do you hold this thing Monsieur Duport?' Seeing his beautiful Strad being crushed by the Emperor's spurs, Duport cried out, 'Sire!' with such anguish that Napoleon smiled and handed him back the instrument. Nevertheless, the damage had been done. Though very well repaired, a small dent in the ribs still remains as a legacy of this rough handling. The instrument descended to Franchomme, who bought it for 25,000 francs, then sold it to Servais, who left it to his son, Joseph, whose widow sold it for 1,000,000 francs. Today, it is in the possession of the great Russian cellist, Mstislav Rostropovich.

A frank and unassuming personality, Louis Duport was well liked by his colleagues. Despite his great success, he remained modest and simple in his tastes. He was also a very humorous and eloquent conversationalist, never short of an audience when talking about the adventures he had experienced on his travels.

Duport was one of the very few string players who retained his tone and technique to the last. When people remarked upon this fact he would say 'All technical skill is acquired and retained by dint of hard work. As for the sureness of intonation, I have to thank Nature alone for it.'[4] To prove the point he would fill a glass to the brim with water and carry it round the room balanced on the back of his hand—without spilling a single drop. He was then almost seventy. Duport wrote a great deal for his instrument, including concertos, a *duo concertante* for piano and cello and three nocturnes, but none remain in the cello repertoire.

In his *Essai sur le doigtes du violoncelle et la conduite de l'archet, avec une suite d'exercices*, he writes:

I have treated with minute detail the subject of double stops. This I have done for two reasons: the first is that, until now, nothing concerning them has been written, and they are so important for a good player; the second, because they have so often served me as an argument, for without an established mode of fingering, double notes are impossible.

This must not be taken word for word, for Corrette, in his *Violoncello School*, though very insufficient, does give directions for double stopping. Nonetheless, Duport's was by far the most important work of its kind at a time when published methods were appearing more frequently, and contains some of the best studies that have ever been written for the instrument. They were mainly aimed at the amateur performer, presumably owing to the increasing popularity of the cello as an instrument for the dilettante. It was Duport who established a well-founded system of fingering and, according to Baudiot, he also invented the fingering for the chromatic scale. Several modern editions of these exercises have been produced and are still considered valuable.

In the preface, Duport gives us some indication of the close relationship that existed between himself and his elder brother. He writes: 'Much will be found that is difficult, but nothing that is impossible to execute, as I have tried everything repeatedly myself. It has also been tried by my brother, who ever was and will be my master.'

CHAPTER III

The French Influence

AMONG BERTEAU'S MANY other pupils there is the sad figure of
Jean Baptiste Janson (1742–1803), who at first met with considerable
success throughout Europe as a soloist and was highly regarded as a
professor at the Paris Conservatoire from its foundation in 1795.
Unfortunately he became involved in the notorious quarrel, at
administrative level, that caused the complete reorganization of the
institution in 1784, and was dismissed. Although only forty-two, he
never recovered from the shock and, following a nervous breakdown, died within the year.

One of Janson's most celebrated pupils, and his successor at the
Conservatoire, was Charles Nicolas Baudiot (1773–1849). He would
appear to have been both versatile and energetic, for as well as an
official post in the Treasury and an appointment as first cellist in the
Chapel Royal he still continued his career as a soloist.

His playing was said to be based on a well-developed technique
and perfect intonation, but lacked power and emotional expression,
a criticism that was often levelled at French cellists at the time.
Baudiot's true vocation was as a teacher, with Norblin and Vaslin as
two of his most celebrated pupils.

An amusing story is told about Baudiot when playing in a concert
given by the famous patron of the arts, Madame Catalini. A
symphony of Haydn was followed by Baudiot's solo which happened to be the Fantasia on the Andante from the same symphony.
Baudiot had no notion of what had gone before. Thinking it a joke,
the audience began to laugh and the poor man was beside himself.
The ensuing embarrassment made him lose control of his playing
and the audience laughed even louder. Finally, he gave up and was
led from the platform in a state of total collapse.

Baudiot wrote a great deal for his instrument, most of which is
now obsolete. His *Méthode*, in which he was assisted by his pupil,
Pierre Norblin, is dedicated to Cherubini, the then Director of the
Conservatoire. The work contains much helpful advice. He thought

overwork injurious to technique, and firmly believed in giving
children the best teachers available. 'It is generally recognized that in
science, literature and art, as well as in our social life, the first
education requires the greatest care, its neglect leaves traces which
sometimes prove indelible.' In his directions for holding the bow,
Baudiot recommends the same hold as the violinists employed,
whereby he places all his fingers on the bow stick in front of the
nut.

The Parisian, Jean Henri Levasseur (1765–1823), studied with
both Cupis and Jean Louis Duport. Since his father was Inspector
General and Vocal Instructor at the Paris Opera, no doubt it had
some bearing on Levasseur being appointed a member of the Opera
Orchestra. Nonetheless his appointment as first cellist in 1789, and
later as a member of Napoleon's Private Music, would doubtless
have been on merit. He even continued as a member of the Royal
Band after the defeat of Napoleon.

Levasseur was also a respected professor at the Paris Conservatoire
and one of the chief contributors to the *Méthode de Violoncelle et de
Basse d'Accompagnement* by Baillot, Levasseur, Catel and Baudiot.
This official instruction book appeared also in German translation
published by C. F. Peters at Leipzig. It is clear, from some of the
comments, that the cello was certainly not a universally familiar
instrument at the beginning of the century. What is of particular
interest is that the directions for holding the instrument, and bow,
are exactly the same as those given in the late nineteenth-century
manuals, except that the spike was not yet in use. It is suggested
that the right foot is bent sideways, inward from the ankle. Bowing
instructions, however, differ widely from the late nineteenth-century methods. The authors condemn the use of the point of the bow
for detached notes, as it is not deemed strong enough to make the
thick cello strings vibrate, therefore giving a hard, dry tone.

Levasseur's most prominent pupils were Lamarre and Norblin.
Jacques Michel Hurel Lamarre (1772–1823) came from a very poor
Parisian family, but his musical talent was so outstanding that at
seven he was taken into the Institute of Pages of the Royal Music
where he received a first-rate musical education. At fifteen he studied
with J. L. Duport and by the age of twenty-two he fulfilled the dual
role of professor at the Conservatoire and cellist at the Théâtre
Feydeau.

Destined for a solo career, Lamarre left Paris in 1801 and his fame
as a virtuoso performer spread all over Europe and Russia, where he
met with great success in Moscow and St Petersburg. In 1815, he

married a rich lady of society, after which he played only at private concerts.

Lamarre much admired the violinist, Pierre Rode (whom Spohr had also much praised), and he was often called 'Rode of the bass'. Fétis, who heard him play frequently, says of him: 'He had a most wonderful execution, but his main strength lay in the rendering of chamber music. He entered more deeply into the spirit of works of that class than any other violoncellist I have ever heard, and he succeeded better than any of them to bring out all the beauties of such compositions.'[1]

On account of his years at the Brussels Conservatoire, Nicolas Joseph Platel (1777–1835) is regarded as the founder of the Belgian school of cello-playing. He was born in Versailles, where his father was a member of the Chapel Royal, and received his first musical training as a singer in the Institute of Pages of the Royal Music. At ten he showed such talent for the cello that his father persuaded his friend, Louis Duport, to give him some lessons. Duport taught the boy for two years, during which time he imparted to him that beauty of tone by which all his students were recognized. When Duport went to Berlin in 1789, Platel became a pupil of Lamarre.

Platel had a series of appointments as first cellist in theatre and opera orchestras and appeared with great success in the 'Rue de Clery' concerts. In 1801, when Duport was in Berlin and Lamarre in Russia, he had no competition on the solo platform and reigned supreme among French cellists.

Platel was an inveterate traveller, and if a town took his fancy he would cancel all future engagements and stay until he felt the inclination to move on. The local inhabitants were fortunate in that he entered into all musical activities, singing, playing the cello and teaching. He was so enchanted with Ghent in Belgium that he once abandoned a very important tour and stayed for seven years.

In 1813 Platel went to Antwerp where he was appointed first cellist of the Opera Orchestra. Six years later he moved to Brussels where he held a similar post in the Royal Opera. In 1826 the Prince de Chimay offered him the post of teacher of cello at the newly-opened Royal School of Music in Brussels at the handsome salary of 500 francs per annum. When the institution became the 'Conservatoire de Musique' in 1831, he was appointed full professor of the cello. Among his many pupils were Servais, Batta and De Munck, all of whom became distinguished soloists and teachers whose influence spread over many generations of accomplished cellists.

The intrigue and jealousy so often found among artists, was quite absent in Platel's nature. He was well-liked by his colleagues, not only for his kindness, but also for his generosity, which was sadly exploited by his associates. It seems that in money matters he was totally incompetent, and when living in Antwerp his debts caused the brokers to be brought in. While they were taking away the furniture, Platel picked up his cello and walked out, not bothering about the rest of his possessions. Some time later, a relative left him a considerable sum of money in gold, which he placed in an old silk stocking and carried everywhere. Ignoring the advice of his wiser friends, he was frequently persuaded to part with sums on loan to anyone with a tale of hardship—sums which were never repaid. Unconcerned, he continued to live in this happy-go-lucky way for the rest of his life.

He wrote a considerable amount of music for his instrument, including five concertos and three books of sonatas.

By the beginning of the nineteenth century, France had acquired a high standard of cello playing and vied with Germany for first place, which, until the latter part of the eighteenth century, had belonged to Italy. Meanwhile, individual characteristics in each country had begun to emerge. Germany favoured a powerful tone and highly developed left-hand technique combined with a serious expression of emotion, whereas the French style corresponded to all the grace and elegance of the Courts of Louis XV and XVI. Tone production looked towards Viotti, who had taken the Italian style of violin playing to Paris and become founder of the French school. As a result the cellists also took to lighter bowing, excelling in spiccato[2] and staccato,[3] akin to the violin technique. Although French cellists had a considerable facility of the left hand, it did not reach that of the German, Romberg, and his successors.

Most prominent among French cellists in this period were Norblin and Franchomme. Louis Pierre Norblin (1781–1854) was born in Warsaw. His father, the famous painter, Norblin de la Gourdaine, had married a Polish woman and settled there. Louis Pierre showed early talent for the cello and in 1798 went to Paris where he studied at the Conservatoire at first with Baudiot and then with Levasseur. He played at the Théâtre Italien and in 1811 became solo cellist at the Opèra, a post he held for 30 years. In 1823 he succeeded his late master, Levasseur, as professor at the Conservatoire and stayed until 1846. His most celebrated pupil was Franchomme.

An excellent soloist and an accomplished quartet player, who took part for many years in the Baillot String Quartet, Norblin also played with the violinist and conductor Habeneck, with whom he founded the Conservatoire Concerts in 1828, renowned for their fine performances of the classical repertoire. Norblin had many interests outside music: his collection of paintings, drawings, prints and coins was said to be the finest in Paris.

One of the greatest French masters of the cello was Auguste Franchomme (1808–84), from Lille. He began his studies under a mediocre teacher, named Maes, at the Conservatoire at Lille, but in 1821 won first prize. He was then elevated into the class of Pierre Baumann, a fine musician who was his principal master. In 1825 he went to Paris and entered the Conservatoire studying under Levasseur and Norblin. Here he also gained first prize after one year. While still a student Franchomme held an appointment at the Théâtre Ambigue-Comique, and was subsequently engaged for the Opéra and the Théâtre Italien as solo cellist.

Solo playing and chamber music had always appealed more to Franchomme than being part of an orchestra and he left the theatre after a few years to devote himself to these fields and to teaching. When the Conservatoire Concerts were founded in 1828, Franchomme became a member of that institution, and solo cellist of the Royal Band. He was second professor at the Conservatoire Royale and, on the death of Norblin in 1846, succeeded him as first professor. Franchomme formed a string quartet with the celebrated violinist, Delphin Alard, and also held chamber-music soirées together with the pianist, Charles Hallé (later Sir Charles and founder of Manchester's Hallé Orchestra).

An intimate friend of Chopin, Franchomme collaborated with the composer on the *Grand Duo Concertante* on themes from *Robert le Diable* and the Sonata Op.65, the latter being dedicated to Franchomme. He combined a full and expressive tone with a brilliant facility of the left hand, and, in addition, possessed the rare gift of a musicianly interpretation of everything he played. His cantilena was said to be most moving and always evoked an enthusiastic response from his audience. Franchomme acquired the famous Duport Stradivarius from the great cellist's son who called upon him saying, 'You are Duport's successor, and you alone should have this instrument'. Nonetheless it did not prevent him asking the astronomically high price of 22,000 francs, about £880 in the currency of the time (1842).

Franchomme wrote a number of works for his instrument, including transcriptions of violin sonatas by Mozart and Beethoven, solos with pianoforte, a concerto, and the celebrated *Twelve*

Caprices Op. 7 which still form part of the standard literature of the cello.

One of Franchomme's students, who became better known as a teacher than as a soloist and who succeeded his master at the Conservatoire, was Jules Delsart (1844–1900), from Valenciennes. He trained many first class cellists, Paul Bazelaire and Henri Casadesus being the best known.

Delsart was heard in London on several occasions, one being the first performance of Popper's *Requiem* for three cellos, in which he took part with the composer and Edward Howell. His writings for the instrument consist of arrangements and editions of classical works including the Violin Sonata in A by César Franck.

Practically nothing is known about the early life of Baudiot's pupil, Vaslin (b. 1794), who entered the Paris Conservatoire in 1808 at the age of fourteen. The following year he was given a place in the orchestra at the Théâtre Variétés and later became a professor at the Conservatoire. Among his pupils was Jacques Offenbach, then a very promising cellist, who later achieved world fame as a composer of opera buffa.

In 1884 Vaslin published his *L'Art du violoncelle*. In the preface he tells us that he was then ninety and had studied for 82 years. The instructions for holding the bow are most explicit, and he condemns the habit of letting the wrist fall below the level of the arm. He also says that he formed his style of playing by watching the violinist Baillot, whom he much admired. This earned him the nickname, 'Le Baillotin'.

Vaslin was the owner of a fine Stradivari cello dated 1725, which, according to Hill, he acquired in 1827 for £160. He parted with it in 1869 but Hill gives an interesting account of his treatment of it in the intervening years. It seems that when he had 'grown old and fidgety'—he was over eighty—he became obsessed with the idea that something was wrong with the neck, in that it was ill-shapen. Gand, Rambeaux and many other Parisian luthiers tried their best to correct the supposed fault, but nothing pleased him. He then tried scraping it down himself—also to no avail. It was finally bought by the well known amateur cellist and instrument collector, M. Jules Galley, who wrote, 'I followed the wanderings of this admirable instrument to the different luthiers with a sad heart, and watched during many years for my opportunity to secure it. At last, in 1869, an offer for £600, plus my own Stradivari, which I valued at £400, obtained it for me.'[4] The 'Vaslin' is at present in the possession of Martin Lovett, cellist of the Amadeus String Quartet.

CHAPTER IV

The Forgotten Genius:
Luigi Boccherini

'TRULY ONE OF the most distinguished instrumental composers of his country . . . he was, in his earlier years, an admirable violoncellist, with an incomparable tone and an expressive musicality which gave to his instrument a magical charm.' This account, reflecting Boccherini's reputation among his musical contemporaries, appeared in the *Leipzig Allgemeine Musikalische Zeitung* in an obituary in August 1805.

A key figure in the development of the art of cello playing in the second half of the eighteenth century, Luigi Boccherini (1743–1805) rendered an immense service to the instrumental music of Italy, Spain and France, and was one of the first in these countries to compose quartets in which all the instruments are employed in obbligato fashion. Even before Haydn, he created a sensation with this type of music.

Born in Lucca, in Italy, Boccherini was the son of a professional double-bass player who had the distinction of being the first to play a solo on that instrument. Not surprisingly, he showed an early talent for music and, when at five years old, he had some cello lessons with his father. By the age of nine he had progressed well enough to continue his studies with the Abbé Vanucci, *maestro di cappella* of the cathedral at San Martino. He made his first public appearance at thirteen, by which time he had surpassed his teacher's knowledge.

Sent alone to Rome, he resided in a religious seminary receiving instruction from G. B. Costanzi, who had been trained in the then fashionable school of the violinist, Tartini, at Padua.

After one year, Boccherini and his father were engaged as members of the Imperial Theatre Orchestra in Vienna. At seventeen he tried his hand at composition resulting in six trios for two violins and cello obbligato (Op. 1 dated 1760 in the catalogue he drew up himself).

A court appointment in Vienna was his for the asking, but Boccherini wished only to return to his native city to promote interest in the cello. Sadly, a humble petition to the Grand Council of Lucca was not even acknowledged. Nevertheless, father and son returned to Lucca, but apart from a few engagements with the orchestras of the Chapel and the theatre, there were no regular jobs. They therefore went back to Vienna where an enthusiastic welcome awaited them. Furthermore, Boccherini was given 66 florins and 2 kreuzer over and above his regular salary. A note against his name on a list of such beneficiaries, reads: 'Luigi Boccherini, violoncellist, gave a great concert at which, with the assistance of his father, Leopoldo, he performed, upon the violoncello, his compositions for one or two violoncellos. This concert ranks him among the virtuosi of the Musik-Akademia.'[1]

Eventually, Lucca and the Grand Council invited Boccherini to take up an appointment as 'player of the violoncello, by the grace of the Most Excellent Council, with a salary of five scudi a month, with the confirmation of the usual obligations and with the stipulation that he shall not enjoy this salary during his absence from the city and state, and that the time of such absence shall not exceed one month, and that only with the permission of Their Excellencies.'[2]

Boccherini was certainly kept busy for his five scudi. Work was divided between the theatre and the Grand Chapel both of which were under the same management. It was also compulsory for artists to provide an accompaniment to the morning meal of their 'Excellent Lordships' of the Council. Besides the religious festivals, they took part in the Election Feast known as 'The Sacks'—so called because the names of the elected magistrates were drawn from one sack; and from another, the order in rotation in which their government posts were to be allotted. It had existed since 1431 and was celebrated by an elaborate ceremony with processions in which music naturally played a very important part.

However eager Boccherini was to take up this post in Lucca, the reality must have been disappointing. Perhaps he felt isolated at being one of a small band of artists, and needed the stimulus from musicians with a similar talent. In any case he played there for the last time in January 1765, after which he and his father made their way to Milan, a centre for many distinguished musicians from neighbouring countries who found it a convenient meeting place.

It is generally agreed that the initial public performances of the very first string quartet took place in Milan in 1765, and that Boccherini was the innovator. In Cambini's *Memoirs* we read:

In my youth, I had the happiness to spend six months in this delightful situation. Three great masters, Manfredi, the supreme violinist of all Italy for playing in an orchestra or in a quartet, Nardini, so renowned for the perfection of his style and for his virtuosity, and Boccherini, whose merits are sufficiently known, did me the honour of inviting me to play the viola with them.[3]

In 1765, when Boccherini was twenty-two, we have the first instance of his being unable to fulfill his duties on account of ill-health. His condition—almost certainly tuberculosis—was to over-shadow the rest of his life. When his father died the following year, Boccherini, left to his own resources, turned to the violinist, Manfredi, who became his friend and musical partner, and with whom he undertook an extensive concert tour throughout northern Italy, arriving in Paris in 1767.

It was a well established fact of Parisian musical life that no artist was invited to perform at a Concert Spirituel unless he had played for the famous Baron de Bagge at his luxurious house in the Place des Victoires. A musical connoisseur and wealthy patron of the arts, the baron held soirées every Friday. He would invite all the visiting virtuosos and talented amateurs who wished to make their débuts in the capital city, gathering the most discriminating musicians of the day to hear them. Here were to be found the cellist, Jean Pierre Duport, and the great violinists, Gossec, Gaviniès and others. The baron would also seize the opportunity to display his own dubious talents to his captive audience. Something of a caricature when performing as a violin virtuoso, he was said to make terrible grimaces and his tone made people wince.

However, the baron was not only impressed with Boccherini's playing, but also took a personal liking to him, inviting him to stay in his house. Here Boccherini came into contact with all the prominent artistic personalities of the lively pre-revolutionary era. Significantly, although he rubbed shoulders with the élite in the salon, he was never presented at court.

In the late eighteenth century, Italian music was beginning to lose the prestige it had previously enjoyed, and fashion favoured German ideas. Now the accent was on spontaneity, simplicity and a feeling for nature. When Boccherini and Manfredi appeared at a Concert Spirituel on 20 March 1786, they wisely aimed to stir the emotions of their audience rather than astound them with virtuosity; and there is no doubt they succeeded, for the audience gave them a rapturous reception. The *Mercure de France*, in April of that year, reports: 'M.

Boccherini, already known to us by his impressive trios and quartets, performed in a masterly fashion, upon the violoncello, a sonata of his own composition.'

In 1769, through the Spanish Ambassador in France, Boccherini was invited to visit Madrid with Manfredi, and here met the Infante Don Luis for whom he composed six quartets (Op 8 of 1769). Early in the following year Boccherini was appointed 'violoncellist of his [Don Luis'] Chamber and composer of music' with the authorization of H. M. Charles III. Under his contract he was bound to write exclusively for his master but was allowed to have his music published. He was paid an annual salary of 30,000 reals, equalling about £350 at the time; a much larger stipend than that of the prince's confessor, personal physician, librarian or the chief officer of his wardrobe. Only one or two secretaries received higher salaries. This was a happy period of security and steady activity which lasted for fifteen years. Boccherini applied himself to his work with enthusiasm and vigour and was fortunate in having, among the musicians at court, the Font family, a father and three sons who, together, formed a superb quartet. Boccherini would join them for performances of his quintets. An early set of six quintets, Opus 11 of 1771, established his fame. No. 5 contains the famous Minuet.

In 1771, Boccherini married Clementina Pelicho who bore him five children, but tragically died of a stroke in 1785. Unfortunately the death of Don Luis the same year put Boccherini in a precarious position. Don Luis' social position had always been somewhat complicated. As a child of ten he had been made a Cardinal and Primate of Spain, but on reaching manhood knew he could not maintain the vow of chastity. In 1776, when he married, his brother Charles III decreed that, whilst he would be allowed at court on special occasions, his wife could not be present. Fortunately he did not deprive Don Luis of his considerable fortune; hence Boccherini's very comfortable appointment.

A petition from Boccherini to Charles III, 'At your Majesty's Feet', asking for Royal Protection to continue receiving his salary, had the desired effect, no doubt because the monarch was upset at the loss of his brother. The King guaranteed his salary as before (now 12,000 reals per year), and agreed that the first vacancy for a cellist in the Chapel Royal should be given to him. His future was assured and the authorities even gave him a dispensation from some performances because of his frequent spittings of blood.

In the early 1780s, a performance of six of Boccherini's quintets had been given in Madrid in honour of the Prussian ambassador of Frederick the Great, an account of which no doubt reached that talented cellist Friedrich Wilhelm, heir to the Prussian throne. In October 1783, Boccherini received a letter from him, accompanied by the gift of a gold box, telling him how much he enjoyed playing his music and that he looked forward to hearing more. At the time Boccherini could do little but accept the compliment gracefully but the subsequent death of the Infante meant that Boccherini could now dedicate works to other patrons.

The Prince was also aware of this fact and in January 1786 lost no time in writing to Boccherini with the news that he had conferred upon him the title of 'Composer of Our Chamber'. This was accompanied by a pension of 1,000 German crowns to be paid annually in return for a specified number of quartets and quintets. When his patron succeeded to the throne of his uncle, as Friedrich Wilhelm II of Prussia, Boccherini reserved the greater part of his new works for his new master, while still receiving his emolument from the Spanish King.

Boccherini's fertile creative powers must never have been in greater demand, for he also wrote for the distinguished Countess-Duchess of Benavente-Osuna, a wealthy patron of the arts whose salon was open to Italian and French influences. As director of the Duchess's sixteen-piece orchestra, Boccherini appeared resplendent in a costume of rich silk velvet and white satin, whilst his musicians had to be content with uniforms of common cloth. Her concerts were high events in the Madrid social calendar and were made even more exciting by the background of jealous rivalry between her and the Duchess of Alba who favoured the music of Brunetti.

We know that Boccherini was remarried in 1787, to Maria Porreti, daughter of his cellist friend, Domingo Porreti. But from 1787 his name disappears from the annals of the Osuna household and reappears only in 1796, in letters from Boccherini to Ignaz Pleyel. Of Viennese origin, Pleyel had settled in Paris and opened a small business for the publication and sale of music. In later years a piano factory was added, and from this grew the firm which became a household name in the nineteenth century.

The avaricious Pleyel was also a composer, so he recognized in Boccherini's compositions an opportunity for his own gain. The 'gentle, patient and polite' Boccherini was delighted at the prospect of a steady market for his writing. Unfortunately it did not work out in practice. From the letters of Boccherini to Pleyel (published in full in the excellent biography of Boccherini by Germaine de

Rothschild) we witness a saga of broken promises and unreliability on almost every count. It seems Boccherini's letters were seldom answered, his manuscripts not returned and money constantly withheld. Despite his suffering over the years, Boccherini continued to address him, 'My dear beloved Pleyel' and sign himself, 'your dear friend and servant'.

Tragedy struck again in 1802 when Boccherini's two daughters died within a few days from an epidemic. Boccherini lost all interest in remaining alive. He was now extremely poor. The pension from Charles III had dwindled to a pittance and his only means of livelihood was from the sale of his works. The unscrupulous Pleyel, as always, kept him short and he died on 28 May 1805 aged sixty-two.

In the obituary, in *Gazette Musicale Générale de Paris*, he was described as 'A marvellous violoncellist. Above all, he charmed us by the incomparable sonority and the peculiarly expressive singing tone of his instrument.'

At the time of Boccherini's death, the romantic age occupied the attention of the younger generation. Spohr thought little of Boccherini's music, and Mendelssohn described one of his quintets as, 'A peruke, beneath which might be seen the smiling features of a kindly old man.'[4]

In his later years, owing to his precarious state of health, Boccherini had abandoned playing the cello, but through his compositions he opened up new horizons in cello writing.

Texture is a dynamic element in Boccherini's chamber music . . . In a sensuous, wholly Latin way, he relished the sound of an ensemble of instruments for its own sake. He used bowed tremolandos extensively in inner parts, to lend movement and vibrancy to the music; he used double stops more for their enriching effect than from harmonic necessity, and triple or quadruple stops to create dramatic accents.[5]

The Dutch cellist Anner Bylsma considers Boccherini to be the greatest figure in the history of the instrument, but stresses that his music must be played on old instruments, a prerequisite not needed for any other composer. He explained why the music does not work on modern instruments: 'If you go for learned modulations and big developments, you won't find them in Boccherini's music, which is why musicologists cannot come to grips with it. Therefore one can hardly find any books about his music.'

He quoted an example from Boccherini's fuller chamber music:

In a quintet, the texture and sensuality of sound is of more importance than the actual themes. All five voices can be heard continuously and are equally delightful for player or listener. In score, there is no music quite like it. One cellist may be carried away just playing an open string where the viola pleasingly doubles the first violin's melody, *ponticello*, the second cello playing *pizzicato arpeggios*, and the second violinist alternating octaves lightly over two strings. Most surprising is Boccherini's use of many different descriptions for 'soft': piano, pianissimo, suave, amorosa, mezzo voce, etc. When loud, his music is 'folkish' and irresistably happy. His pianissimos are often breath-takingly sad, but at the same time, sweet.[6]

Boccherini was one of the first of the Italian school to give expression to the solo and virtuoso aspects of the instrument through the building out of the thumb position into the soprano range. He extended beyond his predecessors the playing of double stops as well as fast passages that require great facility in performance. Bylsma gives a further example: 'Dissonants often appear high upon a lower string where the resolution comes lower on a higher string, not unlike a stopped note to obtain dissonance on a natural horn.'

Until Boccherini's time, the favourite manner of writing was to use the violin clef (as with Mozart and Beethoven), indicating notes sounding an octave lower than written. By using five clefs (soprano, alto, tenor, bass and treble), Boccherini wrote everything as it would sound; there was therefore not so much need to use ledger lines for passages in the highest register.

Boccherini spent so much of his time abroad that his native country was not only deprived of his talent, but also of the personal contact that teaching would have afforded. Had he remained in Italy he would have been to the cello what Corelli and Tartini were to the violin. His withdrawal caused a loss which was never made good, because in Italy there was no one of equal importance to continue his work.

CHAPTER V

Enter the English

THE CELLO MADE a slow start in England. Here the viol reigned supreme until the mid-eighteenth century, mainly because it was regarded as a gentleman's instrument. Rejected by the upper classes, the violin was considered vulgar and fit only for accompanying dancing in taverns and fairgrounds, whereas King Charles I, Lord Francis North, Lord Crewe, and other members of the nobility, could all take their part in a consort of viols.

The first name we encounter playing the 'bass' violin is William Saunders, a member of Charles II's 'Twenty-four Violins' which he had modelled on the French King Louis XIV's 'grande bande'. Having lived in exile at the French Court until the Restoration in 1660, Charles did his best to emulate French taste in everything.

This influence did not spread far outside the Court. It was not until 1733 that the cello superseded the bass viol in English orchestras and, even then, it was mostly played by Italian artists. We have seen already that Burney credited Cervetto and his contemporaries as having brought the cello into favour in England about 1740.

Although these Italian teachers would have had many pupils, few cellists of distinction were to be found in England even late in the eighteenth century. Wasielewski speculates that, at the end of the Civil War, England was far more concerned with colonial politics, and found it easier to employ foreign artists for their musical needs. This may be a part of the explanation but also, during the greater part of the eighteenth century, playing a musical instrument was not considered manly.

A somewhat remarkable exception, Bartholomew Johnson(1710–1814), was a Yorkshireman from Wykeham near Scarborough who lived to be one-hundred-and-four. Around 1770 he appeared as a cello soloist in London and was for 70 years one of the 'town waits'. Highly respected, both as man and musician, 'for the many excellent traits in his character', he celebrated his hundredth birthday with a Jubilee Dinner and musical performance at the

Freemason's Lodge, Scarborough. A medal was struck as a memorial of the event. At about ten o'clock the old man took part in a string quartet, performing the bass to a minuet he had composed upwards of 60 years earlier. The assembly consisted of about 70 important personalities including Lord Mulgrave, who subsequently commissioned a portrait of Johnson by J. Jackson, R. A. This was presented to the Corporation and now hangs in the Council Chamber of the Town Hall. In an obituary, *The Gentleman's Magazine* of 1814 describes him as, 'a celebrated musical character. He possessed to the last a vigorous mind and strong retentive memory.'

There then appears what must be the first musical prodigy on the cello. Unfortunately very little information has survived regarding Benjamin Hallet, who was born in 1743, and always played dressed in women's clothes. A print by James McArdell tells us: 'A child, not five Years old who, under the tuition of Mr Oswald Performed on the Flute at Drury Lane Theatre Anno 1748 for 50 Nights with extraordinary Skill & Applause, and in the following Year was able to play his part in any Concert on the Violoncello.'

The picture in the section following p. 128 shows that he not only held the instrument like a double bass, supporting it with the left hand, but also held the bow at a point at least one-third of its length from the heel; to achieve any technical facility would therefore have been difficult.

In advertisements his name is listed as 'The Child' alongside Mr Garrick and Mrs Cibber, leading lights in the theatre. In 1752, 'At the particular desire of Several Persons of Quality' Benjamin Hallet—now nine years of age—was given 'A Benefit'. Everyone from the leading actor down to the humblest carpenter had his Benefit at some time. After 'A Grand Piece with Kettle-Drums and Trumpets', there is a Solo on the Violoncello by Cupid—alias Benjamin Hallet—who also speaks an epilogue in the character of Cupid. It was announced, 'The house will be made very warm, and illuminated with wax lights'.[1] Hallet received a further Benefit the following year. But at almost eleven no doubt he would have looked incongruous in women's clothes. For whatever reason, his public career appears to have ended there. Perhaps he took up a position in an orchestra somewhere and, dressed as a male, was no longer recognizable?

The London-born John Crosdill (1755–1825) began his career as a choirboy at Westminster Abbey. His father, a pupil of Duport, gave him his first lessons and, at the age of nine, Crosdill appeared as a prodigy at a concert given by Siprutini, when they played a duet for two cellos. In 1768 when only seventeen he was elected a member of the Royal Society of Musicians. A year later he was appointed first cellist in the Three Choirs Festival at Gloucester, a position he held until his retirement, excepting the year 1778 when the younger Cervetto took his place. In 1775 Crosdill continued his studies in Paris under the elder Duport where he was a co-student and friend of the younger. It was Crosdill who persuaded Jean Louis to play in London later in his career.

When the 'Concert of Antient Music' was established in 1776, Crosdill was appointed first cellist. He also became a member of the Chapel Royal, a member of the King's Band of Music and Chamber Musician to Queen Charlotte. It was at this time that he gave cello lessons to the Prince of Wales (afterwards George IV) and, as a result, became a great favourite in court circles and the most fashionable cello teacher in the country. His many pupils included members of the aristocracy and several who later became profes- sional musicians. The Yorkshire-born Robert Lindley and Henry Griesbach from Copenhagen both studied with Crosdill.

He appeared frequently at the 'Professional Concerts' at the Hanover Square Rooms, managed by Lord Abingdon, and was also manager of the 'Ladies Concerts' which took place at the homes of leading ladies of society. Crosdill amassed a considerable fortune, augmented it by marrying a rich lady and retired from public life. He emerged once only from this retirement, in 1821 to play at the Coronation of George IV.

Crosdill was said to have an amiable disposition and showed great generosity towards his fellow musicians. In his will he bequeathed £1,000 to the Royal Society of Musicians—a princely sum at the time.

The London-born James Cervetto (1747–1837), son of Giacobo Basevi Cervetto, received his first lessons from his father and made rapid progress, appearing at the Little Haymarket Theatre on 23 April 1760 at the age of thirteen. It was said that he lacked the fiery temperament and execution of Crosdill but his tone was sweeter and more expressive. This was probably due to the guidance he received from Karl Friedrich Abel, the celebrated gambist who served as a model for many cellists of the time. Burney says of him, 'When a child, and hardly acquainted with the gammut, [he] had a better tone, and played what he was able to execute, in a manner much more *chantant* than his father. And, arrived at manhood, his tone and expression were equal to those of the best tenor voices.'[2]

From 1780 onwards Cervetto played at the Professional Concerts along with Crosdill and his contemporaries, and also with Duport and Baumgarten when they visited London in 1783. According to *Cramer's Magazine* of 1784, in March of that year he had played a concerto of his own composition with 'the power of tone and nobility of style which one is accustomed to hear from this artist'.

Cervetto travelled throughout Europe for seven years playing in the principal cities and meeting with much success. In 1771 he was appointed solo cellist to the Queen's Private Band.

He wrote a considerable amount for his instrument including *Twelve Solos for a Violoncello with a Thorough Bass for the Harpsichord*, and *Twelve Sonatinas and Six Lessons or Divertimenti*. His compositions show a distinct advance in technique over that of the early Italian writers for the instrument, a greater development of passage work and considerable variety in double stops.

James Cervetto evidently inherited his father's longevity and lived to be ninety. His life was one of great comfort with an assured place in society gained for him by his father's fortune.

It is important to remember that there were practically no books of instruction to guide these early cellists. Methods were passed down by word of mouth from teacher to pupil. One of the first tutors was published *c.*1765 by Robert Crome, under the title, *The Complete Tutor for the Violoncello containing the Best and Easiest Instructions for Learners*. In the second edition there is some interesting advice together with an account of what could only be the forerunner of the spike:

> This instrument may be Consider'd as a large Fiddle only held the contrary way, and the fourth string is next to the Bow Hand, as the Body is turn'd downward, the lower part is to rest on the Calves of the Legs supported with the knees, but for the greater ease of a Learner we wou'd advize him to have a hole made in the Tail-pin and a Wooden Peg to screw into it to rest on the Floor which may be taken out when he Pleases.[3]

He is implying that once the learner became an expert he would no longer need the peg. This was written over one hundred years before the introduction of the end-pin or spike.

Another interesting point is that Robert Crome advocates the

modern bow hold. Although by no means generally adopted, it is
clear that it had come into use in the eighteenth century. He also
suggests tying pieces of fiddle string under the strings to form frets
as an aid for intonation. Playford, in his *Easy Guide to the Skill of
Music* (1664), suggested that learners on the violin should do
likewise, a practice carried out successfully by Arnold Dolmetsch
early this century with his young violin pupils.

Yorkshire seems to have been a good breeding ground for cellists.
Rotherham-born Robert Lindley (1776–1855) was by far the greatest
English cellist to this date. His father, a violinist, gave him his first
lessons on that instrument, but at an early age Lindley exchanged it
for the cello. When he was only nine he appeared at the Brighton
Theatre, taking the place of an indisposed soloist. He not only
brought the house down with his brilliant playing, but was invited
back several times to take part in further concerts.

At sixteen he continued his studies with James Cervetto, and in
1794 became principal cellist of the Opera at the King's Theatre in
London and retained that position for 57 years. At the same time he
appears to have followed a solo career without any impediment,
appearing at the 'Antient Concerts' and those given by the Philharmonic Society.

Lindley's friendship with Dragonetti, the virtuoso double-bass
player, lasted for over 50 years. It was said of them: 'Nothing could
compare with the intimacy of their mutual musical sympathy. They
played together at the same desk and at every orchestral concert of any
importance, and Lindley's performance of the accompaniment to
recitative, from a Figured Bass, was most elaborate and ingenious.'
This was already a dying art, so Lindley's reputation as a reliable and
musical accompanist became widespread. He included a great deal of
eighteenth-century music in his repertoire and his performance of
Corelli sonatas with Dragonetti were famous. It is interesting that Van
der Straeten considered it was somewhat strange that Lindley should
include this early music in his repertoire 'at a time when *so many* fine
and important works for the violoncello had been written'.[4]

The French writer Vidal does not seem to have been impressed
with his playing. He describes it as 'cold, and in technique and style
he remained far behind Romberg, Lamarre, Bohrer and Servais'.
The coldness seems to be confirmed in an opinion expressed in the
Berliner Musikzeitung after a performance in Germany: 'Lindley plays
the violoncello as beautifully, with perfect intonation and surety of
technique, as [Robert] Hausmann, but he has not the fire.' Grove is

a little more enthusiastic. 'Lindley's tone was remarkable for its purity, richness, mellowness and volume. His technique, for that date, was remarkable, and his accompaniment of recitative was in its way perfection, though his style was wholly unsuited to *recitativo secco*.' This remark stems from the criticism that in opera he took liberties by over-embellishment in accompanying recitative when all that was needed was support for the vocal line.

When the Royal Academy of Music was founded in London in 1822, Lindley was appointed one of their first cello professors.

CHAPTER VI

Father of the German School:
Bernhard Romberg

ONE OF THE most important cellists in the latter half of the eighteenth century, and the undisputed father of the German school of cello playing, was Bernhard Heinrich Romberg (1767–1841). It was not only his technical skill and musicality that attracted audiences throughout Europe, but also his considerable gifts as a composer. Romberg revolutionized the technique of the instrument exploring its capabilities in a way that looked forward to the demands of the nineteenth century. He was, for the cello, the main link between the classical and romantic periods, forming a bridge between Boccherini and Duport, and responsible for developments later taken up by Servais and Davidov.

Romberg was born at Dinklage in Germany into a distinguished family of musicians who, for several generations, had produced string and wind players, pianists and singers. His father was clarinettist to the Prince Elector at Munster, and his cousin, Andreas, a virtuoso violinist and composer.

Bernhard received his first instruction on the cello from Johann Schlick (c.1759–c.1825), one of the great virtuosos of the late eighteenth century and cellist to the Prince Elector at Munster. After some further tuition from the Viennese, Franz Marteau, Romberg completed his studies under a violinist.

At the age of seven he appeared at a public concert with his violinist cousin, Andreas, with whom he later toured the principal cities of Europe. In 1784, this brilliant pair captivated Parisian society at a soirée at the home of Baron Bagge. At a Concert Spirituel, they made such an impression that the composer, François Philidor (whose consuming passion was chess, at which he was said to be unbeatable), introduced them to the great violinist, Viotti, then at the height of his fame. Romberg would also have heard J. P. Duport in Paris. The French influences both on his playing and composition almost certainly stemmed from this period.

For several years Romberg and his cousin played in the Court Orchestra at Munster, and later moved to Bonn where they met the Ries family, the leading Czech cellist, Joseph Reicha, and Beethoven, who was then organist and violist to the Court. During this time Franz Ries, Andreas and Bernhard Romberg formed a string quartet with Beethoven as their violist. They also played in a piano trio with Beethoven. When the French invaded Germany in 1782, Beethoven and Romberg escaped together working as kitchen boys on a Rhine river boat.

Beethoven thought highly of Romberg and his playing, but the latter had little understanding of his friend's music. Spohr, in his autobiography, tells how Romberg suggested it was impossible to play 'such absurd stuff' as Beethoven's Quartets Op. 18. On another occasion it is claimed that Romberg struggled with one of the Rasoumovsky quartets, failed to understand its meaning, threw it on the floor with the retort, 'Nobody can play that!' Perhaps the most unforgivable legacy of his arrogance is that when Beethoven wanted to write a cello concerto for him, Romberg rejected the offer because he only performed his own compositions.

With the outbreak of the French Revolution, the cousins moved to Hamburg, and from there undertook a long concert tour which included their début in Vienna. Here they were assisted by their friend Beethoven, now living in that city. Romberg played two of Beethoven's cello Sonatas Op. 5 at this concert, with Beethoven at the piano.

Parting from his cousin for the first time, Romberg toured England, Spain and Portugal. At a soirée at the Court in Lisbon, King Ferdinand VII, a good amateur musician, played the violin. The many Spanish influences found in Romberg's later works seem to suggest that his time in Madrid was a happy one.

The success of Romberg's concerts in Paris in 1800 resulted in the offer of a professorship at the Paris Conservatoire. He accepted, but after only two years returned to Hamburg. He subsequently became solo cellist to the Chapel Royal of Prussia, in Berlin, where he often performed with the Duports. Spohr, who heard him at this time, describes him as being 'in the flower of his virtuosity'. The German critic, Rochlitz (never easy to please), also wrote: 'Romberg is the most accomplished of all living violoncellists. . . . Since the time of Mozart, the most discriminating audience has never been as greatly enraptured by any other artist, both as performer and composer.'[1]

Four years later, when the Napoleonic wars put Prussia into turmoil, Romberg was on the move again. It was then that he first went to Russia—he was to make six visits in all—meeting with unparalleled success. Russian critics wrote glowing accounts of his performances and the nobility vied with each other to have him as their house guest. One of the close friendships from this time was with the Count Mathieu Wielhorsky, a fine amateur cellist who also became his pupil. Through his travels in Russia, Romberg did a great deal to stimulate interest in cello playing in that country, especially in provincial towns where he was able to reach musicians who might never have had the opportunity to hear such an artist.

In his maturity, presumably Romberg revised his views on Beethoven. In 1824 he was the first to play the cello part in one of Beethoven's late quartets, the Op.127 in E flat major, commissioned by Prince Nikolay Galitzin.

Clearly, Romberg retained his power well into old age. In 1833 when he was sixty-six, a Vienna critic wrote: 'The artist's consummate skill is truly enchanting. Though of advanced years, he is still the same great master; the only vocalist of the instrument, he seems to take delight in toying with extraordinary difficulties. He will, no doubt, continue as an unsurpassed performer.'[2] Three years later a Munich critic wrote: 'Even time yields to this artist. What he has lost in power, he has made up for in tenderness, sincerity and precision; the totality and perfection of his playing are as surprising as ever.'[3]

With hindsight, it is easy to dismiss Romberg's compositions as being of merely academic interest, but, seen in the light of his time, they were of considerable value. He employed a number of new devices which led other contemporary composers to develop them, and extend the capabilities of the instrument. For instance, he made more use of the thumb position than had any of his predecessors since Boccherini. Romberg also acknowledged J. L. Duport's contribution in establishing a system of specific fingering for the cello, and built upon it to develop left-hand technique to a very advanced level which he then used skilfully in his compositions.

Despite the fact that, for the most part, Romberg was a travelling virtuoso at a time when getting about was both difficult and hazardous, his creative powers were prolific. Besides several operas, his works include ten concertos, six concertinos, sonatas, duets, string quartets, fantasias, divertimenti, variations and countless other pieces. Although not likely to compete with some of the great classics, his concertos in particular are excellent for teaching purposes. Hugo Becker, one of the prominent cello teachers of the first half of the twentieth century, considered that Romberg's concertos were the best possible exercise, especially for the left hand. Many older cellists who were trained during this period well remember the name Romberg as synonymous with 'all those dreadfully difficult concertos'.

Curiously enough his egocentric personality inadvertently served a useful purpose, in that he used the orchestra as an accompaniment only, demanding from the soloist an advanced technique. Indeed, the emphasis is on technique in every concerto. Romberg wrote out all his cadenzas, presumably not wishing to encourage spontaneous improvization. He also advocated sparing use of vibrato, maintaining that if used only when necessary, it had greater effect. He gave similar directions for guarded use of spiccato and harmonics, and criticized Paganini—whom he otherwise admired—for his abuse of harmonics and other tricks.

Romberg completed a cello method in 1839, which was accepted as a manual for the Paris Conservatoire, and subsequently published in Paris, Germany, Austria and England. From this manual we discover that staccato was apparently not a strong part of his own technique, and—according to Van der Straeten—never used in any of his concertos. Romberg maintains that staccato can only be achieved by using a stiff arm or a tightly screwed-up bow, and even then success is doubtful. He writes: 'Indeed, as the violoncellist is so seldom called upon to employ the *staccato*, it would be a great pity that he should spoil his bow hand by practising it to any extent', a recommendation destined to have had a bad influence on many German players who presumably would have passed on this information to their pupils. In short, he belonged to the school of Viotti and Spohr in believing that the instrument should express feeling in good taste and that virtuosity for its own sake was vulgar.

Romberg also extended his inventiveness to the instrument itself. It was he who suggested flattening the right-hand side of the fingerboard to prevent the C string from beating on it when great pressure was placed on the bow. Other modifications, such as the thinning and lengthening of the cello neck and fingerboard and the increasing of the distance between the fingerboard and the table, are also attributed to Romberg.

Another simplification for which Romberg was largely responsible was the reduction of clefs used in music for the cello. Until well into the nineteenth century, Italians and Germans used only the tenor clef in cello compositions, whilst in France only the alto clef was used. Boccherini made use of five clefs. As explained in an earlier chapter, this was largely due to the ambiguous position held by the cello until the end of the eighteenth century. As the compass of cello playing was extended up to the higher positions, it was deemed necessary to use clefs that would make reading easier for the performer. Romberg is also credited with having invented the sign for the thumb.

Romberg played on a Golden Age Stradivari dated 1711. Hill quotes that instrument as being unique in that it has only a single line of black purfling instead of the usual three—two black and one white. Stradivari is not known to have used one on any other instrument. The cello is also exceptional in that its back and sides are of plain poplar instead of the more usual maple. Only a few of Stradivari's instruments are made from this wood—mostly those dating from before 1700. Romberg also possessed two very fine Tourte bows, stamped Romberg 1 and 2 (now owned by Edmund Kurtz), which shows he benefited from the advantages of the fully developed model which emerged in 1780.

Romberg had many pupils, of which the most outstanding were Cyprian Romberg (his nephew), Pierre Norblin, Mathieu Wielhorsky, Adolf Press, Friedrich Kummer and August Prell.[4] Romberg's influence on cello playing in his time, and on musicians such as Dotzauer (founder of the Dresden school), and on several generations of pupils, cannot be overestimated. Hugo Becker, when discussing the great cellists of his own time, said that Romberg, Servais and Davidov were 'the most brilliant creative personalities in the realm of art, whose compositions had a huge impact on the development of cello playing'.[5]

CHAPTER VII

The Dresden School

ALWAYS AN ACTIVE centre of music, the Dresden Court managed
to attract many gifted musicians from other countries, especially
Italy. Consequently the standards were high and the Dresden Court
Orchestra enjoyed an excellent reputation. After the turn of the
eighteenth century, the advent of Dotzauer and what came to be
known as the Dresden school of cello playing brought the study of
this instrument to a peak. Until the beginning of the twentieth
century, Dresden remained a most important centre for cello
playing.

Justus Johann Friedrich Dotzauer (1783–1860) was born at Hasel-
rieth, near Hildburghausen, the son of a minister of the church. He
showed early talent for music and took lessons on the piano and the
violin. The village blacksmith, who played for fairs and dances,
taught him the double-bass, and he is known also to have played the
horn and the clarinet. Ruttinger, the local organist, whose musical
lineage stretched back to no less a person than J. S. Bach, taught the
young Dotzauer music theory. Early cello lessons were, unbelieva-
bly, the responsibility of the Court trumpeter. Thus the early
musical education of young Justus Johann Friedrich was not without
versatility.

Having decided on the cello as his main choice, he was sent to
Meiningen to study with Kriegk, a pupil of the younger Duport.
For a time he was a member of the Leipzig Orchestra, subsequently
joining the Court Orchestra at Dresden. Ten years later he was
appointed solo violoncellist and remained in that post until 1850
when he retired.

In 1806 Dotzauer went to Berlin where he had a period of study
with Romberg, so forming yet another link with the Duports. His
repertoire included many of the concertos by his master. His interest
in string quartet playing led to the foundation of the celebrated
Leipzig Professors' quartet. Even the pernickety Spohr was high in

praise of Dotzauer's qualities as a quartet player, remarking on the purity of his intonation and the perfection of his technique.

Although Dotzauer appeared successfully as a soloist in Vienna, and in all the main towns of Germany and the Netherlands, it is as a teacher that he is best remembered. Among his many pupils were Kummer, Schuberth, Voigt and Dreschler.

In Dotzauer's *Violoncellschule*, like Romberg he holds the instrument between the calves without an end-pin, but from illustrations we see that his position has more freedom than Romberg's, and he appears to hold the bow in a more relaxed manner. The French schools recommended that the bow should be held a certain distance from the frog, whereas in Dotzauer's *Violoncellschule* he appears to be one of the first who insisted that it should be held close to the frog as we do today. Overall, he tried to train his students to use a natural movement throughout the entire length of the bow, which looked forward to the twentieth century.

A prolific composer for his instrument, his many symphonies, operas, concertos, concertinos, sonatas, a Mass and several chamber works have now faded into oblivion. His teaching works are quite a different matter. He wrote three Violoncello 'schools', 180 exercises and caprices, some containing preludes and fugues, and although these are now of only academic interest, the exercises still provide excellent material for the student.

Friedrich August Kummer (1797–1879) was born in Meiningen, the son of a well known oboist who played in the Ducal Band. His first music lessons were on the oboe with his father, but when the latter was promoted to the Chapel Royal at Dresden, Friedrich took up the cello and began studies with Dotzauer. When he applied for admission to the Chapel Royal in 1814, there was no vacancy for a cellist, so he was taken on as an oboist! Three years later, he was admitted to the cello section. When Dotzauer retired, Kummer was appointed solo cellist in his place, a position he held until 1864 having celebrated 50 years with the same orchestra. He retained the post he had held at the Dresden Conservatoire from its foundation in 1856 until his death in 1879. Among his numerous pupils were his sons, Ernst and Max, Bernhard Cossmann, Julius Goltermann, Richard Bellmann and Ferdinand Böchmann.

Kummer was renowned for his diligence and attention to detail, and worked incessantly to improve both the technical and artistic side of his playing. It was said that his quiet and cautious temperament prevented him from rising to the heights of inspiration, but others defended him claiming that the outstanding features of his style were a nobility, lack of affectation and the ability to convey the spirit of the work performed. A critic in the *Allgemeine Musikzeitung* wrote: 'The main attribute is his elegiac playing; how wonderfully Kummer can express it and how frequently he coaxes the listener to this mood.' Van der Straeten agreed that he was a fine cellist, but had one misgiving: 'Unfortunately he remained a stranger to the lighter and more brilliant technique of the bow, cultivated by the French and Belgian school.' It seems that he looked upon *spiccato, staccato* spring bow arpeggios as 'idle tricks'. Van der Straeten apparently learnt this at first hand since he had his early lessons on the cello from a Kummer pupil, Johannes Hoecke, a member of the Cologne Orchestra.

Nevertheless, Kummer became known and admired throughout Europe and Scandinavia, and in Dresden he played in a quartet led by the Polish violinist, Karol Lipinsky. Their 'Quartet Academies', in which they played the music of Haydn, Mozart and Beethoven, became one of the most important activities in this musical city. The press praised their technical mastery, expressive interpretation, and faithfulness to the style of the music played.

Kummer wrote a great deal for his instrument: concertinos, duets, duos, a concerto and a number of arrangements and transcriptions. He had 163 published works, whilst 200 entr'actes for the Royal Court Theatre remained in manuscript. None of this music is ever played, but, like those of his master Dotzauer, his teaching works were of the greater value. His *Violoncello School*, with an appendix of *101 Excellent Studies*, his *Ten Melodic Studies* Op. 57, and the eight *Grand Etudes* Op. 44, are considered by many to be among the finest studies ever written for the cello.

In his 'school' we see a picture of Kummer holding the cello in a manner similar in many ways to that of Dotzauer, but more naturally. It was this naturalness for which Kummer strove. He was beginning to approach the modern idea of placing the fingers on the frog of the bow and he considered the freedom of movement very important. He was, however, inclined to overexaggerate wrist movements when evaluating the role of the arm.

Another Dotzauer pupil, Karl Dreschler (1800–1873) from Saxony, began his career as a military bandsman at Dessau. Friedrich Schneider, Kapellmeister to the Duke of Anhalt-Dessau, noticed his talent and recommended him to his employer who provided the means for some study with Dotzauer. When his training was complete, Dreschler undertook a long and extensive tour of Europe including England and Scotland. In 1826 he was appointed principal cellist of the Dessau Orchestra.

Wasielewski says that Dreschler's performances were characterized as much by faultless purity and refinement as by feeling and tasteful playing which, though not powerful, was graceful and delicate. A very able leader of the cello section in orchestras, he was much sought after as principal cellist in music festivals all over Germany. He was also an excellent teacher, bringing all the expertise of the Dresden school to Dessau, and, through his pupils—the best known being Lindner, Cossmann, Espenhahn and Grützmacher—he consolidated the line through several generations.

Although born in Hamburg, and trained by the elder Prell—a pupil of Romberg—Sebastian Lee (1805–87) spent much of his working life in France. In 1830 he made successful débuts in Hamburg, Leipzig and Frankfurt, but two years later, a warm reception in Paris made him decide to live there. In 1837 he became solo cellist with the Grand Opera Orchestra in Paris, a position he held for over 30 years. On his retirement he returned to his native city, devoting himself to teaching and composition.

Owing to the dual influences of the German and French environment, Lee combined features of both schools in his stylish playing, and also in his *Ecole de Violoncelliste* (Paris 1845). Accepted as a manual at the Conservatoire, the dedication was to its cello professor, Pierre Norblin. With the exception of his *Etudes* Op. 57, which are still used for teaching purposes, Lee's compositions are of little value today. One of his best known pupils was Ferdinand Böchmann.

Karl Schuberth (1811–63), from Magdeburg, the son of Gottlob Schuberth a virtuoso oboist and clarinettist, had his first lessons on the cello at the age of five. He appeared in public as a soloist at eleven, and at thirteen was sent to study with Dotzauer. He enjoyed a successful solo career appearing all over Europe. England and Scandinavia. In 1835 Schuberth went to St Petersburg where he took up a permanent position as Director of the Imperial Band and Inspector of the Music School affiliated to the Court Theatre. He was also appointed Director of Music at the University. In 1863, he went to Zürich for what was to be a period of convalescence, but died there shortly afterwards.

Schuberth's playing was described by Wasielewski as 'exceedingly clever, but in expression more elegant and ornamental than expressive'. Another critic describes it as brilliant but lacking in breadth and grandeur. His compositions, although effectively written for the instrument and useful for the student, would appear to reflect the bleak judgements of his playing. Today Schuberth is remembered mainly for his most famous pupil, the Russian Karl Davidov.

The name of Bernhard Cossmann (1822–1910) is probably best known for his studies which remain in universal use today. Born at Dessau, the son of a Jewish merchant, he was a pupil of both Dreschler and Theodore Müller (cellist of the celebrated Müller String Quartet), and completed his studies with Kummer at Dresden. From 1840 he was principal violoncellist at the Théâtre Italien in Paris, during which period he also made appearances in London, Berlin and Leipzig. In 1847 Mendelssohn appointed him solo cellist for the Gewandhaus Concerts at Leipzig, when he took the opportunity of studying composition with Moritz Hauptmann. In 1849 he undertook an extensive concert tour which brought him to England and Ireland. He played before Queen Victoria at Windsor Castle, and at the Philharmonic Society Concerts in Dublin.

In his Leipzig period, Cossmann formed a friendship with Liszt. In a letter to Wagner, in July 1850, Liszt writes: 'Our cellos will be strengthened by the addition of Cossmann from Paris . . . a member of our orchestra from the 15 August . . . will be an excellent acquisition.' Cossmann played at the first performance of Wagner's *Lohengrin* at Weimar in August 1850, with Liszt as conductor. He was also engaged as solo cellist to the Duke of Weimar and first cellist in the Weimar Orchestra, a position he held for sixteen years.

Wasielewski remarked upon his 'fine, distinct tone' and that he 'manages the fingerboard with ease'.[1] A good soloist and excellent quartet player, it was in this latter field that Cossmann became known throughout Europe. Weimar was the mecca of many distinguished musicians and Cossmann had no difficulty in forming string quartets in this town where the playing was of a very high standard. Joachim, Laub, Singer and other great violinists were at some time leaders of his quartet.

During a tour of Russia in 1866, Cossmann accepted the post of professor at the Imperial Conservatoire, but stayed only four years. He returned to Baden-Baden where he had always spent his summers regardless of his professional domicile. From this time onwards he undertook numerous tours with Brahms, von Bülow, and the famous Austrian soprano, Pauline Lucca.

In 1878 he was appointed professor at the Hochschule at Frankfurt-am-Main, a post he held until his death in 1911. Since his return from Russia he had devoted considerable time to composition and the editing of works for the cello. None of his compositions are remembered today, except his *Etudes de Concert* Op. 10 and his cello studies.

Cossmann was known for his dry humour. Carl Fuchs, who studied with him, said that once, when a pupil was playing Popper's 'Dance of the Elves' with a tolerable left hand but a very heavy bow arm, Cossmann said: 'Very good, but you had better call it "In the saw-mill"!'

The name of the Hanover-born Georg Edward Goltermann (1824–98), a pupil of August Prell, is almost forgotten today, but in the latter part of the nineteenth century he was a well-known touring virtuoso. In 1851 he retired from the concert platform in order to devote his time to composition and conducting. Unfortunately, the decision was probably the wrong one. His compositions are not of any lasting value, but they have a certain advantage in that he wrote with an intimate understanding of the instrument that allows less gifted players to obtain the greatest effect with comparatively small demand on their abilities.

The leading light in cello playing in the second half of the nineteenth century, and the abomination of the twentieth century musicologists for his mutilated editions of the classical repertoire, was Friedrich Wilhelm Grützmacher (1832–1903). Born in Dessau, he received his first musical instruction from his father, a member of the ducal band. His preference for the cello showed itself very early on and he began his studies with Dotzauer's pupil, Dreschler. The Dresden school of cello playing was thus given still greater forward impulse through Grützmacher.

In 1848 he went to Leipzig, playing in a private orchestra, and was heard by the famous violinist, Ferdinand David, who arranged for him to play in one of the 'Euterpe' concerts. When Cossmann left Leipzig in 1850, Grützmacher succeeded him in all three of his professional appointments—solo cellist in the theatre orchestra, the Gewandhaus Concerts and professor at the Conservatoire. For many years Grützmacher also played in the David String Quartet.

Grützmacher left Leipzig in 1860 to take up the position of principal cellist of the Court Orchestra at Dresden. He was also head of the Dresden Musical Society and, from 1877, professor at the Dresden Conservatoire. Despite all these activities he still managed to undertake concert tours in Europe and Russia, where he made the acquaintance of Davidov, to whom he often went for advice.

Grützmacher's playing was characterized by his mastery of technical difficulties combined with a delicate manner of expression and great musicality, and his cantilena was much admired. The one criticism was that his playing had a certain stiffness. Perhaps by today's standards we would have considered his playing nearer to the norm than did some of his contemporaries who excelled in slides and excessive vibrato. Grützmacher's repertoire would also show him to be forward-looking, in that he included sonatas by Beethoven, Mendelssohn, Chopin and Grieg. As a soloist Grützmacher played in the first performance of Richard Strauss's *Don Quixote* in Cologne in 1898.

A gifted teacher, Grützmacher trained many young cellists who later became well-known. His younger brother, Leopold, his nephew, Friedrich, Emil Hegar, Johann Klingenberg, Wilhelm Fitzenhagen and Hugo Becker all studied with him in Dresden. There is no doubt that the activity of these and other cellists helped to carry forward the high principles of the Dresden school. Closely allied with the Viotti school of violin-playing, combining a sound technique with developed musicality, it also attempted to improve the general repertoire by replacing drawing-room pieces with music of real value. Solo, chamber and orchestral playing were seen as a musical whole, and teaching and performance united with this aim in view.

Although once widely used, Grützmacher's compositions are almost unknown today. However, his transcriptions, studies and arrangements of the classics provided, at the time, a much needed extension to the repertoire, and it is to his credit that he brought about a renewed interest in the music of composers who had been completely forgotten. He vandalized Boccherini's concertos by taking samples from four different works to form his edition of the Concerto in B flat, unfortunately still used today. Brave cellists such as Anner Bylsma and Maurice Gendron have researched into the originals and have dared to redress the balance; but habit dies hard and many modern players are unaware of the inaccuracies in the edited version. Nonetheless, Grützmacher did at least bring Boccherini into the public view. Had it not been for his 'arrangements' that genius might be remembered only for one minuet. A much more blatant example is Grützmacher's 'concert' version of Bach's Solo Suites, which he completely reorganized with additional chords, passages and embellishments which inexcusably distort the composer's work. On the other hand, he must be given some credit for having been one of the first in modern times to look at the Bach Suites as concert pieces rather than as studies. The cadenzas he wrote for the Boccherini B flat Concerto, and the Haydn D Major (little) Concerto are still played today and prove that he had a thorough knowledge of his instrument and its capabilities. His *Twelve Etudes* Op. 72 and *Daily Exercises* Op. 67 (later edited by Hugo Becker) still occupy a place in the teaching literature.

CHAPTER VIII

The Dresden Influence

A PUPIL OF Grützmacher at Dresden, Johann Klingenberg (1852–1905) should be mentioned for his one contribution to cello playing: his 'Dotzauer-Klingenberg' tutor, in which he amalgamates three volumes of Dotzauer with exercises by Duport. It is probably the most systematic and thorough work ever compiled for the instrument.

Klingenberg held several important appointments in ducal bands at Wiesbaden and Brunswick, but concentrated upon editing music, mainly for the publisher Litolff at Brunswick. He used to relax by taking solitary walking tours in the Tyrol. In July 1905 he went out as usual but never returned. His valise, which he always sent on by post to his next halting place, was also not recovered, and it is generally presumed that he was robbed and murdered.

One of the great chamber-music players of the latter part of the nineteenth century, Robert Hausmann (1852–1909), was born in Rottleberode in the Harz Mountains, and at nine received lessons from Theodore Müller, cellist of the Müller String Quartet. When the Berlin Hochschule was founded in 1869, Hausmann was one of the first pupils to study the cello, and proved to be one of the best. He studied under Wilhelm Müller until the latter's death in 1871, and succeeded him as first professor of the cello. Joachim, a violin professor at the same institution, took Hausmann to London. It was here that he met and studied with Piatti, with whom he became closely attached. He was a frequent winter visitor to Piatti's villa at Cadenabbia in Italy.

Hausmann appeared in London with the Philharmonic Society and on a number of occasions at the old St James's Hall, receiving a warm response from audiences and critics. He was a member of the Dresden String Quartet, and in 1878 joined the Joachim Quartet with which he was associated until Joachim's death in 1907. The 'London' Joachim Quartet, the principal quartet of the Monday and Saturday 'Pops', was an independent group, of which Piatti was the cellist.

On 18 October 1887, Hausmann and Joachim gave the first performance of the Brahms Double Concerto at Cologne, with the composer conducting. Brahms had written the concerto in an attempt at reconciliation with Joachim, from whom he was estranged when Brahms sided with Joachim's wife in their divorce suit. After the performance of the concerto Hanslick described Joachim as 'the king of all violinists' and Hausmann as 'a virtuoso cellist of hardly lower standing'. Brahms had long been an admirer of Hausmann's playing.

Hausmann once took the Dvořák Concerto to Brahms and they played it together. Afterwards, Brahms said, 'Had I known that such a concerto as that could be written, I would have tried to compose one myself.' Brahms had long promised to compose a new work for Hausmann, but no concerto materialized. However, he wrote his second sonata, Op. 99 in F major, for him, and it was first performed from the manuscript on 14 November 1886 in the small hall of the Musical Society in Berlin by Hausmann with the composer at the piano. Max Kalbeck wrote in the *Presse*:

It is difficult to imagine how happy we are to hear this brilliant composition performed so professionally before the rest of the musical world will be able to enjoy it. The creative spirit is still hovering over the manuscript, and the composer's personality arises right in front of us. No stranger stands between the work and the listener, and that is why there appears a picture true down to the tiniest details for those who perceive it sincerely and ingenuously.[1]

Max Bruch's beautiful *Kol Nidrei* was also dedicated to Robert Hausmann.

Hausmann's playing combined an excellent technique of the left hand with a great facility of the bow and a tone that was rich and powerful. He was a highly gifted musician who excelled in the performance of chamber music, and contributed to the literature of his instrument by publishing carefully revised editions of classical studies. His edition of the Bach Suites for solo cello (1898) had the merit of being closer to the original text than most.

Hausmann played on one of the most beautiful Golden Age Stradivari cellos—dated 1724. Known today as the 'Hausmann', it is owned by Edmund Kurtz.

Friedrich Wilhelm Fitzenhagen (1848–90) was born in Seesen in the Duchy of Brunswick where his father was musical director. From the age of five he took lessons on the piano, the cello and the violin; and on account of the frequent emergencies that occurred in the small ducal band he played, in addition, several wind instruments.

At fourteen, Fitzenhagen began serious study of the cello with Theodore Müller and completed a period of advanced study with Grützmacher in Dresden, where he was also engaged for the Chapel Royal.

In 1870 he played at the Beethoven Festival at Weimar and attracted the attention of Liszt who tried to tempt him to join the orchestra in that town. But Fitzenhagen had accepted an appointment as professor at the Imperial Conservatoire in Moscow, and thereby embarked on the most important period in his career. At the time he was regarded as the premier cello professor in Russia and was appointed solo cellist to the Russian Imperial Musical Society, and director of the Moscow Music and Orchestral Union which organized many concerts where he appeared as soloist.

Fitzenhagen wrote more than sixty works for his instrument: they include four cello concertos, a suite for cello and orchestra, a string quartet which was awarded the prize of the St Petersburg Chamber Musical Union, and many salon pieces.

On 30 November 1877, Fitzenhagen gave the first performance of the Tchaikovsky *Variations on a Rococo Theme* Op. 33 for cello and orchestra, which was dedicated to him. Tchaikovsky allowed him a great deal of freedom in modifying the solo cello part, and he altered the sequences of the variations. In Tchaikovsky's original version the D minor variation came third out of eight but Fitzenhagen, seizing the opportunity to stun his audience, switched the seventh and the third, and simply did away with the final variation.

Fitzenhagen must have felt pleased after a performance at the Wiesbaden Festival in June 1879, for he wrote to Tchaikovsky, 'I produced a furore with your variations. I pleased so greatly that I was recalled three times, and after the Andante variation (D minor) there was stormy applause. Liszt said to me: "You carried me away! You played splendidly," and regarding your piece he observed: "Now there, at least, is real music!" '[2]

The variations were to be printed in full score in 1889. Anatoly Brandoukov, who was visiting Tchaikovsky, found him in a bad mood. The composer showed him the proofs saying, 'That idiot Fitzenhagen's been here. Look what he's done to my piece—he's altered everything.' When Brandoukov asked what he was going to do about it, he retorted, 'The devil take it! Let it stand as it is!'[3]

Consequently, the Fitzenhagen version became part of the standard repertoire, but there has been an interesting recent development due to the researches in Moscow of the Russian cellist Victor Kubatsky. He subjected the manuscript to X-ray experiments and discovered that Tchaikovsky's text had been inked over. The original was subsequently published and has been recorded by Sviatoslav Knushevitzky.

Gradually the original began to supersede the vandalized version, but old habits die hard, and many cellists still prefer the Fitzenhagen edition. The young British cellist Raphael Wallfisch now plays the original version and has also made a beautiful and convincing recording.

Nonetheless, as a teacher Fitzenhagen was held in high esteem. He trained a number of excellent cellists, including the Polish Joseph Adamowski (1862–1930), who went to America in 1889 to join the newly-formed Boston Symphony Orchestra, and was one of the founders of the orchestra's pension scheme. Adamowski also formed the string quartet that bore his name, and taught at the New England Conservatory in Boston.

Ludwig Lebell (b. 1872) attracted the attention of musical circles in Vienna with his precocious piano playing at the age of three. He took up the cello at fifteen with Popper in Budapest and was said to be one of his favourite pupils. In 1896 he made his British début at the Queen's Hall Promenade Concerts in London and followed this with appearances all over the country. An excellent teacher, he was for many years in charge of the chamber-music classes at Trinity College in London, and many of the older generation of British string players recall to this day his tuition with much gratitude. He composed a number of works for his instrument, including a sonata and *Twenty Studies* Op. 13. He also published revised editions of studies by Kummer and Dotzauer.

Emil Hegar (1843–1921), from Basel in Switzerland, was one of Grützmacher's best pupils at Leipzig. When only twenty-three he was appointed principal cellist at the Gewandhaus Orchestra and teacher at the Conservatoire, and had many pupils who later followed distinguished careers. The more prominent of these were Klengel, Heberlein and Rensberg. Johann Svendsen dedicated his lovely concerto in D major to Hegar, but it was seldom played because it lacked technical display for the soloist.

Hegar's career was cut short by a nervous complaint of the left hand. He turned to his second love, singing, and was professor of that subject at the Conservatoire at Basel until 1907.

CHAPTER IX

'Paganini of the Cello':
Adrien Servais

ALTHOUGH THE CELLO was introduced into Belgium and Holland at about the same time as in France, it made considerably less progress. William de Fesch, born in the Netherlands at the end of the seventeenth century, is the first cellist of any importance. He was also organist and choirmaster of Antwerp Cathedral, and composed and played the violin. In 1731, he went to London where he met with some success as a composer. His writings include six suites for violoncello, Op. 8, and, according to Fétis, a Mass for two choirs with orchestra for which he wrote a cello obbligato.

One of the strongest influences on the Belgian school of cello playing, through his teaching at the Brussels Conservatoire and his dazzling solo performances, was Adrien François Servais (1807–66). Born at Hal near Brussels, he was the son of an organist who gave him his first musical instruction on the violin. Through the patronage of the Marquis de Sayre he was later sent to Brussels to study with van der Planken, leader of the Opera Orchestra. When Servais heard Platel, he was so enchanted by the sound of the cello that he abandoned the violin, entered the conservatoire as Platel's pupil and was awarded the first prize after only one year. He went on to become Platel's assistant in 1829.

Servais played in the Opera Orchestra, and made solo appearances but attracted little attention in his own country. Three years later in Paris his playing caused a sensation, and his performances at the Philharmonic Society concerts in London the following year were equally triumphant.

However, Servais was a perfectionist and, feeling the need of a final polish, he returned to Brussels for a further two years of study. It was then that his playing reached the highest level, with a faultless technique, a graceful and flowing bow arm and warm and expressive tone. His compositions for his instrument not only reflect these characteristics but also explore new elements of cello technique that he had developed during this period of maturation.

In 1836, Servais revisited Paris and was received with even greater adulation. He subsequently toured all over Europe receiving rave reviews everywhere. A Leipzig critic wrote of 'the enormous power of his *fortissimo* and the exquisite tenderness of his *pianissimo*', and compared the 'incredible technique and excellent accuracy of the left hand' to that of Paganini. Servais, like so many cellists who had begun on the fiddle, placed his left hand on the fingerboard in the manner of violinists. He had also heard Paganini in Paris and was known to admire his playing. In fact, he was nicknamed 'Paganini of the Cello'.

A prolific composer, Servais wrote three concertos, fantasias, duos with piano and violin (in which he collaborated with the violinists Léonard and Vieuxtemps), caprices and many transcriptions. He composed only for cello, his works being full of innovatory techniques, using every device to provide colour and brilliance in his music. His compositions today are mainly of use in teaching but their historical significance must not be underestimated.

In 1839, Servais visited St Petersburg for the first time, where his superb playing appealed greatly to the Russian audiences. There is no doubt that his performances in the capital and provincial towns of Russia stimulated interest in the cello in that country, leading to the development of links between Russia and Belgium in much the same way as did the playing of Vieuxtemps and Wieniawski for the violin. Servais visited Russia ten times in all, undertaking long and extensive tours, and married in St Petersburg in 1849.

A singing tone would seem to have been a feature of his playing even in the highest positions as well as in the bass. A Viennese critic wrote: 'Servais' aim is not to cast dust in his audience's eyes, but to enrapture the heart.'[1] If this seems rather excessive in its praise, we can look at that laconic master, Berlioz, for his opinion. In 1847, he wrote:

In the second concert we discovered a first class talent, of Paganini's standing, which amazes, touches and fascinates by its courage, flights of feeling and vehemence: I am speaking of the great violoncellist, Servais. His singing is heartfelt, without any exaggerated emphasis, with grace and without affectation; he makes short work of the most incredible difficulties: he never allows error in his tone quality, and in the passages when the instrument has to play its highest notes, reaches an impetuosity which the bow of a master violinist would find it hard to manage.[2]

When Platel died in 1848, Servais succeeded him as cello professor at the Brussels Conservatoire. From this time, although his tours became less frequent, he never reached the point of abandoning his wider audiences. Over a period of 40 years, at a time when travel was extremely difficult, Servais gave frequent concerts in various European countries.

Servais will also be remembered for his invention of the spike or end-pin. Apart from the crude device suggested in Robert Crome's tutor, the only other aid was to rest the base of the instrument on a footstool, but this was very early on in its development. In old age, Servais grew very fat and found it difficult to support the cello with his legs. Since it allowed the arms more freedom, the spike revolutionized cello technique. Another very important development following the invention of the spike was that women were at last able to play the instrument with dignity. Prior to this very few 'ladies' dared sit straddled around the cello, and had no option but to play it 'side-saddle'—so to speak.

Servais played on a magnificent large-pattern Stradivari cello dated 1701, which is one of the few which has not been reduced in size. It is also the sole example of the master's work in cellos of that year. In their book, Hills point out that it is the only instrument that combines the grandeur of the pre-1700 cellos with the more masculine build that Stradivari favoured in his earlier years. Furthermore, the ribs on this instrument are the deepest of any cello made by Stradivari.

When this cello came into the hands of the Parisian dealer, Vuillaume, Servais immediately fell in love with it. The large instrument seemed almost made for him, a tall, well-built man, but the price—12,000 francs, and moderate for the time—was quite beyond his means. However, the Princess Youssopova, a wealthy Russian admirer, bought it and presented it to him. The instrument subsequently became almost as famous as its owner, and the tone that he drew from it was remarked upon by all who heard him. Servais also made experiments with different bridges. He found that an exceptionally narrow bridge added brightness to the tone, often lacking in large sized instruments.

Towards the end of his life, Servais was criticized for his over-romantic playing and his 'unending sugary vibrato', especially in Russia where the young Davidov was emerging. Inevitably musical tastes change: both music lovers and musicians were becoming more knowledgable and advancing beyond the demands of the drawing-room which had so well set off Servais' romantic virtuoso style. The spirit of the new age, new aesthetics and profound meaning and significance were the qualities that were now being looked for in music.

In 1866, the last Russian tour that Servais undertook extended to Siberia. As a result of over-exertion, he became ill and died shortly afterwards at his home town of Hal.

His many pupils inherited much of his fine technique and expressive style; among them were his son Joseph, Jules De Swert, Ernest De Munck and Joseph Hollman.

The significance of Servais' role in the history of the art of the violoncello, is that through his performing style and his compositions, he created a unity that symbolized the epoch of romantic virtuosity in which he flourished.

CHAPTER X

Belgium and Holland

THE FOUNDATION OF the Belgian school of cello playing by Platel, and its further development by Servais, began to attract students to the Brussels Conservatoire, but there were still a number from the Netherlands who preferred to go abroad. One of these was Pierre Alexandre Chevillard (1811–77), from Antwerp, who was accepted into the Paris Conservatoire at the age of nine to study with Norblin and took first prize at sixteen. After a period as first cellist at the Théâtre Gymnase, and a number of concert tours, he returned to make a very successful début in Brussels, where critics praised his brilliant technique and refinement of style.

Chevillard was not only a fine player but also concerned with the artistic aspect of his profession. He tried hard to interest Parisian musical circles in Beethoven's late string quartets—which were quite unknown to them—but failed, mainly through the lack of intelligence among his colleagues. Finally, through the help of Maurin, Sabbatier and Mas—who shared his aims—he founded a string quartet called 'Société des derniers Quatuors de Beethoven', and gave some private concerts. Their singularly musical interpretations attracted a steadily increasing audience so that eventually they were encouraged to perform in the Salle Pleyel. Here they found a large and enthusiastic following, especially among amateur quartet players, and subsequently toured all the main cities of Germany where they met with a similar response. In 1859, Chevillard succeeded Vaslin as professor at the Paris Conservatoire.

A cellist who had considerable influence on the development of Dutch cello playing was Jacques Franco-Mendes, born in Amsterdam in 1816 into a Portuguese Jewish family. He showed early talent and at thirteen went to Vienna to study with Joseph Merk, cellist in the Imperial Chapel there. After touring in Europe with his brother Joseph—a fine violinist—he was made Chamber Cellist to the King of Holland, and later became the Royal Solo Cellist. In 1845, when he took part in the Grand Festival in Bonn for the unveiling of the

Beethoven Memorial, he left the critic of the *Allgemeine Musikalische Zeitung* unimpressed with his solo performances. He took up permanent residence in Paris and died there in 1860.

Franco-Mendes wrote a great deal for his instrument; two of his string quintets and a string quartet received first prize from the 'Netherlands Society for the Advancement of Music'. One of the most talented of his pupils was Charles Appy.

Born in The Hague in 1834 of French parentage, Charles Ernest Appy was that rarity among string players, a late starter who achieved fame. He took up piano studies at fourteen, and a year later turned to the cello, taking lessons at first from the Belgian, Charles Montigny, and then Merlen, principal cellist of the Amsterdam Orchestra. He completed his studies with Franco-Mendes and enjoyed a busy career both as soloist and principal cellist in a number of orchestras, including that at the Crystal Palace in London.

In 1862 Appy joined the Coenen String Quartet, where for nine years he performed frequently with some of the greatest artists of the day, including Clara Schumann. For almost twenty years he was professor at the 'Maatschappij tot Bevordering van Toonkunst' in Amsterdam.

Alexander Batta (1816–1902) was born in Maastricht in Holland and had his first lessons on the violin from his father. Like Servais, when he heard Platel play he was so taken with the cello that he abandoned the violin and became Platel's pupil at the conservatoire. He shared the first prize with De Munck in 1834.

In Paris he heard the famous tenor, Rubini, and decided to model his playing on the singing tone of this artist. Unfortunately, Rubini, in common with many of the singers of his time, indulged in slides and excessive rubato. Batta's playing derived little musical benefit from this imitation, but it made him the darling of the Parisian salons where he was lionized, particularly by the ladies.

Batta owned a magnificent Golden Age Stradivari cello, dated 1714, which he acquired in 1838. It seems that Servais had been eulogizing a certain cello in the possession of Thibout, the Parisian luthier, and asked Batta to come and look at it. Then playing an Amati that he liked, Batta was not interested in another instrument. However, once he set eyes on the Strad and heard its voice he was so enchanted that he became obsessed with the idea of owning it. He told his story to a rich friend, a Monsieur Place, who bought it for the very reasonable price of 7,300 francs, and presented it to Batta. Throughout his life, Batta received many offers far in excess of this sum, the most tempting being that of a Russian nobleman who gave him an open cheque from Rothschild's, begging him to fill in the figure. But he steadfastly resisted until he was eighty, when he sold it to Hill's for £3,200. So consuming was his passion for this instrument that he insisted upon taking it personally to the station from which Mr Hill was to leave. When the train was about to depart, he kissed the instrument reverently before handing it over to its new owner.

The Belgian François De Munck (1815–54) was one of the most promising cellists of his generation. The son of a teacher and bandmaster, he received his first instruction from his father, and at ten studied with Platel at the Conservatoire in Brussels. In 1835 he was appointed Platel's assistant, and when Platel died a few months later, De Munck succeeded him.

In his youth, De Munck's playing was said to be distinguished not only by perfect intonation but also by an intensity of feeling combined with an apparent ease in surmounting all difficulties. Sadly, he fell far short of his early promise. It seems that he was far more interested in pursuing what Grove describes as 'a somewhat disorderly course of life'. As a result he neglected more and more the study of the cello, and his health became affected. In 1848 he had to resign from his post at the Conservatoire, and was succeeded by Servais. In a last effort to reinstate himself De Munck was engaged for a time in the orchestra at Her Majesty's Theatre in London, but through failing health he finally returned to Brussels and died shortly afterwards.

Fortunately, his younger son, Joseph Ernest De Munck (1840–1915), was better organized. He appeared in public at the age of eight and made his London début two years later. He studied with Servais at the Brussels Conservatoire, and afterwards travelled as soloist playing concertos with Juillien's orchestra in Great Britain. With his brother, Camille, he gave the first performance of an unpublished duo for violin and violoncello by Vieuxtemps at a 'Saint-Saëns' Concert in Paris, and was also the cellist of the Maurin String Quartet for two years.

In 1871 he went to Weimar as solo violoncellist of the Grand Ducal Chapel, where he became friendly with Liszt. He married the singer, Carlotta Patti, and resided for some time in the USA. He then settled in England and was professor of cello at the Royal Academy of Music in London until his death in 1915.

Jules de Swert (1843–91), from Louvain, was one of the best of the Belgian cellists and Servais' most prominent pupil. He received his first lessons on the cello from his father, a choirmaster at the cathedral in Louvain. Servais heard him and offered to take him as his pupil at the conservatoire, where he became 'Laureat' at fourteen. He pursued a successful career as a soloist appearing throughout Europe and held several appointments in German cities, including Weimar and Berlin where he was first cellist of the Chapel Royal and professor at the Hochschule. He also went to Bayreuth where, at Wagner's request, he formed the orchestra in which he was principal cellist. He spent some time in Dusseldorf where he played in a trio with Clara Schumann and Leopold Auer. Their performance of both classical and modern music was said, at the time, to have been unequalled.

Van der Straeten recalls hearing him play Bach's sixth solo suite, and the impression never faded. In appearance he was short, square-built and muscular, looking more like a prize fighter than a musician, but as soon as he took up his bow he was transformed. Van der Straeten writes, 'His tone was superb, powerful yet full of sweetness, and technical difficulties were unknown to him. He was an excellent musician, who never lowered his art to mere firework displays.'[1]

A cellist who achieved fame in a somewhat less orthodox manner was Auguste van Biene, born in Rotterdam about 1850. He studied with Servais at the Brussels Conservatoire and came to London in 1867 where he played for some time in Sir Michael Costa's orchestra. He then became what was probably the first cellist to appear successfully on the music-hall stage throughout the British Isles. Later he wrote and produced a play called 'The Broken Melody', in which he acted the part of a Russian cellist who played popular melodies interspersed with the dialogue. This met with resounding success and as a result earned him far more money than he would ever have achieved as a serious soloist. There is in existence a recording of the theme, 'The Broken Melody', played by Van Biene complete with an obbligato of sobs.

Edouard Jacobs (1851–1925), from Hal, at first studied the double-bass at the Brussels Conservatoire, turning to the cello at twenty, first with Gustave Libotton, and later with Servais. He toured for some time in Europe and for eight years was a soloist at the Weimar Chapel Royal. In 1879 he was appointed second professor at the Conservatoire and, on the death of Servais, succeeded his master as first professor. He later extended his touring to London where he appeared at the Queen's Hall. For many years he was engaged for the season's concerts at Pavlovsk, near St Petersburg.

An excellent soloist, Jacobs was known for his powerful and beautiful tone. He was also a fine chamber-music player and, together with Hermann, Coëlho and Van Hamme, instituted the original series of concerts at the Palais de Beaux Arts in Brussels. These concerts are today regarded as the most important in the musical life of the capital city.

Joseph Hollman (1852–1927), from Maastricht in Holland, started his career as a 'pensionnaire du Roi', a title given to youngsters of promise who were educated at the expense of King William III. Hollman then studied with Servais at the Conservatoire at Brussels where he took first prizes in almost every subject. Finally he attended the conservatoire in Paris under Leon Jacquard.

He subsequently toured in Europe, Scandinavia, Germany and Russia, and in London gave a series of concerts at the Bechstein Hall with Saint-Saëns at the piano. The composer greatly admired Hollman's playing and dedicated his second cello concerto (in D minor Op. 119) to him. Hollman gave the first performance at the Singakademie in Berlin in 1903. He was also the first to play Bruch's *Kol Nidrei* with orchestra in England.

Hollman wrote two concertos and a number of short pieces, popular in his day, but now forgotten. His contemporaries said that his playing was distinguished by its powerful tone and impeccable technique, but two contrasting opinions of his playing come from more recent sources. In his youth Pierre Fournier lived above the Hollmans in Paris. He has given an evocative description of the Dutchman's practising, 'The instrument grated, blew, boomed, whistled, wheezed, coughed and sometimes even sneezed. In short, all the symptoms of a head cold were accurately parodied by the bow of Monsieur Hollman.'[2] The other comes from Bernard Shaw. 'Hollman . . . played an aria of Bach's as only a great artist can play that great composer's music. I am not fond of the violoncello: ordinarily I had as soon hear a bee buzzing in a stone jug; but if all cellists played like Hollman, I should probably have taken more kindly to it.'[3]

Royalty seemed to have been attracted to Hollman, and in the course of his travels he collected numerous distinctions and awards. He was a favourite of Queen Victoria who presented him with a magnificent diamond ring, and the Prince of Wales (later King Edward) gave him a tie pin with his initials set in diamonds surmounted by the crown.

Hollman also had an eye for the ladies. William Van den Burg, the Dutch-born American cellist, recalled that when he was out for a stroll, even at the age of eighty, he could not resist turning his head when he sighted a pretty girl.

Isaac Mossel (1870–1923), from Rotterdam, was not only admired for his virtuosity and elegant style of playing but also respected as a musician. Mossel had begun his studies at eight with Louis Kohler and Oscar Eberle and toured as a soloist before taking up an appointment as principal cellist at the Konzerthaus in Berlin. He subsequently served in the same capacity in the Berlin Philharmonic Orchestra. In 1887 he went with Davidov on his last tours through Germany and Holland, and a year later was appointed solo cellist to the Concertgebouw at Amsterdam, teacher at the Conservatoire and at the school of 'Maatschappij tot bevordering van Toonkunst'. He was also a member of the Amsterdam Conservatoire String Quartet. Mossel owned a beautiful Nicolas Amati which he used alternately with an Alexander Gagliano.

Although none became world famous, several generations of the Franco-Dutch family of Hekking have contributed their talents to the advancement of cello playing. Charles Hekking, born in the Hague in the middle of the nineteenth century, toured successfully throughout Europe and was solo cellist at the theatre. He also taught at the Conservatoire in Bordeaux.

His nephew and pupil, André Hekking (1866–1925), born in Bordeaux, toured extensively as a boy of fifteen and was praised both for the richness of his tone and the integrity of his interpretations. He finally settled in Paris and devoted himself to teaching. He taught at the Ecole Normale de Musique and at the American Conservatory at Fontainebleau. In 1919, he became a professor at the Paris Conservatoire.

The best-known member of the family was Charles's son, Gérard Hekking (1879–1942). Born at Nancy, he studied at the Paris Conservatoire, carrying off the first prize in 1899 at the age of ten. He was a member of the Opera Orchestra and then lived for some years in Amsterdam where he was principal cellist in the Concertgebouw Orchestra under Mengelberg. During the 1914–18 war he served for four years with the French Army and in 1927 became professor at the Paris Conservatoire. Hekking was an excellent teacher—one of his many pupils was Maurice Gendron. He was also a great friend and supporter of young composers, believing that the instrument will only progress if sufficient new repertoire is written for it; a view not shared by many of his contemporaries.

A contemporary of Hekking's, Iwan d'Archambeau (1879–1956), was the cellist of the Flonzaley Quartet from 1903 until it disbanded in 1929. With Adolfo Betti as leader, Alfred Pochon as second violin and Ugo Ara, viola, it became one of the most celebrated quartets of the time.

Born at Herve in Belgium he was the youngest son of the famous composer Jean Michel d'Archambeau and had his first lessons on the piano. He was sixteen when he turned to the cello and commenced studies with Alfred Massau at the Verviers Conservatoire. He subsequently studied with Edouard Jacobs at the Brussels Conservatoire and with Hugo Becker in Frankfurt. He also took an intensive course of instruction with Bernhard Cossmann in string-quartet playing.

D'Archambeau had always hankered after a virtuoso solo career and his musical ability certainly made him eligible. But the activities of the Flonzaley proved so fulfilling that he never regretted his decision to join them.

However, a year before the great farewell tour, undertaken by the quartet in 1928, d'Archambeau had been asked to perform the Haydn D major concerto at the Verviers Festival. It was such a success that he was encouraged to take up his solo career once more—at the age of fifty. By devoting himself to practising six hours a day he was able to meet the demands of his 'second début', in October 1930, when asked by that great American patron of the arts, Mrs Elizabeth Coolidge, to play in a series of six concerts at her Chicago Festival. His programmes included performances of several of the Bach Suites, and sonatas by Hindemith and Locatelli. The success of this venture led to a series of concerts in Boston, New York and other American cities.

However, these were the years of the great depression when all the performing arts suffered. He was therefore forced to return to Europe, where, from this time, he followed a highly active solo career until his death in 1955. He also made recordings, not only with the Flonzaley, but of the Bach Suites which are of historical interest. He also recorded duos for cello and violin with his son Pierre d'Archambeau, now an American citizen.

A great chamber-music player, who in the course of his career gave over 2,000 concerts, was the Belgian Robert Maas (1901–48). He appeared as a soloist at twelve and was a pupil of Jacobs at the Brussels Conservatoire. For many years he was a member of the famous Pro Arte String Quartet formed in 1912 by the Belgian violinist, Alphonse Onnou. He happened to be in Belgium when war broke out in 1939—the other members had stayed in the USA—and suffered terrible privations. He played in cafés and lived in constant danger of being deported because he refused to play for the German troops.

It was at a party in New York after the war that he met the violinist Henri Temianka, then seeking a cellist for a string quartet that he contemplated forming. In his delightful autobiography *Facing the Music*, Temianka describes his playing of one of the Bach Suites.

> I knew instantly that I was in the presence of a master, a great cellist, and a great artist. His style of playing was monumental. There was a throbbing, indestructible rhythm that drove the music on to its inevitable destiny . . . Yet, for all his dramatic power and fervor, his playing was characterized by classic reserve and impeccable taste.

It was a chance visit by Maas to Emil Herrmann, the New York violin dealer, that brought him sight of the four Stradivari instruments that had all been part of Paganini's collection. Herrmann was prepared to sell but only if the instruments were to be kept together. One of the violins had been sold to Paganini by the Count Cozio di Salabue, and was his concert instrument, the viola was the one for which Berlioz wrote *Harold in Italy*. The cello—dated 1736—was the last instrument made by Stradivari, at the age of ninety-two.

Mrs William Andrews Clark, widow of the copper king and United States Senator, purchased the four instruments outright and presented them to Temianka to form the 'Paganini' string quartet. For two years Maas was the cellist of this remarkable and highly successful group. But during the interval at the Memorial Concert of Alphonse Onnou, his lifelong colleague and friend, he collapsed in the wings and died from a heart attack. He was only forty-seven.

CHAPTER XI

'Czar of Cellists':
Karl Davidov

IN RUSSIA, FOLK-MUSIC had always been an integral part of national life, but it was not until 1713, when Peter the Great brought in singers from outside, that harmony was introduced to the then universally unison singing of the Russian people. In 1720, the German Duke, Carl Ulrich of Holstein-Glottop, sought asylum at the Russian court and brought with him his small private band of musicians. In addition to the violins, violas d'amore, cellos and basses, there were wind, brass and percussion instruments. The Czar invited them to play regularly at court, and it was this band which formed the nucleus of what later became the Chapel Royal. Peter's son, Peter II, a great lover of music, took up the study of the cello under Riedel, a German from Silesia who, about 1727, was appointed court master of fencing and cello playing. He was also a member of the orchestra in St Petersburg and remained there until 1740.

The Czarina Anna, also a music-lover, brought in several prominent artists from abroad, who became the first teachers of the Russians in the art of cello playing. Among these were the Italians, Gasparo and, later, Giuseppe dall'Oglio from Padua, who was succeeded in 1763 by another Italian, Cicio Polliari, and in 1770 by Chorchewski.

The cello soon gained favour amongst the Russian aristocracy, and one of its first and most important exponents was Count Mathieu Wielhorsky (1787–1863), a Polish nobleman whose family had settled in Russia after the partition of their country by Frederick the Great in 1772. Wielhorsky had early shown musical talent and studied piano and theory before taking up the cello. At one time he housed Romberg in his palace for two years in order to obtain his services as a teacher. Held in high esteem by his contemporaries, many dedicated works to him. Servais' famous *Morceau de Concert*, the Vieuxtemps *Duo Brilliant*, for violin and cello with orchestra,

Op. 39, and Mendelssohn's Second Sonata—one of his best chamber works—were all composed for Wielhorsky.

At his death in 1863, Wielhorsky left his extensive library to the St Petersburg Conservatoire and his Stradivari cello to Karl Davidov. Hill tells us that the cello was originally obtained from Count Apraxin in exchange for 'his Guarneri cello, 40,000 francs (equal to £1,600 in 1902) and the handsomest horse in his stables'. This is the instrument that was given to the young Jacqueline du Pré by an anonymous donor at the start of her brilliant but tragically brief career.

Karl Davidov (1838–89), one of the first great Russian masters of the cello, was born in Goldingen, in the province of Latvia, the son of a doctor who was also a good amateur violinist. Since music-making was an integral part of their family life, he was exposed to its influence from a very early age. He began piano lessons at five and the cello at twelve with Heinrich Schmidt, principal cellist at the Moscow Theatre. He later went on to study with Karl Schuberth, Director of the Imperial Band and of Music at the University.

Due to the family's insistence that he complete his formal education before embarking upon further musical studies, Davidov took a degree in mathematics at St Petersburg University. At twenty he went to study composition with Moritz Hauptmann at the Leipzig Conservatoire. An interesting outcome of this period is that Hauptmann's advanced ideas on musical theory had a profound influence on Davidov, not only as applied to composition, but in his later work on the development of cello technique. His mathematical knowledge was particularly helpful in understanding his teacher's ideas on acoustics and harmony, and his grasp of 'several phenomena which result from cello tuning in fifths'.[1] Davidov was one of the first to link technique with the anatomical and physiological aspects of teaching, also explored by Becker and carried further by Feuermann and Casals.

Davidov's original ambition was to be a composer, but when unexpectedly asked to substitute for Grützmacher in a Mendelssohn trio at a private concert with Ferdinand David and Moscheles, he was an instant success. He also played solos on the same occasion. Subsequently, when invited to play in a Gewandhaus concert, to perform his own first concerto Op. 5, he received a tremendous ovation. Clearly, it was as a cellist that the future beckoned.

When Grützmacher moved to Dresden, the 22-year-old Davidov took his place at the Leipzig Conservatoire as professor of cello. He also began a series of concert tours travelling all over Europe and

England where he was described as the greatest cellist of his time. Tchaikovsky called him 'The Czar of Cellists'. Critics frequently complimented him on his perfect intonation, even in the highest positions. Julius Klengel used to say, 'I only understood what cello playing signifies after hearing Davidov in St Petersburg in my youth.'[2]

Nonetheless, Davidov could not always bring about the desired effect. In November 1869, when he played the Schumann Concerto for the first time,[3] conducted by Balakirev, the critic, Serov, who was known to dislike Schumann, wrote, 'Even the exceptional virtuosity of Davidov could not save this musical rigmarole'.[4]

Apparently Davidov had little need to practise. The violinist, Leopold Auer, who led the St Petersburg Quartet with Davidov as cellist, claimed that he could play without practising for months. His students recalled that often, before a performance, Davidov would bring his cello to class and ask them to play-in his new strings, because he had no time to spare!

In 1876, Davidov and Tchaikovsky were both candidates for the Directorship of the St Petersburg Conservatoire but Davidov was chosen. His reign was marked by his concern for the poorer students and he greatly increased the number of scholarships awarded. He also brought about the provision of free lodging for needy students.

Davidov was appointed 'Soloist to His Majesty', a title awarded only to the most important artists in Russia at the time. He was also cello soloist at the Italian Opera when Wieniawski was solo violinist.

Davidov's appointment at the Conservatoire was suddenly terminated in 1887, when he became involved in a love affair with a beautiful young student pianist. Forced to leave the country, he undertook a series of concert tours abroad where he was again greeted with all the enthusiasm he had enjoyed in his early youth. He returned to Russia the following year, and, with the pianist Safonov, made an extensive tour of all the principal towns. But in January 1889, at the age of fifty, he was taken ill in the middle of a recital of the Beethoven sonatas and was unable to finish the performance. He died a few days later.

It was said that Davidov's technique was equalled by few and surpassed by none. But he never tried to dazzle his audiences with pyrotechnics. The virtuoso side of his playing was always subservient to the musical expression. His rich and powerful tone, and absolute purity of intonation were the hall-marks of his playing.

Davidov made a considerable contribution to the development of the technique of the bow and, as a result, laid down important rules.

He also shared the opinion of so many great players in the past, that the influence of violin technique upon the cello is significant. Davidov would advise his pupils to 'listen attentively and observantly to the best violinists, as it was to them that he owed all he had learned'. Many modern cellists abhor the idea of learning from violinists; indeed some claim that a cellist who has studied with a violinist develops bad fingering habits that are difficult to break. It is more likely to have been the phrasing and singing tone of the violinists that the early cellists tried to emulate.

Improvements in the technique of playing in thumb positions across the lower strings were brought about by Davidov (later called 'The Davidov hinge'). He also employed the device of using one string alternating natural harmonics with the adjacent open string (used originally by Romberg), to be found in his most popular composition *At the Fountain*. He wrote numerous other solos for the cello, most of which became an integral part of the cellist's repertoire until early in our present century. Davidov also wrote four concertos, which deserve attention by those who claim that the cello literature is limited.

At the Imperial Conservatoire, Davidov trained a number of foreign students including Carl Fuchs, Leo Stern and Hanus Wihan, the dedicatee of the Dvořák Concerto. His favourite Russian pupil was Alexander Wierzbilowicz (1850–1911), who became one of the most outstanding Russian cellists of his time. Born in St Petersburg, he was principal cellist of the Imperial Opera and toured successfully all over Europe. Later he became solo cellist to the Czar. He was appointed professor of cello at the Conservatoire and cellist of the St Petersburg Quartet led by Leopold Auer. Unfortunately he had a reputation for heavy drinking, but it seems to have made little difference to his playing which was, by all accounts, full in tone and of astonishing facility.

The Russian Anatoly Brandoukov (1859–1930), best known as the dedicatee of Tchaikovsky's *Pezzo Capriccioso*, was a student of Fitzenhagen's at the Moscow Conservatoire. He toured Europe for some time, before settling in Paris in 1890, where he appeared to enjoy the social round rather more than cello playing.

Tchaikovsky greatly admired Brandoukov's playing and in the late summer of 1887 sent the few pages of manuscript of the *Pezzo Capriccioso* to him to see if it was cellistically viable. In the same way that Fitzenhagen had meddled with the *Rococo Variations*, without consulting the composer, so Brandoukov made his own modifications and gave the Paris première in 1888. It was published in this form later that year. However, some of the more discerning of present-day cellists are now reverting to the original Tchaikovsky manuscript.

The Cherniavsky family from Kiev boasted several highly talented musicians. The father, Abraham Cherniavsky, a musical scholar and conductor in the Ukraine, played a variety of musical instruments and taught all his nine children to play at least one. Mischel Cherniavsky (1893–1982) was the most gifted. He learnt the violin at the age of four, and shortly after had lessons on the cello with Wierzbilowicz in St Petersburg. Subsequently he studied with Joseph Sulzer in Vienna, Popper in Budapest and finally with Herbert Walenn in London. Walenn had high hopes of his young pupil whose talent he declared to be 'heaven-sent'.

The family was most famous for its Cherniavsky Trio, which achieved international status with the violinist Leo, the pianist Jan, and cellist Mischel at nine, seven and six years old respectively.

When the trio disbanded in 1933, each followed his own individual career; Mischel Cherniavsky settled in London and took British citizenship. He went round the world five times and played under almost every famous conductor. During World War II he worked tirelessly for the various war relief funds, taking part in hundreds of concerts.

After the war, Cherniavsky resumed his solo career and successfully revisited all the continents where his family had appeared as children: South Africa, Australia and India. In 1958 when he appeared with Sir Thomas Beecham at the Royal Festival Hall in London, the *Daily Telegraph* critic wrote, 'Cherniavsky's fiery and graceful style, exquisite sense of phrase and rich variety of tone suggested a perfect sympathy with the conductor's own taste.'

Mischel's grandson, Fyodor André Cherniavsky, now living in Atlanta Georgia, USA, says:

I knew my grandfather Mischel to be a unique kind of individual of compelling character. One was immediately struck by his dynamic energy and playful fantasy. He was an expert joker, humourist and raconteur. His enthusiasm was contagious and his intensity unflagging. He had a total recall of dates and details of his concerts and it was fascinating to hear his personal accounts of the many artists he encountered at the time.[5]

All three brothers shared an emotionally volatile temperament and displayed a restlessness of spirit. Perhaps, for them, music was a means of transcending their environment and a passport to an experience of the world at large. Their music-making was essentially performance-orientated and emphasized communication through emotional excitement and virtuosic brilliance. Their real success lay in the pioneering work as a trio during their early years, virtually as musical gypsies. They specialized in travelling to out-of-the-way places, often under gruelling conditions. Here they were often responsible for bringing music to people who otherwise would never have the opportunity to hear a live performance of anything.

Boris Hambourg (1885–1954), from Southern Russia, came from a family of distinguished musicians. His father, Michael, was a well-known pianist, his brother Mark, an even more famous pianist and another brother Jan was a solo violinist.

Hambourg studied the cello with Herbert Walenn and Hugo Becker, and Joachim was impressed when he heard him at a pupils' concert in 1902. Boris also spent some time with Ysaÿe in Belgium as, like so many other cellists, he considered a great deal was to be gained from studying violin technique. This resulted in his abandoning many of the accepted theories.

Hambourg was one of the few musicians of his era to take an interest in works by early composers, and his series of historical recitals at the Aeolian Hall in London were well researched and presented.

CHAPTER XII

The Bohemian Touch

THE CZECHS HAVE a long and lively musical history. When travelling in Bohemia in 1772, Burney remarked upon the musical achievements of the 'common people'. He describes how he went into a school where children of both sexes aged from six to eleven were 'reading, writing, playing on violins, hautbois, bassoons and other instruments'.[1] This small country has produced a very high proportion of great musicians, many of whom were some of the greatest virtuosos of the eighteenth century. The first cellist we know of is Johann Čermak, living in Warsaw in 1790. The cellist, Joseph Fiala, heard him and remarked upon both the excellence of his playing and the beauty of his cantilena.

Then came the Nerudas, a family of accomplished musicians stemming from Johann Georg Neruda (1716–80), who excelled on both the violin and the cello, and was for 30 years master of the Chapel Royal at Dresden. He also composed a considerable amount of music for the cello. Two of his sons and his brother were all distinguished musicians. The line culminated in the famous violinist, Wilhelmina (Wilma) Neruda (later Lady Hallé). Her brother, Alois, was for many years cellist at the National Theatre in Prague and later at the Imperial Opera in Vienna. Another brother, Franz Neruda, born in 1843 at Brunn in Austria, started the violin at five and turned to the cello at twelve. He and his sister, Wilma, became famous as prodigies in their travels throughout Europe. He later enjoyed an equally successful career as a touring soloist. He made frequent visits to Manchester and London, where he often took Piatti's place at the 'Pops'. Neruda had studied originally with his father but he also came into contact with Servais. Both his playing and his compositions show the influence of the Belgian master.

Ignaz (Hynck) Mara (c.1721–83) was a pupil of E. Viceslaus Petrik, and considered one of the most important cellists of his time. In 1742, Mara went to Berlin and, through the influence of Franz Benda, his countryman and leader of the Chapel Royal, was appointed to the King's private music. Mara combined beauty of tone with great expression; his compositions, which appear to have been much appreciated in his day, remained in manuscript. Two of his sonatas for cello and bass are in the Royal Library at Berlin.

Ignaz's son, John Baptist Mara (1744–1808), was an artist of extraordinary talent. He had his first lessons on the cello as a small child and, when appearing as a soloist, attracted the attention of that famous protector of musical art, Prince Henry of Prussia, who engaged him as one of his chamber musicians. His handsome appearance and engaging manner captivated all who came in contact with him, especially the famous singer, Gertrude Elisabeth Schmeling, who later became his wife. Unfortunately his happy-go-lucky disposition led him down hill and he squandered all their combined earnings, of which his wife's were the more considerable. Through his excesses he was dismissed from his job, his marriage broke up and his career, which had started so brilliantly, was finished. He ended up in Holland, an incurable dipsomaniac. He could be found every night in the lowest of sailors' haunts, playing for drink money. His compositions remained in manuscript and are in the Imperial Private Library in Berlin.

Joseph Reicha (1746–95), from Prague, uncle of the composer, Anton Reicha, was appointed musical director of the court and theatre orchestras in Bonn in 1785. Beethoven, then only fifteen, played viola in both ensembles.

One of the most romantic figures in the history of the cello was Joseph Fiala (1751–1816). He was born in Sochowitz, which formed part of the feudal estate of the Countess Netolitsky, a tyrannical and vicious woman who, like so many other sovereigns of the time, exploited her subjects to the limit.

Early signs of musical talent caused the Countess to take him to Prague to study with John Stiastny, oboist, and father of the two cellists, Jan and Bernard Stiastny. He also had some lessons with the cellist, Werner. In the Countess's house, he was treated as a servant and put to wash dishes, much in the same way as Lully in the Court of Louis XIV. This exasperated Fiala, who was fast developing into a virtuoso on both oboe and cello, and he managed to escape to the protection of Count Hartiz at Ratisbon. The furious Countess lured him back to Prague where she made his life intolerable. He escaped a second time but was captured by a body of armed men who threw him into prison. The Countess then hit on the diabolical scheme of having all his front teeth pulled out so he could no longer play the oboe. The gaoler obviously had more human feeling than his high born mistress and hid him at his own house, at the same time sending word to the Emperor about the Countess's dreadful plan. The Emperor, who knew of Fiala's talent, ordered his immediate release.

In 1777, when he was a member of Prince Wallenstein's orchestra in Vienna, Fiala was heard by the Elector Max Joseph of Bavaria who persuaded him to go to Mannheim. There he married Josepha Prochaska, the daughter of one of the court musicians. In 1778 he was engaged by the Bishop of Salzburg, where he became acquainted with both the Mozart family and Michael Haydn, brother of the more famous Josef.

His gentle and refined nature appeared to have won him the friendship of all the distinguished people with whom he became acquainted, but his musical talent repeatedly brought his life into jeopardy. It seems that the Archbishop admired his oboe playing so much that he commanded him to play as many as twelve concertos in an evening. This over-exertion caused the rupture of a blood vessel and Fiala had to abandon playing for a considerable period. In fact, he could never again play the instrument for any length of time, and henceforth devoted himself to the cello and the viola de gamba. He toured extensively playing both instruments, and, in 1792, settled in Donaueschingen as principal cellist to Prince Fürstenburg. He remained there until his death in 1816.

The Kraft family occupy an important place in the history of the cello. Anton Kraft (1752–1820), born in Rokitzau, in Bohemia, originally expected to become a lawyer, but made such progress on the cello with Werner that he was engaged for the Chapel Royal in Vienna. Haydn obtained a place for him in the Court orchestra of Prince Esterhazy, and when his patron died he took up a similar appointment with Prince Grassalkowitz in Vienna.

In 1793, with Ignaz Schuppanzigh as leader, Prince Lichnowski as second violin, and Franz Weiss on the viola, he founded the famous string quartet which played at the Prince's house every Friday morning. They performed the string quartets of Haydn, Mozart and, later, Beethoven under the direction of the composer. Beethoven greatly admired Kraft's playing and dubbed him 'Die alte Kraft' (the ancient power). He was the cellist whom Beethoven had in mind when he composed his triple concerto in C major Op. 56. The proposed pianist was Beethoven's pupil, the Archduke Rudolph and the violinist, Karl August Seidler. The concerto was given its first performance—presumably with an orchestra—in a private house in 1805 by these three artists, published in Leipzig in 1806 and dedicated to Prince Franz Josef Lobkowitz. The first public performance was given in Leipzig in 1808, with the pianist, Müller, the violinist, Mattei, and with Dotzauer as cellist. In April 1809, Kraft played Beethoven's Third Sonata in A major Op. 69 with the composer.

Kraft's studies in composition with Haydn led to the controversy as to whether he or Haydn wrote the D major Cello Concerto; a matter still open to speculation today. His own compositions consist of a number of sonatas, which 'may be taken as an example of the height of the German eighteenth-century school continuo sonata development'.[2] He also published a Concerto in C, several Grand Duos, works for baryton and a Divertimento.

The significance of Kraft's influence is that he brought the Czech traditions to Vienna and combined them with those of the Viennese classical school. He was known for his beautiful singing tone and depth of expression which he combined with a faultless technique.

Anton's son, Nicolaus Kraft (1778–1853), studied with his father and was sent by Prince Lobkowitz to Berlin to complete his studies with Jean Louis Duport. He also followed a distinguished career as a chamber musician in the Lobkowitz Chapel, and as a soloist. Unfortunately, in 1834, owing to an injury to his right hand, he had to abandon his public career. But as a composer he made a useful and varied contribution to the literature of the cello.

The elder of the two Stiastny brothers from Prague, Bernhard Wenzeslaus Stiastny (1760–1835), is the least important. As in the case of the Duports, the younger surpassed the elder both in talent and achievement.

Jan Stiastny (1774–c. 1826) received his first instruction from his brother, whom he greatly admired. He held a number of important appointments in royal bands, from which he was allowed leave to undertake concert tours. He also visited England where he met Crosdill and Lindley. His Concertino Op. 7 was written for Lindley and his trios and Duos Concertante, Op. 8 are dedicated to Crosdill.

Although Jan Stiastny's playing was reputed to be brilliant and extremely musical, his public appearances were rare. He was one of those unfortunate artists who, though very gifted, was usually too nervous to appear in public. His colleagues would say that the only way to hear Stiastny play was to gain access to the house where he lived and listen outside the door. However, his contribution to the development of cello playing through his writings should not be overlooked. His six duos for two violoncellos, in two series (published by Schott), show ingenuity and imagination, and even today deserve a place in the violoncello literature.

Bernhard Stiastny's successor as first professor of cello at the Prague Conservatoire was Jan Nepomuk Hüttner (1793–1840) who held the post until his death in 1840. He in turn taught many gifted Bohemian cellists including Jindřich Schmidt (1810–62), for many years principal cellist of the Bolshoi Theatre Orchestra and teacher of Davidov.

Another was Frantisek Hegenbarth (1818–87), whose studies with Hüttner were financed by Prince Kinsky. Hegenbarth was later appointed solo cellist successively at the theatres at Graz, Linz and Lemberg, and from 1852 to 1865 he was professor of cello at the Mozarteum at Salzburg. He was also an accomplished chamber-music player, performing in a trio with Bedřich Smetana and Anton Bennewitz, and in a quartet with Bennewitz, Hřimaly and Deutsch. The most celebrated of his many pupils were Heinrich Grünfeld and Hanus Wihan.

Hanus Wihan (1855–1920), born in Poliza, Bohemia, was admitted to Hegenbarth's class at the Conservatoire in Prague at thirteen. According to Van der Straeten, he completed his studies under Davidov, for whom he retained a lifelong admiration, but it is not clear whether in St Petersburg, or when Davidov was living in Western Europe. At eighteen he was appointed professor at the Mozarteum in Salzburg, and played in a number of orchestras including the famous Bilse orchestra which later became the Berlin Philharmonic. He was also a member of the Chapel Royal at Sondershausen near Weimar where he formed a close friendship with Liszt. When he later became a soloist of the court orchestra at Munich, he met Wagner, von Bülow and Richard Strauss, all of whom much admired his playing. Strauss dedicated his *Romance* for cello and piano to Wihan.

A close connection exists between Czech music and the performing art of Wihan. His contacts with Smetana and Dvořák greatly influenced the artistic development of all three. Wihan's was further reinforced by his practical studies with Davidov, then the leading figure of the Russian school of cello playing. Thus he was amply prepared to apply high technical and artistic standards to all his undertakings, the most notable example being the founding in 1891 of the Czech String Quartet which stayed together for over 40 years and was considered one of the greatest quartets of the era. The original members of the quartet were the violinists, Karl Hoffmann and Josef Suk (who married Dvořák's daughter and whose grandson, Josef Suk is the celebrated violinist), the violist, Oskar Nedbal and the cellist, Wihan's own pupil, Otakar Berger. When Berger's health declined, Wihan succeeded him, and after Berger's death in 1897, he retired from teaching to devote himself entirely to quartet and solo performances. Ginsburg writes, 'Playing in the ensemble, Wihan possessed the art of subjugation of his mastery and brilliant individuality to the interests of the artistic whole.'[3] Zeděnek Nejedlý, writing in the periodical *Smetana*, [No. 10] in 1915, declares, 'The Czech Quartet and Wihan—these are two names that history will link eternally, and if we consider the Czech Quartet to be the summit of Czech performing art, this only means that, for us, Wihan is the maestro whose name will always be in the first rank of the Czech musicians of our time.'

Anton Dvořák wrote his *Rondo* Op. 94 for Wihan, and it was first performed in a Czech town called Hrudim, when the cellist was touring with the composer and the violinist, Ferdinand Lachner. They also played transcriptions of Dvořák's piano works, including two of the *Slavonic Dances*. It was for Wihan that Dvořák wrote the very attractive cello part in the Dumky Piano Trio Op. 90 (1891). As for the Cello Concerto (Op. 104), there was little doubt whom the composer had in mind. It seems that when composer and cellist worked together, Wihan offered some modifications many of which Dvořák accepted.

Wihan first performed the concerto with the composer at a private house in Luzany in August 1895, when the members of the Czech Quartet were present. It was published by Simrock in 1896, and the first public performance took place in London in March 1896 at a Philharmonic Concert with Dvořák conducting, but with the English cellist, Leo Stern, taking the solo part. Many stories have circulated offering reasons for this substitution, and most claim that Wihan and Dvořák fell out just before the performance. But Lev Ginsburg, referring to letters from Dvořák published in 1957 by the British scholar John Clapham, maintains that the London date clashed with concerts already contracted by the Czech Quartet and could not be changed. Their friendship continued on the warm and friendly basis on which it had always existed, and Wihan performed the concerto in 1899 at the Hague, in Amsterdam and Budapest, all with Dvořák conducting. A critic in the local newspaper, *Pester Lloyd*, wrote of Wihan's 'technical perfection, refined musical taste, brio and verve', and also of his 'powerful and robust tone'.

Hanus Wihan talked with enthusiasm to his pupils about his studies with Davidov, particularly concerning the natural way of playing in which the Russian cellist had trained him. He would advocate the free movement of the right arm which made it easier to produce a natural flowing sound. He called it the 'breathing' of the bow. Certainly all the descriptions of his playing, commenting on his long line and expressive tone, would seem to bear this out. But also, like Davidov, he was absolutely opposed to virtuosity for its own sake. He preferred to bring out the richness and beauty of the music itself and, when needed, made virtuosity his servant.

When Hanus Wihan retired from the Bohemian Quartet in 1914 he was replaced by Ladislav Zelenka (1881–1957), a figure greatly respected by Czech musicians in the early twentieth century, but almost unknown outside his native country. At one time the Bohemian Quartet was a household name throughout the world: they once appeared at the British Court with Paderewski and were paid £500, an enormous fee at that period.

Zelenka was born in the small town of Modřany near Prague and first studied the violin, proceeding later to the cello. Wihan heard him play and was so impressed that he offered him a place at the Prague Conservatoire. Wihan had a similar experience with Becker, who saw him as a future soloist and refused any payment for lessons.

The young Zelenka had other ideas. Modest and retiring by temperament, he had no ambitions for a solo spotlight. He preferred to serve art rather than strive for personal glory, so he joined the Ševčik Quartet and deputized on occasions for Wihan in the Bohemian Quartet, eventually succeeding him.

Besides playing the cello, Zelenka came in useful as a guardian for Josef Suk who was very absent-minded. Suk liked to compose during train journeys and in hotels, so Zelenka packed his luggage and made sure he left nothing behind. He also rosined his bow for him. The quartet would seem to be self-sufficient in yet another capacity for the violist, Herold, was an accomplished instrument maker and carried out all necessary repairs on the spot.

When age and illness curtailed the activities of the individual members of the quartet, Zelenka took more and more to teaching. From the Prague Conservatoire he was promoted to the Master School and eventually appointed Director of the entire institution. After World War II he was also made Director of the newly established Prague Academy of Musical Arts.

Despite his chosen field of chamber music and teaching, Zelenka was apparently a superb soloist. Bernard Vočadlo, in a touching centenary tribute in *The Strad* of December 1981, tells us that his interpretation of the Dvořák Cello Concerto was acknowledged as the undisputed standard by which other well-known Czech cellists were to be measured. He describes one of these performances as 'magnificent and authentic'.

Vočadlo considered that, as a teacher, Zelenka had few equals:

> He was very strict, yet incredibly human. He would work in minute detail but appreciated individuality and originality. With him, time was forgotten; his favourite students had lessons lasting the whole morning or afternoon twice a week. I even had, during one summer holiday, the rare privilege of a lesson every day for a month in return for rowing the master round his favourite fishing haunts.[4]

Zelenka's students found his studies and exercises invaluable, but during his lifetime he refused to publish them. After his death, a devoted band of his pupils saw that this was remedied. In the West, up to the present time, only his thumb position exercises are in print.

CHAPTER XIII

'Sarasate of the Cello':
David Popper

'FULL CREDIT IS due to Popper that the cello is today a virtuoso instrument and will remain so in the future. He expanded the former limits of technical possibilities and enriched the cello literature with interesting, effective compositions, which, almost without exception, are used in the repertoire of cellists all over the world.'[1] This colourful tribute appeared in a Viennese newspaper when David Popper took up his appointment as the first professor of cello at the Royal Hungarian Academy of Music at its opening in 1886. At the time, Viennese audiences were the severest critics in Europe.

David Popper (1843–1913) was born in the old ghetto of Josephstadt in Prague, the son of a Cantor in two synagogues which served some nine thousand Jews. Those were the days when, if Jews crossed the barrier into the city proper, yellow stars of identification were obligatory.

At the age of three Popper was able to imitate very accurately his father's chanting, and at five could improvise on the piano. A year later he began lessons on the violin, and at twelve obtained a place at the Conservatoire in Prague, with the proviso that he took up the cello instead of the violin. He was placed in the class of Julius Goltermann, once a student of Kummer in Dresden and therefore standing in a direct line from Romberg and Duport.

At eighteen, Popper was employed in the Chapel Royal of the Prince of Hohenzollern at Löwenberg in Lower Silesia, and later was elevated to 'Kammervirtuoso'. In appreciation, Popper dedicated his *Six Character Pieces* (Op. 3) to his patron. Wagner and Berlioz, who both had at some time conducted the Löwenberg Orchestra, expressed admiration for Popper's playing.

On 24 January 1864, Popper was invited to give the first performance of Robert Volkmann's Cello Concerto in A minor (Op. 33) with Hans von Bülow conducting. Volkmann explored new fields in the employment of the cello as a dramatic instrument, almost operatic in declamation, and in so doing, represented a formidable challenge to the young player. There were at the time many first-class performers from which Von Bülow could have chosen: Grütz-macher, Cossmann, Goltermann (Popper's teacher), Piatti and Davidov, then only five years senior to Popper. Normally a hard man to please, von Bülow wrote to Joachim Raff in January 1864 that it was 'an extraordinary pleasing performance . . . remarkable talent, beautiful tone and great technique. . . . He has a promising future'. The critics echoed this opinion praising his 'rich, expressive, and beautifully produced tone'. Popper was just twenty-one.

He first appeared in Vienna in 1867, at a concert put on by the American impresario, Bernard Uhlmann, a not over-popular figure with the German musicians, who feared he would bring a commercial element into their sacred preserve. A year later, when the 25-year-old Popper was engaged as principal cellist to the Imperial Opera Orchestra, he was the youngest ever to have been appointed in that capacity. A glance at the names of his predecessors, Josef Weigl—a godson of Haydn—Nicolaus Kraft and Joseph Merk shows how highly he was regarded.

In his new domicile Popper could do no wrong, and was securely under the wing of von Bülow, then a very powerful force in Vienna. Nonetheless, his sponsors received good value for their money: during a ten-month season, there were some 225 performances and rehearsals daily from 10 am until 2 pm. There were also rehearsals for the Philharmonic Concerts which took place on Sunday afternoons throughout the season. In addition, he gave a series of eight concerts with the Hellmesberger Quartet, with Joseph Hellmesberger (also leader of the orchestra), Adolf Brodsky and Sigismund Bachrich.

In December 1868, after a performance of the Volkmann Concerto, Herman Starcke in the *Neue Zeitschrift fur Musik*, wrote: 'Vienna has had, until now, no cellist to boast about, and none was received with such enthusiasm, other than some foreign artists who appeared on transitory visits. We can congratulate ourselves on the recent acquisition of this artist.' Hanslick went even further: 'The violoncello has produced only two outstanding virtuosos, both foreign-born—Davidov from St Petersburg, and Popper from Prague.'[2]

Popper left the Vienna Opera Orchestra in 1873, in order to fulfil concert tours all over Europe, England and Russia—which he had first visited in 1865. He appeared to be a man of inexhaustible energy, travelling and composing non-stop: his published opus numbers amounted to 60 by 1880. His salon pieces were extremely popular and no cello recital would be complete without one or two as encores. Even today, his 'Elfentanz', a charming virtuoso piece requiring a faultless technique, can evoke an incredulous response from the audience. It is interesting that in the early development of the cello, players transposed violin music, whereas in Popper's case, celebrated violinists such as Auer, Sauret, Hermann, Neruda, Halíř and others made their own personal transcriptions of his pieces, a special favourite being his concert study 'Spinning Song'.

In Steven De'ak's biography of Popper, there is a touching story of the time when Popper was playing in Odessa in the mid-eighties. A prosperous looking gentleman knocked on the door of the artists' room and asked him if he would play Bruch's *Kol Nidrei* for him. This was the time when Alexander III had perpetrated wide persecution of the Jews. Popper played the melody as he had remembered his father singing a Hebrew chant on the Day of Atonement, and his solitary auditor, moved to tears, thanked him by pressing a thousand roubles into his hand.

The year 1886 was an eventful one for Popper. In the summer he married a young Czech girl from Prague (his previous marriage, to the pianist Sophie Menter, had ended in divorce), and in the autumn he took up his new appointment as cello professor at the Royal Hungarian Academy of Music in Budapest. There were two music schools in Pest, the National Conservatory and the Theatre School, but aspiring musicians tended to study abroad in Vienna, St Petersburg, Leipzig or Paris. It was Liszt's idea to have a Hungarian Academy and eventually it was founded in 1875 with him as President. Instruction was offered in general musical subjects but at first the only instrument taught was the piano. When a string department was opened in 1886, the young violinist, Jenö Hubay, was appointed as its head, Popper becoming its first cello professor. Bartók, Dohnányi and Fritz Reiner were students at the time, and Kodály, also a student, recalled that since the enrolment of string students was rather slow to begin with, the two professors could often be found in the coffee house across the street playing billiards! However, once the flow had started, Popper had all the students he needed. He seldom had more than seven or eight at a time, who met twice a week for three-hour sessions. He also gave private lessons for which he charged a high fee. He now had an international reputation and saw no need to sell himself cheaply.

In the very first season, Hubay and Popper founded the string quartet that bore their names and was often known as the 'Budapest'.

The two musicians were highly compatible. Through his experience in the Hellmesberger Quartet, with its reputation for elegance and refinement, Popper's playing blended well with that of Hubay's, which was strongly influenced by Vieuxtemps. Their first concert, on 10 November 1886, took place after only three weeks' rehearsal.

The quartet was often joined by Brahms in concerts, and as a trio they introduced a number of his chamber works at a time when his music was thought to be difficult both to perform and to understand. The Cello Sonata in F Major (Op. 99) had received its first performance by Hausmann in Vienna in November 1886. Popper played it with Brahms a month later. De'ak tells us that he once asked Popper how Brahms was as a pianist. He replied that there were quite a few inaccuracies 'in spite of his great pianistic technique' and that 'he was loud, too!'[3]

In 1890, Gevaert, the Belgian composer and musicologist and Director of the Conservatoire in Brussels, rearranged the Haydn Concerto in D major (published in its original form in the 1840s), augmented the orchestration and added a cadenza for the soloist. It aroused Popper's interest and he performed it in Munich, replacing Gevaert's candenza with one of his own. Well received by both press and public, it soon took its place in the standard repertoire.

In 1891 Popper undertook 29 concerts in a tour of England, Scotland and Ireland. At the Edinburgh concert a critic reported that his first appearance in Scotland aroused much interest and that a large number of local cellists was present to hear him. 'He is far and away the greatest exponent of the art of cello playing who has ever appeared in Edinburgh.'[4] His London concerts drew similar praise. Critics wrote of him fully justifying the high expectations formed of his abilities. 'His tone is both sweet and silky . . . he might not inaptly be styled the Sarasate of the Violoncello.'[5]

George Bernard Shaw, known not to be over-fond of the cello, had obviously revised his opinion after hearing Popper at St James's Hall in London on 21 November 1891: 'There is no lack of novelty about his style to Londoners, and he is, on his own plane, the best player in the world, as far as we know, here.'[6] At this performance he was joined by the Englishman Edward Howell and the Belgian Jules Delsart in his own *Requiem*, for three cellos and orchestra, conducted by F. H. Cowen.

When, in 1892, Popper returned to his birthplace, Prague, he was warmly received by his compatriots. The critic from the *Prager Tageblatt* summed up his contribution to the world of cello playing: 'Only Popper succeeded in elevating the instrument above the sphere of pure melody and short-lived cantilenas, by including characteristics and moods for our modern musical needs, in powerful performances . . . What he could not find he replaced by his rich inventiveness. He became the creator of an entirely new cello literature.'

One Sunday morning in 1900, a 19-year-old student of piano and composition arrived at Popper's apartment to accompany a rehearsal for a forthcoming concert. His name was Béla Bartók. Popper and the young pianist performed together at a charity concert to raise money to build a sanatorium for the poor of Budapest. After the performance Bartók wrote to his mother, 'Am very glad that I had the chance to play with a real artist at last, and became acquainted with a delightful man. . . . At the end of the first rehearsal he told me that I am a good sight-reader, and thanked me five times for coming to his house.'[7]

The advent of Casals made a deep impression on Popper. He admired his playing and appreciated that the younger cellist once boasted that he had played practically everything that Popper wrote. However, he was less enthusiastic over some of Casals' techniques. Steven De'ak describes going to a Casals concert with Popper in Budapest, and how he appeared puzzled that Casals had quite a different bowing technique from that of the loose wrist and straight thumb in vogue at the time. He also noted that Casals used far fewer overt slides than did Popper's generation. When Popper and De'ak returned by the underground train, conversation was somewhat limited. De'ak says that Popper mumbled about 'beautiful tone . . . excellent technique' and 'splendid intonation', and finally said: 'In spite of all these, he did not touch my heart!'[8]

The death of Popper's only son, from tuberculosis in 1911, was a terrible blow. In 1913, Popper slipped on a frosty pavement, fractured his right arm and, although he eventually resumed teaching, never fully regained the use of his arm.

Popper received honours in almost every country in Europe in the course of his career. In the very title-conscious Austro-Hungarian Empire in which he lived, titles of real value were always bestowed by the Emperor himself. The highest honour, 'Hofrat' in German, was awarded him on 5 August 1913, in honour of his seventieth birthday which fell on July 18. He enjoyed the title for two days only. On August 7 he had a heart attack and died during the night.

It is not generally known that Popper was also a first-class pianist, and he made great use of the piano in his lessons. If necessary he would pick up his cello to illustrate a point. An evocative example of his musical knowledge is given by Van der Straeten who had invited him to his home following a Philharmonic Concert in London at which Popper had played. Emil Sauret had been asked to play, and chose the first movement of the Beethoven Violin Concerto. As no copy of the music was at hand, Popper sat down at the piano and, without a moment's hesitation, commenced the opening tutti, playing by heart. To everyone's astonishment he played the whole accompaniment from memory with a delicacy of touch, a beauty and such phrasing as would put many a solo pianist to shame. Moreover, it was evident from the way he treated the various instrumental entries that it was not the piano part but the orchestral accompaniment which he remembered.

As a composer he achieved world fame. He wrote four concertos—of which the E minor Op. 24 is a very fine work—a string quartet, a suite for two cellos and countless salon pieces, some of which are still played today. His greatest contribution to the development of cello technique is his *Hochschule des Violoncellspiels* which was published in four volumes of ten studies each and appeared between 1901 and 1905. It remains one of the most important milestones in the development of the art of cello playing, and is still widely used by teachers all over the world. It provides a balance between the music itself and technical innovation. Many of the studies explore the technical difficulties that Popper had encountered in the music of his contemporaries, such as Wagner, Liszt, Berlioz, Schumann and others.

Of his many pupils the best known are Arnold Földesy, Jenö Kerpély, Ludwig Lebell, Adolf Schiffer—the teacher of Janos Starker—and Mici Lukács, one of his very few female pupils. Steven De'ak, Popper's biographer, also studied with him from 1911–13.

As a man, Popper was tall and handsome with an irresistible platform charisma. He was not only a good conversationalist with a variety of subjects at his disposal, but also had the rare quality of being a good listener. Very little is known of his private life. Most of his letters were lost in a fire and—although the diaries of his contemporaries point to some amorous undercurrents—to the world, he appeared a model of propriety.

The life of Popper marks the period which saw the transition from the romantic virtuoso style to the flourishing of interpretative art. Having overcome mere virtuoso interests, he was the first to play the concertos by Haydn and Schumann as well as providing some of the most enchanting salon pieces in the literature of the instrument.

CHAPTER XIV

'Grand Master of the Cello': Alfredo Piatti

AFTER BOCCHERINI, THE first name of any consequence in Italy is Giuseppe Rovelli (1753–1806), a distant relative of Alfredo Piatti. Born in Bergamo, he studied in Milan where, until his death, he remained in the service of the Duke of Parma. One of his pupils was Vincenzo Merighi (1795–1849), considered to be the founder of the Lombardian school of cello playing. Merighi was professor at Milan Conservatoire from 1826 to 1849 where Piatti, Alexander Pezze and Guglielmo Quarenghi were his students. The story of how he acquired his Stradivarius cello, now known as the 'Stanlein' (c. 1707), must surely represent the bargain of the century. Walking one day through the streets of Milan, Merighi saw a man pushing a barrow with a cello balanced precariously upon it. He stopped him and bargained successfully for the somewhat dilapidated instrument, offering a sum equivalent to today's £5. In 1834–35, Paganini bought it from him and later sold it to Vuillaume who resold it in 1854 to Count Stanlein, no doubt for rather more than the original outlay. It has since been restored to immaculate condition and is now owned by Bernard Greenhouse, formerly of the Beaux Arts Trio.

Although little is known of the history of the de Casella family, they appear to have made some contribution to the art of cello playing in their country. Pietro Casella (1762–1844), head of a long dynasty of cellists and founder of the Turin school, was born in Genoa, and in 1831 became a member of the Court orchestra. Among his pupils were his sons, Cesare Giovacchino (1819–86), and Carlo Casella (d. 1886). The latter was said to be a virtuoso who went to Spain and followed a distinguished career in the Court in Madrid. He wrote a number of compositions for his instrument, mostly of the salon genre, but even today his six *Grandes Etudes* Op. 33 serve as excellent studies. He died in Lisbon.

Cesare Casella (c. 1849), born in Oporto, a son of Carlo Casella, was a distinguished cellist still living in Paris in 1886. Last in the line is the composer, Alfredo Casella (1883–1947),son of Cesare, who wrote two cello and piano sonatas and a concerto for cello and orchestra. The first Sonata Op. 8 (1907) was dedicated to Casals.

By far the most important of the nineteenth-century Italian cellists was Alfredo Piatti (1822–1901), born in Bergamo, son of Antonio Piatti, leader of the local orchestra. He studied the violin with his father and cello with his great-uncle, Gaetano Zanetti, whom he succeeded in the orchestra at the age of eight. Two years earlier he had distinguished himself at the house of the Count Vertova of Bergamo when he played in a string quartet. At ten he was accepted as Merighi's pupil at the Milan Conservatoire where he studied for five years. In September 1837 he made his début playing his own concerto at a Conservatoire concert, and a year later gave a concert at La Scala which was so renumerative that he was able to embark upon a European tour. He appeared with phenomenal success in Vienna and other cities, but in Pesth was taken ill and had to sell his cello to pay for his food and lodging until he was well enough to leave. On his way home, he met Liszt who invited him to share a concert in Munich. The success of the event—in which Piatti played on a borrowed instrument—prompted Liszt to organize further concerts in Paris in 1844. It was here that he presented Piatti with a fine Amati cello.

On 31 May 1844, Piatti made his introductory appearance before a London audience at a morning concert at Her Majesty's Theatre, and the critics immediately acclaimed him as an artist of the first rank. On 24 June he made his official début at a Philharmonic Society Concert, playing a *Fantasia* by Kummer. He was placed on the programme to follow Mendelssohn, who gave a particularly brilliant account of the Beethoven G Major Concerto. Despite the challenge, the 22-year-old must have acquitted himself well enough, for the *Morning Post* critic wrote, 'Piatti's magnificent violoncello playing won universal admiration, by the perfection of his tone and his evident command over all the intricacies of the instrument.'

After this concert, Moscheles, the pianist with whom Mendelssohn was staying, invited Piatti to his house, as Mendelssohn wanted to play a sonata with him. Piatti went along prepared to play the Sonata in B flat, but Mendelssohn brushed it aside and produced a new sonata in D major then only in manuscript.

From 1844–5 Piatti toured the United Kingdom, Italy and other European countries, and in spring 1845 went to Russia with the pianist, Theodore Dohler. Concerts featuring the two artists were

highly successful both in St Petersburg and Moscow, and critics
almost ran out of superlatives in describing Piatti's overall excellence:
'His developed technique, sonority, pleasant tone, rare purity,
refined taste, abundance of feeling and expression, and the most
charming singing which one can hear on a primarily singing
instrument.'[1]

A confirmed anglophile from his first visit, Piatti appeared regularly in London and the main provincial towns. He played frequently
as principal cellist with the Italian Opera Orchestra in London, and
in a quartet in which Heinrich Wilhelm Ernst was leader, Joachim,
second violin, and Henryk Wieniawski the violist. He also took part
in the concerts of the London Beethoven Quartet Society.

Apart from one season when he broke his right arm in a carriage
accident, for the rest of his life Piatti appeared regularly at the Pops,
then held at St James's Hall in Regent Street, and devoted entirely to
chamber music. Joachim, Ludwig Straus, Zerbini and Piatti formed
the original 'London' Joachim string quartet which was permanently
engaged for the Pops. At the time, it was claimed that for nobility
of style, beauty of tone and perfection of ensemble, that combination
was never surpassed.

In 1858 Piatti revisited Vienna and achieved a success equal to that
of his début there twenty years earlier. Hanslick praised his 'sincerely
and deeply felt' playing, 'which remains serious and virile with all
its heartfelt feeling'.[2] Piatti was also complimented for not attacking
his instrument with too strong a hand, so that his playing lent itself
to alterations of tone-colour.

Van der Straeten heard Piatti in 1897–8, at one of the last Pops in
which he appeared, playing his own arrangement of a violin sonata
by Haydn 'with a nobility of style which was quite monumental. It
was free from all sentimentality.'[3] Van der Straeten also found it
remarkable that Piatti's perfect intonation and agility of the left hand
remained well on into old age.

Throughout his performing career he was offered important
teaching posts in his native Italy, but he refused, preferring to spend
most of his time in England. In latter years he spent the winter
months at his Villa Caddenabbia on Lake Como.

Despite the demands of his concert appearances, his teaching
career was long and influential. Although ostensibly a professor at
the Royal Academy of Music in London, his attendances were
sporadic: most of his other teaching was private, and tailored to fit
his concert schedule. The German cellists, Robert Hausmann, Hugo

Becker and Leo Stern all studied with Piatti and acknowledged the debt they owed to him. One of his favourite pupils was the British William Whitehouse.

In 1892, pupils from all over the world came to Milan to pay homage to their much beloved master on the occasion of his Seventieth Birthday Concert. Many internationally celebrated musicians, including Verdi and Arrigo Boïto, the Italian poet and composer, were also present.

As a man he was reserved and quite unapproachable by those who tried to make profit from his celebrity but, if he met with sincerity, he was most helpful. Van der Straeten admitted that he personally owed a great debt to Piatti who was always ready with assistance and advice throughout the years when he was researching for his various books on the cello and its literature. Piatti's favourite pastime was a good game of whist, at which he was a very skilled player who never missed a point that could be won by finesse and judicious play.

With the exception of his *Tarantella* Op. 23, a first class virtuoso piece, his compositions in general are of little value today. However, it should be remembered that he was responsible for making arrangements of works that, but for him, would never have seen the light of day. His object was to enrich the repertoire of the instrument by replacing the salon and empty virtuoso music that was so fashionable at the time. He was the first to publish eighteenth-century works, including sonatas by Locatelli, Porpora, Veracini, Ariosti, Marcello and Boccherini. Unlike Grützmacher, Piatti endeavoured to preserve as much of the original as possible. When preparing the piano part he would adhere to the directions indicated by the composer's figured bass, and he very rarely resorted to imposing unnecessary bowings and fingerings, so prevalent in most nineteenth-century editions. His interest in early music led to a meeting with that legendary pioneer, Arnold Dolmetsch, of whom he became a close friend. He had been taken to one of the Dolmetsch concerts in the 1880s and was greatly impressed by Hélène, Dolmetsch's eleven-year-old daughter who played Simpson's *Divisions on a Ground* on the viola de gamba. It was Dolmetsch who helped Piatti in his transcription of the Simpson gamba variations for the cello. Piatti also compiled an edition for cello and piano of the first suite by J. S. Bach, an exercise that would not have met with Dolmetsch's approval.

Nonetheless, the virtuoso elements in Piatti's writing are of historical interest since they give some indication of his mastery of the instrument. He employed rich passage-work in both legato and staccato, and made great use of 'bouncing' bow technique. Piatti's *Twelve Caprices* are still of value today in the teaching literature.

He played in the old manner, without a spike, holding the cello between his knees. Judging by pictures he also favoured the low elbow position for the right hand.

A fine judge of good instruments, for many years Piatti played on a Pietro Giacomo Rogeri dated 1717, but in 1867 he acquired—as a gift—the instrument he had coveted for nearly 25 years, a Stradivari made in 1720, and one of the master's finest instruments.

It was on a visit to Dublin in 1844 that Piatti came across the cello which was to become his favourite instrument. It had been brought from Cadiz to Ireland by a wine merchant, and remained in a music shop for some time, after which it was sold for £100 to a professor from Dublin.

When Piatti first saw the instrument it was owned by a cellist named Piggott, who would not part with it. After Piggott's death it passed through many hands and was then bought for £350 by General Oliver, an intimate friend of Piatti, who had refused to sell it to Vuillaume for £1,000. One day the General asked Piatti which of his valuable collection of instruments he considered the best. Without hesitation Piatti chose the Strad, whereupon the general said, 'Take it home, keep it, enjoy it.' Piatti was reluctant to take advantage of such spontaneous generosity, but the next day it was delivered to his house with a note from the General asking for its acceptance in the kindest terms. The General was later godfather to Piatti's only child, Rosa.

During the latter part of Piatti's life, Robert von Mendelssohn, nephew of the composer, offered Piatti £2,000 for the Strad. Mendelssohn was refused, made his offer *carte blanche*, but Piatti never parted with his beloved instrument. After his death in 1901, his daughter Rosa, knowing that the instrument would spoil if it were not played, reluctantly sold it to Mendelssohn for £4,000.

All these details were given to William Whitehouse by the Contessa Rosa Constanza Piatti-Lochis. It appears also that when Piatti first had this cello, he took it to Paris to show Vuillaume. The latter suggested restoration—where the bridge had indented the table, and marks where the left hand comes against the ribs etc.— but Piatti politely refused his offer to revarnish and make it 'good as new'. However, Mendelssohn could not resist the temptation to have it restored, and, in addition, had a new neck grafted on to it.

Piatti was one of the last of the old romantic school of cello players combining brilliant technique and good taste. Wasielewski wrote, 'He is not only the most important cellist in England, but belongs altogether to the highest rank of artists of the present time.'[4]

CHAPTER XV

The Twin Peaks:
Julius Klengel and Hugo Becker

BY THE END of the nineteenth and beginning of the twentieth
century, the German school of cello playing was firmly in the lead.
A number of excellent players emerged as soloists, chamber and
orchestral musicians, many of whom were also first-class teachers.
Two names stand out from the others, twin peaks in the development of the art of cello playing—Julius Klengel and Hugo Becker.
Both represented the Dresden school, stemming from Grützmacher,
and as such had similar artistic tastes; their seriousness of interpretation and rejection of the romantic virtuoso style of playing encouraged interest in the employment of teaching aids and editions. But
in approach, they were worlds apart. Becker, who concentrated on
the scientific aspect of teaching, made considerable researches into
anatomy and physiology. Klengel was far more empirical in
approach.

The son of a lawyer and fine amateur musician who was a close
friend of Mendelssohn, Julius Klengel (1859–1933) had all the
advantage of being born in that hive of musical activity, Leipzig.
His grandfather, and many generations before him, had been professional musicians and his brothers and sisters were all able to play an
instrument. From his earliest childhood, chamber-music ensembles
in various combinations were possible within the family.

Klengel had his initial musical instruction from his father and his
first lessons on the cello with Emil Hegar, principal cellist in the
Gewandhaus Orchestra and a pupil of Grützmacher and Davidov.
At fifteen he became a member of the Gewandhaus Orchestra and
in 1881, at twenty-two, was promoted to principal cellist. That
same year, he was appointed 'Royal Professor' at the Leipzig
Conservatoire. He remained with the orchestra until 1924, and, to
celebrate his fifty years' service, Furtwängler conducted a jubilee
concert with Klengel playing the cello part in a double concerto for
violin, cello and orchestra that he had composed for the occasion.

Klengel appeared many times in Russia, the first in 1882 when he performed his own concerto with the orchestra conducted by Anton Rubinstein. He gave the first Russian performance of the Haydn D Major Concerto in 1887 at St Petersburg, and took part in a number of chamber-music concerts including some with the St Petersburg Quartet led by Leopold Auer. In 1889 he returned to Russia with the Brodsky Quartet in a series of concerts in which well-known Russian pianists also appeared. When he played Beethoven's C major Sonata with Vassilij Safonov, a critic commented upon the artist's 'dazzling success' with the Moscow audience. In 1911 a cello competition was held to celebrate the fiftieth anniversary of the Russian Music Society; he was invited to sit on the jury.

A contemporary, Hugh Butler, writes:

As a performer Klengel ranked very high on the musical as well as on the purely technical side. He made his effects by subtlety of accent and emphasis rather than by violent contrasts or emotional climaxes. He was a fine and scholarly musician, with an admirable taste and sense of style, and nowhere was this more conspicuous than when he took part in chamber music or interpreted such music as the Beethoven sonatas or the Bach solo suites. His least strong point was quality of tone, which, though clear and effective, was a little lacking in beauty.[1]

A varying opinion is expressed by his pupil, S. S. Dale: 'Above all, his tone was astonishing although some critics found it overpowering. His system of tone production is nowadays in abeyance, killed off I think by the use of steel strings. In Klengel's time the gut string was supreme.'[2]

Klengel had extremely sensitive musical faculties, no doubt due to his early exposure in the home to music of all kinds. His knowledge of chamber music was so vast that it was claimed he knew every part of each instrument in all the standard repertoire. It was well known that, whichever piece they chose, Klengel could accompany his pupils on the piano, playing everything from memory.

As a composer he contributed much to the literature of his instrument, and in this respect it is important to remember that Klengel was in close contact with other eminent musicians of his day. Joachim, Brahms, Rubinstein and Reger all had a considerable influence on his musical thinking. He wrote four concertos for cello and orchestra, two for two cellos and two for cello and violin, a sonata, caprices and a *Hymn for Twelve Cellos*, dedicated to the memory of the conductor, Artur Nikisch. He also wrote a number of teaching works, some of which are still in use: his *Technical Exercises in all Keys* (1909) for development of finger and bowing techniques, and *Daily Exercises* (1911) are the best known. He also made editions of sonatas and concertos from the classic repertoire and an edition of the Bach solo suites. It is a common misconception today that Casals was the first to bring the Bach solo suites before the public. S. S. Dale tells us that Klengel was teaching Bach to his cello students as long ago as 1880. The Beethoven sonatas were also a regular part of his repertoire.

Today, Klengel is mostly remembered as a teacher. Throughout his years at the Leipzig Conservatoire he gave some fifty lessons a week, and could name among his students many who later achieved world fame: Emanuel Feuermann, Guilhermina Suggia, Paul Grümmer, Joachim Stutschewsky, Edmund Kurtz, Gregor Piatigorsky and William Pleeth were all students of Klengel at Leipzig. Piatigorsky writes: 'I marvelled at Klengel's art of teaching by really not teaching. At lessons one seldom heard suggestions or discourses on music from him. He let a student play a piece to the end and said, "Fine", or in a severe case, "Watch your left arm, young man!"'[3] William Pleeth confirms this view: 'What I loved about him was he was actually a very simple man. He had no whims, no sophistication. He was very honest and I loved him for it. Klengel never encouraged us to copy, and if you look at the wide range of playing from his many pupils you will see how different we all are.'[4]

Hugo Becker (1864–1941) was born in Strasbourg in Alsace, son of Jean Becker, the famous violinist and founder of the Florentine String Quartet. He began on the violin and piano at the age of six taking lessons from his father, but at nine he heard a cello solo that made such an impression on him that he begged to be allowed to take up that instrument. He learnt first with Kanut Kündinger, a first class musician at Mannheim; and at fifteen he was offered the post of second cellist in the Court Orchestra of that city. A year later, he studied for a few months with Grützmacher in Dresden.

In 1880 he toured successfully with his father, brother and sister as the 'Jean Becker Family Quartet'. Van der Straeten heard them at Wesel on the Rhine and describes a performance by the young Becker of the Concerto in A minor by Goltermann as having 'a perfect command over the technical difficulties and in a very artistic style'.[5] Like Klengel, Becker's background of chamber music in his home from early childhood must have had considerable bearing both on his musical development and his taste. With his sister and brother he formed a permanent trio which was as well known as the family quartet had been. A further influence came about through some lessons from Piatti, whom he met in London in 1882.

From 1884–6 Becker was solo cellist of the opera orchestra in Frankfurt and in 1895 he was appointed first teacher of cello and director of the chamber-music class at the Hochschule in that city. It was at this time that he formed a trio with the pianist, Daniel Quast and violinist, Willy Hess. He also played in the Frankfurt String Quartet until 1906 with Hugo Heermann as leader.

In addition, Becker undertook a busy concert schedule. He visited Russia three times, and in the season 1900/01 toured the USA. From 1891 onwards he played in London every year, deputizing for Piatti and eventually replacing him. Becker also had success in London with two very distinguished colleagues in the Ysaÿe–Becker–Busoni Trio. After their second recital, on 21 November 1901, the *Morning Post* wrote that it was 'wholly delightful. Such ensemble playing could certainly not be surpassed.' Each artist also played solos, and Becker's playing of a sonata by Valentini 'galvanized [it] into life with extraordinary success'. Of the Beethoven Trio in B flat, the *Daily Telegraph* waxed poetic: 'It brought out the beauty, tenderness and sublimity of a work which the ancient Greeks, had they possessed and understood it, would have enshrined and worshipped.'

During the first decades of the present century, Becker achieved a reputation as a great teacher, although he was often criticized for his pedantry. One student described him as 'a dry old stick'. From 1902 he taught at the Royal Music Academy at Stockholm and after Hausmann's death in 1909 succeeded him at the Hochschule in Berlin. Among his many pupils were Enrico Mainardi, Johannes Hegar, Paul Grümmer, Arnold Földesy, Boris Hambourg, Beatrice Harrison, Herbert Walenn and Herbert Withers.

As he grew older his solo appearances diminished but he remained a member of some important chamber ensembles, playing in trios with Ernest Dohnányi and Henri Marteau, and later with Artur Schnabel and Carl Flesch.

Becker's compositions are of no great consequence; but his edition of the Bach solo suites attracted a certain interest at the time. His *Mixed Finger Bowing Exercises, Etudes* and *Six Special Etudes* are still in use today.

He had direct and indirect links with other great musicians of his time, among whom were Brahms, Joachim and Schumann. Reger dedicated his second solo suite in D minor Op. 131 to Becker.

A Russian critic described Becker's playing as being classic rather than romantic, and also pointed out that it was his timing and the ease with which he surmounted difficulties that was so remarkable. Von Bülow, a close friend, used to say he was the only cellist who played with virility. The significance of this assessment is that early in the present century, the cello was deemed an 'instrument of the soul', and most appreciated when it expressed sentimental feelings. Becker disagreed and, in his book, *Technique and Aesthetics of Violoncello Playing* written in collaboration with the physiologist, Dr Dago Rynar, he states: 'The violoncello is a virile instrument, able more than any other string instrument to embody, along with the repleteness of feeling, its chivalrous, vigorous and exalted content.'

Becker was one of many music teachers of this era who began to explore the physiological aspects of performance and how best these could be aligned with the most natural way of playing. His works represent a masterly attempt to solve some of the difficulties by treating the technical and aesthetic problems as a whole. With his wide experience as a performer and teacher he was able to draw on examples from the eighteenth to the twentieth century composers in his methodological analyses. Dvořák and Richard Strauss were both heartily in accordance with his analysis of the Concerto in B minor and *Don Quixote* respectively.

Becker owned two Stradivarius instruments. The 'Cristiani', dated 1720 which he acquired in 1884, the year of his father's death, and one made in 1719, now known as the 'Becker'.

One of Klengel's pupils who contributed greatly to the art of cello playing, both by teaching and performing, was Paul Grümmer (1879–1965). Born in Gera in Germany, he was the son of a court musician, who gave him his first lessons on the violin when he was eight. At fourteen, he studied the cello with the court musician Friedrichs and the cellist, Emil Böhme, who played in the Municipal Orchestra. A year later he went to the Leipzig Conservatoire under Klengel and completed his studies with Becker.

In 1902 he made a successful début at a London concert where he appeared before the King and Queen, and followed this with an extensive tour of Great Britain, Europe and America. He often appeared with many of the most famous artists of the day: Wilhelm Backhaus, Jan Kubelik, Franz von Veczey, Bronislaw Huberman and Vasá Prihóda all played with Grümmer.

He settled in Vienna in 1905 where he was soloist in the orchestras of the Concert Society and the Opera House. From 1919–30 he was the cellist of the Adolf Busch String Quartet and, during that time, performed the Brahms Double Concerto with Adolf Busch.

Teaching was an important part of Grümmer's musical life. From 1907–13 he taught at the Viennese Musical Academy, and again from 1940–46 and at the Hochschule of Cologne and Berlin in the twenties and thirties. In 1946 he settled in Switzerland where he continued teaching until his death in 1965.

Max Reger, Wolf-Ferrari, Alexander Tcherepnin and other composers dedicated works to Grümmer. His own writings were confined to an edition of the Bach solo suites together with the facsimile of the original manuscript, *Exercises for Advanced Cellists*, and a *Method for the Viola da Gamba* (1925). He helped considerably to revive the art of viola da gamba playing, and was a fine soloist on that instrument, played with ensembles of early instruments and gave recitals with the harpsichordist, Wanda Landowska.

A distinguished teacher, Carl Fuchs (1865–1951) was born in Offenbach near Frankfurt, the son of a leather merchant who hailed originally from Amsterdam. He started on the cello at nine, with Robert Riedel, and at sixteen studied with Cossmann at the Frankfurt Conservatory. Devoted to his teacher, Fuchs was grateful that besides those 'dry' Romberg Concertos, which were then *de rigueur*, he learned the Schumann Cello Concerto which had a cataclysmic effect on his life. Shortly before leaving the Conservatory, he played it at one of the examination concerts, not knowing that Clara Schumann was present. She expressed her approval for his sensitive interpretation and a warm contact was established, which led to further meetings for chamber-music evenings at the pianist's home. Later, when Fuchs was going to England, Clara Schumann gave him a letter of introduction to Karl Hallé (afterwards Sir Charles) in Manchester.

In the autumn of 1885, Fuchs went to St Petersburg to study with Davidov, having had some preparatory lessons that summer in Thuringia.

He arrived for his first lesson at the Conservatoire in a carriage and pair, so as to ensure the safe transport for his valuable Bergonzi cello. Davidov was highly amused and advised him in future to use one of the second-rate cellos provided by the institution.

His first lesson with Davidov—at which Fuchs played his A minor Concerto—so pleased the composer that he invited him to perform it at a soirée at his house before a host of eminent musical friends. The room was heavily carpeted and draped with massive curtains, so that, with the additional crowd of people, the sound of the cello was almost lost, a deep disappointment to both of them.

When Davidov had to leave Russia, following his affair with a student, Fuchs, never over fond of Russian social life, left also. Travelling with Davidov to Leipzig, he met Adolf Brodsky and Klengel, and attended a party that the latter gave for his famous colleague, where 'all those in Leipzig who had so much as had a cello between their knees appeared'.[6] Eighty cellists were said to have been there: on every step of the staircase stood a cello case.

Fuchs was always enchanted by Davidov's playing and the ease with which he overcame the greatest difficulties. He would quote Davidov as saying that anyone could play song-like melodies, but 'art was needed to produce passage-work clearly and with a good tone'.[7]

The turning-point in Carl Fuchs's life came in 1887 when, armed with his introduction to Hallé from Clara Schumann, he took up his abode in England, which was to become his second home. On his first visit to Manchester he appeared as soloist with the Hallé Orchestra. Since, at that time, continental pitch was lower than English, he had to tune his cello a semitone higher, and he remembered that it took him some time to adjust to the strange sensation. Curiously, today the situation is reversed.

Fuchs was appointed principal cellist of the Hallé Orchestra and gave its first performance of the Lalo Concerto, the *Rococo Variations* by Tchaikovsky and Strauss's *Don Quixote*. He remained a close friend of the Hallés throughout their association with the orchestra. When the Royal Manchester College of Music was founded in 1893, Sir Charles Hallé appointed Fuchs its first professor of cello.

For many years, Fuchs played with the orchestra under Hans Richter, Hallé's successor, and he told some amusing stories about the conductor's incongruous attempts at the English language. In German one word, *Fleisch*, suffices for both meat and human flesh. Once, when the cellists were not giving enough body to a *pizzicato* passage, Richter commanded, 'Please do not play with the nail. Play with the meat!'

He also recalls the occasion when another conductor—albeit a budding one—asked him if he would play a concerto at a forthcoming concert with the Hallé at St Helen's in Lancashire. 'St Helen's!' said Fuchs, 'Beecham's Pills?' 'Yes,' was the dry rejoinder. 'That's my name.'

It was indeed the young Beecham, whose father had engaged the Hallé for his son to conduct as his 21st birthday present. Fuchs regretted that, owing to a previous booking, he was unable to accept the engagement which was to mark the beginning of the career of one of the most colourful characters in the English musical scene for the next fifty years.

Shortly before Hallé died, Adolf Brodsky came to Manchester to take over the leadership of the orchestra and teach at the College of Music. Brodsky had made himself a reputation for quartet playing in Leipzig, so it was not long before he formed one with the available forces in Manchester. Cosmopolitan in its personnel, Brodsky, Briggs, Speelman and Fuchs hailed from Russia, England, Holland and Germany respectively. Destined to become one of the most famous English quartets, their concerts were highly successful. When they appeared in the capital in a performance of Beethoven's late quartets, despite the fact they came from the provinces the critics declared that not until now had Londoners known what quartet playing was. Busoni, Siloti, Backhaus and Percy Grainger were some of the eminent musicians who played with the Brodsky String Quartet in their regular Manchester concerts, the entire proceeds from which were devoted to helping poor but gifted students of the College.

When war was declared in 1914, Fuchs and his family were visiting relatives in Germany. His wife and children were allowed to return to England by a circuitous route, but Fuchs was taken prisoner, and released only under supervision until the war was over. The long separation from his family caused a nervous breakdown, but the doctor who attended him became interested in the cello and Fuchs found considerable therapy in giving him lessons.

Fuchs was a modest, kind and gentle man. Never a great soloist, he was a fine and sensitive chamber-music player and an excellent teacher. One of his pupils at the College, Jan Kerrison (later the wife of Archie Camden, the virtuoso bassoon player—also long associated with the Hallé Orchestra), said, 'Fuchs had endless patience with his students, and his wealth of musical knowledge was astounding, especially in chamber music. His string quartet classes were an absolute joy.'[8] It seems that his speciality was what he called 'handbowing' in which he used the entire hand as opposed to the wrist when great strength was needed.

Fuchs played for many years on what he thought was a Carlo Bergonzi made in 1720. But it is known that Bergonzi never made any cellos and that those believed to be by him were made in his workshop by Matteo Gofriller. Fuchs was undeterred by the ambiguity, and writes, 'Although this friend was born in the reign of King George I, our friendship still flourishes.' He came by this instrument through Cossmann, his master, who secured it from one of his pupils, Josef Diem, a shepherd in the Bavarian Alps, who later became a cellist of some reputation.

Josef Diem (1836–94) was born in Kellmunz in Bavaria. As a boy he was a herdsman with an innate love of music. He first mastered the flute, then the violin and at fifteen joined a band of strolling players, with whom he eked out a meagre living. In Switzerland, a wealthy Jewish landowner recognized his talent and sponsored his attendance at the Munich Conservatoire where he studied the cello with Hippolyt Müller for three years.

Diem's début at Augsburg was so successful that a Nuremberg manufacturer presented him with a Guarneri cello. It was after this that he went on to Weimar to complete his studies with Cossmann. In 1866 he was appointed professor of cello in Moscow and continued to tour in Europe and in Great Britain. In 1872 he went to America for a few years, and returned to Constance in Switzerland in 1889, where he founded a school of music.

The German story would not be complete without a mention of Edmund Van der Straeten (1885–1934). Born in Düsseldorf into a noble Dutch family, he began his musical studies when very young. Principally a gamba player, he also had lessons on the cello with Johannes Hoecke, a pupil of Kummer and completed his studies at the Guildhall School of Music in London with Gustav Libotton and Louis Hegyesi, a pupil of Franchomme.

His family were opposed to him taking up music as a profession, but fortunately he discovered he was temperamentally unsuited for a solo career, and happily confined his activities to chamber-music playing. Van der Straeten is best remembered as a scholar, researcher and writer. In the light of more recent discoveries, his writings are somewhat dated, but nevertheless remain of value in the history of the cello and its literature.

CHAPTER XVI

The British Element

ALTHOUGH GREAT BRITAIN produced a number of excellent chamber-music cellists in the latter half of the nineteenth century, there were no great soloists. Fortunately there were some first class teachers, most of whom received their training in Germany, who were able to pass on their expertise to their pupils. But it was a slow process.

A teacher who became immensely popular in Great Britain in the late nineteenth century was the Belgian-born Gustav Libotton (1842–91). He studied at the Brussels Conservatoire with Servais, and as a young man caused a sensation in St Petersburg when he appeared there in 1864. He later became professor at the Brussels Conservatoire and first came to London in 1873.

He frequently appeared as a soloist in orchestral and chamber-music concerts and was said to be a brilliant player. But by nature he was shy and retiring and did not enjoy the virtuoso life. He much preferred teaching, and in 1880 was appointed professor of cello at the Guildhall School of Music where he had upwards of 60 students, a remarkable achievement when the cello did not enjoy the popularity it does today.

Sadly, he died of tuberculosis at the age of forty-nine. Piatti was always a firm supporter of Libotton and knew his value as a teacher. It was he who opened an account at Coutts, his personal bank, as the first subscriber to a Memorial Fund.

Most prominent among the early cellists in Great Britain was Edward Howell (1846–98), who came from a family of singers and instrumentalists spanning several generations. It was Edward's elder brother Arthur—a double-bass player—who, on the death of Dragonetti, joined the cellist Charles Lucas and Robert Lindley in the performance of the Corelli Sonatas (two cellos and double bass) in 1850.

A pupil of Piatti, Howell held a number of important appointments including Musician-in-Ordinary to the Queen, first cellist in the

Queen's Band, and the Leeds and Three Choirs festival orchestras. From 1872, Howell was a member of the Covent Garden Theatre Orchestra, and for many years principal cellist of the Royal Italian Opera. When David Popper gave the first performance in England of his *Requiem* for three cellos and orchestra at St James's Hall in 1891, Howell took part with the composer and Jules Delsart. Howell taught at one time at the Royal College, the Guildhall and the Royal Academy, and it was there that he had as his pupil, Herbert Walenn who eventually succeeded him. He arranged Romberg's treatise as *A First Book for the Violoncello*, at that time a very useful contribution to the teaching literature.

Piatti's favourite pupil, the London-born William Edward Whitehouse (1859–1935), started on the violin with Adolphus Griesbach but turned to the cello at thirteen, when he became a pupil of Walter Pettit, principal cellist of the Queen's Band. In 1878 he entered the Royal Academy of Music where he studied with Piatti and Pezze and gained the Dobrée Prize after only one year. In 1882 he became assistant professor of cello at the Royal Academy of Music and full professor a year later. He also taught at the Royal College of Music and King's College, Cambridge.

Highly regarded both as a soloist and chamber musician, Whitehouse—commonly known as 'W. E.'—appeared many times in the Pops, often deputizing for Piatti when he was abroad. He also played with Joachim and toured extensively with the violinist, Simonetti and the pianist, Amina Goodwin as The London Trio. The list of his pupils contains many of the best-known names at the beginning of the twentieth century: Herbert Withers, Warwick Evans, Ivor James and Felix Salmond, and among the ladies, Kate Ould, Beatrice Evelyn and Beatrice Harrison.

Another Piatti student, Leo Stern (1862–1904), was born in Brighton into a musical family, the son of a violinist and conductor. His mother was a pianist. As a boy he played the drum in the orchestra of the Brighton Symphony Society and took lessons on the cello with Hugo Daubert. A chemist by profession, he remained an amateur until the urge to take up music as a career became too strong. He studied for two years with Piatti, and spent a further year with Klengel and Davidov in Leipzig. From this time onwards he became a full-time professional soloist touring with the singers, Mesdames Patti and Albani.

In Prague he came into contact with Dvořák and, when Hanus Wihan was unable to play in the first performance of his Cello

Concerto, the composer selected Stern. The première took place at a Philharmonic Concert on 19 March 1896, with the composer conducting. The *Musical News* of March 28 considers the piece is concerned as much with the orchestral aspect as with that of the solo instrument. 'Indeed, in many places, the solo was quite obscured by the elaboration of the orchestral parts.' The critic goes on to say that it cannot be doubted that 'it is a noble and important work', and that 'its Adagio is one of the most beautiful movements we possess in the whole range of music, [but] it is open to doubt, whether, as a concerto for the violoncello, the work generally presents a satisfactory example of this type of piece.' Stern's performance appears to have satisfied all the critics. The *Musical Courier* says that he 'played the solo part with much expression and faultless intonation'.

A long-forgotten cellist, highly regarded in his day, is William Henry Squire (1871–1963). Born in Herefordshire, Squire had his first musical instruction from his father, a gifted amateur violinist. He made his first public appearance as a prodigy at the age of seven, and in 1883 won a founder-scholarship to the Royal College of Music to study the cello with Edward Howell and composition with Hubert Parry. He also had an occasional lesson with Piatti.

Squire made his début at a concert given by the Spanish composer, Albéniz, at the St James's Hall in London, the success of which led to an increasing number of engagements. His orchestral début took place playing the Saint-Saëns Concerto at the Crystal Palace in 1895. That same year he was appointed principal cellist of the Royal Opera Orchestra at Covent Garden, and subsequently filled the same position in most of the leading British orchestras. He was professor at the Royal College of Music from 1898–1917 and held a similar post at the Guildhall School of Music from 1911–17.

Squire was one of the first solo cellists to make a number of recordings, of which the Elgar Concerto conducted by Hamilton Harty (1936) was considered by many to be the best available at the time. To modern ears, his playing sounds 'old-fashioned', but in his day he was considered to be in the first rank as a soloist and chamber-music player. Fauré thought sufficient of his playing to dedicate his *Sicilienne* to Squire.

He was also a composer of some substance. He wrote a cello concerto, two operettas and many short pieces in a popular style. His *Twelve Easy Pieces* are still used by many teachers today.

★

Herbert Walenn (1870–1953) was born in London into a family of artists and musicians and received his musical education first at the Royal College of Music, then with Edward Howell at the Royal Academy of Music, completing his studies with Becker at Frankfurt. He soon gained a reputation as a soloist and chamber musician, appearing frequently at the Pops. He made his début at one of these with Lady Hallé, and was subsequently cellist of the Kruse String Quartet. Walenn was a highly respected and loved teacher who generated much affection from his students—especially at the Royal Academy where he taught for many years. A number of his pupils became famous: Zara Nelsova, Boris Hambourg, Mischel Cherniavsky, Douglas Cameron, Boris Rickelman and Giovanni Barbirolli who later, as John Barbirolli, achieved an international reputation as a conductor.

Walenn's methods were unorthodox in that he taught very little technique, and even then referred his pupils to books. Milly Stanfield, his student at the Academy, and author of *The Intermediate Cellist*, says: 'He did some very strange things on the cello, but his tone was magical. He also had a tremendous talent for drawing out the good in people. It was a joy to learn with him because he was such a warm and lovable man.'[1]

Walenn's personal contribution to the development of the art of cello playing in England cannot be overestimated. He promoted the cello in a way not previously conceived. A good psychologist, he encouraged amateur players who would never have got very far, and in so doing raised the standards of playing in that hitherto neglected area. He was founder, in 1919, and director of the London Violoncello School where, in the early 1920s, in addition to the opportunities for solo performances, he instituted a series of concerts with up to a hundred cellists taking part. Casals' *Sardana* for sixteen cellos was written for the school in 1927. However, the work received its most hallucinatory performance at the Tonhalle in Zurich when Casals conducted 120 cellists, led by Tortelier, gathered to pay homage to Le Maître for his seventy-fifth birthday.

A touching tribute to Ivor James (1882–1963) came from an obituary in the *R. C. M. Union Magazine* in 1963 'He truly felt music to its very depth and centre. He communicated his musical intention to his pupils in some remarkable way which seems impossible to put into words.' James, or 'Jimmy' as he was known to everyone, was a pupil of William Whitehouse at the Royal College of Music, where his potential as a teacher was soon

The cello played in horizontal position (from a
fresco at Roccapietra near Varallo)

Family making music by Jan Miense Molenaer,
mid–seventeenth century

'The Quartette Party',
eighteenth century

Giacobo Basevi
detto Cervetto

J. L. Duport, from a drawing
by J. Denon

Robert Lindley from an
original lithograph by
Charles Baugniet

Benjamin Hallet

Alfredo Piatti

David Popper

Hugo Becker

Julius Klengel

Carl Fuchs

1898: The young Casals in a string quartet led by Crickboom, with
Galvez (vla) and Rocabrunna

The young Beatrice Harrison with Elgar

May Mukle

Below left: Felix Salmond (caricature by Virginia Quarles Wendt)

Below: Diran Alexanian

recognized. Once when Whitehouse was absent, James was put in charge of the class with quite remarkable results. On completing his studies he joined the English String Quartet in which Frank Bridge played viola.

James's gifts as a teacher became more and more evident and, in 1919, he became Whitehouse's assistant at the College; many were convinced that, from this time, a new era of cello teaching had begun. James could always find some words of encouragement for the less talented—an attitude that stemmed from his need to share with others his own innate love of music. But he could be firm when a pupil was not pulling his weight. Harvey Phillips recalled an occasion when he received a report which read, 'He seems to keep his brains in his cello bag, and forgets to take them out. I want a far higher standard from him.'[2]

James would never tolerate anything approaching exaggeration or poor taste. He would tell his pupils to consider the line of the music, believing this to be the first essential if an interpretation is to carry conviction. But he was also aware that it was imperative for a student to build a strong technical base so that the interpretation could be effective. He taught for 34 years at the Royal College, and his teaching extended to all branches of music with perhaps an emphasis on chamber-music making. Among his many pupils were Thelma Reiss, Harvey Phillips, James Whitehead, Amaryllis Fleming and Martin Lovett of the Amadeus String Quartet. Another was Helen Just, of the English String Quartet and a professor at the Royal College, whom he married in 1928.

James was also a pioneer of the summer school as a place of vacation study. Today there are such courses all over the country specializing in every aspect of music, but at the time virtually nothing was available outside the colleges. James directed the first of its kind at Westminster College, Cambridge, in 1929, sponsored by the British Federation of Music Festivals. During the 1939–45 war it moved to Downe House near Newbury.

Undisputably, Ivor James contributed greatly to the art of cello playing in Britain, and his work in the field of chamber music was invaluable. His illustrated lectures on chamber music in which he analysed great chamber works with his characteristic approach, combining scholarship with humour, were welcomed in educational centres everywhere. During the darkest days of the 1939–45 War his lecture-concerts on the late Beethoven string quartets, organized by Myra Hess, at the National Gallery in London, were described by one cellist as 'being invaluable for keeping people sane'. In 1957, together with Sir John Barbirolli, he represented Great Britain on the international jury of the first Casals Competition in Paris.

Everyone who knew James remarked upon his warmth of personality and his unflagging interest in his pupils. He became the elder statesman of cello playing in England, and although over eighty was still lecturing two months before he died. A favourite quotation of his was, 'Music is a kind of inarticulate, unfathomable speech, which leads us to the infinite, and sometimes allows us to look beyond.'[3]

A very promising young cellist who could easily have followed a solo or chamber-music career, but eventually became one of our great conductors, was Giovanni Battista Barbirolli (1899–1971), born in London into an émigré Italian family with generations of musicians to its credit. Young 'Tita' first learnt the violin at four, but when practising he would wander from room to room, much to the annoyance of his patriarchal grandfather. Barbirolli explained: 'One day he jumped into a hansom cab and drove to Withers to buy a quarter-size cello. He sat me down and put it between my knees and said, "Now you'll have to sit down. You can't practise the damn thing walking about!"'[4]

Tita made excellent progress on his new instrument and won a scholarship to the Trinity College of Music in 1910 to study under Edmund Woolhouse who had been a pupil of Lindley. His first public appearance was at the age of ten in the Queen's Hall at a college concert, playing one movement from the Georg Goltermann Concerto. A critic, though praising the performance, commented upon the small sound. In later years Barbirolli made the characteristic remark that since it was a small cello played by a small boy in a large hall, that was not surprising. Nonetheless, as a prodigy he had a considerable impact on Edwardian society and, in 1911, at the age of eleven, he made some recordings with his sister Rosa at the piano. One of the pieces is *The Broken Melody* by August Van Biene.

Barbirolli entered the Royal Academy of Music in 1912, on an Ada Lewis Scholarship, to study with Walenn. Milly Stanfield—a fellow student—said he was the best cellist in their class, and that they used to ask him to play through their concertos before they started learning them. Some 50 years later, Lionel Tertis recalled Barbirolli playing the Saint-Saëns Concerto in A minor Op.33, 'Most amazing, quite wonderful technically and musically. He was a prodigious prodigy who could play my head off when he was eleven and a half.'[5]

Barbirolli's first professional experience was gained in the pit, in theatres and cinemas and, at sixteen, he became the youngest member of Henry Wood's Queen's Hall Orchestra. His first solo recital was in 1920 in Dublin and there followed a number of solo engagements with orchestras up and down the country. His own expression was that he 'played everywhere but in the street'. One of his happiest youthful recollections was at the Theatre Royal, Drury Lane, when Anna Pavlova was giving her ballet season. Her famous dance to the music of Saint-Saëns' 'Swan', with cello obbligato, was apparently too difficult for the solo cellist to tackle. Barbirolli was brought forward from the back desk and played it so movingly that Pavlova split her bouquet of tiger lilies and threw half down to the young cellist. She asked to see him afterwards and Barbirolli always remembered that her handshake was like a grip of iron.

Another greatly loved teacher who took up his chosen field at twenty-five and died suddenly at the age of seventy when on tour with the National Youth Orchestra, was Douglas Cameron (1902–72), known to everyone as 'Duggie'.

Born in Dundee, Cameron was fifteen when he first took up the cello, and two years later won a scholarship to study at the Royal Academy with Herbert Walenn.

On leaving the Academy he became cellist of the Kutcher String Quartet and a member of Henry Wood's orchestra. Once Herbert Walenn brought along Casals when Cameron was playing the solo in the William Tell overture. They stood in the wings and, after listening for a while, Casals said, 'That boy will make good!' Cameron met Casals on many future occasions. One happy one was when he was invited to represent England in the Casals International Competition, when it took place in Israel. Cameron was for some time cellist of the Blech Quartet, and subsequently founded his own New London String Quartet with Erich Gruenberg as leader.

That same year he became a professor at the Royal Academy of Music, and found that his chamber-music and teaching left no time for orchestral playing. He gave recitals with his pianist daughter, Fiona, and during the 1939–45 War, he led the cello section in, and played concertos with the National Symphony Orchestra conducted by Sydney Beer. He also played concertos under many famous conductors, including Rudolf Schwarz, Norman Del Mar and Sir Adrian Boult. His performance of the Elgar Concerto with the BBC Symphony Orchestra conducted by that great Elgarian, Sir John Barbirolli, was described as 'superb'. Cameron had known Elgar and had studied the bowings and fingerings with him. When

Beatrice Harrison recorded the concerto in 1928, Cameron had been a member of the orchestra.

Cameron coached the cello section in the National Youth Orchestra for many years and taught at a number of summer schools. One of the frequent visitors who sat in on his classes was Emanuel Feuermann who greatly respected his approach to teaching. He had the great gift of being able to bring out the best in his pupils so that they developed in their own way. He never tried to impose his own style of playing on them. Consequently, irrespective of talent he was able to encourage them to their utmost potential. And as such they were not recognizable as 'Cameron' students. Paul Tortelier was once judging one of the competitions at the R.A.M. when virtually every cellist was in the running for the prize. This intrigued Tortelier who thought them all equally good yet so different stylistically. He asked who their individual teachers were; when told that most were from the same professor he could scarcely believe it.

Duggie was one of the most popular teachers of his time. He loved life, good food and wine, and smoked like a chimney. He was a great raconteur and his after-dinner stories were a constant source of enjoyment to his fellow musicians. His many students included Florence Hooton, David Strange, Douglas Cummings, Derek Simpson, Keith Harvey, Thomas Igloi, Christopher van Kampen and Julian Lloyd Webber.

When Cameron died, the Academy asked the cellist Lilly Phillips, a fine quartet player in her own right—whom he had married in 1924—if she would take on his pupils on a temporary basis. She is still there, in 1987, fulfilling a busy teaching schedule.

CHAPTER XVII

'Freedom with Order':
Pablo Casals

UNQUESTIONABLY, THE GREATEST impact on twentieth-century cello playing was made by the Catalan, Pablo Casals (1876–1973). He not only revolutionized the technique of the instrument, but changed the entire way of thinking about the cello and its capabilities.

Casals was born in Vendrell, in Tarragona, Spain, the son of an organist, and from a very early age was surrounded by music. As Casals described it, 'Music was for me an ocean in which I swam like a little fish. Music was inside me and all about me; it was the air I breathed from the time I could walk.'[1]

He had his first piano lessons when he was four, sang in the church choir when he was five and took up the violin at seven. By this time he had also written his first composition,[2] and was only prevented from playing the organ because his feet could not reach the pedals. When he was nine, this glorious moment arrived and the mightiest of instruments was added to his list.

At eleven, Pablo heard the cello for the first time, played by one José García in a trio at a concert in Vendrell. From the first notes he was captivated, and told his father, 'That is the most wonderful instrument I have ever heard. That is what I want to play.'[3]

He was sent to study with García at the Municipal School of Music in Barcelona when he was twelve, and in a short time the boy was earning pocket money of four pesetas a day playing light music in a trio at the Café Tost. Even here, with his own knowledge of Bach, Beethoven and Brahms, he began, subtly, to improve the repertoire. Eventually, he persuaded the owner to have concerts of classical music for one night a week and they turned out to be immensely successful, people travelling long distances to attend.

At the music school, too, he was beginning to change the order of things. He noticed something awkward and unnatural in the stiff-armed playing generally accepted at the time as correct. In order to keep the elbows close to their sides, pupils of both cello and violin were given books to hold under their arms whilst playing.

One day, when browsing in a music shop, he picked up a bundle of old scores, tattered and discoloured with age. Although only thirteen, he immediately recognized something extraordinary. He had stumbled across the Six Suites for Violoncello Solo by J. S. Bach. He had never heard about them from his teacher or any other musician, but the discovery revolutionized his musical outlook. He spent the next twelve years practising them until he felt he was ready to present one in public. Since the re-discovery of Bach by Mendelssohn, the nineteenth-century attitude to Bach made people look upon the suites as studies. A sidelight on this attitude is that in order to make them palatable, Grützmacher, Piatti and Schumann made editions with piano accompaniment, but Schumann's was never published.

In 1894, with a letter of introduction from his friend, the composer, Albéniz, to the Count de Morphy (an accomplished musician and great patron of the arts), he went to Madrid. The Count presented the young musician to the Queen who provided the means for him to enter the Madrid Conservatory of Music. Here he studied composition with Tomas Breton and chamber music with the celebrated Jesus de Monasterio, who was also Director of the Conservatory. Knowledge of harmony gained at this stage gave substance to his intuitive modelling of intonation. His exceptional talent for counterpoint later bore fruit in many compositions.

At the same time, he received private instruction from the Count, not only in music, but in all the arts, philosophy and mathematics.

Three years later it was decided that the young man should complete his cello studies at Brussels Conservatoire, then the most important string teaching centre in Europe. An incident during a brief visit there, gives an insight into the nature of the man who was later to stand out against Franco's dictatorship in Spain. It seems that the Director, François Gevaert, impressed with Casals' playing, recommended him to the cello professor, Edouard Jacobs. At the session next morning, the professor waited until the class was over and then beckoned to Casals, saying in a patronizing manner, 'So, you are the little Spaniard that the director spoke to me about. Do you wish to play?' Casals said he would be glad to. Then the professor asked if he knew certain pieces, rattling off a long list, to which he truthfully replied that he knew them all. The professor turned to the class saying, 'Well now, isn't this remarkable! It seems that our young cellist plays everything. He must be really quite amazing!' He then asked Casals to play *Souvenir de Spa*, by Servais, a virtuoso piece that was regularly played in the Belgian school. Casals, by now incensed, nevertheless decided to oblige. As he played, the room fell silent and when he had finished the students were too stunned even to applaud. Visibly shaken, the professor took him aside, glowed about his talent and offered to take him in his class, promising him the first prize. The angry young man retorted, 'You ridiculed me in front of your pupils. I do not want to remain here a moment longer!'[4] He left for Paris the next morning.

This impetuosity brought repercussions. When the Queen heard that her prodigy had thrown away the chance to study in Brussels, she withdrew her support. There followed a very difficult time when Casals had to work as second cellist in the music hall, the Folies-Marigny, in the Champs-Elysées. In order to buy food, his mother had to take in sewing and was often working well into the night. She also sold her hair to make a few extra francs.

Finally, they returned to Barcelona and, that same year, the Casals family fortunes took an upward turn. His old professor, José García, retired from the Municipal School and Casals was offered his post. He was just twenty-one. There followed teaching at the Liceu School of Music and an appointment as principal cellist in the Opera Orchestra. It was also during this time that he formed a quartet with the Belgian violinist, Mathieu Crickboom, the violist Galvez and the pianist and composer Enrique Granados.

Casals had never drawn a line between teaching and learning; for him teaching was in fact learning. Therefore he continued to work on his study of technique, determined not to be hampered by the restrictions of the past. He advocated learning from the past, but not to be dominated by it. His secret was that he always believed in trying to achieve the best possible effects on the cello by using technique as a means, not an end in itself. He would say, 'The purpose of technique is to transmit the inner meaning, the message of the music. The most perfect technique is that which is not noticed at all.'[5]

He taught his students the methods of fingering and bowing that he had begun to develop in his own days as a student. He taught the importance of relaxation and how to exercise the left hand so as to create a balance between tension and relaxation. His exercises for relaxing the hand and arm for a fraction of a second during performance were found to be of inestimable value.

In 1898 came what Casals called 'The Disaster': the final crumbling of the Spanish Empire in the Spanish-American War. Effects on the

population were widespread, and the young musician had his first
sight of the casualties of war. This was doubtless the origin of his
lifelong devotion to peace. It is interesting that 'Pau', the diminutive
for Pablo, by which he was known to his friends, is also Catalan for
'peace'.

The following year, he made his London début playing the Saint-
Saëns Concerto under August Manns at the Crystal Palace. He also
played at the homes of a number of society hostesses who, in
accordance with the prevailing fashion, gave private concerts. He
was invited to play for Queen Victoria at Osborne House, her
summer residence in the Isle of Wight. Casals recalls that the
atmosphere was rather formal with no applause between pieces and
only a 'polite clapping' at the end. However, many years later he
was given a telegram by Queen Maria Cristina sent to her by Queen
Victoria after the concert. It seems she had found it *entzückend*—
'charming'.

In the autumn of that same year came what Casals describes as the
turning point in his career. His friend and patron, the Count de
Morphy had introduced him to Charles Lamoureux, founder and
director of the famous orchestra that bore his name. When the
young cellist arrived, Lamoureux was busy over a score and barely
looked up, while at the same time indicating he should play. After
the opening phrase of the Lalo concerto, Lamoureux put down his
pen and listened attentively until the movement was finished.
Lamoureux had a physical disability that made leg movements
difficult, but he limped towards the young cellist, threw his arms
around him, and, with tears in his eyes, said, 'My dear boy, you are
one of the elect. You will play in my first concert next month.'[6]

The concert took place in October 1899 at the Château d'Eau with
the Lalo concerto. In December Casals appeared again in the
Concerts Lamoureux at the Théâtre de la République playing the
Saint-Saëns concerto. Both concerts were received with tumultuous
applause. In the 1930s, the veteran French cellist, Joseph Salmon,
recalled that performance as 'unbelievable! . . . Like listening to the
work for the first time . . . Casals made it sound *easy*. We cellists
were dumbfounded.'[7] Although he did not realize it at the time,
Casals was later convinced that the initial appreciation by Lamoureux opened the way for his future success.

He settled happily in Paris—then the cultural centre of the world.
He described it as a mecca of activity, as the home and workshop of
men of arts and letters. His circle of friends included the painters
Degas and Eugene Carrière, the philosopher Henri Bergson, the

writer Romain Rolland and musicians, Ysaÿe, Thibaud and Cortot. He also became closely associated with the composers, d'Indy, Enesco, Ravel, Schoenberg and Saint-Saëns.

The pianist Harold Bauer became a very close colleague and friend. Casals gave more concerts with Bauer than with any other musician and felt that they complemented one another perfectly. From the first meeting an instant rapport existed between them.

In 1901 Casals made a highly successful trip to the United States with the American singer, Emma Nevada, and the French pianist Léon Moreau. They gave 80 concerts, sometimes playing in the most remote places. Here Casals was struck by the attention given in the USA to musical education in schools, the bands and choral groups. He was also impressed with the feeling of equality among the people. No doubt this appealed strongly to his republican upbringing and beliefs, but it must be said that he also enjoyed the favours of the royal family in Spain and a warmly reciprocated lifelong friendship with the Queen of the Belgians.

In 1905, with his friends Thibaud and Cortot, Casals formed the trio that will probably remain one of the greatest in the history of music. It was a collaboration that lasted for 30 years. When they began playing together, Casals was twenty-eight, Cortot, twenty-seven and Thibaud, twenty-four. He writes, 'We understood each other perfectly in our music, and we formed a marvellously gratifying team—not only as an ensemble but as friends. We began the custom of devoting one month each year to travelling together to give chamber-music concerts, and our trio soon became widely known.'[8] They were responsible for some of the earliest recordings of chamber-music for the gramophone. Their superb interpretation of the Schubert trio in B flat was one of the first which helped to dispel the early prejudice among the anti-gramophone league. Casals always insisted that he preferred to play chamber music rather than solos—he never fully overcame his nerves before a solo concert.

The first Russian tour came in 1905—rather an unfortunate time since it coincided with the Revolution of that year. Bound for Moscow, he was diverted to St Petersburg when, due to a strike, all Moscow trains had come to a halt. In St Petersburg, he deputized for a cellist who had been stranded in Moscow for the same reason. The circumstances of the concerts—conducted by Alexander Siloti—were dramatic. Due to the general strike there was no electricity, so the hall was lit by candles. However, the audience gave Casals a warm response. During the three weeks of concerts the atmosphere in the day time was tense and ominous, while sporadic gunfire could be heard throughout the night.

During the First World War Casals remained in New York, returning to Barcelona in 1919, with the intention of improving the poor state of music in his own country. Shocked at the low standards of playing in the two existing symphony orchestras in Barcelona, he offered to co-operate in any way they wished and to provide financial backing if necessary. The conductors of both orchestras protested that there was insufficient local talent to build a better orchestra and that in any case, Casals had been away too long to be capable of assessing the situation. But he had always considered that cello playing in isolation was limited in its scope, whereas, when harnessed to conducting, which had always appealed to him, the one gave an extra dimension to the other. So, with funds provided from his own savings, and after months of auditioning and organization, he founded the Orquestra Pau Casals.

When Spain became a Republic in 1931, he spent a few happy and secure years in his splendid home in San Salvador. But the outbreak of the Spanish Civil War in 1936 meant that, owing to his political affiliation, he was no longer safe in his own country. General Queipo de Llano, one of Franco's aides and chief propagandist for the fascists, once broadcast that if he caught Casals he would put an end to his political activities by cutting off both his arms at the elbows. Casals ignored the threat and soldiered on, playing in hospitals and giving concerts to raise money for the Republicans. When the fall of Barcelona was imminent he was summoned to a ceremony at the University to receive an honorary doctorate. The city was already being bombed by Italian planes and the faculty members were in the process of evacuating their families. But with a hand-written document—there was no time for printing—they were at least able to honour their most famous and beloved son. A few days later, with a sad heart, he was persuaded to cross the Pyrenees to the little French town of Prades, where he lived in exile for over twenty years.

Conditions at Prades, especially in the winter, were grim. One of his pupils recalled arriving dressed in his best suit. Casals looked very serious and said he would give him some advice. The young man waited agog for the words of wisdom to fall from his lips but all Casals said was, 'Dress warm. It can be very cold here.' The student later discovered that this was no understatement. Three jerseys plus an eiderdown were often necessary to keep out the cold. Prades itself is in a valley, but the wind—known as the Tramontane—is frozen by the ice as it blows over the nearby mountains, on its way to the Mediterranean. As the winter progresses the wind becomes colder and colder.

After the 1939–45 war, Casals was again invited to England, and was greeted with tremendous enthusiasm throughout the country. The concert which remained most clearly in his own memory was one at the Royal Albert Hall in June 1946 when he played both the Schumann and Elgar concertos with Sir Adrian Boult conducting the BBC Symphony Orchestra. When he left the hall, the crowd in the street outside was so dense that it was some time before the police were able to get him to his car. It did not bother Casals. His warmth of personality responded to the people who had waited for him. He admitted he could have remained for hours among 'those radiant faces'.

He also spoke to his fellow countrymen in Catalonia in a BBC broadcast. He concluded his message with 'The Song of the Birds', a Catalan folk-song. This was to become forever identified with him and henceforth he always played it at the close of every concert performance. It was also the name of his house in Prades, *El Cant dels Ocells*.

When the British Government recognized Franco's régime in Spain, Casals decided that he could no longer appear in England, and even interrupted his recording of the Haydn D Major Concerto. The test pressings of the first two movements give a tantalizing taste of what we lost. He was later offered honorary degrees by both Oxford and Cambridge but regretfully declined them for the same reason. Throughout the war he had steadfastly refused to play in Nazi Germany, and remained obdurate in his vow that he would never play in any country which recognized Franco. Shortly after his final concert in this country, Sir Stafford Cripps approached him in Paris with an offer to discuss the situation. Casals' reply was characteristic. 'We would not understand each other. We would speak different languages. You would speak about politics, and I would speak about principles.'[9]

On his seventieth birthday, Casals received messages from all over the world. From the Soviet Union he received a cable signed by Prokofiev, Shostakovich, Khachaturian and other Soviet composers. Great Britain broadcast a special concert. Sir Adrian Boult spoke on behalf of the thousands of musicians and music lovers who sent their greetings, and Sir John Barbirolli conducted 50 cellists in the *Sardana* that Casals had written for the Walenn Violoncello School in 1927.

Due to the energy and enthusiasm of the violinist, Alexander Schneider, who became one of Casals' most trusted friends, a festival to celebrate the 200th anniversary of Bach's death was held in Prades. Suddenly, this sleepy little town became alive with eager travellers from all over the world drawn towards soloists of the calibre of Szigeti, Stern, Serkin and Istomin. Franco forbade Spaniards to cross the border, but, undaunted, they crossed the Pyrenees secretly on foot. There was even an elderly shepherd who brought his sheep with him over the mountains.

The first festival was such a triumph it was decided that it should become an annual event. The second, held in Perpignan, was equally successful. The festival of 1953, held in the Abbey of St Michel de Cuxa, was especially glittering with an orchestra composed of soloists, leaders of world-famous string quartets and prestigious orchestras. The wind was provided by the Philadelphia Orchestra, and Tortelier led the picked cello section. The highlight of this festival was, perhaps, the recording of Casals' marvellous interpretation of the Schumann concerto. Intensive rehearsals over a period of three weeks were intended to lead to a recording without conductor, but it was rightly felt that things would go better with one. Eugene Ormandy happened to be on holiday in the South of France and agreed to 'keep order' but, at the time, declined to have his name on the label as it was certainly not his interpretation.

At the 1952 festival Casals first met a young cellist, Martita Montañez from Puerto Rico. Casals' mother had been born in Puerto Rico and he was very excited to discover that the two families knew each other. Three years later, Martita returned to Prades to study with him, and they were married in 1957 in Puerto Rico. It was here that Casals was to live with his young wife for the remainder of his life. He returned to Prades each year until 1966, which was the last festival he attended. In 1960 he was invited by Rudolf Serkin to give master classes at Marlboro, in Vermont USA, and returned there for many years. His master classes were given at a number of schools and universities in the USA, and after settling in San Juan, Puerto Rico, he started a festival there, too.

Over the years, many famous cellists from different countries came to him to study or seek advice, including Guilhermina Suggia, Emanuel Feuermann, Gaspar Cassadó, Maurice Eisenberg, Raya Garbousova, Pierre Fournier, Paul Tortelier, Bernard Greenhouse,

Christopher Bunting, Maurice Gendron, Amaryllis Fleming, Rostropovich and many, many others.

Casals owned a Gand, a Tononi and a large pattern Stradivari cello, but much preferred his Gofriller. He also possessed a magnificent Ruggieri presented to him by that colourful patron of the arts, Mrs Jack Gardner of Boston.[10]

There are few words that can encompass the measure of Casals' contribution to cello playing in the twentieth century. Juliette Alvin, the French cellist and pioneer of the Music Therapy movement, who attended his master classes in Paris, seems to sum up the essence of that contribution. She writes:

> Pablo Casals possesses the supreme gift of a great teacher: vision which transcends the subject. His teaching breaks through the narrow boundaries of a specialized field and extends to all branches of human activity. To him, life and music which expresses it, are one. They repose on the same ethical and philosophical principles.[11]

An ex-pupil, Christopher Bunting, says:

> He felt himself to be temperamentally in accord with the ideas of the French philosopher, Henri Bergson, especially those concerning the *Elan Vital* and 'Freewill in Time'. Far from being an indulgence in amorphous speculation they led him in his personal development to a coming-together of instinct and method, to a consciousness-in-action, to a science of musical performance. Thus all elements, pitch, rhythm, dynamics were weighed in a conscious awareness infused by instinct.
>
> Thus he proposed an 'expressive intonation' whereby the pitch of notes was chosen in relation to several interacting factors. For example, the difference between the major and minor third was accentuated, the accentuation being enhanced as the speed of the music increased. Ascending and descending scales, expressive of differing moods were intoned differently. Time factors were also consciously chosen, avoiding a robotic pulse. Casals instinctively understood the dramatic value of delay—if only by a millisecond. He would speak of 'posing' a note.
>
> He would 'sculpt' every note dynamically with what he called the 'natural diminuendo'. Just as there is a recognizable distinction between the lowing of cattle and the articulate tone-colour of a great lieder singer, so was Casals' playing distinct from the

unguency of a cello-playing dedicated to a seamless flow of beguiling sound.

Need it be said that without the synthesizing virtue of a vital instinct this intervention by the conscious mind may lead to embarrassing results.[12]

Christopher Bunting recalls that when he first went to Casals he was not on his wavelength at all.

The reason for this initial bewilderment was that Casals was using an electron microscope, so to speak, whereas I was merely using a magnifying glass . . . Later I began gradually to be able to respond to his way of looking at music with its extraordinary blend of analysis pushed to an almost fanatical extreme and a very strong intuitive power which achieved the vital synthesis . . .

Casals was a fount of music and it was really a question of how much one could take . . . This relentless drive towards an ideal was miraculously combined with endless patience and great gentleness. His motto, 'Freedom with order' should perhaps speak to us with increasing force in the confused times in which we live.[13]

CHAPTER XVIII

The European Vanguard

THE EARLIEST KNOWN public 'concert of musick on sundry instruments' in North America took place at Boston on 30 December 1731, and a number of private musical societies subsequently sprang up in and around the Boston area. One of the earliest of these was the Handel and Haydn Society, founded in 1815 by the German, Gottlieb Graupner, who had settled in America in 1797. In 1810, he formed the Philharmonic Society of Boston, which became the first orchestra to present regular concerts of classical works. In 1865, the Harvard Musical Association organized an orchestra of 50 musicians who gave ten concerts each season under their conductor, Carl Zerrahn, until 1881 when it was overtaken by the newly formed Boston Symphony Orchestra. But the main body of the players at that time were German in origin. Americans who wanted to undertake serious musical studies had no option but to go to Europe, which meant Leipzig, Berlin or Brussels. An expensive exercise that few could afford.

Consequently there would not have been many indigenous cellists in the orchestras and no outstanding names are mentioned in the solo field. However, as the 'land of opportunity', America has always attracted émigrés from both Eastern and Western Europe. In music, the one-way traffic has been particularly active in the early twentieth century so that present American teaching methods are firmly based on the best European traditions.

One of the earliest émigré cellists, Victor Herbert (1859–1924), is remembered today only as a highly successful composer of operetta. Born in Dublin, he inherited artistic gifts from his mother's side of the family. When she was widowed and remarried a German physician, the family settled in Stuttgart.

As a boy Victor showed talent for music but preferred to study medicine, though since his family could not afford the training, he turned to music, taking his first lessons on the cello. At fifteen, he studied with Cossmann in Frankfurt for two years, then entered the

Stuttgart Conservatoire under Max Seifriz. Even as a student he was already composing songs, playing in orchestras and chamber-music ensembles and appearing as a soloist. In 1885 he became a teacher of cello at the newly-formed Music School in Stuttgart and, following several European tours, was appointed solo cellist of the Court Orchestra there. Here he met and married the opera singer Thérèse Forster, and in the Autumn of 1886 they sailed for the USA. They had both been engaged by the Metropolitan Opera, she as a *prima donna*, he as principal cellist of the orchestra under Anton Seidl.

Impressed by the wealth of opportunity in this young and enthusiastic country, Herbert became very active as an orchestral player, chamber-music player and teacher. In 1889 he was appointed to the faculty of the National Conservatory of Music established by Jeannette M. Thurber, where Dvořák was later director. Herbert also appeared successfully all over the country as a conductor. In March 1894 he was soloist in a performance of his own Second Cello Concerto in E minor Op.30 with the New York Philharmonic Society Orchestra—to whom it was dedicated—conducted by Anton Seidl. It was said that Dvořák was so impressed with the work that he composed his own concerto in a similar form.

An accident to his left arm caused Herbert to abandon his cello playing, but as a conductor he became busier than ever. As resident conductor of numerous American orchestras, he raised one, the Pittsburgh Symphony, to a standard said to compare favourably with its counterpart in Boston.

Another important aspect of his influence on the musical world of his time was that he worked tirelessly for the improvement of the copyright laws for composers. He was an eloquent speaker, with an innate Irish charm, and it was his testimony that brought about the amendment of the American Copyright Law of 1909. Herbert was also one of the founders of the American Society of Composers, Authors and Publishers in 1913.

In retrospect, the fame of his popular pieces and his many operettas has overshadowed what was a most important contribution to the development of music in his adopted country. He was one of the most outstanding solo cellists of his time, a first class conductor and a composer of taste. His social reforms were, for the period, distinctly radical and he was also one of the first to recognize the potential of the phonograph, and made several early recordings, both as cellist and conductor, in which he was greatly assisted by Thomas A. Edison.

★

Willem Willeke (1880–1950), born in The Hague, Holland, began his musical life as a child prodigy, playing both piano and cello, performing the Haydn D Major Cello and Schumann Piano Concertos at the same concert. By the age of fourteen he could play all the Brahms cello works and took part in performances of Brahms' chamber music with the composer at the piano.

Despite this precocity, he sought a career in medicine and took degrees in Bonn and Vienna. It was only on the advice of Joseph Joachim that he was persuaded to abandon medicine in favour of music. There then followed a series of highly successful appearances in Scandinavia where he played the Grieg Sonata with the composer at the piano. He then toured Europe and the USA and performed the Strauss Sonata once again with the composer at the keyboard. He held many appointments as solo cellist with famous orchestras, including the State Opera and Royal Philharmonic in Vienna, and in addition was Royal Cellist to the Emperor Franz Joseph. For a time, he was also principal cellist of the Royal Opera House Orchestra at Covent Garden.

As a conductor he held a number of important posts throughout Europe, and in 1907 went to the USA as cellist with the Kneisel String Quartet. When it disbanded in 1917, Willeke founded the 'Elshuco' Trio, which took its somewhat cryptic name from the first two letters of Elizabeth Shurtleff Coolidge, renowned patron of the arts in the USA. (Shurtleff, her husband's middle name, was later replaced by Sprague, her own maiden name.) Mrs Coolidge sponsored the first Berkshire Festival of Chamber Music in 1918 at her home in South Mountain, where she built a Temple of Music, a hall specifically designed for chamber music. Willeke was the first Musical Director of the festivals, and when he died in 1950, his widow, Sally, took his place. The festival has continued in an unbroken line to the present time.

Willeke became the principal teacher of cello at the Institute of Musical Art, which was taken into the Juilliard School in 1926. Of his many pupils, one of the best known was Marie Roemaet-Rosanoff. His edition of *Thirty Solo Pieces for Violoncello With Piano Accompaniment*, published in 1909, was an extremely popular collection during the first quarter of the present century.

The Belgian, Horace Britt (1881–1971), made his American début as a soloist with the Chicago Symphony Orchestra in 1907. Thirty years later he joined the faculty of the University of Texas at Austin and remained their most distinguished cello professor until his death.

Britt was born in Antwerp into a family of professional musicians. His father was a composer and musicologist and his mother a singer. He was taught *solfeggio* at six, and at seven began his studies on the cello with Gustave Faes. He made his first public appearance a year later.

A pupil of Jules Delsart at the Paris Conservatoire at eleven, at fourteen he won the *premier prix* with a performance of Davidov's very difficult Concerto in B minor. A year later he appeared as soloist with both the Orchestre Colonne and the Orchestre Lamoureux. Introduced by the great Spanish violinist Sarasate, he made a triumphal London début followed by an extensive tour of the provinces.

After a recital tour of the Far East—he was the first to give cello recitals in Asia—he arrived in the USA where he made solo appearances with many leading orchestras. He was principal cellist of the Metropolitan Opera Orchestra for many years, and at the invitation of Gustav Mahler joined the New York Philharmonic in the same capacity. In San Francisco he was principal cellist of its Symphony Orchestra and cellist in the string quartet led by Louis Persinger.

Chamber music had always been of paramount importance to Britt and over the years he was cellist to the Letz and Mischa Elman Quartets. In the late 1920s and 1930s he played with Casals, Maurice Ravel, the flautist George Barrère, the harpist Carlos Salzedo, Myra Hess, Georges Enesco, Artur Schnabel, Harold Bauer and many others. He was guest cellist of the London String Quartet and soloist with Casals' orchestra in Barcelona where he introduced Bloch's *Schelomo* to Europe in 1927. In the late thirties he formed the Britt Sextet, sponsored by Elizabeth Sprague Coolidge, in order to introduce the rarely performed sextet by Vincent d'Indy, and subsequently the entire string sextet repertoire.

Britt's first teaching appointment was in 1924 as professor of cello and chamber-music at the newly-formed Curtis Institute in Philadelphia. In 1947 he joined the faculty of the University of Texas and also founded the University of Texas String Quartet. In 1964 he was made Professor Emeritus and remained in Austin until his death in 1971. Two of his pupils, now active teachers, were Phyllis Young and Claude Kenneson.

Marie Roemaet-Rosanoff (1896–1967), like Britt, was of Belgian origin. She came very early to the USA where she studied with Willem Willeke at the Juilliard School, and later became his assistant.

Shortly after the 1914–18 war, she left for Europe with her Russian born husband, the cellist, Lieff Rosanoff (1885–1974). Together they studied with their idol, Casals, both in Paris and at Vendrell in Spain. On returning to America, the Rosanoffs— through their teaching—were mainly responsible for bringing Casals' style to that country. A great team, for many years they ran a summer school in Connecticut for their students. One of these was young Martita Montañez, who Lieff Rosanoff suggested should have a period of study with Casals, little thinking that she would end up by becoming his second wife.

Apart from her teaching at the Peabody School of Music in Baltimore and the Third Street Music School in New York, Marie Rosanoff played in the Musical Art String Quartet for over twenty years. It was the quartet-in-residence at the Institute of Musical Art when Walter Damrosch was President, and used four Stradivari instruments; the cello was the 'ex-Becker', known as the 'Pawle', because when Hill's book was written it was owned by a Mr Pawle.

One of her many gifts as a teacher was an ability to steer the young through the period when they want to give up because things become difficult. She gave endlessly of her time, and immediately recognized talent lurking under a shy exterior. She knew instinctively that the young can feel threatened if too much pressure is put upon them. Stephen Kates, who studied with her from the age of eleven, says, 'She never trampled on me for not playing in tune, or berated me for bad preparation. With her it was always nourishment and support.'[1]

After her death, Casals said: 'Marie Rosanoff was an exceptional woman, a true artist, extraordinary cellist and a kind human being. All those who knew her will always remember her and consider it a privilege to have been her friend.'[2]

No account of émigrés to the USA could exclude Ennio Bolognini (1893–1979), one of the most charismatic figures in the musical world, and probably one of the greatest cello talents of his era. He was born in Buenos Aires, Argentina, son of Egidio Bolognini, amateur cellist and Italian correspondent of *Figaro* who was a close friend of Toscanini—who later became Ennio's godfather.

Ennio first learnt the cello with his father, and finished his studies at the St Celicia Conservatory in Buenos Aires under José García, teacher of Casals. He made his solo début when he was twelve, and at fifteen won first prize in an Ibero-American International Contest.

His prize was a fine cello by Luigi Rovatti (dated 1910), a pupil of Rocca.

When Saint-Saëns was in Buenos Aires he accompanied the seventeen-year-old Bolognini at the piano for 'The Swan'. A few months later, when Richard Strauss was visiting the city, he played with him in a performance of his Sonata.

Bolognini attracted many friends in the top echelons of the musical world. Heifetz, Horowitz, Victor Herbert, Maurice Ravel, Caruso, Puccini and others. He shared an apartment in Buenos Aires with Arthur Rubinstein—their third room-mate was Bolognini's lifelong friend, Andrés Segovia.

In 1921 he was given an honarary doctorate of music by the University of Buenos Aires and spent the next two years playing and conducting in Chile before emigrating to the USA. Although he appeared as a soloist with a number of American orchestras, including the New York Philharmonic under Toscanini, it was not as a cellist that he entered the country, but as the sparring partner for Luis Firpo in preparation for his fight with Jack Dempsey. Bolognini was once welter-weight champion of South America. He excelled in every kind of sport and was also a licensed airplane pilot. He flew his own private plane and at one time worked as a stunt flyer.

Just before the 1939–45 War, Bolognini was a co-founder of the Civil Air Patrol. Although almost fifty, he trained cadets to fly B-29 bombers throughout the War. In Argentina he had flown World War I Italian-made biplanes. He continued to fly, well into his eighties, and would proudly show his membership card for the exclusive 'Quiet Birdmen' pilots' organization.

Bolognini was tall, well built and extremely handsome. Paradoxically, despite his athletic attributes, he was a *bon vivant*, who loved good food and wine. He was also a compulsive gambler. He spoke five languages fluently and could converse in Hebrew, Greek, Japanese, Hungarian and Russian as well as in some fifteen Italian dialects.

Nevertheless, built into this extraordinary character was an outstanding talent as a cellist. In the late twenties he lived in Philadelphia playing in a cinema, and went on to become principal cellist of the Chicago Symphony, where he took his dog to every rehearsal.

Bolognini's exit from the Chicago Symphony came about because of his linguistic prowess. The Russian composer, Glazounov, was appearing as guest conductor, and throughout the rehearsals used Bolognini as interpreter. On the day of the concert he walked on to the platform but was seized by stage fright. He skirted the podium and went straight to Bolognini and grasped him by the hands. Bolognini talked to him calmly and quietened him down, but Glazounov held on, still terrified. Finally he conducted the concert, but afterwards the manager accused Bolognini of trying to share the limelight. His fiery Argentine temper flared up and they were suddenly minus their principal cellist.

Bolognini soon found work in an ensemble in a night club named 'Yar' run by an émigré Russian prince who happened to be a Romanoff and first cousin to the late Czar, Nicholas II. He also looked exactly like the English King George V. Bolognini's orchestral colleagues were frequent visitors and enjoyed seeing him perform some of his technical tricks. It is said that there was nothing he could not achieve on the cello. One night he asked for requests from the patrons and someone shouted, 'The Swan!' He obliged by playing the first four bars on the same bow with a luscious full and pure sound. The request had been made by Emanuel Feuermann, who could believe neither his eyes nor his ears; his resounding 'Bravo!' was a treasured memory for Bolognini.

He was also an accomplished conductor, having learnt the art from Toscanini himself. He founded symphony orchestras in a number of places in the US where none had existed previously. In Chicago's Grant Park he held the record for being the most popular conductor. He would boast that the only people who ever beat his record attendance of 60,000 were Lily Pons and Heifetz who each had attracted 100,000.

There are many stories about Bolognini's unpredictable behaviour. Once he had been engaged to play in the Ravinia Festival, an open air event held just outside Chicago. Apparently at the rehearsal he and the conductor had an altercation which resulted in Bolognini being fired. In the evening he completely wrecked the performance, flying his plane, buzzing and diving throughout the proceedings. He had the effrontery to land in the parking lot and, due to his phenomenal strength, it took almost a dozen policemen to arrest him.

From 1951 until his death in 1979 Bolognini lived in Las Vegas. Here he played in one of the casino orchestras, and in 1963 founded the Las Vegas Philharmonic Orchestra. It was the first serious orchestra the city had known and, not surprisingly, a shortage of sponsors and patrons brought it to an end five years later.

Stephen Kates met him in Las Vegas and was astounded by his playing. 'It was beautiful beyond words. He had enormous hands and could play anything at will—and with a fantastic tone. His style was unique. The purest sound I have ever heard on the cello from anyone.'[3] He was also an accomplished guitarist and could play flamenco music on the cello using his fingers in *pizzicato* as on the guitar.

Soon after this meeting, Kates saw Casals and brought him Bolognini's greetings. Bolognini knew Catalan and had been engaged as page turner on Casals' first American tour. Casals' eyes opened wide. 'Bolognini! The greatest cello talent I ever heard in my life!'[4] That, unsolicited from Casals, was not to be ignored. Feuermann is reputed to have said, 'For my money, the world's greatest cellist is not Casals, Piatigorsky or myself, but Bolognini!'

One of the people who knew him well is the American cellist, Christine Walewska, now living in the Argentine. She not only studied with him but is also the dedicatee of six pieces Bolognini composed in which the cello is played in the style of the flamenco guitar. She regularly gives his *Serenata del Gaucho* as an encore and stuns her audience with her own and the composer's virtuosity. She has the exclusive right to perform these pieces. Piatigorsky and other leading solosts tried repeatedly to obtain permission, but it was Bolognini's wish that Walewska should have the sole rights for performance.

Bolognini's Rovatti cello is now in the Smithsonian Institute in Washington, and, like its donor, is unique. On its table there are fifty-one signatures by musical celebrities from Ezio Pinza, Kreisler, Heifetz, Stern, Szigeti to Victor Borge and Liberace. Naturally the signature of Jack Dempsey also appears.

Few young cellists today are even aware of his existence. But for those who knew him, there are affectionate memories of an eccentric but genial and generous companion and, above all, a cellist of incomparable ability and charm. Claudia Cassidy of the *Chicago Tribune*, not known for flattery, wrote, 'No more beautiful tone is being drawn from the instrument today. It is a tone so alive in magnetism, so rich in color, so pure in intonation, and so patrician in line that, like any other tone so remarkable, it is always heard with a fresh shock of pleasure. The very first note makes the audience sit up and take notice.'[5]

Maurice Eisenberg (1902–73), best known as a teacher, was also, at one time, a very accomplished soloist. He divided his time between Europe and the USA. He was born in Königsberg, into a Russian-Polish family who emigrated to the USA shortly afterwards. He took up his musical studies very late, and was ten before he had his first lessons on the violin, but changed to the cello when he was twelve. He made up for lost time, for within a year he won a scholarship to the Peabody Institute in Baltimore.

Unfortunately when serious illness in the family brought about financial problems, the thirteen-year-old boy felt obliged to help. So for the next two years he attended high school and the Conservatory by day and played every night in a dance band at a cabaret.

His fortunes changed when Stokowski noted down his name when examining students at the Peabody. Shortly afterwards he was given a place in the Philharmonic Orchestra. At eighteen he became principal cellist with the New York Symphony (later the Philharmonic) Orchestra under Walter Damrosch.

At twenty-one he began to find inadequacies in his own playing and did not know how to put things right. A meeting with Casals solved the problem. He resigned from the orchestra and went to Europe where, on the great man's advice, he studied with Klengel, Becker and at the Ecole Normale in Paris with Alexanian.

He made a successful début in Paris in 1926 and followed it with similar appearances in Europe and in London, where he often had the pianist, Gerald Moore, as his partner. In March 1946, when he performed the Boccherini Concerto in B flat with the L.S.O. at the Albert Hall with Sargent conducting, he was praised by the critics for the 'scintillating virtuosity' of his interpretation, and 'its delightful blending of dignity, graciousness and humour. Playing of this kind sets a standard for the younger generation.'[6]

On his return flight across the Atlantic he was asked by the Vice President of the airline to play for the passengers, the performance to be broadcast to America, live. This must surely be the first time that a cello recital took place 8,000 feet up in the air.

Eisenberg eventually turned to teaching as a full-time occupation, considering it more important to pass on to his students some of the knowledge he had gained through his own early struggles. He was professor at the Juilliard School in New York and at the Ecole Normale in Paris. He also gave master classes at International Courses in Cascais in Portugal. Eisenberg's teaching was greatly influenced by Casals, with whom he enjoyed a close and lifelong friendship.

Eleanore Schoenfeld (b.1925) is regarded as one of the most important cello teachers in the USA. She is professor of cello and Chairman of the String Department at the School of Music at the University of Southern California in Los Angeles.

Born in Berlin, into a musical family of Russian and Polish origin, she was, at fourteen, the youngest student to be admitted to the Hochschule in that city. With her violinist sister, Alice (a pupil of Karl Klingler), she has performed the Brahms Double Concerto all over Europe. Since Eleanore also studied chamber music with Klingler—Joachim's favourite pupil and member of his famous string quartet—the sisters feel they have a direct link with Brahms, whose illuminating remarks were passed on to them by their teacher. It was for Joachim and Robert Hausmann that Brahms wrote the concerto.

As the Schoenfeld Duo, they continue to perform and coach both in the USA, where they emigrated in 1952, and in Germany, directing the Karl Klingler Seminar, a summer course devoted to chamber music.

Schoenfeld is also Co-ordinator of the biennial Piatigorsky Seminar for Cellists held at the University in June. This was established after Piatigorsky's death in 1976 as one of the activities of the Gregor Piatigorsky Chair in Violoncello, founded in 1974 in recognition of his brilliant achievements as an artist and teacher.

CHAPTER XIX

Across the Atlantic:
Felix Salmond

BY FAR THE most direct impact on American cellists for almost a thirty-year period came from the British-born Felix Salmond (1888–1952). 'The touching beauty of his tone, the liveliness of his temperament and the deep sincerity of his musicianship, were qualities that made him both an inspiring performer and teacher.'[1]

It was in the latter capacity that Salmond exerted his unique influence on American cello playing through his long tenure at two of the country's leading conservatories, the Juilliard School in New York and the Curtis Institute in Philadelphia. This influence is still active in both of these schools through his students, the late Leonard Rose and Channing Robbins in New York, and Orlando Cole in Philadelphia. His teaching now encircles the world with third generation students, two of the best known being Lynn Harrell and Yo Yo Ma.

He was born in London into a family of professional musicians: his father Norman Salmond was a well-known baritone and his mother, an accomplished pianist who had studied with Clara Schumann. From such an environment it is not surprising that he always stressed the singing qualities of the cello. In an address to his students at the Curtis Institute, he once said: the cello is '*par excellence* the great singer and poet of the trio and is unequalled by the piano or violin in its variety and range of tone colour and in its capacity to express music of nobility, tenderness, and declamation. The violoncello can sing soprano, contralto, tenor and bass, and it is capable of equal beauty of tone in all of these registers.'[2]

Salmond began his cello studies at twelve with London's foremost teacher of the time, William Whitehouse—a student of Piatti. At sixteen he won a scholarship to the Royal College of Music, where he continued with Whitehouse as his professor. At nineteen he went to the Brussels Conservatoire for a further two years' study with Edouard Jacobs.

At Salmond's début recital at the Bechstein Hall in London 1909, his mother played the piano, and they were joined by the composer, Frank Bridge on viola and the French violinist, Maurice Sons, for the Brahms Piano Quartet in G minor. They also gave the first performance of Frank Bridge's Phantasie Trio in C Minor. The enthusiastic response from critics led to many solo engagements. During the years immediately following the First World War, he was also building a reputation as a fine chamber-music player, and in 1919 he took part in the first performance of Elgar's String Quartet, led by Albert Sammons.

His friendship with Elgar inspired the composer to entrust to him the première of his cello concerto. They worked closely together, and Elgar accepted much of Salmond's advice on cellistic viability. The first performance, which unfortunately was a disaster, took place on 27 October 1919 at the Queen's Hall with the LSO conducted by the composer. The remainder of the programme was conducted by Albert Coates. Something of a *prima donna* who liked the sound of his own voice, Coates often lectured his players for up to 40 minutes before a rehearsal. On this occasion, Coates ran over his allotted rehearsal time by well over an hour, and Elgar, who could be fiery when roused, almost exploded. It was only the fact that poor Salmond had painstakingly worked for months preparing his concerto, which prevented him abandoning the entire project. Sir John Barbirolli, then a young cellist in the orchestra, confirmed Coates's pontifical manner on this occasion. Naturally, the work was under-rehearsed, and neither audience not critics were greatly impressed. The critic, Ernest Newman, never one to mince his words, wrote, 'the orchestra made a public exhibition of its lamentable self.' *The Times* thought it was 'not a work to create a great sensation', and the *Daily Telegraph* bemoaned its 'lack of exaltation . . . lack of surprise'.

S. S. Dale, writing about the Elgar Concerto in *The Strad* 50 years later, recalled that first performance:

Let it be clearly understood that the fault was not that of Felix Salmond, a most brilliant cellist, with a powerful tone, a remarkable range of dynamic gradations, an acute and penetrating intellect, and a most accomplished technique. It does not speak much for English audiences that Salmond never had his due in England; and to be recognized at his true worth he had to emigrate to the United States, where he was responsible for the training of many of America's finest cellists today.[3]

Despite his undisputed acceptance by American cellists, there is no doubt that his memories of the Elgar Concerto were too painful for Salmond, and he never performed it in America. Orlando Cole, who studied with Salmond at the Curtis Institute and knew him for 27 years, confirms that he rarely taught it. 'As a student, I was never urged to work at it. In the thirties there were no recordings of it available in America and, looking at the score, it appeared to our immature taste to be a very ineffective sort of work. Of course, we misjudged it entirely.'

Orlando Cole recalls that, although normally a kind man, Salmond could also be a tyrant: 'Lessons were the agony and ecstasy. When you did something right it was fine, but you had to go through hell when you didn't. I had a hard time in the beginning. He would say, "What makes you think you can play cello? . . . You're wasting my time and your time. You have no talent!"' But Cole made progress and remained devoted to his teacher for the rest of his life, continuing Salmond's work at Curtis to the present day.

Cole explained how Salmond's methods differed from those of other teachers.

He always aimed for beauty of sound, and he achieved it with a different kind of bow arm. At that time, the German school used a lot of wrist in string crossing and produced a dry nasal sound— if one judges from recordings made by Klengel and Becker. Even Suggia had it occasionally. Salmond made a much more modern sound—he didn't slide around like the previous generation, with heavy *glissandi* and so on. His was much more tasteful playing. I always think he was much more under the influence of Casals—at least he greatly admired him.

When it came to bowing, Salmond's maxim was simplicity. He recommended a relaxed approach and warned against over-use of the wrist. His own playing was noted for this quality.

He derived power from having his thumb bent on the bow with the fingers together, not spread out. His bow-change was so simple—not at all like the German or the French School. They played with a caved-in straight thumb. Salmond derived power from a bent thumb. I think this is very important. I advocate power from the thumb resisting pressure from the first finger— more than just the weight of the arm.

His choice of repertoire was also innovatory for that period.

> He taught the great music of the cello literature. Up to that time, sonatas had been regarded as recreational—played in the home or at private concerts—rather than works for public performance. He introduced the sonatas of Beethoven, Brahms and Franck on his programmes. He didn't favour the Popper pieces and the show-off lollipops that were then staple diet in the cello literature. He didn't teach the Romberg or the Davidov concertos, and he didn't even know the Popper Etudes—which I think was unfortunate. He taught us the Franchomme and the Piatti Caprices because he had learnt them with Whitehouse. He also taught us the Bach Suites, which were rather scorned by the German School who treated them as études that were 'good for you', but not as something to perform.[4]

Salmond made some recordings of a number of short pieces including Bruch's *Kol Nidrei*, and the Beethoven A major and Grieg sonatas. His recording of the Schubert B flat Trio with the pianist, Myra Hess and the violinist, Jelly d'Aranyi has been transferred to LP.

Salmond was known for his amiable personality and a modesty unusual for an artist of his eminence. He was also culturally well-rounded and would encourage his students to widen their knowledge outside their own field. He once said, 'Develop your taste for the sister arts: go to see great pictures, great movies (there are a few!). Read great literature, as well as all you can about the great music masters, their lives and works.'[5]

The list of some of Salmond's pupils, now prominent as players and teachers, reads like a musical *Who's Who*. Besides those already mentioned there was Stephen De'ak at the Curtis Institute, Bernard Greenhouse, formerly of the Beaux Arts Trio, Alan Shulman, now a distinguished conductor and composer, Daniel Saidenberg, Samuel Mayes, for many years solo cellist of the Philadelphia and Boston Symphony Orchestra and professor at the University of Michigan, Richard Kapucinsky, now professor at Oberlin College, Frank Miller, formerly Toscanini's solo cellist and principal cellist with the Chicago Symphony, and Tibor de Machula, who was successively principal cellist with the Berlin Philharmonic and Concertgebouw Orchestras.

Daniel Saidenberg was born in Winnipeg in 1906 into a family where everyone played an instrument. His first teacher was a pupil of Klengel and at fifteen he went to the Paris Conservatoire into the class of André Hekking. At seventeen he entered the Juilliard School under Salmond and completed his studies with Feuermann, whom he considers the greatest cellist he has ever met.

When only eighteen he won the Naumberg Competition in New York and made his professional début as a soloist the same year. He spent four years with the Philadelphia Orchestra and succeeded Alfred Wallenstein as principal cellist of the Chicago Symphony Orchestra in 1930.

Saidenberg enjoys a distinguished career as a chamber musician. He has been a member of the Kroll String Quartet, and joined both the Budapest and Juilliard String Quartets in quintet performances. Although he has made a number of solo appearances that have elicited praise from critics, his conducting career has somewhat eclipsed his cello playing. In 1947 he formed his own group, the 'Saidenberg Little Symphony', and toured with them for many years. He is also head of the cello department at Chicago Musical College.

Saidenberg owns a superb Stradivari cello dated 1719 which once belonged to Hugo Becker.

Orlando Cole was born in Philadelphia in 1908. He had been learning the cello for only two years before becoming one of the initial intake of students at the Curtis Institute at its opening in 1924. When Felix Salmond joined the staff in 1925, Cole was one of his first students. He graduated in 1934 and from 1938–42 became Salmond's assistant.

In 1942, Cole and several of his colleagues founded the New School of Music in Philadelphia where they specialized in chamber music and orchestral training. After the war he returned to teach at the Curtis Institute from 1952 until the present time. He was also cellist of the Curtis String Quartet, which started out under quite another name, 'The Swastika'. In 1927 there was nothing untoward about the title, which had been suggested to Mrs Bok—of the founding family of the Curtis Institute—by her friend, Rudyard Kipling. In 1932, when the symbol was beginning to have sinister connotations, Josef Hofmann, the pianist and director of the Institute, agreed to the renaming of the group. The quartet travelled throughout North America and Europe giving some 3,000 concerts, until they disbanded in 1980. They gave first performances of Samuel Barbers's serenade for string quartet, *Dover Beach*, also his Cello Sonata and String Quartet. In England they broadcast for the

BBC and took part in King George V's Jubilee celebrations. Cole recalls one concert at the house of Lady Astor, when Prince Arthur of Connaught, anxious to show he knew what was what, said to them, 'We have enjoyed your performance today. I hope that next time you come you'll play the New World Symphony.'[6]

Cole had many students who are now solo cellists with more than a dozen leading American orchestras, or members of prominent quartets. He also taught Lynn Harrell who writes: 'I was seventeen when Orlando Cole took me into his home to live. My mother had just died; my father had died two years before. His support and gentle family love helped me to survive a very hard time. In his teaching it was his intense feeling and awe of the great repertoire—including non-cello repertoire, that expanded my entire musical view.'[7]

Another of his students who is steadily climbing to the top is Marcy Rosen (b. 1956) from Phoenix, Arizona. She has won a number of awards and has appeared all over the US as a soloist with leading orchestras. She is also a fine chamber musician and has performed with famous artists such as Isaac Stern, Yehudi Menuhin and Oscar Shumsky.

One of Cole's maxims in teaching is that he believes in a good foundation. He is aware of how easy it is for a teacher to rely on the innate talent of highly gifted pupils for his successes, but knows that it is the 'average' student who needs the most help. He considers that if one provides a student with a sound foundation, while at the same time working towards a musical goal, the less talented will benefit as much as the rare 'natural' talent. He always takes into consideration the individual physical make-up of each student and stresses that adjustments have to be made accordingly. For this reason he is not much in favour of a student reading about the basics of string playing without supervision. Even when accompanied by photographs, he feels that such aids have their limitations.

The cello on which Cole has played for some years is the famous 'Sleeping Beauty' Montagnana. Made in Venice in 1739 it had previously been used by Piatigorsky for twenty years.

Another Salmond pupil, who has devoted much of his time to chamber music and composition, is Alan Shulman, born in Baltimore in 1915. His family were all musical, and in order to form a trio with his brother and sister, who played piano and violin respectively, Alan was directed to the cello at the age of eight. As the Shulman Trio they were extremely active, performing in several

Baltimore theatres and over the radio, and were one of the pioneers in radio commercials. When he graduated from the Juilliard School he joined the cello section of the newly-founded NBC Orchestra under Toscanini. During his time at the Juilliard and with the orchestra he continued to play in string quartets. He was cellist of the Kreiner Quartet until 1938 when he left to co-found the Stuyvesant String Quartet who specialized in playing contemporary music.

Shulman has always enjoyed an active musical career and, for the past twenty years or so, has been associated with a number of prominent chamber-music ensembles and orchestras. He has taught at the Juilliard School and many other institutions throughout his country. One of his main interests has been organizing seminars, and concerts (and conducting) for the study and performance of works for cello ensemble. He has also directed several workshops for young cellists sponsored by the Violoncello Society of which he was a founder member and has served as President, Board Member and Editor of the Society's *Newsletter*.

Shulman has contributed considerably to the literature of his instrument. He has composed over fifteen works for up to eight cellos. He has also made a number of transcriptions and piano accompaniments to unaccompanied études. His Cello Concerto, dedicated to 'The People of Israel', written for Leonard Rose as soloist, was given its première by that artist on 14 April 1950 at Carnegie Hall with Dimitri Mitropoulos conducting the New York Philharmonic.

Shulman's *Elegy—in Memoriam: Felix Salmond* was performed at the Violoncello Society's 30th Anniversary Multiple Cello Concert, New York in May 1986. It was dedicated to Fortunato Arico, Jascha Bernstein, Pierre Fournier, Harry Fuchs, Frank Miller, Leonard Rose and Mischa Schneider, all of whom had recently died.

CHAPTER XX

'The Jewel In the Crown':
Emanuel Feuermann

ONE OF THE greatest cellists of the twentieth century was Emanuel Feuermann (1902–42), born in Kolomea in Galicia, Poland, the son of a self-taught musician who played both the violin and cello. He had a few lessons on the violin from his father, but persisted in holding it downwards like a cello. His father fixed a makeshift peg and, impressed with what he heard, bought him a small cello. Nevertheless, the family's attention was fixed on his elder brother, Zigmund, a prodigy on the violin, and in order to launch him, they moved to Vienna in 1908.

At nine years of age Munio, as he was called, had some lessons with Friedrich Buxbaum, principal cellist in the Vienna Philharmonic Orchestra and member of the famous Rosé String Quartet. Later he studied with Anton Walter at the Music Academy in Vienna.

The most significant event in the young boy's development was hearing Casals at his début in Vienna in 1912. Although he knew about great cellists, such as Popper and Davidov, he realized that Casals was 'truly recreating the instrument'.[1] He rushed home demanding that his mother should buy the music of the Boccherini B flat and the Haydn D major concertos. Between lessons he worked incessantly at them, and it was from these rather rough but intensely individual performances that his teacher became aware of his potential.

In February 1914, at the age of twelve, Munio made his début, playing the Haydn D Major Concerto with the Vienna Philharmonic Orchestra conducted by Weingartner, and was much praised by the critics. But after the first flush of excitement had died down, his family paid scant attention to his playing, and he joined his brother on a tour with their father. In 1917, Feuermann went to Leipzig to study with Klengel, who remarked on the paucity of his repertoire, which appeared to comprise little besides the cello part of the Brahms Double Concerto. This may have been an exaggeration, but it was significant of the way he played second fiddle to his brilliant brother who, sadly, never fulfilled his early promise. Over-exploited in his childhood, Zigmund later suffered from mental illness and died of a brain tumor at the age of fifty-two.

Feuermann studied for two years with Klengel and benefited enormously from his particular style of teaching. Like the great violinist, Leopold Auer, Klengel had the gift of bringing out the best in his pupils while preserving their individual personalities. Of Feuermann, Klengel wrote, 'Of all those who have been entrusted to my guardianship, there has never been such a talent . . . our divinely favoured artist and lovable young man.'[2] In retrospect, Feuermann regarded those two years as his most fruitful period of study—the time when he became truly at one with his instrument. He divided his daily practice into sessions in which he would study theory, play the piano and build repertoire. This is all the more remarkable since at the time he was hungry for knowledge in the broadest sense, and used every spare moment to repair his neglected education. He remained an avid reader for the rest of his life, preferring reading to practising.

When Friedrich Grützmacher the younger, nephew of the more famous Friedrich, died suddenly in 1918, Klengel suggested the sixteen-year-old Feuermann should succeed him as professor at the Gürzenich Conservatoire at Cologne. The executive committee were thrown into confusion at what appeared a ridiculous proposal from the normally logical and trustworthy Klengel. At his audition Feuermann proved to be all that Klengel had promised. Next morning they described their young professor elect as 'truly a talent of the utmost rarity. In spite of his age we have decided to appoint him to the faculty. Feuermann will be a brilliant jewel in our crown.'[3] But there was one proviso: whilst the appointment carried all the responsibilities of his predecessor, and an excellent salary, the title of professor was withheld. The post also included compulsory membership of the Gürzenich String Quartet, the members of which were older men. It seems that on more than one occasion their teenage cellist had to be woken up during evening rehearsals that went on past his bedtime.

Between 1920 and 1929 Feuermann had performed in some 300 communities and given over 1000 concerts. His first recordings also date from this period. In 1925 he was the first foreign artist to appear in the Soviet Union. The critics admired his playing but complained about the lack of contemporary works in his repertoire. Three years later when he appeared in Moscow with Artur Schnabel, playing the sonatas of Beethoven and Brahms, he was acclaimed for his 'musicality and profundity'.

In October 1929, Feuermann was appointed cello professor at the Hochschule in Berlin, where he was sought after by students from all over the world. During this period he met many great artists, played the Brahms Double Concerto with Carl Flesch, and was associated for some time with the very talented pianist, Franz Osborn. He formed a string trio with the violinist Joseph Wolfstahl and Hindemith on the viola. It was his relationship with these two fine players that moved him to see further possibilities in his own performance. 'They discovered and shaped each other's playing through the fact that each was in a class by himself on his instrument.'⁴ The few recordings that Feuermann made in 1930 with Wolfstahl show that the outgoing and ebullient violinist had considerable influence on the rather shy cellist, and their association, had it lasted, might have provided more superb recordings for posterity. Unfortunately, Wolfstahl died in 1931 from a severe attack of influenza at the age of only thirty-one.

When Szymon Goldberg took Wolfstahl's pace, the new ensemble assumed quite a different character. Goldberg was a less dominating personality than Wolfstahl, and their mutual attitude one of musical dedication, as can be seen in their recording of Hindemith's String Trio No. 2.

This happy state was short-lived, for the darkness that would soon descend upon the whole of Europe was edging closer with the rise of Hitler in 1933. In February the Reichstag was burned. The purge of Jewish musicians began, and it became clear that Feuermann would not have his contract at the Hochschule renewed. There was violent opposition to this incredible prospect. Several members of the faculty protested and many students, both Jews and Gentiles, threatened to resign. But to no avail. In April, when he was in Vienna on the last lap of a concert tour, he received a letter from the director of the Hochschule saying he was being given 'leave of absence' until the expiration of his contract.

Feuermann had first performed in England in 1927. Ten years later, when he appeared at a Promenade Concert at the Royal Albert Hall, playing the Brahms Double Concerto with Antonio Brosa and the BBC Symphony Orchestra conducted by Sir Henry Wood, a reviewer wrote:

I do not think there can any longer be doubt that Feuermann is
the greatest living cellist, Casals alone excepted . . . His facility is
only one facet of a musicianly equipage that amounts to genius; it
is allied to a powerful, rich tone and a sweeping type of phrasing
that is Titanic in conception . . . In Feuermann we have a
spectacular virtuosic artist of the front rank, the Wieniawski, shall
I say, of the cello.[5]

On 2 January 1935, he made his début in New York playing the
Haydn D Major Concerto with the Philharmonic Orchestra con-
ducted by Bruno Walter. The critical reaction was not encouraging.
Olin Downes in the *New York Times* wrote;

Mr Feuermann played (the Haydn Concerto in D major) with a
sonorous tone, with amply sufficient technique, but not in distinguished style, not with the grace, the transparency, the classic
proportion that the music implies. It would be interesting to hear
Mr Feuermann in other works. His reputation justifies expectation
of more distinctive qualities than he displayed last night, though
the audience greeted him cordially and called him back repeatedly
after he played.

Even less impressed, Samuel Chotzinoff wrote in the *New York
Post*, 'I liked Mr Feuermann very much for his cool and accomplished technique, his firm but not extraordinary tone, his musicianly but not imaginative phrasing. He is a distinct addition to an
already large circle of good cellists. But he is, as yet, no Feuermann.'
(Ger. Fireman) The fact that Chotzinoff also described him as 'the
celebrated Russian violoncellist' did not endear him to the artist.
Eight days later, on 13 January, Feuermann made his recital début
at the Town Hall with Fritz Kitzinger as his pianist. Discouraged by
the critics, the public stayed away. But the small audience occupying
only half the hall were the most discriminating for any musician. It
was composed of solo, principal and rank-and-file cellists from
every corner of the city and beyond. They had heard on the
grapevine that here was cello playing in the superlative class, and
they wanted to witness the miracle. They sat enrapt, and roared
their approval after his opening with the Valentini Sonata in E
major. At the end, they recognized that they were in the presence of
a master, and would not let him go.
Perhaps the most significant outcome of the evening was that

both Downes and Chotzinoff changed their opinion. Downes conceded:

> Difficulties do not exist for Mr Feuermann, even difficulties that would give celebrated virtuosi pause. It would be hard to imagine a cleaner or more substantial technic, which can place every resource of the instrument at the interpreter's command. And there is, of course, more than technic. There is a big tone, finely sustained in singing passages, and warm. There is palpable sincerity, earnestness, musicianship attained as the result of exacting study.[6]

Chotzinoff not only amended his error regarding Feuermann's nationality but admitted that he had to 'eat his words':

> What else can I do but say that as a virtuoso on his instrument Mr Feuermann seems to be miles ahead of his colleagues. I have heard more sensuous tones on the cello but never so amazing a technique. The bowing in spiccato and staccato, the masterfully dexterous left hand would be astonishing even in a virtuoso of the violin. Indeed, Mr Feuermann plays the cello like a great violinist. In addition, he can summon passion that is sincere and a style that reflects a patrician musical personality. I feel better, now that this report is off my chest.[7]

Despite this success, followed by offers to play all over the US, Feuermann still hankered after living in England. In Cologne in 1935 he had married Eva Reifenberg, the daughter of one of his oldest friends. Her family were still in Germany and his own were in Vienna. England would have been a convenient half-way point, but British audiences had not so far been over-responsive to his playing.

This all changed when, in May 1938, he played *Don Quixote* at the Queen's Hall with the BBC Symphony Orchestra conducted by Toscanini. *The Strad* critic was enthusiastic, 'Feuermann is the soloist par excellence for this work; he possesses such huge reserves of technique, his mastery of the instrument [is] so thorough and searching, his tone so remarkably pure, round and rich'.[8]

This, and other overwhelming reviews, brought offers of engagements for return visits; but it was all too late. At the time Feuermann and his wife were living in Zurich where he was given special permission to hold master classes at his home.

When the *Anchluss* was signed in Austria, his family were trapped in Vienna. In September 1938, his friend, Bronislav Huberman, managed at the eleventh hour to get them out, and into Israel. At the end of that year, Feuermann arrived in New York with his wife and daughter. A month later they applied for citizenship.

Over the years Feuermann had worked with a number of gifted pianists: Fritz Kitsinger, Wolfgang Rebner, Albert Hirsch and his sister Sophie. Soon after his arrival in the US, NBC Artists offered to sign him up for exclusive management with Franz Rupp, a brilliant pianist who had for many years played with Kreisler. They were an ideal pair. Feuermann, somewhat intense, often arrogant and with an icy wit; Rupp, engaging, equable and experienced, a man who could meet him on equal terms both musically and in performing standards. They had an excellent working arrangement that benefited enormously from the fact that they could joke with each other. Franz Rupp says of his erstwhile partner:

Artistically, he was a wonderful player. In my opinion, he was the greatest cellist of them all. I played with Casals, and many others, and I still think he was the greatest. He was also an excellent teacher. As a person he was quite different. I could never warm to him in the same way as with other musicians with whom I've played. But when he played, for me he was a god.

Rupp also reminds us that, at the time, the cello was not accepted as a solo instrument in the same way as was the violin. 'It was Feuermann and Casals who made it so. This was the reason why, when I was offered a contract to accompany the singer, Marian Anderson, in the season 1941–42, I had to accept. With Feuermann I had only twelve concerts a year and that was simply not enough to compete with such an offer.'

Rupp admits that he learnt a great deal from Feuermann about phrasing. 'We fought from time to time but when it came to the music I forgave him everything.' Rupp compared him with Kreisler who didn't like to practise:

I was not one for over-rehearsing myself. But with Feuermann we had to work everything out in the minutest detail. He left nothing to chance. And that was why it was so wonderful. The tone, the technique—perfect like pearls. He was not a man with a great deal of temperament. But in everything else, it was just perfection. From the musical aspect, Feuermann was, in my opinion, the greatest musician I have ever met.[9]

Feuermann's widow—now Eva Lehnsen—maintains that he did not like to practise. She has several letters that read 'You will be surprised and proud of me—I practised today for two hours!' She explains, 'But the moment he played with a pianist, or with a group of musicians, either in chamber-music or with an orchestra, he was very particular to work out every detail. Only then would he feel comfortable and the anxiety he felt before a performance "that something might happen" left him.' She also points out that in Europe he had a faithful following, but that in America he could not afford a bad concert. 'In this country he felt that every concert was a challenge.'[10]

In December 1939 Feuermann was engaged for the historic recording of the Brahms Double Concerto with Heifetz, and Eugene Ormandy conducting the Philadelphia Orchestra. This is a full-blooded example of a meeting and fusion of three great talents. The results no doubt inspired RCA to make further recordings, with Heifetz, Feuermann and Rubinstein, of the Brahms Trio in B major Op.8, the B flat Major Op.97 by Beethoven, and the Schubert B flat Major Op.99. The Dohnányi Serenade in C major Op. 10 with Heifetz and William Primrose (viola) is yet another example of the consummate artistry of three great musicians.

In 1941, Feuermann was appointed professor of cello at the Curtis Institute of Philadelphia. In the summer of that year, in a rented house in California, he gave master classes to the many students who were now coming from all over the world. In his biography of Feuermann, Itzkoff makes an interesting observation on the way in which Feuermann and his students were affected by the situation.

The distance between the master's playing and the students', in spite of their talent, was so huge that for many the situation was an inhibiting one . . . Feuermann tried his best to translate his unique technical and physical solutions of the problems of the instrument to the special circumstances of the student. But, for Feuermann, the technical and the musical were so intertwined that he found it almost impossible to solve a technical problem for a student without bringing in a musical problem or to go after a musical problem without becoming enmeshed in a technical one.[11]

Students normally had no difficulty in understanding Feuermann's musical approach, but his explanations of the physical aspect were more difficult for them to grasp. He would show them what he was doing, and analyse everything.

The legacy of Feuermann's teaching (was) a musicianship deriving from the seasoned use of the finest technical equipment in the service of the most refined sensual delineation of the composer's ideals, combined with an awareness of how the body must respond to the demands of the instrument in order to achieve the musical goal.[12]

This approach is clearly indicated in a piece Feuermann wrote for *Who's Who in Music* (1941), and reprinted in a commemorative issue of the *Newsletter of the Violoncello Society* in 1972.

When I took lessons from Julius Klengel he thought I was using strange and unusual fingerings only on account of my long fingers. It did not occur to the dear old man that I had purely musical reasons in mind. Twenty years ago when I started concertizing, the public and even critics often disliked my way of playing. Because of my efforts to eliminate the usual noise which, in their opinion, was inseparable from the sound of a cello, they frequently criticized me for 'playing violin on the cello'. The tradition even among music-minded people was to pity the cellist for trying to compete with the violinists; a cello recital was expected to be a boring affair. The public preferred to hear small pieces: some badly arranged minuet or a slow piece with *schmalz*.[13]

On the occasion of her seventy-fifth Birthday Concert, Raya Garbousova remarked on the influence that can be seen in young people through the old recordings of Feuermann, 40 years after the death of a young man who died at thirty-nine. She contends that this is because it is *modern* playing.

Eva Lehnsen gives us some insight into the personal character of this man who seems to have made conflicting impressions on people who knew him.

He loved teaching at the Curtis, just as he had loved it at the Hochschule in Berlin. He adored fast cars—the faster the better. But he also liked routine—normality. He liked to belong to a group, but his life as an artist imposed a solitary discipline. Whereas he liked to go early to bed, only seldom could this be achieved. The family was for him the most important thing in his life. He loved being with them at the weekend, and set it aside for doing something different. A typical example was that on Sunday he would carefully make a parting in his hair—which was very sparse anyway. But it was Sunday and therefore had to be celebrated by being different![14]

On 25 May 1942, six days after a minor operation, Feuermann developed a wholly unnecessary peritonitis, and died. The loss to the world of music was irreparable. Although only a slight memorial to his genius, his recordings—re-issued during the 1980s—remain as an example of his inestimable contribution to the art of cello playing.

CHAPTER XXI

The Last Great Romantic: Gregor Piatigorsky

A GIANT OF a man, over six feet four in height with a warm and colourful personality of similar dimensions, Gregor Piatigorsky (1903–76) was not only a great cellist but also one of the most popular musicians of his generation. Born in Ekaterinoslav, in Russia, into a poor but musical family, his father was a fiddler who gave him his first lessons on the piano and violin.

One night, his father took him to a symphony concert where he saw and heard the cello for the first time. In his autobiography, Piatigorsky writes, 'From that night on, armed with two sticks, a long one for the cello and a short one for the bow, I pretended to play the cello . . . Those magic sticks lifted me into a world of sound where I could call every mood at will.'[1]

At seven years of age he was given a real cello and took some lessons from a local teacher named Yampolsky. At nine he was appearing in concerts as a soloist. An interesting incident dating from this time was when a pupil of Klengel, visiting the Piatigorsky home and hearing the prodigy, warned, 'Listen carefully, my boy. Tell your father that I strongly advise you to choose a profession that will suit you. Keep away from the cello. You have no talent whatsoever.'[2]

Fortunately nobody took the remark seriously, especially when 'Grisha' was awarded a scholarship to the Moscow Conservatory, where he studied with Gubariov, and later, Alfred von Glehn, a pupil of Davidov. He also had some private lessons with Anatoly Brandoukov.

From the age of eight, and throughout his time at the conservatory, the young Grisha was obliged to earn money for his family. Most evenings he accompanied his father playing in night clubs, and even wrote for the silent movies. He always regarded this as the most difficult time of his young life.

At fifteen, two years after the Revolution, he was engaged as principal cello of the Bolshoi Theatre in Moscow, the youngest ever to have held that position. Significantly, the quartet in which he played was renamed The Lenin.

Despite the support he received from the Soviet authorities, he was refused permission to travel abroad to study, so he took the law into his own hands. Many years later the *Daily Telegraph* published a verbatim account of his defection to Poland (his command of English was still somewhat limited):

> When the Bolshevik Revolution breaks out I am boy; everyone is running away, so I take cello and with musical companions go to frontier in cow's railway carriage. On the way we perform for Red soldiers. We have hall packed with soldiers, no room left. We play for them—beautiful Debussy—thing like that. At the end only two of audience remains. I do not think they understand Debussy. One night we go across border. I carry cello over shoulder. Suddenly bing-bang-bang! Two soldiers shoot at us. My health remains goods, but poor cello—finished. Shots not hit. There is with us lady opera singer. She is awfully fat. As she hears bangs, she jumps up on shoulders. Puts big arms round neck . . . Cello is no more!

The following year, Piatigorsky went to Berlin where he had some unsuccessful lessons with Hugo Becker. From there he proceeded to Leipzig and was only marginally more happy with Klengel. It was on Klengel's advice that he returned to Berlin in 1924 but, still very poor, he suffered the rigours of bad lodgings and was exploited by grasping landlords. He even spent some nights on a bench in the Tiergarten. The situation improved when he found employment playing in a trio at 'Ruscho', a small Russian café near the Kurfürstendamm. He recalled the acute embarrassment he felt when he saw artists like Feuermann and his contemporaries at the tables. However, it was not a wasted experience. One day Furtwängler heard him there and engaged him as principal cellist for the Berlin Philharmonic Orchestra, a post he held until 1929, when he resigned to follow his now rapidly expanding international solo career.

During this time he not only undertook solo appearances with orchestras in Europe, Asia and the USA, but also played chamber music with some of the greatest artists of the day. He formed a trio with Schnabel and Carl Flesch and played privately with Milstein and Horowitz.

Piatigorsky's first recital in the USA was at Oberlin, Ohio, on 5 November 1929, and his first solo appearance with orchestra was with the Philadelphia Orchestra under Stokowski. On 29 December 1929, he made his New York début playing the Dvořák concerto with the New York Philharmonic under Mengelberg. The Americans took him to their hearts at once, and loved the warmth of both his playing and personality. When Hitler rose to power, Piatigorsky had no doubt as to where he would make his permanent home. He became a US citizen in 1942.

His first appearance in Great Britain was at the end of 1935 when he gave three recitals to packed audiences at the Grotrian Hall in Wigmore Street, his fame having preceded him through recordings for HMV. He premièred a great many new works and a number of composers dedicated works to him. He met Prokofiev in Germany when they played the composer's *Ballade* together and he subsequently asked the composer for a cello concerto. The Op.58 (1938) was first performed in Boston with the Boston Symphony Orchestra under Serge Koussevitzky. Prokofiev wrote to Piatigorsky from Moscow, 'Do whatever you find necessary. You have *carte blanche.*' Apparently, Prokofiev was not happy with the composition as it stood, and subsequently used the material for his Symphony-Concerto for Cello and Orchestra Op.125, premièred by Rostropovich. Darius Milhaud dedicated his *Suite Cisalpin* for cello and orchestra, composed on Piedmontese song themes (1954), to Piatigorsky, and he gave the first performance of Hindemith's last cello composition, the Sonata for Cello and Piano (1948).

The Walton concerto, dedicated to Piatigorsky, was the result of considerable co-operation between composer and soloist—much of it was uncellistic until Piatigorsky suggested modifications. The concerto received its first performance in Boston with the Boston Symphony Orchestra under Charles Munch on 25 January 1957. Piatigorsky came to England especially for the European première at a Royal Philharmonic Concert on 1 February 1957, with the BBC Symphony Orchestra conducted by Sir Malcolm Sargent. The concerto was well received on both sides of the Atlantic.

Parallel to his phenomenal success on the concert platform, teaching always remained a very important part of his career. From 1941–49 he was head of the cello department at the Curtis Institute in Philadelphia, where his friend, the violinist, Efrem Zimbalist, was Director. He taught chamber music at the Berkshire Music Centre in Tanglewood, Mass, and from 1962 until his death was head of cello at the University of Southern California Music School.

The violinist Henri Temianka once questioned Piatigorsky about his approach to the students, technically and otherwise. He replied:

My main desire is to make them *people*, artists who are happy in their profession, so that they become real servants of art. And I find that that is the most difficult thing, because it goes hand in hand with all the technical and musical development. What really matters is, how they will use their art as human beings in a productive life. Actually, everything hangs together. For instance, you cannot be a stupid person and a great player; you cannot be a mentally unhealthy person and produce something of value in our difficult profession.

Although he paid attention to the technical details of how to hold the bow, he maintained, 'You cannot learn how to *learn*, you must learn how to *feel*.' He was adamant in his rejection of anything that was dry and scholastic and thought that a scientific explanation was pretentious. Discussing scales, he said:

When I was young I was studying with teachers who pestered me with scales! Of course you understand that no exercise is a waste of time. I know very few bad exercises. But for me, my point of view is always the end effect, the purpose. This purpose is always to make music. For instance, I don't believe in any set fingering for the scales. I try to convey to my students that they must learn to play scales *musically*, and not to think of the bowing they are using.

He considered boredom the greatest enemy of art, and when he felt that his pupil was bored, he knew he was not teaching him properly. He never objected to students using fingerings which he did not. 'Sometimes I don't use them because I don't think they are musical but very often it's because I can't play them. But if this student can, I don't interfere. I can only listen and envy; and I let him know it.'[3] Above all, he wanted his students to think for themselves and not be mimics.

Nathaniel Rosen studied with Piatigorsky when he was thirteen years old and the year spent on Goltermann's A Minor Concerto was, for him, an unforgettable experience:

For the first time I began to learn what it really meant to play the cello. Piatigorsky worked with me tirelessly, all the time inspiring me with the desire to play the Goltermann as if it were, in fact, the greatest cello concerto ever written. In that way, my desire was translated into an important tool in learning to express myself and in developing the technique required to accomplish this end.[4]

Piatigorsky's friendship with his students was an integral part of his teaching. Rosen and many others comment upon his ability to advise them on problems other than musical ones. He was twice invited to sit on the Jury of the International Tchaikovsky Competition in Moscow, in 1962 and 1966, and several of his pupils won prizes. He was also greatly impressed by the attention the Soviet régime paid to musical education. In 1962, the Violoncello Society of New York offered him the supreme accolade by the inauguration of the Piatigorsky Prize to be given biannually to deserving young artists.

When asked who he thought was the most important cellist from the past, Piatigorsky had no doubt. 'For me there was only one supremely great cellist in early times and, in the same person, a great composer for the instrument. He was Boccherini.'[5] On one occasion he refused to record Boccherini's B flat Major Concerto because he did not have the original score: not surprisingly, he considered the Grützmacher edition too free.

Sound production was of the greatest importance for Piatigorsky. He loved a beautiful singing tone and, for the most part, achieved it. But he felt also that the cello should not be denied variety of tone. He knew the great bass singer, Chaliapin, quite well and had performed with him. On one occasion, Chaliapin remarked, 'You sing very nicely on your cello, Grisha, but try to speak more on it!'[6] Perhaps there is an echo here of Casals' 'natural diminuendo'?

Piatigorsky owned two magnificent Stradivari cellos: the 'Batta', dated 1714 and the 'Baudiot', dated 1725. The latter, made when the master was eighty-one, is similar in build to the 'Piatti' Stradivarius. It was sold by Baudiot's widow in 1850 for 10,000 francs (£400 at that time).

Piatigorsky was a walking legend, described by all who knew him as a very special human being, with unique warmth and charm of personality. As a raconteur he was unsurpassed. He would have all his colleagues in fits of laughter over his experiences, especially when he came off badly himself. When he died of cancer in 1976, the musical world was shattered. At a concert given in his memory at the Caspary Auditorium, Rockefeller University, New York, in

November 1976, Janos Scholz (President Emeritus of the Violoncello Society) said:

> As a performer, he was what in German one would call an *Urtalent*, constantly bubbling like a fountain, giving us with both his hands lovely music, most happily and beautifully interpreted. His nature was a jolly one, fundamentally, being endowed as he was with an explosive sense of humour, something we could never detect in either Casals or Cassado. . . . On stage he was a supreme performer with an unsurpassed presence and sense of projection. Nobody who saw him will ever forget how he carried his instrument on high—like a fiddle—while pointing his bow like a rapier.[7]

Piatigorsky will also be remembered for his continuous support of new compositions, and the programme building that came as a result. In an obituary, Milly Stanfield describes him as:

> The last of the great romantic cellists; and probably his most beneficial influence on his younger co-instrumentalists lay in reminding them, through his example, that élan should never be sacrificed to the desire for more speed. Although certain classicists and purists may at times have been surprised at some of the liberties he took, which affected the rhythm and occasionally the phrasing, all must have appreciated his sincerity and spontaneity.[8]

CHAPTER XXII

The Unique View

'IN A MOUNTAIN-RANGE, does anyone expect the peaks to be of the same height? But—the view from each is unique.'[1] Elizabeth Cowling's comment aptly focuses attention on certain musicians who, although not always breathtaking in their public performances, deserve to be called 'great' if only for their ability to pass on their expertise to the younger generation. In fact, early struggles to master a particular aspect of technique, have often led to an added dimension to their approach to teaching. The violinists Carl Flesch and Otakar Ševčik certainly came into this category.

One of the most controversial teachers of the twentieth century, Diran Alexanian (1881–1954), was born in Constantinople of Armenian parents. He studied with Grützmacher in Leipzig, where as a student he played chamber music with Brahms and the great violinist, Joseph Joachim. When only seventeen he played the solo in Strauss's *Don Quixote* with the composer conducting, the success of which led to further concerts in whicn he played concertos under Nikisch and Mahler.

In 1901 Alexanian settled in Paris where he met Casals, who noticed that he used revolutionary fingerings which were close to his own ideas. They then discovered that these ideas extended to general technique and interpretation. In 1922 Alexanian published his treatise, *Traité théorique et pratique du violoncelle*, and in 1929, his analytical edition of the Solo Suites of Bach.

It was at the Ecole Normale in Paris, where Alexanian was in charge of the 'Casals' class from 1921 to 1937, that he put his controversial ideas into practice. His methods attracted students from all over the world and his influence spread beyond his immediate pupils. Maurice Eisenberg and Antonio Janigro were students of his and Piatigorsky, Fournier, Georges Enesco and Feuermann frequently sat in on his classes. William Van den Burg, a student of his at the Ecole Normale, recalls that one day Feuermann came to the class and played the Dvořák Concerto 'marvellously but like an alarm clock'.[2] He and Van den Burg became friends and Feuermann confided that he was taking lessons with Alexanian, even though he was himself professor at the Hochschule in Berlin. Many years later, when Van den Burg was solo cellist with the Philadelphia Orchestra, Feuermann told him that his time with Alexanian was 'like going to the laundry'.

In 1937 Alexanian went to the USA where he achieved considerable success at the Peabody Institute in Baltimore and the Manhattan School of Music in New York. Here Bernard Greenhouse, David Soyer, George Ricci, Raya Garbousova and Alexander and Mischa Schneider were a few of the many fully professional artists who either attended his classes or sought his advice.

It seems that one either loved or hated 'Alex', as he was universally known. He encountered much opposition from the establishment at the Conservatoire who openly called him a charlatan. The teachers were still using antiquated techniques of the nineteenth century, when slides were the order of the day and no one ever paid any attention to the relationship between the physical construction of the student and his ability to handle the instrument. For those who benefited from his teaching there is the strong belief that he opened up new horizons, but his contribution to the art of cello playing has still to be recognized.

The British cellist and teacher, Antonia Butler, studied with him in Paris from 1926–29, and is convinced that the people who derived the maximum benefit from his teaching were those who stayed more than a year.

> Many people were frustrated because they were torn to pieces, and couldn't stay the course. I remember that the first six months were very difficult and I despaired of ever achieving anything. What I, and so many others did not realize was that he broke down in order to rebuild, and you had to be patient. At the beginning of the second year you felt that you were beginning to absorb something and could make it part of your own intelligence. Up till then you were groping. He could be very sardonic and sometimes quite nasty, but he could also be very kind.

Eventually, Butler came to admire Alexanian and respected him for his impeccable musicianship.

> All his ideas on technique were to express the music. He would always avoid unmusical and unnecessary slides—such as we were

brought up on. As far as possible, he advised us to make a slide sound only if you wanted it as a means of expression. He also worked out ingenious ways of shifting on semi-tones and changing the bow if necessary. He showed us that it is possible without upsetting the phrases.[3]

He insisted upon his students knowing exactly the harmonic progression and structure of the Bach Suites before attempting to play them. His fingerings, too, were *sacrosanct*. Although quite revolutionary at the time, his left-hand exercises were of considerable value, and these and many of his ideas have now become part of our technical vocabulary.

Another student of Alexanian, Edmund Kurtz (like Antonia Butler), came directly from Klengel. 'There is no doubt that Alexanian put you into a strait-jacket. It was difficult to stay with him and remain yourself. His is a very complicated system and in my own case it took many years of performing in public before I could honestly feel "myself" again.' Nonetheless, Kurtz considers that Alexanian is the most important influence in the development of cello technique in the wake of Casals. 'He has written one of the most important books about the cello and how it should be played, and also the first to make an edition of Bach's Suites for unaccompanied cello, with an attached facsimile of the manuscript.'[4]

Raya Garbousova regards her studies with Alexanian as one of the most important influences in her musical life.

I do not necessarily mean the actual learning of the instrument, but it was his whole attitude to music and its meaning. We sat for hours just talking and this led to most important revelations. I know many famous musicians of today who were in desperation when he died. His knowledge was tremendous. His playing was not attractive, but that is unimportant.[5]

The Rumanian-born Edgard Feder, conductor, composer and editor now living in New York, and a close friend, recalls that Alexanian much enjoyed good food and drink. His hobby was cooking. When he was in New York, he and Edgard Feder had a steady date for lunch every Saturday and the main topic of conversation was the exchange of recipes and culinary ideas. Alexanian was particularly fond of oriental cuisine and he and Feder were frequent visitors at The Golden Horn, a Turkish restaurant in New York that no longer exists. Feder tells us that Alexanian was a slow eater and a meal could easily stretch over two hours.

Edgard Feder was born in Bucharest, son of the well-known music publisher and impresario, Jean Feder. He began his music studies very early and was a pupil of Dimitrie Dinicu at the Royal Conservatory in his native city. He also studied composition and conducting with the Italian, Alfonso Castaldi. Feder completed his education in Paris taking doctorates in Law, Economics and Philosophy, at the same time continuing his cello studies with Alexanian. His Cello Concerto was premièred in France with Pierre Fournier as the soloist.

Another interesting aspect in the development of cello playing comes through two pedagogues who, though both born in Europe, first came together in the USA. The Yugoslavian Rudolf Matz and the Italian Luigi Silva (1903–61) did not meet until they were in their early fifties and worked together for only seven years. Yet their combined efforts in individual teaching, and the publication of teaching literature has made a valuable contribution to the training of present and future generations of cellists.

Rudolf Matz, born in 1901 in Zagreb, had his first lessons on the cello with Umberto Fabbri and later at the Academy of Music in Zagreb with Juro Tkalčić, who had been trained in Paris. He also studied piano, composition and conducting.

Matz freely acknowledges the debt he owes to Václav Huml, a pupil of Ševčik in Prague, and professor of violin at the University of Zagreb for 50 years. Matz's association with Huml, first as a student and later as a colleague, was in his estimation crucial, both in his development as a cellist and in the evolution of his ideas on cello technique.

As a young man Matz was an enthusiastic and gifted amateur athlete and, at one time, a world-class sprinter. He is convinced that his early athletic training and his later collaboration with Ana Maletić, choreographer and teacher of eurythmics, enabled him to learn more about the human body and how it worked. He was therefore able to refine his concepts of pedagogy, basing them on the anatomically correct and physiologically natural use of the body and its muscular propensities.

Matz had experienced considerable frustration in his own early cello instruction and, inspired by Huml's approach to violin teaching, he began to explore some of the many unsolved problems of cello teaching. He was helped and further motivated by his meeting with the brilliant young Italian cellist, Antonio Janigro. He encouraged Matz to write and publish his findings, since they were much in line with his own training in Milan and Paris.

In 1943, Matz wrote the work that would make his name known throughout the world, *The First Years of Violoncello*. The first three volumes were published in 1946 and continued to appear intermittently until 1971. It has been described as the best cello method since the publication of Duport's *Essai* (*c.*1806). Matz's method is based on the two kinds of motion involved, physiological movements and non-physiological movements, and how these can be related to the individual relationship between the cellist and his instrument. He advocates two three-part rules to facilitate the study of the cello (and other instruments):

1. While playing the cello, we must constantly be alert:
   a. To notice at once each and every mistake and imperfection
   b. To recognize the cause
   c. To know how best to correct the error
2. While playing the cello, everything that happens must be:
   a. Pleasing to the eye
   b. Harmonious to the ear
   c. In accordance with anatomy and the rules of phsysiology.

Matz's own conclusions speak for themselves:

Thus far the cello has yet to complete definitively its evolution—as have the piano and violin. As a consequence, nowadays, our instrument is being played in diverse, often contradictory ways, following the tradition prevailing in different countries. In the meantime, if teachers were but to observe and obey the rules and laws of rational cello playing based on a physiological approach, the prospect for the future more than likely would be that cellists in every part of the world could raise the level of their playing, and the large differences presently in evidence should gradually tend to disappear, in so far as the relationship between cellists and their instruments is concerned.[6]

Matz's researches brought him into contact with many musicians and scholars from other countries. He was appointed professor at Zagreb Academy in 1950 and taught there until his retirement in 1973. In 1955–57 he spent two years in the US where he was able to have close contact with performers and pedagogues, one of the most significant being Luigi Silva, who had first become acquainted with his work around 1953 when Pablo Svilokos, a student of Janigro's in Zagreb, came to study with Silva at Yale University. When Silva saw the first few volumes of Matz's *First Years of Violoncello* he wrote to him in September 1954 that he considered it one of the most important contributions to cello teaching in our time. 'Now I feel we have finally *the* modern method of which I have often dreamed and which, in due time, will supplant all that has been printed.' Thus began their unique partnership, conducted mainly through correspondence for the seven years of their association.

Once when Matz had written most of the newsletter he sent every Christmas to his colleagues and friends in the US, he sat down and played through Bach's C Major Suite. He closed thus: 'I was inspired by this music and for a while was completely possessed and felt as if the music were lifting me away from the earth into a heavenly euphoria. If there is such a thing as happiness I must have experienced it at that moment in its full beauty.'

In a more recent interview, Matz discussed his ideas on his chosen profession:

My experience has shown me that music has a very great influence on people. This was the crucial factor which led me to devote my life to music and especially to teaching and to showing people how to discover beauty in music. I believe that an understanding of the inherent beauty of music enriches human character and gives it a wider humanistic base. It is this humanism which I wanted, with the help of music, to develop in people.[7]

Luigi Silva was born in Milan into a family of professional singers. His father, also a pianist and conductor, gave his son his first lesson on the piano when he was five. Three years later, Luigi turned to the cello, and later still received his formal musical education at the Conservatory in Rome. He then wanted to study further with one of the best teachers in Europe, and auditioned for most of them. These would certainly have included Klengel and Becker. It is interesting that none would accept him: they all told him that his hands were too small and his constitution was too frail. Arturo Bonucci at the Liceo in Bologna was the only one willing to risk taking on this presumably 'unteachable' young man. Silva went on to receive two degrees at Bologna, which included a master's in teaching, the field that was to become the consuming passion of his life.

Silva's first employment as a professional cellist was in the Rome Augusteo Orchestra and subsequently as principal cellist with the Opera Orchestra in Rome. In 1930 he was cellist of the Quartetto di Roma, one of the most celebrated chamber-music groups in Europe, at one time rivalling the famous Pro Arte String Quartet.

In 1933, Silva won the Boccherini Prize, the first national contest for young concert artists, and it is possible that his lifelong interest in the compositions of Boccherini stemmed from this event. That same year, Silva began teaching and, although his performing career was very healthy, he found that his interests lay more and more in pedagogy. Between 1933 and 1940 he was professor at conservatories in Teramo, Padua, Venice and Florence.

In 1939, Silva, his wife and his parents emigrated to the USA where they eventually became US citizens. From 1941–49 he taught at the Juilliard, Mannes and Hartt schools of music, the Peabody Conservatory and Yale University, often commuting to all in the same year.

Elizabeth Cowling, who went to Silva for some lessons when she was already a professional teacher herself, writes:

Silva had extraordinary gifts as a teacher. . . . Though an Italian, he spoke English very well and could express himself and say exactly what he meant. . . . [He could speak and read Italian, French, German, Spanish and English.] Of course Silva illustrated during lessons in a very inspiring way, though he never tried to overawe a student with his own incredible virtuosity. But his great gift was in sensing the individual and his particular problems and finding ways to solve them. He wanted to guide each student into his potential as a performer, not to make carbon copies of himself.

One cannot compare Silva's teaching with that of Feuermann, Casals or Piatigorsky, who all taught cellists who were already advanced. For the most part, Silva taught young people just learning to play the instrument, many of whom came from culturally barren environments. Often their first encounter with real music was at their lessons. Cowling points out that his own particular interest in developing the left-hand technique almost certainly arose from his early problems with his small hands. 'His compensations . . . came through developing greater fluency and accuracy in shifting and a much greater use of thumb position. Silva's hand moved like lightning in shifting; many of his reviewers commented on this fluency, as they did on the accuracy of his intonation.'[8]

Joel Krosnick, cellist of the Juilliard String Quartet, studied with Silva when he was ten, and retains today an unusually deep affection and respect for the man who built for him a virtuoso equipment that he considers will serve him the rest of his life.

He had his own four-octave scale system with fingerings that were always the same going up and coming down. All the scales and études came with preparatory exercises governing shifting and hand shape to assure that a real discipline was given to the hand and brain along with the learned notes. The shape of the hand had a specific interval shape in different registers. I always remember at my second lesson he gave me the 'jet plane' exercise. I had not played in thumb position at this stage, and the 'jet plane' was taking off in an octave slide up and down the cello. Naturally the octave was very difficult to maintain. But once mastered it was of inestimable value.

He was unfailingly kind, but very persistent. He kept precise notes of which exercises and scales he'd given me for each hand, études, pieces etc. He represented and gave me an orderly approach to the cello and its techniques—which I have shaped and augmented in my own way—but the cellistic thinking was clear and brilliant. He had real pleasure in 'the cello', and what he could do with it. I still remember going to his apartment shortly before his untimely death and finding him playing a late Popper D major étude which called for short octave arpeggiandos jumping up and down the cello. At that point—about 1960—he no longer played in public, but he played this fabulously. He smiled and said to me: 'You know it brings me much pleasure that I can still play something like that.'[9]

Silva made transcriptions for cello of the 42 Kreutzer studies and the 24 Paganini caprices and the *Variazioni di Bravura* on themes from Rossini's opera *Moses*, also by Paganini. But his greatest contribution is a treatise for which he began researching in the 1930s and started writing in 1950. It is the fundamental thesis of this work that the history of left-hand technique, and the evolution of fingering systems are intimately connected to the manner of placing the hand in relation to the fingerboard. He gives detailed analyses of literature from the eighteenth century up to the middle of the twentieth century. He continued to work on his treatise until his death.

Meeting Rudolf Matz had an immediate impact on Silva and his work. By the same token, Matz's work also benefited from this relationship. The incomplete treatise, with added material from Matz, remains in first draft and is called: 'History of the "Posture" of the left hand in the neck positions of the violoncello in accordance with the "Natural" confirmation of the hand, and resulting systems of fingering.'

Another Italian cellist with strong Yugoslavian connections is Antonio Janigro, born in 1918 in Milan. He started to learn the piano at the age of six, and two years later he was presented with a small cello by Giovanni Berti who also gave him some instruction. Within twelve months he was sufficiently advanced to attend Gilberto Crepax's class at the Verdi Conservatory in Milan. At the age of eleven, Antonio played for Casals who suggested he should study with Alexanian in Paris. In his letter of recommendation Casals wrote:

A brilliant instrumentalist with a fine sense of style, and, I hope, sufficiently determined, he should become a shining exponent of our chosen instrument.[10]

At sixteen, Janigro left for Paris and the Ecole Normale and basked in its rich musical environment. Besides Casals as the main inspiration, there was Alfred Cortot, Jacques Thibaud, Paul Dukas, Nadia Boulanger, Stravinsky, Joseph Salmon, Georges Enesco and Bohuslav Martinů. Two of his fellow students were Dinu Lipatti and Ginette Neveu.

Immediately after his graduation, Janigro started his career as a soloist, playing in recitals with Dinu Lipatti and Paul Badura-Skoda. Such beginnings presaged well for the future, but when war broke out in 1939, he was on holiday in Yugoslavia and therefore forced to remain there. Fortunately Zagreb Conservatory recognized the talents of their captive guest and offered him the post of head professor of cello and chamber music. This turned out to be an important development for both Janigro and the Yugoslavs. Undoubtedly, he was responsible for the establishment of a modern cello school in that country. It was in Zagreb that he first met Rudolf Matz, and between them they founded a cello club and organized two cello congresses.

When war was over, Janigro resumed his international career and

extended his tours to the USSR and South America. After his début
in the USA in 1956, a critic wrote:

> With simplicity, with modesty and with disregard for exemplary
> performance he masters his instrument in the most miraculous
> way . . . He never gives the impression that he is making any
> effort. In his hands, the cello never labours, never becomes
> breathless, never pants, is never exhausted. . . . There is always
> an atmosphere of calm serenity, and the most daring technical
> feats seem to be child's play . . . nobility, balance, depth, charm
> and unwavering evenness . . . are little short of miraculous.[11]

In common with many cellists, Janigro always felt that the
repertoire for his instrument was limited. When Zagreb Radio asked
him to form a symphony orchestra, his skill as a conductor soon
became clear and he was offered engagements by many of the
leading orchestras in other parts of Europe. Janigro continued solo
appearances, either with conductor or directing from the cello,
which led quite naturally to founding the *I Solisti di Zagreb*, a body
of twelve string players who were to become one of the leading
ensembles of its kind. He still lives in Zagreb and enjoys a busy and
varied musical life (he has made over 50 recordings), but unfortunately is seldom heard in the West.

CHAPTER XXIII

Versatility par Excellence:
Bernard Greenhouse and Leonard Rose

TO PLAY CHAMBER MUSIC in a small group is one of the severest tests of musicianship. When one such combination is regarded the world over as impeccable from every standpoint, we have music-making of a very high order. Two solo cellists who later concentrated on chamber music at this level are Bernard Greenhouse and Leonard Rose, with the Beaux Arts and Istomin–Stern–Rose trios respectively.

Bernard Greenhouse (b. 1916) had three elder brothers who already played the piano, violin and flute. 'I was never asked. My father said "You'll play cello"—so at the age of nine, I had my first lessons.' For the young boy this was 'an enormously exciting experience' and from this moment he has never ceased to love the sound of the cello. His training period is particularly interesting because his four teachers, Salmond, Feuermann, Alexanian and Casals, each represented a different approach which, individually and collectively, he considers have benefited both his playing and his teaching.

His first serious studies were at the Juilliard with Felix Salmond. Then came two years with Feuermann, whom he found very demanding. 'As an instrumentalist there was no one greater. I got from him just what I needed by way of handling the instrument. His left-hand technique was something quite extraordinary. His bow arm, too, was superb—it was great natural playing.' At the time his approach to the left hand was rather tight. 'I had been concerned mostly with beautiful sound, so there was a lack of facility in my playing which I think he was able to change. I was startled at the ease with which he handled the instrument. I tried to emulate it in my own playing, and to fathom the secrets that make the difference between a natural and an acquired technique.' Greenhouse is convinced that his was not a natural technique, but close observation of Feuermann enabled him to make improvements to the point where, some time later, after one of Greenhouse's New York recitals, Salmond told a friend, 'At least the boy has learned to *play* the instrument.'

In 1942, two major events changed the course of his life. Firstly, Feuermann's tragically early death left him without a teacher and, secondly, he joined the US Navy where he served for three years. During this period he began sporadic studies with Alexanian. 'I was enormously impressed with his musical ideas so I arranged to coach with him each time before one of my New York recitals, the first of which took place in 1946. I found his advice invaluable, not only on programme but on so many of the musical aspects.'

Although Alexanian became mentor and close friend of Greenhouse they were not always in agreement.

> After playing for two or three hours in the evening we would go out to dinner—Alexanian was a great gourmet—and we would continue discussions which occasionally became arguments— mostly on cello technique. He was a great man but more of a musical mentor than a technical adviser. I felt that many of his ideas on technical matters were old-fashioned and could be rather destructive unless the person working on them had strong convictions on how to play the instrument. . . .

'He was a musical genius and pedagogue, not a great cellist.' It would seem that Alexanian also lacked business sense for he would never accept a fee from Greenhouse. 'I decided the only way to repay him was to take him on a gourmet tour throughout Europe. I rented a car in Le Havre and we drove through France going from one great restaurant to another. We finally came to Prades. Casals and Alexanian had not met for some twelve years—since their time together at the Ecole Normale. It was quite an emotional reunion.'

Casals arranged to play that same evening for Alexanian and Greenhouse, accompanied by the pianist Eric Itor Kahn who happened to be visiting.

> Afterwards there were discussions on some of the finer musical points and the arguments between the two of them went on until two in the morning ending without any conclusion. A month later we were in New York and Alex showed me a card from Casals, saying, 'You were absolutely right in your interpretation of that phrase.' Casals had a great respect for him. It was fascinating to have been part of that discussion.

Greenhouse's own first encounter with Casals was in 1946 when he had just come out of the Navy.

I hadn't wanted to go back to my old style of living without trying to see the great man. I took the troop transport to Europe, but having failed to obtain a positive answer from Casals, I went to Paris and enrolled at the Fontainebleau School. I had written twice to Casals and been turned down both times. After the third attempt I received a reply giving me precise time of arrival saying he would hear me play providing I donate $100 to the Spanish Refugee Fund.

The outcome was two years' study with Casals. At first he was the only student. 'I was one of the first of many people who had tried to study with Casals. At the time he wasn't much interested in teaching. I was fortunate because my lessons were very frequent— and long—sometimes four hours several times a week.' Modestly, Greenhouse adds, 'It was just a matter of luck, I think, that he agreed to accept me. I think he wanted someone young to speak with—many of the sessions were half playing half talking. His life story was told in much greater detail than has ever been published. It was a wonderful experience—not only the music but the relationship between a great master and a young student.'

Greenhouse is in no doubt as to what he owes to Casals. 'I think I learnt from him that music is creative, not a question of repetition.' He cites an example of how Casals made him learn the Bach D Minor Suite indicating precise bowings, fingering, dynamics and phrasing. He was given three weeks to learn it perfectly from memory and then play it to Casals, who reproduced the exact vibrato and tone colour that had been directed. Then Casals told him to change every phrasing, dynamic, fingering and bowing.

I was astonished that this man could remember for weeks what he had told me, play it and then change everything in order to show that playing a Bach suite was a creative process. It didn't apply only to Bach—but to everything I played. It taught me that I should never make up my mind that there was an absolute way to play a phrase and have it set in my mind so that I would finally lose the feeling of inspiration. This was typical of Casals.

A very active solo career followed this period. A feature at each of his New York appearances was that he included a first performance of a work by a modern composer. But chamber music had always been a very important part of Greenhouse's musical life. 'I enjoyed many years of solo playing, but I did not feel that I am the kind of person who could be satisfied with the very limited repertoire and at the same time meet the demands in that field. I was very keen to play the quartet literature and for many years I played in various ensembles, one of which was a quartet with Oscar Shumsky. We also played the Brahms Double Concerto together.' In addition, the lonely touring life, the endless meetings with conductors and administrators, did not appeal to him. 'Apart from my great interest in making music I am rather a private sort of person, and that was one of the reasons why I have divided my career as I have. I still enjoy playing recitals, especially with my colleagues in the trio.'

Originally, the group began quite casually at Tanglewood, in 1955, with the pianist, Menahem Pressler and violinist, Daniel Guilet. 'We started with the same idea as so many other soloists—getting together for a few performances and then going our own ways on solo tours. At first it worked like that, and then Columbia Artists asked us to play in a series of ten concerts which soon blossomed into 80 in a season. At the time there were a few quartets, but it was thought impossible to make a living with a trio.' They were so successful in the following years that they decided to try their luck in Europe. In London they played at the Royal Festival Hall in 1958 to an audience of 300, and the press described them as 'a pale trio'. Not an encouraging start.

The Beaux Arts played all over the world, and gave some 130 concerts a year in the US. They celebrated their thirtieth anniversary in 1985 and Greenhouse retired from the Trio during the 1987 season. But he always found time for a busy teaching career, at the Juilliard and Manhattan schools of music, and at the New York State, Hartford and Indiana universities. He retired from teaching in 1986 and has plans for his 'twilight years'. Greenhouse has several homes on Cape Cod in Massachusetts, and hopes to build one or two more.

I would like to start a cello colony for people who have finished their doctoral or master's programmes at university to have somewhere to go where they can settle down and practise their instrument. I'm planning to have eight or ten cellists to come and work during the winter. It's a lovely setting and I think a little different from teaching at university where students have the problem of working on five or six academic subjects besides their music. I'll be available for advice and there will be a pianist in residence.[1]

The Fritz Kreisler arrangement of the Paganini Concerto includes a beautiful cello solo. Many years ago, when Kreisler was rehearsing with the Cleveland Symphony Orchestra under Artur Rodzinski, he stopped the orchestra immediately following the cello solo to congratulate the performer on his playing. It was the young Leonard Rose (1918–84), later to become a distinguished soloist and respected teacher, whose untimely death was a sad loss to the music world.

Born in Washington, into a family of émigré Russians from Kiev, he had his first instruction with his father, an amateur cellist. At ten he took lessons with Walter Grossman at the Miami Conservatory and later studied with his cousin, Frank Miller, then principal cellist with the NBC Symphony Orchestra in New York. At sixteen he won a scholarship to the Curtis Institute where he was a pupil of Felix Salmond, and two years later became his assistant.

Stephen Kates, who studied with Rose, says:

Rose's training was certainly in the tradition of Salmond. Very thorough. He was very much interested in instrumental finesse, tone colour, expression, lyricism. What he tried to do with his own students was to make very clear a certain kind of lyricism in their playing, where the quality of sound and level of music making had to be watched constantly.[2]

Rose's path led him to the top via the orchestra, and he would constantly remind his students that it was probably the best way to gain experience. At twenty he became principal cellist to the NBC Symphony Orchestra under Toscanini and after one season went to the Cleveland Orchestra under Rodzinski. When Rodzinski became principal conductor of the New York Philharmonic Orchestra, in 1943, Rose followed him and stayed as their principal cellist until 1951. It was with this orchestra that he made his solo début at the Carnegie Hall, in 1944, playing the Lalo Concerto. His last appearance as an orchestral member, and his first in Britain, was at the Edinburgh Festival. He then began touring as a soloist, making his début at the Royal Festival Hall in London in 1958 playing the Brahms Double Concerto with Isaac Stern and the London Symphony Orchestra conducted by Josef Krips. An account in *The Strad* tells us that the concert was not as well attended as was expected. It suggests possible lack of appeal of the concerto, but considers the name of Isaac Stern should have guaranteed 'a good show'. Stern is complimented on his luscious tone, and Rose on his 'even more luscious cello tone'. He is described as 'an American cellist who is not yet known here, but who must certainly be watched for'.[3]

Rose's solo appearances took him all over the world and he was heavily committed to teaching, both privately and at the Juilliard School where he had been professor since 1946. Lynn Harrell, Stephen Kates and Yo Yo Ma are three of the many fine cellists who have been trained by him. Kates recalls:

> He loved to demonstrate at the lessons and liked his students to aspire to the same musical convictions that he held dear. And because there was a great deal in his students that needed finishing, it was inevitable that they should adapt mannerisms of his playing. A great deal of his success was that his students would fall into this beautiful and natural way of playing. He loved everything that was simple and direct and I suppose he considered that at some time in one's career, imitation was crucial.

Kates is convinced that Rose had a special gift to make his students play better, and generally speaking came out of a lesson 'feeling like a million dollars. He had a wonderful way to make you play better that was not methodology, but he gave you confidence. He made you feel good about yourself when you were doing it.'[4]

Despite this gift of making his students happy, Rose had firm ideas about cello technique. There has been much controversy as to whether cellists can learn from violinists or not. Certainly in the past centuries there are a number of examples of cellists claiming they have learnt from the best fiddlers. Some string players today believe that all should hold the bow as the violinists do, with the little finger on top of the stick. Rose disagreed and conceded that violinists may hold their bows this way but that cellists cannot. 'The stick should never go above the second joint of the index finger. Between the first and second joints is, I feel, a good starting point.'[5]

On vibrato Rose also had definite views. He felt that vibrato should be performed by the lower arm 'with the pad of the fingers as a pivot, and the upper arm moving only passively'. He also pointed out that he preferred that way for the violin also—and that Kreisler always made his vibrato that way. 'With the forearm vibrato, one can get many types of color and much subtle variety. If the vibrato is relaxed, one can play with any width and in any speed.'[6]

Rose was a firm advocate of practice. He admitted to have practised as much as four to five hours a day, even when on tour. He believed that this is the only way to prepare to give the best possible performance for the audience. He also believed in playing for an imaginary audience before going on stage. He would often rehearse a programme two or three times before facing the real audience. He was an inveterate planner, in that he attended to every minute detail before giving a performance and once said: 'I do not believe in relying on last minute inspiration in public performance. One should put as much effort into the planning of a work, not only musically but technically. The chances for success are much greater. After successfully planning one is able to express the emotional content of the work more fully.'

Rose's playing was admired for its romantic lyricism and expressive phrasing, his skilful use of rubato all based on an impeccable technique. His recordings of the Schumann Concerto with the New York Philharmonic conducted by Bernstein and the *Rhapsody* by Bloch with the Philadelphia Orchestra under Eugene Ormandy, are explicit examples of these qualities. There are also many with the Istomin–Stern–Rose Trio.

Rose played on a superb Amati cello dated 1662, whose 'luminous tone' has been likened to 'a ribbon of spun gold'.[7]

CHAPTER XXIV

The Italian Quartet

ITALY TENDS TO export its talent in exchange for gifted foreigners, so the balance of excellence is maintained. Four cellists who have helped to achieve this equanimity are the Spaniard, Gaspar Cassadó; the Italian, Enrico Mainardi; the Rumanian, Radu Aldulescu, and Amedeo Baldovino, born in Egypt of Italian parents.

Gaspar Cassadó (1897–1966) was probably Casals' youngest pupil when he studied with him in Paris in 1910. He was certainly the only prominent Spanish cellist after Casals. Born in Barcelona, the son of Joaquin Cassadó, a well-known organist and choirmaster, he received his first musical instruction from his father at the age of five and two years later took lessons on the cello with Dionisio March, cellist of the Mercedes Chapel in Barcelona where his father was employed. He appeared at a public concert at nine. Shortly afterwards Casals heard him and offered to give him some lessons. The Municipality of Barcelona awarded him a scholarship to go to Paris in 1910 where, in addition to his private studies with Casals, he took lessons in composition with Manuel de Falla and Maurice Ravel.

During the 1914–18 war the family returned to Barcelona, but after the cessation of hostilities Cassadó undertook a number of international concert tours which established him as one of the leading soloists on his instrument. He played under most of the leading conductors; Weingartner, Furtwängler, Wood, Beecham and others; and his performances of the Brahms Double Concerto with Huberman, Szigeti and Jelly d'Aranyi were hailed as outstanding. He toured for some time with Giulietta von Mendelssohn, and it was with her that he gave the first performance of his *Sonata in the Spanish Style* at the International Music Festival in Venice in 1925.

Italy had a special appeal for Cassadó and he settled in Florence where he lived for over 30 years. He became one of the founder-artists responsible for the Accademia Chigiana Music Courses at Siena in 1932, and headed the advanced master-class there in 1947.

Of his London début, it was said, 'He gave the impression of having stepped into the world with his cello and bow in his hands.'[1] And Grove tells us that 'his tone is of mellow quality and his technique neat and sparkling, but what impresses his audience most are his qualities of subtle phrasing and classical balance of interpretation'.[2]

Cassadó first visited the Soviet Union in 1962 as a member of the Jury of the Tchaikovsky International Competition. He was invited again in 1966 when he gave recitals with his pianist wife, Chieko Hara, appearing in Moscow, Leningrad, Kiev and Riga. Lev Ginsburg writes:

The attractive features of Cassadó's performing act were its nobility, delicate musicality, spirituality and true artistry. In his playing, emotion and élan were combined with convincing musical thinking, whether it concerned the unity of the form of the work or an individual phrase. The romantic animation of Cassadó's interpretation coexisted well with classical austerity and restraint.[3]

In his compositions, Cassadó's writing for his instrument is very effective. The best known of his short pieces are *Requiebros* and *The Dance of the Little Green Devil*; and his transcriptions of classical and romantic pieces are a valued addition to the repertoire still extensively used today. His Concerto in D minor, dedicated to Casals, requires a brilliant executant and deserves a place in the cello repertoire.

On 21 January 1964, at the Wigmore Hall London, Cassadó made an unusual dual première. He presented six unpublished cello sonatas by Boccherini played on the Stradivari cello of 1709, once owned by the composer. The performance was given together with the pianist, Eve Barsham, who had discovered the manuscripts in the archives of the Duke of Hamilton in Scotland. There were eleven cello sonatas in all, six of which had not been published.

Cassadó had planned to celebrate his seventieth birthday in Kiev playing the Brahms Double Concerto with David Oistrakh, but when the disastrous floods devastated Florence, where he had spent so many happy years, he made an exhausting tour of the area—against the advice of his doctors—and died soon afterwards of a heart attack.

A colourful character whose achievements as a teacher are underestimated today is the Italian, Enrico Mainardi (1897–1976). Born in

Milan, his father gave him a small cello when he was three and he had his first lessons a year later. At eight years of age he appeared in public playing a Beethoven sonata and, as a prodigy, toured Italy, appearing in Bologna accompanied by the composer Respighi. At thirteen he played the Saint-Saëns Concerto at one of the London Promenade concerts with Sir Henry Wood conducting.

At sixteen, Mainardi took part in the Bach–Reger Festival held in Heidelberg, an experience which became a turning point in his musical life. He had chosen to play the Bach Solo Suite in C major, and apparently impressed his audience so much that, in 1936, Alexander Berrsche recalled the occasion, remembering that there was considerable anxiety in the audience when they noted the extreme youth of the young man who had taken on such a task, but who fulfilled it admirably.

The 1914–18 war interrupted Mainardi's concert tours, so he put his cello aside for four years. When he took it up again he found he had forgotten how to play. The beautiful sound he had made instinctively in the past, now completely eluded him. In disgust he entered the Academia di Santa Cecilia in Rome to study composition and piano. It was only at twenty-four that he decided to tackle the cello again and went to Berlin to study with Hugo Becker. He later described to his pupils how he had been forced to re-learn, consciously, what he had been able to do instinctively as a child. This obviously gave him an unusual understanding of the difficulties encountered by the talented youngsters who, after puberty, have to think consciously about what they are doing. This period in Mainardi's career made him exceptionally good at analysing and curing technical problems experienced by his students.

On his return to Italy, he resumed his career and, in addition to solo work, he played in a number of distinguished duos and trios. From 1929–31 he played under Erich Kleiber at the Berlin State Opera and the Dresden Philharmonic Orchestra, and in 1933 was appointed professor of cello at the Accademia di Santa Cecilia in Rome. When Becker died in 1941, Mainardi succeeded him at the Hochschule in Berlin.

For some time Mainardi's name disappeared from the musical scene, only to emerge in the post-war years through appearances with Dohnányi and Wilhelm Backhaus, and for many years with the pianist, Carlo Zecchi. The trio he formed with the pianist, Edwin Fischer and the violinist, Georg Kuhlenkampff became world famous. When Kuhlenkampff died in 1948 his place was taken by Wolfgang Schneiderhan.

Mainardi was always well known as a performer in Germany, Italy, Switzerland and Scandinavia. Only in France and England was he better known as a teacher. Of his many pupils, the British cellist, Joan Dickson, now a professor at the Royal College of Music, describes him as 'of tremendous personality and exuberant vitality, with a wonderful gift for expressing musical ideas in illuminating, if sometimes ungrammatical language.'

In 1950, at the age of twenty-seven, Dickson decided she was not making the progress she wished. She had heard about Mainardi's gifts as a teacher so, when he came to play at the festival in Edinburgh, where she then lived, she decided to have a lesson with him. It was a turning point in her life. In particular, his explanations as to how one should approach unaccompanied Bach, opened doors that hitherto had been closed to her.

Dickson knew that her salvation as a musician lay in Mainardi's hands. She went to study with him in Rome during the following summer and many summers to come, eventually becoming his assistant. 'I never had a moment's doubt about the wisest decision I ever made.'

A man with such a powerful personality could easily have imposed his stamp upon his pupils, but he would not allow this to happen. 'The only thing he imposed upon his pupils were his standards and his own deep sense of commitment to an unending search for truth in music.' Apparently he was reluctant to let his pupils see his fingerings and bowings because he preferred to discuss the principle of fingering in relation to interpretation. He wanted them to learn to be imaginative and individual in their use of fingerings. This principle he also followed for interpretation. If a pupil instinctively played a phrase a certain way, he would say that if the instinct was right, one could always find justification in the score. He taught how to interpret the printed page so that, if challenged, his pupils could give a reason for what they were doing.

He was insistent that the entire score of any work should be known. Any pupil who turned up for a lesson on a concerto without a score was in for some sharp admonition. He would always discuss the work as a whole—never the cello part alone. He had a remarkable ability to evoke orchestral sounds on the piano and in addition had a great gift for describing music in words. This again was unusual, since English was his fourth language. Dickson says that he made people hear things in music that they'd never heard before. 'For the first time I became aware of how the shape of a phrase is governed by the harmony; he made analysis meaningful to those who had hitherto looked upon the dissection of music as a purely academic exercise which had nothing whatsoever to do with inter-, pretation or performance.'[4]

Mainardi had firm ideas on the role of the interpretative artist. He would tell his class never to forget that they were servants of the composer and should seek to convey the meaning of the music rather than try to achieve personal success. In that respect their whole bearing on the concert platform was relevant, including the way they dressed. Indeed, his sartorial splendour showed that this was a subject on which he was well informed.

His clothes were always chosen in the best of taste and, in his latter years, he wore a flowing black cloak reminiscent of a character out of a Verdi opera. He was an extremely handsome man with a mass of white hair and was well aware of the charismatic effect he had on people, especially the ladies. A great raconteur, he loved to accompany his stories with dramatic gestures, and his humour pervaded everything. Curiously enough, all the histrionics were absent on the concert platform. Here he was the serious musician interpreting serious music to what he hoped was an appreciative audience. Unfortunately, he overestimated the intelligence of the average concertgoer who might have preferred a little more show-manship. Consequently, he remained much more appreciated by musicians than by the general public.

Amedeo Baldovino was born in Alexandria, Egypt, in 1916, of Italian parents, and took his first cello lessons at five years of age on a small cello specially made for him. His teacher was a pupil of Francesco Serato, who was known for the elegance of bowing which he combined with a remarkable left-hand technique.

When his family moved to Bologna, Amedeo attended the G. B. Martini School of Music where he studied with Camillo Oblach. He made his first public appearance at the age of ten and followed this with a number of other concerts in and around Bologna. He graduated with the highest honours at fourteen and from this time began to play outside Italy as a soloist with the Concertgebouw, Berlin and Czech Philharmonic orchestras under some of the world's leading conductors.

Although only twenty, after six years of highly successful concert giving, Baldovino decided he wanted to devote some time to the study of composition. And, because of the emphasis placed on music in his formative years, he now felt the need to enlarge his general education to include philosophy. He spent a further four years at the

G. B. Martini School and graduated in 1940 with a degree in composition, after which he resumed his performing career, interrupted yet again by military service during the 1939–45 war.

In 1951, Baldovino was chosen by the violinist, Giaconda de Vito, as her partner in a performance of the Brahms Double Concerto with the Philharmonia Orchestra conducted by Sir Malcolm Sargent. From this point his reputation as an international soloist grew steadily. After he gave a recital at the Wigmore Hall in London in March 1959, *The Times* critic wrote:

The features of this cellist's style which are most striking are his very full and rich tone, wonderfully steady intonation, and immaculate bowing. In short, he has a masterly technique: and, what perhaps is even more important, he has the kind of musical personality which can put such a technique to very rewarding use.

His Bach suites glowed with life. Mr Baldovino lived their every note, and it was good to hear this great music played so passionately. There was nothing of the museum curator about this artist's approach to music.

Despite his success as a soloist, Baldovino's love of chamber music never diminished. In 1957 he collaborated with the violinist, Franco Gulli and the violist, Bruno Giuranna to form the Trio Italiano d'Archi which appeared successfully all over Europe and in the USA. However, when, in 1962, he was asked to take the place of Libero Lana of the famous Trio di Trieste, he left the Trio Italiano.

One of the main hazards of running a small group is staying together long enough to achieve the perfect ensemble. Baldovino has some advice for the young on this score.

There are many young people who try to form a group and could make a success of it eventually, if they had the patience to overcome the initial difficulties. You must try to find an equilibrium between the members of the group and you must have the will to survive together. Many of the problems are imagined, and I am of the opinion that this is the hardest obstacle to overcome. We also live in a period when young musicians have too many temptations. They have an open world all too ready to respond to their desire for quick economic returns. It is certainly a very different situation from the times when groups like the Trio di Trieste and the Quartetto Italiano studied on their own with only

the stars to guide them. To initiate a career then was more
demanding than it is now.[5]

Now, Baldovino devotes his time to chamber music and teaching,
combining both on the many courses for which he is in demand. He
has had twenty years of teaching at the Conservatories in Perugia
and Rome, and succeeded Enrico Mainardi at the S. Cecilia Academy
in Rome until 1984. He gives master classes throughout Europe.

Baldovino owns and plays three very beautiful cellos, a Tononi, a
Postiglione and the 'Mara' Stradivarius of 1711, 'an extraordinary
instrument of unique perfection that has given me joy for thirty-two
years of my life'. However, the 'Mara' was once nearly lost in a fog.
In July 1963, in order to meet a concert commitment, the Trio di
Trieste were forced to take the night ferry that ran between the two
cities of Montevideo and Buenos Aires. The airports had been closed
because of bad weather. They took off in thick fog and, at 4.30 a.m.
ran into a submerged wreck. When fire broke out, there was no
option but to throw themselves overboard wearing life-saving
jackets. Of the 450 passengers, 140 were drowned. After presuming
that all cargo had been lost, a few days later they learned that
miraculously the cello case had been recovered. When it was opened,
there was the cello, but in pieces, unglued and almost unrecogniza-
ble! It was taken to Hill's in London where, after a nine-month
restoration operation, the instrument emerged intact with all its
previous characteristics unchanged.

The Rumanian-born Radu Aldulescu, now an Italian citizen, is one
of that country's most distinguished acquisitions. Born in Piteasca,
Rumania, in 1922 he took up the cello at six years of age and at
twelve entered the Royal Music Conservatory in Bucharest to study
with Dimitrie Dinicu. He graduated at seventeen with three major
prizes and that same year made his professional début playing the
Haydn D Major Concerto with the Bucharest Radio Symphony
Orchestra.

At only nineteen Aldulescu was appointed solo cellist in the State
Opera Orchestra of Bucharest, a position he held until 1945 when
he found his solo career, and teaching, began to overtake his
orchestral work. In 1964 he became Gaspar Cassadó's assistant in
Santiago de Compostela in Spain and, at the same time, made his
London début playing the Dvořák Concerto with the BBC Sym-
phony Orchestra. Three years later he was given the Harriet Cohen
International Music Award as 'the best foreign cellist appearing in

England'. He subsequently toured West Germany, France, Greece and Spain, appearing as a soloist with leading orchestras and in recitals.

The decision to leave Rumania came in 1969, and Aldulescu is unequivocal as to the reasons. 'There was a necessity for me to have more space to move. My career had come to the point where it was essential for me to make myself known in the west.'[6] He chose Italy because of the similarities between that country and his own.

In 1972 Aldulescu formed the Trio d'Archi di Roma with the violinist, Salvatore Accardo and the violist, Luigi Bianchi. He frequently performed with the celebrated pianist and conductor, Carlo Zecchi. In addition to being in demand for international festivals and seminars, he teaches regularly at the International Academy of Music in Rome and the Conservatoire Européen de Musique in Paris.

Aldulescu was greatly influenced by Piatigorsky and Cassadó, because he felt an affinity with their temperament, tone and imagination. Certainly his own playing clearly shows this trend. Critics universally praise the glowing warmth of his tone, sensitive phrasing and technical ease. Perhaps the essence of his playing is the blending of intimacy and sincerity with a strong individual statement about the music itself. What comes across is a personal point of view, loved by his audiences everywhere.

CHAPTER XXV

Ladies on the Bass Line

AT THE TURN of the eighteenth century, the violinist Ludwig Spohr discouraged his wife from playing the violin because it was 'an unbecoming instrument'. If this is true of the violin, what would he have thought of the cello which was deemed not only unbecoming but hardly respectable? Since the spike was introduced quite late in the nineteenth century, a lady had either to straddle the instrument like a man or cope with it side-saddle. Paul Tortelier recalls that his first teacher, Béatrice Bluhm always used the more modest method, and this was in the twentieth century.

One of the first known female cellists was Lisa Cristiani (1827–53), a Parisienne of considerable charm who was an elegant and sympathetic but small-toned player. She toured successfully throughout Europe and Scandinavia, and the King of Denmark conferred the title of Chamber Virtuosa upon her. In Leipzig in 1845, she attracted the attention of Mendelssohn, who not only accompanied her solos but dedicated the beautiful *Song Without Words* Op. 109 to her. Tragically, Cristiani contracted cholera in Siberia whilst on a tour of Russia and died within a few days. She was only twenty-six.

Her beautiful Stradivari cello, dated 1700, and known as the ex-Cristiani, once belonged to Hugo Becker. The present owner resides in the UK but wishes to remain anonymous.

Gabrielle Platteau was one of the first women to play the cello in public in Belgium. Little is known about her except that she was said to be a pupil of Servais at the Brussels Conservatoire and, in 1875, died in her early twenties, like Cristiani. Van der Straeten once heard her in Cologne and recalled that she was an outstanding performer with a fluent and brilliant technique and a sweet but never powerful tone. She made a successful début at the Crystal Palace in London in 1873.

In Britain, the first name we encounter is that of Beatrice Eveline, born in Wales in 1877. At nine years of age, she won first prize in the National Eisteddfod defeating nine male competitors. She later won an open scholarship to the Royal Academy of Music where she studied with William Whitehouse. In 1908 she made a successful début at the Queen's Hall Ballad Concerts in London and subsequently toured Europe as a soloist.

The London-born May Mukle (1880–1963) is regarded as the true pioneer of women cellists in Britain, becoming the first to achieve international status as a concert artist. She hailed from a family of practising professional musicians who proudly claimed some gipsy blood. Her father, Leopold Mukle, an expert in organ-building was also the inventor of the penny-in-the-slot mechanical music machine.

May was already performing in public at nine. She supported herself from the age of eleven by taking any engagement that came her way, and at thirteen studied with Pezze at the Royal Academy of Music where she carried off all the prizes available to cellists. At seventeen she was elected an A.R.A.M.—a rare honour for one so young.

Mukle soon became known throughout Britain as a soloist of exceptional gifts and subsequently toured Europe, Australia, Asia, Africa and the USA meeting with great success. In Vienna, Max Kalbeck called her 'the female Casals', and *The Times* described her as being 'in the very front rank of living violoncellists'.

Although primarily known as a soloist she also derived much pleasure from playing chamber music, and was a very accomplished performer. Many times she joined Thibaud, Tertis and others in private performances of chamber music. In his memoirs Arthur Rubinstein mentions her 'beautiful playing' of a Brahms' String Sextet when she joined Albert Sammons, Eugene Goossens, Lionel Tertis, Gertrud Bauer (sister of Harold Bauer) and Augustin Rubio in a private performance at the house of the celebrated actress, Ruth Draper. He also mentions another occasion when she played both of the Brahms' sextets with Thibaud and Paul Kochanski on violins, Tertis and Pierre Monteux on violas and Felix Salmond as first cello.

Over the years she was a member of a number of well known string quartets, including the English Ensemble with the violinist, Marjorie Hayward the violist, Rebecca Clarke and the pianist Kathleen Long. She also had a long and active association with the distinguished American violinist, Maud Powell. They toured South Africa and America as the Maud Powell Trio with Mukle's sister, Anne, as their pianist and enjoyed an enormous success.

Mukle was well known for her support of the work of contemporary composers and was responsible for first performances of the Ravel and Kodály duos in Great Britain. She also premièred Gustav Holst's *Invocation* in 1911 at the Queen's Hall in London. Ralph Vaughan Williams dedicated his *Six Studies in English Folk Song* for cello and piano to Mukle, and she gave the first performance on 4 June 1926 with her sister, Anne, at a concert mounted by the English Folksong and Dance Society at the Scala Theatre in London.

May Mukle played on a magnificent Montagnana which had been presented to her by an anonymous donor who invited her to choose any cello from the Hill collection. Although it was a large instrument, she never had any difficulty in handling it and produced from it a powerful and beautiful tone.

Lyndon de Lecq Marguerie, now teaching cello at Oxford, was probably Mukle's only pupil. She was primarily a performer, but Marguerie studied with her for several months and recalls that her vivacious and warm personality was in complete contrast to her platform persona which was rather reserved. Absorbed in the music she made no outward show.

Apart from her considerable talent as a performer, she was remarkable in her generosity towards her younger colleagues, particularly those of her own sex. She knew that her pioneering had paved the way for women to take up the cello and she enjoyed their successes. It was nothing unusual for her to lend her Montagnana to a gifted youngster who was appearing in an important concert.

The close proximity of her London flat to the Wigmore Hall, and the openness of her hospitality, meant that it became a little mecca for visiting musicians. Vaughan Williams, John Ireland and Ravel were frequent visitors. Casals, also a close personal friend who much admired her playing, went there on a number of occasions.

The story of how she acquired the flat is characteristic. A small block originally intended as an office building was erected in Bulstrode Street off Marylebone Lane in London, and Mukle decided it would better serve music if it were divided into flats. She used her most persuasive manner to convince the agents that by letting the entire premises to musicians there would be no problems about noise when practising and the landlords would be reasonably sure of long tenancies. She won the day. The four floors were converted and soon occupied by a few of her closest friends and colleagues.

May Mukle's fellow professionals were also greatly indebted to her for her vision in founding the M.M. (Mainly Musicians) Club in a converted basement adjacent to Oxford Circus Tube Station. It provided a meeting place and a restaurant which was particularly useful in the early days of the 1939–45 war when it was also used as an air-raid shelter. She had an innate sense of fun which contributed greatly to the friendly atmosphere and, unless playing in a concert or rehearsing, she was in charge almost every night, braving the air-raids, tin helmet at the ready. Unfortunately her business sense did not match her other gifts and, after some fifteen years, the club was closed down.

With the end of the war in 1945, she resumed her nomadic wanderings, and on her last tour of Africa was seriously hurt in a car accident. Then almost eighty, in spite of a broken wrist and other injuries she gradually and painfully resumed her playing. In 1959 she even undertook a short tour of the USA. One of the people who chanced upon one of her concerts in Burlington, North Carolina, was the cellist Elizabeth Cowling: 'It was fascinating in several ways, one of which was that she and her accompanist, Mrs Pearl Sutherland Ideler, were touring in the old manner of "barn-storming", that is, they found their own place to play in, in this instance a church, mimeographed their own programmes, and put a plate at the back of the room for contributions. (There was no charge for the concert).' She played a varied programme which included the Elgar Concerto which was 'simply beautifully played.'[1] An interesting observation from Cowling is that although Mukle's technique was of the pre-Casals era, her eminent musicality over-rode the old-fashioned fingering techniques with its many slides. She also noted that her arms were free, not held close to the body as was sometimes the case in those days.

The May Mukle Prize, founded in her memory by friends and admirers all over the world, is awarded each year to a cello student at the Royal Academy of Music in London, where she distinguished herself so many years ago.

Following closely in the steps of May Mukle were two women cellists who achieved international reputations. They were the Portuguese, Guilhermina Suggia (1888–1950), and the British, Beatrice Harrison. Born in Oporto, Suggia was the daughter of an eminent physician. Her family expected her to acquire and exploit the social graces of her class, but as a young child she decided that music was much more important, and made her first public appearance playing the cello at seven. By the age of twelve she was principal cellist in the Oporto City Orchestra, and a year later became the cellist in Moreira de Sa's String Quartet. In 1901, under the patronage of the Portuguese royal family, she was sent to study in Leipzig with Klengel.

While in Leipzig Suggia played as a soloist with the Gewandhaus Orchestra under Artur Nikisch and made her first European tour, settling in Paris from 1906–12 where she studied with Casals. It was often rumoured that they were at one time married, but there is no evidence of this. Ginsburg recalls them playing the Moór Concerto for two cellos in Moscow under Mikhail Ippolitov-Ivanov.

In 1914 she settled in London remaining for many years performing and teaching. She was known for the nobility of her phrasing and 'tone of a masculine power seldom heard from a lady violoncellist'.[2] Milly Stanfield, who heard her many times, writes, 'Her natural gifts and instincts led her to excel in colourful, emotional music and her performance of the Lalo Concerto was unforgettable.'[3]

In October 1930 she was the soloist in the Saint-Saëns Concerto with the BBC Symphony Orchestra under its new director, Adrian Boult, conducting at the Queen's Hall for the first time. The *Daily Telegraph* critic was impressed: 'Madame Suggia played her part of the concerto as though the whole literature of cello music held nothing so divine. She seemed, too, to inspire the orchestra with the same feeling.'[4] It seems she was recalled to the platform many times.

One of the first exponents of Casals' unique mode of cello playing, Suggia remained a staunch advocate of his principles all her life. However, her pupils seemed to vary in their opinion of her teaching. Some claim that she had limitless patience and generosity in imparting her knowledge. Others say she was often negative in her directions and that they derived little benefit from their study with her.

In 1923 Augustus John painted the portrait which now hangs in the Tate Gallery, her personality captured for posterity. In this portrait 'her poise, temperament and force of character all seem to be blended'.[5] In the earlier part of her career Suggia played on an outstandingly beautiful Domenico Montagnana, but the instrument she is playing in the John portrait is her Stradivarius, dated 1717, which she bequeathed to the Royal Academy of Music, to be sold for the foundation of a scholarship for cello students at that institution. When it was purchased in 1951 by Edmund Kurtz for £8,000, Hill's made an unusual gesture in waiving their normal fee so that the gift should remain intact. It is now one of the most coveted awards for young cellists.

During the Second World War, Suggia retired to Portugal, emerging only once in 1949 to appear at the Edinburgh Festival.

Beatrice Harrison (1892–1965) was born in Roorkee in the North West Province of India where her father was serving as Colonel in the Royal Engineers. Her mother sang and played the piano, having been denied a professional career as a singer. She vowed that if any of her children should show musical talent she would nurture it to maturity. As it happened she had four daughters, all of whom were highly gifted. Eventually they all became professionals, Margaret and May were violinists and Monica was a singer.

According to her biographer, Beatrice begged to be given a cello to play when quite a baby. However, piano lessons at two, followed by the violin were *de rigueur* in the Harrison household. She had to wait until she was eight for the cello and, although it was a full-size instrument which she found difficult to hold, she soon adapted to it. A year and a half after her first lesson, she won the Associated Board's Gold Medal competing with four thousand of all ages.

When Beatrice was eleven, she and her sister May entered the Royal College of Music on scholarships. With unusual foresight, Colonel Harrison realized his duty lay with his daughters' careers and not with the army. No doubt egged on by his ambitious wife, he took the unprecedented step of retiring from the army to join her in the nurturing and promotion of their children's talents. At the time this would have been a unique gesture in the wealthy upper-middle-class to which they belonged.

Annie Harrison organized the girls' lives, meticulously planning every minute of their day. When mother was away, the girls were obliged to keep a strict account of their activities. They practised, learnt harmony and counterpoint, took lessons in general education, including French and German, rested on backboards, went for walks and played games. Surely no musicians since the eighteenth century could have had more concentrated training.

Their social position brought them into contact with royalty, and it was as a teenager that Beatrice met the shy Princess Victoria, daughter of King Edward VII and Queen Alexandra. The Princess had a passion for music and the two became instant and life-long friends.

Beatrice Harrison made her London début when she was fifteen playing the Saint-Saëns Cello Concerto at the Queen's Hall with Henry Wood and his orchestra. In her diary that evening she writes:

'Had 20 bouquets. Mr Wood was very pleased. *The Times* critic said
I was a musician through and through.'⁶

A year later she left the RCM and was sent to study with Becker
at the Hochschule in Berlin. Germany was then the mecca for
musicians, with Berlin and Leipzig as the main centres. She is one of
the few who seem to have good words for Becker, having found
him an excellent teacher. At seventeen, she became the youngest
competitor and first cellist ever to win the coveted Mendelssohn
Prize.

When she was ready to be launched it was Annie Harrison who
organized concerts and tours with the skill of a present day entrepre-
neur. Ahead of her time by several decades, she was an astute
business woman and promoter who not only brought her daughter
success, but understood the need for her to be left to concentrate on
her music.

Beatrice Harrison's first appearance in Berlin was with her sister
May, playing the Brahms Double Concerto in the Beethoven Hall
under Heinrich Noé in March 1910, followed by a recital début at
the Bechstein Hall. In December of that year she played the Dvořák
Concerto at the Singakademie with Becker conducting, and gave
many recitals with the pianist Eugene d'Albert, whose affinity with
marriage had led him to five unsuccessful attempts. He asked
Beatrice Harrison to become his sixth wife, but she declined. Cyril
Scott and several other prominent musicians had also proposed to
her, but there was never room for a man in her life.

If the mother was dedicated, her daughter was equally so.
Working with her cello was what she enjoyed most. Practising was
not only a joy but a necessity. Occasionally at a social gathering she
would become preoccupied and moments later would slip away to
play her cello in another room.

In June 1911, she made her adult début with Sir Henry Wood and
the Queen's Hall Orchestra, playing three concertos, the Dvořák,
the Haydn D Major and Tchaikovsky's *Rococo Variations*. The critics
raved and promised her a brilliant future.

Despite her formidable routine, Beatrice Harrison managed to
find time to be presented at Court—an important event in English
Society at the time. Her dress was made by Paquin, one of the
leading French dressmakers. As she stepped forward to make her
curtsey to the King and Queen, she describes the scene as being like
an Arabian Nights' fantasy. It seems that many rajahs were present
and their jewels and magnificent robes were 'unbelievable'.

In the winter of 1913, she was invited to play in the USA. She was the first woman cellist to play at Carnegie Hall and the first to be engaged as soloist with the Boston and Chicago Symphony orchestras. Concerned almost as much with her appearance as with the performance, she writes, 'For the Philharmonic Orchestra under Stransky at the Carnegie Hall I wore an organdie frock trimmed with diamanté and a wreath of red roses on my head. Fritz Kreisler and his wife were staying at the same hotel and Mrs Kreisler was so kind, showing me how to make up for the platform.'[7]

The friendliness of the Americans greatly appealed to her, and she was overwhelmed by proposals of marriage. She wrote in her diary, 'One quite nice man, somewhat lacking in sense of humour, offered me his heart and his banking account. I should have not minded his banking account but the heart I could not cope with, so had to refuse both!'[8]

Beatrice notes that the Americans overcame their prejudice at seeing a woman play the cello, and she was re-engaged for a second tour which took place early in 1915 after the outbreak of war in Europe. Mrs Harrison and her daughters—May, as Beatrice's accompanist—were booked to return on the Lusitania leaving in late April. However, a nightmare about a shipwreck made such an impression on Mrs Harrison that she cancelled the bookings and transferred to a small American cargo ship which took three weeks. The Lusitania was torpedoed on 7 May.

Beatrice Harrison enjoyed a lifelong friendship with the composer Frederick Delius and he wrote his Concerto for Violin and Cello for her and her sister May. She recalls that originally there were many passages in unison which rendered them technically almost unplayable. At a meeting with Delius, with Philip Heseltine (Peter Warlock) at the piano, May and Beatrice advised the re-writing. 'Heseltine banged out the orchestral part, while I, hot and anxious, played each passage over and over again until Delius was satisfied that it corresponded perfectly with the violin.'[9] At this time Delius also promised her something for cello only and she premièred the Cello Sonata at the Wigmore Hall in October 1918.

Although Delius wrote his cello concerto for her, it was first performed, in Vienna, by Serge Barjansky. Nonetheless Delius was adamant that Harrison should give the first British performance, and this took place on 3 July 1923 at the Queen's Hall with Eugène Goossens conducting. An account comes from Gerald Moore in his book *Am I Too Loud?*, where he writes about her poignant and luscious cantabile so well suited to Delius's music.

Her playing of one heavenly phrase of the Cello Concerto lingers
in my memory although it is thirty years since I heard the work.
She sang on her instrument and had an infallible instinct for
feeling where the muscle of the music slackened, where it tight-
ened again, where it accumulated tension till the climax was
reached. No woman cellist I have ever heard had, at once, a tone
so powerful and sweet.[10]

Beatrice Harrison was clearly very sensitive to Delius's requirements in the concerto and later gave an interesting analysis of mood
in the *Musical Bulletin* of August 1927. 'The artist must be inspired
by a wealth of musical imagination to be able to interpret this music.
It would seem almost impossible to describe this wonderful work
adequately.'[11]

An association with Elgar began shortly after the disastrous first
performance by Felix Salmond of his Cello Concerto in 1919, when
he approached her to ask if she would make a recording for HMV.
This was an abridged version acoustically recorded. In 1928 she re-
recorded the concerto complete for HMV, with Elgar conducting as
before. This second record is of vital historical interest, since
Harrison observes all the composer's directions regarding dynamics
and tempi which often differ from present-day interpretations.

Soon after that recording Elgar asked her to play the concerto
with him at the Queen's Hall, a prospect that delighted her. It seems
that again she was meticulous about her clothes and bought a new
'frock' for every concert. For the Elgar she chose 'heavenly turquoise
blue chiffon' which 'suited the cello so well'. Patricia Cleveland-
Peck, editor of Harrison's memoirs, tells us that she also wore blue
underwear for this concert, and at all future performances of the
Elgar, she wore blue knickers because she felt they were lucky.

It was at Foyle Riding, a country cottage at Oxted in Surrey
which became the Harrisons' final home, that Beatrice hit the
headlines by playing her cello in duet with a nightingale. One
summer evening she took her cello into a wood in their grounds—
which were tended by six gardeners—and played *Chanson Hindou*
by Rimsky-Korsakov. She found she was not alone: 'Suddenly a
glorious note echoed the notes of the cello. I then trilled up and
down the instrument, up to the top and down again: the voice of
the bird followed me in thirds! I have never heard such a bird's song
before—to me it seemed a miracle.'[12]

When the duet was repeated night after night, Beatrice suggested
recording the phenomenon. With difficulty, she persuaded Sir John

Reith, the then Director of the BBC, to send a team down to their home. It is now one of the historic items in the '2LO' archives. Beatrice playing the *Chanson Hindou* in duet with the nightingale was heard by a million people in London, Italy and France, and was also recorded by HMV. Following this event her name became famous and she received letters from all over the world.

Today Beatrice Harrison tends to be remembered only for her cello and nightingale feat. But in her day she was considered by many to be one of the greatest women cellists alive. Not only did she play the traditional repertoire but she was also a staunch supporter of the work of contemporary composers. She introduced the Cello Sonata by Arnold Bax, with Harriet Cohen at the piano, and gave the first performance of John Ireland's Cello Sonata. She also gave the first British performance of the Kodály Solo Sonata in May 1924.

An enthusiastic ambassador for British music, she gave first performances of the Delius Sonata and Concerto and the Elgar Concerto in America and several European countries. When she introduced the Kodály Solo Sonata in New York, the critics were enthusiastic.

As a person she was kind and cheerful, modest about her own talent, with no hint of jealousy regarding her fellow artists. The cello and its music were for her the 'meaning and purpose' of her life. After her mother's sudden death in 1934, she went into retirement at her country cottage, and never fully recovered from the loss.

Her achievements are aptly summed up in *The Strad*: 'The apex of her concert career coincided with the resurgence of British music in the first three decades of the century. In this field her influence is comparable with that of Lionel Tertis on the viola.'[13]

CHAPTER XXVI

The French Tradition

THE BEST TRADITIONS of cello playing established in France in the nineteenth century were perpetuated by a number of gifted artists, of whom Maurice Maréchal (1892–1964) was an outstanding representative. His contacts with distinguished contemporary composers, combined with his own illustrious musical gifts, did a great deal to promote interest in French music on a world-wide scale.

Maréchal was born in Dijon in Burgundy and had lessons on the cello as a young child. By the age of ten he was performing in public and at fifteen won first prize playing Davidov's Second Concerto. He completed his studies at the Paris Conservatoire under Jules Leopold-Loeb, graduating at nineteen with the Premier Prix.

His first employment was with the Lamoureux Orchestra, initially as deputy principal cellist and then as soloist. Consequently, as a very young man he came under the influence of conductors such as Artur Nikisch, Felix Weingartner and Richard Strauss.

During the 1914–18 war, he served throughout as a private. There is an amusing account of how he persuaded two of his fellow soldiers—who happened to be carpenters—to make him a cello. He gave them precise directions, and a primitive though workable instrument emerged. For the rest of the war Maréchal frequently entertained his comrades with this cello made from a powder chest. After he was demobilized, Maréchal settled in Paris with his American wife, Louise Perkins, and toured extensively.

Maréchal's interest in and involvement with contemporary composers probably did more than any other cellist of the time to put French music on the map. In the twenties he was closely associated with Maurice Ravel when the composer was working on his Sonata for Violin and Cello, and together with the violinist, Hélène Jourdan-Morhange, he premièred the work on 6 April 1922. A year later he gave the first orchestral performance of André Caplet's *Epiphanie*, a very difficult symphonic work for cello that, for the time, used unusual cello technique. After a second performance at a

Concert Colonne he was invited by Leopold Stokowski to play it with the Philadelphia Orchestra in the USA.

Le Monde Musicale, obviously delighted at their compatriot's success in New York, wrote, 'His ineffably beautiful tone, artistic fantasy and poetic depth made for a superb interpretation. I have never heard such a faultless rendering of the Debussy Sonata. . . . In Fauré's *Elégie*, Maréchal displayed a noble simplicity and depth of feeling that were far removed from sentimentality.'[1]

By the thirties Maréchal had gained a reputation that placed him high in the ranks of first-class soloists. Unfortunately, war once again interrupted his musical activities. His sympathies were strongly with the resistance movement, and he refused to play in Germany. He would not even take part in radio programmes broadcast by French cities under German occupation. When Gérard Hekking died in 1942, Maréchal took his place as cello professor at the Paris Conservatoire.

Unfortunately, Maréchal developed a muscular disease that affected his right arm and playing became more and more difficult. His last concerts were given in 1950, but his teaching activities and appearances on international juries continued to the end of his life.

As a teacher he was both loved and respected. He never sacrificed artistic intention for technical perfection. Christine Walewska, who studied with him, recalls a remark he made to her just before she had to play the Haydn Concerto in the Conservatoire Competition: 'Play as you feel. If passages are written piano but you want to play them forte, without hesitation play them in the way your intuition prompts you. Play surrendering yourself wholly to the music you are performing, and with much liberty.'[2]

The musicologist, Marc Pincherle, characterized Maréchal as one of the most outstanding representatives of French performing culture. Lev Ginsburg writes:

He was the first in a modern school to link together rarely combined qualitative and quantative elements: on the one hand, powerful tone and on the other refined shading. . . . Outstanding French composers of his time asked Maréchal to be the first performer of their cello works, the majority of which they dedicated to him. . . . If the contemporary French cello school so prospers (from the point of view of European classification apparently, it surpasses our violin and piano schools), it's to a great extent, to Maurice Maréchal's credit.[3]

André Navarra is one of the few cellists who had no further tuition after the age of fifteen and, from this time, worked entirely on his own ideas. Born in Biarritz in 1911 into a musical family, he began learning solfège at seven, closely following with lessons on the cello. At nine he was accepted into the Toulouse Conservatoire, and graduated four years later with the First Prize. He then went on to study at the Paris Conservatoire with Jules Leopold-Loeb, where, at fifteen, he also took first prize.

During Navarra's self-development period, he was fortunate to come into contact with a number of well known musicians who either lived in or visited Paris. He greatly admired Feuermann, and in varying ways he was influenced by Arthur Honegger, Florent Schmitt, Jacques Ibert, Alfred Cortot and Jacques Thibaud. Later, Casals did much to help him achieve a greater artistic maturity.

Navarra's first professional experience came in 1929 when he was only eighteen, as cellist of the Kretly String Quartet. He played with them for almost seven years, and also formed a trio, known as the B.B.N. Trio, with the pianist G. Benvenuti, and the violinist René Benedetti. His solo début, playing the Lalo Concerto with the Colonne Orchestra, was in Paris in 1931. Two years later he became principal cellist of the Grand Opera Orchestra.

In 1937 he won the coveted First Prize at the International Competition in Vienna: quite an achievement for a cellist *sans* professor. A flurry of engagements followed, but the 1939–45 war brought his career to a halt. During this time he served in the infantry and his cello remained in its case.

After the war Navarra toured successfully throughout Europe, Asia, USA and the Soviet Union, and played under almost every great conductor, including Gabriel Pierné, André Cluytens, Karl Böhm, Charles Münch and John Barbirolli. His recording, with Barbirolli and the Hallé Orchestra, of the Elgar Cello Concerto has become a classic.

Navarra's playing is known for its romantic fervour and singing tone combined with technical mastery. His brilliant bowing technique is the envy of many of his contemporaries, and he seems to be able to play with an endless legato in the slowest passages. This facility has often been put down to the fact that he studied with Carl Flesch, which he denies:

But I have, it is true, drawn inspiration from the Flesch method . . . by taking some principles and adapting them to the study of the cello. . . . Fiddlers have centuries of trial and error behind them, scores of master technicians to blaze the trail—Viotti, Tartini, Paganini and the moderns, Flesch, Ševčik etc.—in comparison with which the art of cello playing is singularly devoid of schools in the same context. It is still, one might say, in its infancy. In this comparatively neglected aspect (with the notable exception of Casals' efforts), there is an immense and quasi-virgin field for future violoncello pioneers.[4]

In his younger days, Navarra looked more like an athlete than a musician. He is of the opinion that, ideally, cellists should be of a stocky and robust build, able to dominate the instrument without undue effort. He speaks from experience, for he was once a promising middle-weight boxer, and swimming used to be his favourite sport. His personality is mercifully free from arrogance or affectation, but he can be fierce when a student is not paying attention to his remarks.

Teaching is now his main activity. He continues to hold his professorship at the Paris Conservatoire and for twenty years has taught at the Summer courses at the Accademia Chigiana at Siena, and in the Autumn master classes at St Jean-de-Luz. He has also taught in London, and still gives master classes in Vienna, and other European cities. Navarra does not intimidate his pupils with his own superiority either of technique or experience; neither does he work above them, but with and for them. One might almost say that he comes to terms with their endeavours.

The British cellist Alexander Baillie studied with Navarra both in Italy and in Vienna and thinks he is one of the few who teaches a comprehensive 'school' of cello playing that works.

In a way he puts his students through the mill—which for some can be harmful as well as productive. It takes some time to understand what he means with his teaching methods. I think that we have a very high standard of musicianship in the UK and, coming from that background, I was able to benefit more from Navarra's technical discipline than some of the European students. One must realize that his approach is a means to an end, not an end in itself. He is simply determined that his students should play the instrument well.[5]

His students admire his 'magic touch' and happy temperament. But perhaps the most repeated comment is that he has a quick,

sympathetic intuition of difficulties, and never requires of his pupils
a task he is incapable of performing himself, immediately, and with
skill.

Pierre Fournier (1906–86) was one of the few players who was
equally admired by his colleagues and the general public. Known as
'the aristocrat of cellists', not only for his lyrical playing but for his
impeccable taste in all things artistic, Fournier was born in Paris, the
son of a General, and as a small child took piano lessons with his
mother. Following a mild attack of polio at the age of nine, his
doctor advised he should change to an instrument where he would
not need to use his feet. He turned to the cello and made sufficient
progress to win a place at the Paris Conservatoire, where he was
first a pupil of Paul Bazelaire, and later Anton Hekking. He
graduated in 1923, at seventeen. Already he had a bow arm that was
the envy of his older colleagues. It is said that Fournier and Tortelier,
who were friendly rivals, once met after a recital given by the latter.
Fournier said, 'Paul. I wish I had your left hand', to which Tortelier
replied, 'Pierre, I wish I had your right'.

In 1925 he made a successful début with the Colonne Orchestra in
Paris and followed this with appearances all over Europe. By the
early thirties he had achieved a considerable reputation well beyond
his native France. In 1937–39 Fournier directed cello studies at the
Ecole Normale, and from 1941–49 was professor at the Paris
Conservatoire.

It was after the 1939–45 War that his career became established
internationally. He made some sensational appearances in England
in chamber concerts with Schnabel, Szigeti and William Primrose.
Together they played practically all the chamber music by Schubert
and Brahms. Szigeti calls them unforgettable 'peaks of musical
experience',[6] and recalls that, when they began rehearsing for the
first Edinburgh Festival in 1947, the rediscovery of Fournier's
'immense talent' was a revelation to him. He had last heard him in
the middle 1930s and was now 'tremendously impressed by the
Apollonian beauty and poise that his playing had acquired in the
intervening years'.[7] At this same festival there was a sad reversal of
twentieth-century technical resources when all audible traces of the
Brahms–Schubert cycle by this distinguished quartet were lost for
ever because the acetates on which the BBC recorded the series had
deteriorated.

In 1948 Fournier made his first tour of the USA and immediately
won the respect of the New York critics. The *Boston Globe* talked

about his 'satiny tone' and the 'utmost grace' of his phrasing, and
that 'everything was set forth with equal excellence'. As his career
gained momentum, he was forced to resign from his teaching post
in Paris. He appeared for the first time in Moscow in 1959 performing concertos by Haydn, Schumann and Lalo with the Moscow
State Philharmonic Orchestra. Lev Ginsburg, who was at these
concerts, describes his playing in the Haydn as showing 'buoyant
musical images and clarity of form'. The Schumann Concerto was
'notable for its poetry and integrity'. And of the Lalo, 'His romantic
interpretation, vivid musical phrasing, clear-cut bowing, broad
breadth of the bow, graceful and lustrous passages of full tone—
everything was aimed at revealing the content.'[8]

Fournier admitted to having a broad outlook on repertoire and
was as happy playing the music of Bach, Boccherini, Beethoven and
Brahms as that of Debussy, Hindemith and Prokofiev. Many
contemporary composers have dedicated works to him, including
Martinů, Martinon, Martin, and Poulenc. When discussing the Bach
Suites he would never underestimate their significance, but warned
against 'dry and congealed' performances. Although his own interpretations were reserved, they were also animated and flexible.

As a teacher, Fournier was always insistent upon a velvety and
fluid tone, and a high elbow for the bow arm. He believed in
holding the bow firmly but always allowing the hand and arm to be
free. He advocated Ševčík violin exercises for perfecting bowing
technique.

Most of his ex-pupils find it difficult to pinpoint the essence of his
teaching. It appears that most of it was very personal and intangible.
The British cellist, Margaret Moncrieff, studied with him for a year
in 1949 and remembers him as a kind and considerate teacher who
treated his pupils as equals and never made them feel small. 'He
taught each pupil in a different way. He would always go straight to
the music and this was the core of everything that happened during
a lesson. There were certain things that he felt strongly about.
Rhythm was of prime importance and he disliked players taking too
many liberties with rubatos.'[9]

Another British pupil of Fournier, Richard Markson, says:

He was a very shy, rather retiring man who, although his ego
was substantial enough, never flouted it in an extravagant way.
He was a natural cellist with a wonderfully fluid bow arm, and he
produced a beautiful sound. He also had a dry sense of humour. I
remember once when he played part of the slow movement of the

Dvořák at one of my lessons, his wife came in and said how moved she was. Fournier said dryly, 'I am the "slow movement" cellist. Everyone says how much they like my slow movements. I wonder what is wrong with the other ones.'[10]

A significant aspect of Fournier's musical development was that throughout his life he associated constantly with other distinguished musicians of his time. When Cortot was living in Neuilly, Fournier would play chamber music every Friday night with him and Jacques Thibaud, or whoever happened to be available. Fournier also enjoyed friendships with Furtwängler, Karajan and Kubelik. He had a lifelong association with Wilhelm Kempf and their recording of the Beethoven Sonatas has become a classic. But it was Schnabel who actually helped Fournier on to the first rung of the ladder when he made his début in New York. Schnabel spread the word that a superb young cellist was shortly giving a recital there. The first recording he made of the Beethoven Sonatas was also with Schnabel.

When he was seventy-eight, Fournier gave a recital at the Queen Elizabeth Hall in London. A critic wrote, 'Fournier's perceptive sense of phrasing and his still easy command of the fingerboard transformed his recital into an object lesson in fluency of playing.'[11] He died in January 1986.

Through his master classes on television, Paul Tortelier (b. 1914) has become a household name in Britain—a far cry from his humble beginnings in one of the poorest districts of Paris. His father was a carpenter and cabinet-maker who played both violin and mandoline. At six Paul was given a cello because his mother had once heard Francis Touche play in a café and decided that if she had a son, he would become a cellist. *Maman* Tortelier dominated and protected her son, following every avenue that might bring him advancement. The command, 'Paul, ton violoncelle!' was the signal for practice that survived even after he was married.

Paul took his first lessons on the cello from Béatrice Bluhm, an advocate of the Franco-Belgian school of playing; and she instilled in him the flexible wrist and free bow arm of that school. At the age of nine, he studied privately with Louis Feuillard—a pupil of Delsart—for three years and then entered his teacher's class at the Paris Conservatoire, transferring at fourteen to Gérard Hekking who took the adult students. Tortelier remembers that Hekking had a wonderful feeling for colour and, like Casals, could make Bach dance: 'Hekking, being Dutch, had the kind of vigorous rhythmic feeling one finds in paintings by Brueghel. This rhythm is something you have in your blood . . . freedom in between the beats—but never disturbing the regular lilt of the dance.'[12]

At sixteen Tortelier graduated with first prize, but he was already a seasoned professional. Since the age of twelve he had contributed to the family finances by working at week-ends at a cinema playing accompaniments for the silent films. Subsequently he became a freelance, playing night after night in brasseries and cafés all over Paris (once he was even called upon to impersonate Maurice Chevalier), but after two years he secured his first orchestral job, as sub-principal cellist with the Orchestra of the Paris Radio, and made his solo début playing the Lalo Concerto at the Concerts Lamoureux.

That same year he re-entered the Conservatoire to take a three-year course in harmony under Jean Gallon, who was the first to make him understand music from the composer's point of view. 'He believed that liberty is not license.' Tortelier deplores the credo of the present time which advocates freedom in everything. He considers that, in the same way as apprentices prepared colours for their masters in the Renaissance, so musicians should begin by studying the great masters of their own field—Bach, Mozart, Beethoven—who all began with strict rules. Gallon would say 'fetters foster genius',[13] and would make his students write only for the human voice which, though limited, was an excellent discipline.

From 1935–37 Tortelier was a member of the Monte Carlo Symphony Orchestra, and here he played under Toscanini and Bruno Walter. It was also in Monte Carlo that he played the solo in *Don Quixote* with Strauss conducting. Soon he was undertaking solo engagements all over Europe, Africa, America and Asia playing under most of the world's greatest conductors, but in 1939 the war brought everything to a halt.

In July 1945 Tortelier played for Casals, who was visiting Paris for the first time after the war, and five years later he was invited to lead the cello section of the orchestra during the first Prades Festival, commemorating the bicentenary of Bach's death. This association with Casals, which later grew into a firm friendship, was to have a profound and lasting influence on Tortelier's artistic development. He recalls that he once asked Jean Gallon what he found extraordinary about Casals' playing, and Gallon began tapping rhythmically on the table wtih his fingers, demonstrating the percussive effect of his articulate left hand. Tortelier says that it gave more freedom to the bow which was then not so responsible for clear articulation. 'Casals was probably the first cellist to use his left hand in the manner of a pianist—that is, by normally placing only one finger on the string at a time, rather than keeping all the fingers clamped down. This allowed the fingers to vibrate freely.'[14]

When Tortelier was forty and at the height of his performing career, he was playing in Israel, and he became dramatically aware of the efforts the Israelis were making to secure the establishment of their country. He made an immediate decision to stay and share their experiences, even though he himself came from an old liberal-minded Catholic family. For one year the Torteliers and their two children settled in Mabaroth, a Kibbutz a few hundred yards from the enemy border, living in a wooden hut, occasionally working in the fields, and taking part in their rota duty of meal service.

From 1956–69 Tortelier was a professor at the Paris Conservatoire and held the same appointment at the Folkwang Hochschule in Essen from 1969–75. He was recently appointed Honorary Professor of Music at the Central Conservatoire of Peking, the first Westerner to receive this honour.

Richard Markson, who studied with Tortelier for six years from the age of twelve, is grateful for everything he learnt during that time.

At the very first lesson, he put the cello on his knee and said, 'Here we have a keyboard. It is the logical position for the hand and all fingers must be equal.' I am sure this—the 'square hand', Casals approach—contributed greatly to the clarity of his technique.

He spent a great deal of time at the piano on which he would try to make us aware of the harmonic tendencies in whatever we were playing. He would never allow an audience in his classes, which were four hours long every two days, and vastly superior to anything that was available in Britain at the time. Tortelier also believed strongly in the idea that one must learn to play when very young while the physical reflexes are still supple.

Tortelier's appearances on British television attract a wide audience, many of which know nothing about music. In such appearances there is always the danger of his exuberant personality creating an image that detracts from the more serious side of this many-faceted musician. Markson confirms this risk.

Strangely enough, although he has this tremendous ego on television, he possibly has more humility towards his art than any other musician I know. He is a very serious musician and a dedicated teacher.

These master classes provide no clue as to the way he really taught. He is a musician to his fingertips and has a sound knowledge of harmony, counterpoint and, since he is also a composer, he knows exactly how the wheels go round. He could entertain one for hours with an analysis of Strauss's *Don Quixote*. Without any reference to the music, he would explain exactly what Strauss had done with the harmonies, texture and how it all fitted together. This is something one never sees on the media.[15]

Tortelier is a man of boundless energy and enthusiasm, who has retained his sense of wonder well past his seventieth birthday, and his respect for every man as an equal partner is rare in such an artist. He is a brilliant raconteur and has considerable knowledge of art and literature which he has acquired entirely by his own efforts. His philosophy lies in a saying of Rodin, 'The more simple we are, the more complete we shall be, for simplicity signifies unity in truth.'

One of his students tells a nice story about his down-to-earth sense of humour, and how mistaken is the impression that he is completely in the clouds and absent-minded. After a performance of the Haydn D Major in Edinburgh, a small boy came backstage and asked Tortelier what images he used for the Haydn? Tortelier sat down and talked for some time to the child about merry-go-rounds and children falling off and so on. The child went away misty-eyed saying he'd always remember that image every time he heard the concerto in future. As he closed the door, Tortelier turned to his student and said, 'How leetle does he know that all I think about in the 'aydn is the dangair of the sheefts!'

Today, Tortelier continues to travel the world, performing and teaching, and still finds time for composing. He is one of the few performing cellists who writes extensively for his instrument. His many works include a Sonata Brève (*Bucephale*) for cello and piano, *Alla Maud* for two cellos and piano or string orchestra and a Concerto for Two Cellos.

One of France's most promising and elegant players in the immediate post-war period was Maurice Gendron, born into a poor family in Nice in 1920. His mother played the violin in the pit of the local cinema, and it was here that he gained his first experience of hearing music. An unusually bright child, Gendron could read music at three, and at four was given lessons on the violin, which he disliked. At five he was given a quarter-size cello and took to it immediately.

Maurice's first lessons were with Stephane Odero who took him to hear Feuermann when he was ten. The boy was moved to tears and henceforth regarded Feuermann as his idol. At eleven he studied with Jean Mangot at the Nice Conservatoire and graduated with first prize at fourteen. At seventeen, he was lent a cello, given a rail ticket and 1,000 francs, to enable him to study with Gérard Hekking at the Paris Conservatoire. However, he had to sleep in unheated lodgings, and he sold newspapers in order to live.

During the 1939–45 war, Gendron was exempted from military service because malnutrition had made him unfit. Undeterred, he joined the Resistance and resolutely refused to play in Germany, a decision which nearly had him deported.

Through playing in a private concert with Jean Neveu, the pianist brother of the violinist, Ginette, he met many of the great painters, writers and musicians who had formed their own community in that city. Jean Cocteau, Braque, Marc Chagall and Picasso were to become his personal friends. Francis Poulenc and Jean Françaix, two of the many musicians whom he knew at this period, contributed considerably to his musical development, and he and Françaix gave recitals together for over 25 years.

Another close musical partnership was with Dinu Lipatti, the young Rumanian pianist who died at the age of thirty-three from leukemia. Gendron regards their collaboration as one of his great musical experiences: 'We rehearsed very little . . . with Dinu it was a perfect rapport. In Brahms, for instance, in soft passages, he never covered the cello—which is so very important. He could do it naturally without being superficial—because the music demands it. Not the cellist.'[16] They had planned to make recordings together, but were prevented because Lipatti was fighting a losing battle against illness.

Immediately after the war, through the art historian Kenneth Clark, Gendron met Benjamin Britten and Peter Pears in Paris. As a result, his solo début took place on 2 December 1945, at the Wigmore Hall in London, with Britten as his partner in sonatas by Fauré and Debussy. Sharing the same platform were two young Frenchmen, also at the start of what were to become distinguished careers in music—the singer, Pierre Bernac and the composer and accompanist, Francis Poulenc.

That same month, Gendron gave the European première of

Prokofiev's First Cello Concerto with the London Philharmonic Orchestra conducted by Walter Susskind, and subsequently played it everywhere. 'That', he says, 'is how I started my career. Nobody wanted to hear me, but they did want to hear the Prokofiev.'[17]

Concerts with Sargent and the LPO soon followed and his New York début took place at a memorial concert for Feuermann playing the Dvořák and the Haydn D Major Concertos. His association with Britten and Pears resulted in two appearances at the Aldeburgh Festival, the last occasion being when Gendron substituted for Rostropovich who had suddenly been taken ill. He also formed a trio with Yehudi and Hepzibah Menuhin that lasted for 25 years. They had first met when Menuhin, Britten and Gendron played the Beethoven and Mozart trios together.

Gendron has the unique experience of being the only solo cellist conducted by Casals on a commercial recording. He had visited Prades soon after Casals took up residence at the Villa Colette. Impressed with the younger man's playing, Casals congratulated him on not copying his own interpretation of the Bach Solo Suites. When Phillips asked Gendron to record the Boccherini B Flat Major and Haydn D Major Concertos with the Lamoureaux Orchestra, he suggested Casals as conductor. The recording company doubted if he would break with tradition and conduct another cellist, but Casals accepted immediately. This performance is also unique in that both concertos were played from the original scores which Gendron had discovered in the Dresden State Library. The final result was acclaimed by the critics and has remained a classic recording.

Undoubtedly, the musician who has exerted the greatest musical influence on Gendron is Emanuel Feuermann.

> I shall never forget the first time I heard him. It was quite unlike anything else I had ever heard. Not only was his technique wonderful, but his playing was so honest. He never compromised. Whatever difficulties he had, whether they were with the bow or the left hand, he never cheated. For me he is the image of perfection and it is what I've been trying to do all my life.[18]

Gendron has a lasting regret that he never studied with his idol. He met him several times and Feuermann repeatedly invited him to become his pupil but the financial means were never available—until it was too late.

When teaching, he tries to put Feuermann's ideas into practice with his own students. He has been a professor at the Paris

Conservatoire since 1970 and has taught in Saarbrücken, at the Mozarteum in Salzburg, the Academie Maurice Ravel in St Jean de Luz and at the Menuhin School in Surrey.

Gendron's own playing has always been distinguished by perfect technique combined with expressive tone quality. He pays great attention to phrasing, and his interpretation of French music in particular has a lucidity and a transparency that places it in a class by itself.

CHAPTER XXVII

American by Choice

FOR EVERY HUNGARIAN reputedly born with a violin under his chin a fair number have also taken early to the cello, and later followed distinguished international careers. America is one of the main countries where the musical life has been greatly enriched by their migration.

Three, who took out American citizenship, have something in common besides their mutual origin. Janos Scholz, the late Gabor Rejto, and Janos Starker were all students of Adolf Schiffer—a pupil of, and later assistant to the great David Popper at the Franz Liszt Academy of Music in Budapest.

One of the most loved and respected figures on the American cello scene, Janos Scholz, was born at Sopron in Hungary, an old Roman town on the Austro/Hungarian border. His grandmother came from Trieste, and he is proud of his quarter Italian heritage. He describes himself as 'a real Austro-Hungarian who still feels strongly his Hungarian roots'.

Scholz's family had lived in Sopron for 200 years and could boast many generations of amateur musicians. Janos, who had his first lessons at seven, was a fifth generation cellist, and the first professional. Every member of his family played an instrument, so from earliest childhood playing chamber music was a natural part of his environment.

In order to have a dependable profession to fall back on, should his musical ambitions not come to fruition, his family insisted that he have solid training at agricultural college. Scholz took his cello with him and, between classes in forestry and sugar-refining, he found time to practise. When he received his diploma he handed it to his mother and announced that he was going to Budapest to become a musician.

On graduating from the Royal Conservatory, he embarked upon a professional career, playing with local orchestras and in chamber-music groups. In 1932 he became the cellist of the celebrated Roth

String Quartet, and, when the portent of war cast its ominous
shadow over Europe, they took up an invitation to play in the USA.
It was in fact an exodus, for the other three members of the quartet
were Jewish. Scholz left Hungary with only a suitcase and his cello
and, following their successful tour, the quartet received American
citizenship.

When the Roth Quartet disbanded in 1939, Scholz continued his
career as soloist, chamber musician and principal cellist with the
City Center Opera in New York. He also played with the New
York City Symphony under Stokowski and the young Leonard
Bernstein. He confesses to prefer chamber music to any other form
of music-making: 'I was reared in chamber-music playing from the
beginning and I feel most at home sitting in a quartet concert playing
the bass for one of the great quartets.'[1] A treasured memory is
performing with Bruno Walter as pianist in the Archduke Trio of
Beethoven. He often played trios at home with Szigeti and Bartók:
'Szigeti was rather a shy man and Bartók hardly ever opened his
mouth to speak. It took them ten minutes before they were able to
select a piece of music.'[2]

In 1937 Scholz was invited to become a professor at the Conservatory in Budapest, but declined. A similar offer in 1948 was still not
accepted. However, he returned to see his family in 1973, and a
former pupil, who was now a professor at the Conservatory,
persuaded him to serve on the jury of an international competition
in Budapest.

Scholz was one of the founder members of the Violoncello Society
in New York in 1956 and served as its president from 1962–67. In
1973 he was the recipient of an award presented by the Society on
his seventieth birthday and his fortieth concert anniversary in North
America, 'in recognition of his dedication and contribution to the
Art of the Cello'.

For the past 25 years Janos Scholz has been active as a juror and
chairman of many international music competitions. His concert
appearances became less frequent but nonetheless continue. 'I still
play,' he says. 'The rest of my generation are either gone or retired.'
At seventy he flew to Budapest where he was busily engaged for ten
strenuous days.

First I played the Schubert C Major Quintet with the Bartók
Quartet in the great series of commemorative events of the
Hungarian Radio. Then, I gave a talk at the 'Society for Hungari-
ans Living Abroad' at the Ministry for Foreign Affairs. Following

Beatrice Harrison with her dogs

Emanuel Feuermann with Franz Rupp

Guilhermina
Suggia

Below: André
Navarra

Thelma
Reiss

Below: Maurice
Gendron

Gregor
Piatigorsky

Zara Nelsova

Bolognini's cello

Hideo Saito

Tsuyoshi Tsutsumi

Janos Starker

William Pleeth

Lawrence Foster
shortly before his
death

Mstislav
Rostropovich

Jacqueline du Pré with Sergio Peresson

that, I had a long interview session with the principal fellow of the Hungarian Radio and played the Debussy Sonata with an excellent pianist Marta Szaboky . . . By January 10 (1980) I was back in New York, where I repeated playing the Schubert Quintet with the Bartók Quartet, this time at the Pierpont Morgan Library.[3]

He is known at the Pierpont Morgan Library in two capacities: as a musical artist, and as one of their twenty Honorary Fellows—recognized by scholars all over the world. In 1973 he donated to the Library his valuable collection of Italian master drawings, which is said to be one of the finest in the world amassed by a private collector. His New York apartment is crammed with material acquired over a lifetime of collecting. Besides drawings, there are books, manuscripts, catalogues, sheet music, portfolios and a unique collection of 250 cello and gamba bows, all authentic specimens dating from 1740 to 1880 with examples from France, Germany, Italy and England. Each bow is described in minute detail on a card with a picture and measurements. Many of them have been restored to original playing condition by Scholz himself or by bow experts working under his guidance. This collection will eventually go to the Smithsonian Institution in Washington.

He has also fine examples of gambas and cellos. The instrument he plays upon at the present time is a 1731 Stradivarius, formerly owned by Joseph Hollman.

In 1981, the University of North Carolina at Greensboro conferred upon him the degree of Doctor of Humane Letters, *honoris causa*: 'For the diversity and distinction of your contributions to the arts, for bringing the best of the Old World to the New, and for the care and preservation of invaluable collections.' One part of the citation would seem to be particularly apt: 'Hungarian by birth and American by choice, you have shared your talents with your new countrymen in ways profoundly generous and practical.'[4]

A resident of the USA from 1939 until his death in 1987, Gabor Rejto was born in Budapest in 1916. He received his first instruction from Frederick Teller, a local teacher whose ideas, for the time, were exceptionally forward looking. At sixteen Rejto entered the Academy of Music under Schiffer, and two years later, with his Artist's Diploma, he embarked upon a European concert career.

At this time Budapest was an important centre for music, and Rejto felt he was privileged to have been there when visiting artists such as Heifetz, Huberman, Piatigorsky, Feuermann and Backhaus all played regularly in that city. He was similarly influenced by the great conductors, Klemperer, Furtwängler and Toscanini who also frequently appeared there.

At twenty, he went for two years' study with Casals, first in Barcelona and then in Prades. Like so many already experienced professionals, he had the naive notion that he would begin with enlarging his repertoire. 'We worked for almost a month on basic technique, not even basic literature, but *technique*. He really revolutionized the approach to the cello and at that time it was very modern.' Strangely enough Rejto found that the principles of his first teacher—whom he always considered very advanced, were reinforced when he began with Casals.

It was quite a revelation how carefully Casals went about everything to make cello playing similar to the violinist's technique. He was unique in this approach. His explanations were always logical . . . nothing was ever left to chance and he was able to explain with such attention and such love that it was never boring.

Gradually the musical ideas began to emerge; but it took me some time before I could incorporate and develop these ideas in my own playing. It was a wonderful experience and has always been the foundation on which I have based my own teaching.

Rejto was one of the first to admit that the strong influence of someone like Casals could be a danger because of the temptation to copy the master. The musical world is full of Casals' imitators, some of whom have managed to gain an impression with only a few lessons. 'I am sure that I have not consciously tried to imitate Casals, but irrespective, he remains one of the greatest influences of my musical life.'

Rejto held professorships at the Manhattan and Eastman schools of music and from 1954 until his death was professor of cello at the University of Southern California. He was also the cellist in a number of fine string quartets, including the Paganini and the Hungarian, and a founder member of the Alma Trio—in residence at the University of California. His chamber-music experience attracted many students to the Cello Workshops which he held throughout the USA.

At the 25th Anniversary Conference of ASTA (American String Teachers' Association) Gabor Rejto was chosen Artist-Teacher of the Year. Not surprisingly, when a questionnaire was sent out covering the entire USA he was one of three teachers with the greatest number of students. His classes seemed to flourish wherever he was based. He felt that if there were a reason it was because 'you cannot treat all students on the same level. They are all different. You must be really involved with them and be aware of their individual needs. Not only from the instrumental approach but also from a personal angle. You have to be a psychologist as well as an instructor.'[5]

Born in Budapest in 1924 of Russian parents, Janos Starker was given a cello at the age of six. 'My two brothers were violinists so I had no choice.'[6] When he was seven he entered the Franz Liszt Academy under Schiffer. Of this vintage era, with Jenö Hubay, Béla Bartók and Zoltán Kodály on the teaching staff and Erno Dohnányi as director, Starker says:

They created an institutional spirit. Not every student was a genius, but we had a core of teachers whose beliefs and musical understanding were identical, though they spoke differently about it. These musicians represented the kind of musical traditions which later came to the west. We could claim a line that reached back to those who know how the masterpieces in our repertoire should be played, because many had learnt from the composers themselves.

By far the most important influence on Starker at this time was Leo Weiner, who taught chamber music at the Academy.

Single-handed, Weiner was the person most responsible for the learning and understanding of music as a language by every prominent Hungarian musician who has appeared in the last fifty years. Antal Dorati, Eugene Ormandy, Georg Solti, Géza Anda, Gyorgy Pauk, the list is inexhaustible. He was not only the greatest pedagogue who ever existed, and though he travelled little, he knew everybody in his field.

At the age of eight Starker took on his first pupil, and as a veteran of twelve he had increased that number to five. His performing and teaching activities have always been parallel, a situation which proved to be enormously helpful in his later career. 'I had to explain why something is bad, or how to put the thumb here instead of there. For this experience I am eternally grateful.'[7] Meanwhile, as a

child prodigy, he appeared regularly in concerts, making his professional début playing the Dvořák Concerto at fourteen. In 1939 he
left the Academy (without graduating) and began playing concerts
in Hungary.

During the 1939–45 war, Hungary was a member of the Nazi
bloc. Conditions for following a solo career were so difficult that
during the final year of hostilities, he abandoned his cello altogether.
Picking it up again in the autumn of 1945, he became principal cellist
of both the Budapest Opera and Budapest Philharmonic orchestras.
In February 1946 he left Hungary and performed a concert with
resounding success in Vienna. Despite hardship, Starker remained in
Austria in order to prepare for the October 1946 Geneva Cello
Competition where he was awarded the bronze medal.

While in Austria Starker came to a terrifying conclusion.

I played like a blind man. What happens to the bird who sings
and doesn't know how it sings? That's what happens to child
prodigies. They wake up and ask themselves dangerous questions
about *how* they do it—and have no answers. I nearly had a
nervous breakdown. Consistency is the difference between the
professional and the amateur. I was grown up and could no longer
depend on instinct.[8]

Starker's successes in Vienna and Geneva brought him several
offers of concerts, but afraid to perform on stage alone, he went to
France where he joined a string quartet. It was during this period
that he began to think out his own ideas for developing the
technique of his instrument. He tried out his theories about
bowing, phrasing, breathing and the distribution of muscle-power
on his friends, many of whom were experiencing similar problems.
So began a lifetime of analysis and application, with perfection as
his ultimate goal—a target that he has never abandoned whatever
the circumstances.

By October 1947 he had regained his confidence in his skills and
resumed solo appearances, but travelling on a Hungarian passport
was virtually impossible. So, unhappy with the political climate in
Hungary, he stayed in the West.

After two years, living in Paris, he emigrated in 1948 to the
USA. Antal Dorati, then conductor of the Dallas Symphony,
invited him to be his principal cellist. After a single season, Fritz
Reiner offered Starker the job of principal cellist at the Metropolitan
Opera, a position he held for four years. When Reiner became
conductor of the Chicago Symphony Orchestra in 1953, he took

Starker with him as principal cellist. Starker worked for nine years under the man he considers one of the world's really great conductors. 'Playing with Fritz Reiner was one of the great joys of my life.'[9]

In 1954 Starker became an American citizen. With the outbreak of the Hungarian Revolution in 1956, he brought his family to America, and that same year made his recital début at the Wigmore Hall in London. Critics wrote about the 'intensity of his musical thought' and the 'electrifying mastery' with which he presented the Kodály Solo Sonata Op. 8.

Two years later, he resigned from the Chicago Symphony. He felt the time had come to resume the solo career that had already suffered so many interruptions. In retrospect he realizes that it was quixotic in the extreme, but maintains that he was never in doubt that he could make a living as a soloist.

Shortly after his resignation, Wilfred Bain, then Dean of Indiana University Music School in Bloomington, asked him to join the faculty. 'I agreed to go for two years as a kind of probation period. I saw Bloomington as many people still see it—a sleepy little midwestern town where nothing really happens. I thought I would stay not more than two years. This was in 1958, I'm still here and I think I shall be buried here.'[10]

The security of a university appointment helped Starker to re-embark upon his solo career. After his New York recital début, with pianist Mieczyslaw Horszowski at the Metropolitan Museum in April 1960, that astute critic from the *New York Times*, Harold Schonberg, remarked on his warm and colourful tone 'perfectly produced on any string, in any position. . . . He is a complete technician whose left hand always hits the note dead center and whose right hand wields a bow that is completely responsive.' He further commented on the fact that Starker is a musician who is responsive to style whatever the composer and that he was 'in sympathy with the text and the message'.[11]

Today, more than 25 years later, and with thousands of concerts and close to 100 recordings in between, Starker's reputation as soloist and teacher attracts students from all over the world. He gives full credit to the university for having enabled him to achieve this state of affairs: 'Bloomington is unique in what it offers the students. They have some of the best professors in America, all of whom are also internationally known performing artists.' He proudly points to his colleague and friend, Josef Gingold, like

Starker, a Distinguished Professor: 'He is the greatest violin teacher alive!'

Starker's own approach to teaching leaves no one in doubt as to his aims.

Every student has his or her individual way of playing, and it is the teacher's duty to help them to think for themselves. You give them the elements and teach them to understand why something does not work. I'm not coaching, I'm teaching. I do not want a sausage factory where they all come out alike. Students who have been taught this way will disappear because they have never been taught to think. The only thing you can recognize in my students is that they appear to be in control of their instrument when they are performing.

At the present time we are experiencing 'The Golden Age' of cello playing. Since the advent of players like Casals, and Feuermann—who, in my estimation, achieved the highest possible standards of playing—we are producing some incredibly fine cellists everywhere. But to become a concert artist is quite another matter. The great artist needs not only the elements of instrumental playing, which are rhythm, perfect intonation and tonal colour, but also many other qualities.

Starker admits to having a list of 40 prerequisities, including personality, stamina and the ability to get the musical message over to the audience. He maintains the first essential ingredient is absolute mastery of the instrument from the technical point of view. *Then* comes musical understanding.

This is the language of music. In order to communicate with differing audiences you must vary your musical language.

I am not only interested to teach the best students—those who win competitions—to satisfy my own pride. I am much more concerned that the continuity of teaching should be maintained on an increasingly higher level. Well-trained students will teach all over the world and teaching standards will naturally be raised. If I can be remembered as someone who has played a small part in consolidating good cello playing in the twentieth century because I used my knowledge to the best of my ability, it will all have been worth while.

In the past, some of Starker's critics have accused him of being a cold player. He refutes this idea by saying that some performers throw themselves around in an impassioned display because the audience finds it attractive. 'If you direct all your energy into the music itself there is no need to make all those gestures to convince people. If you are doing your job properly the music will speak for itself. I am much happier if after a concert people say "What beautiful music Schubert wrote", than "How well Starker plays".'[12] Whilst Starker's impeccable technique and seemingly effortless playing certainly confirm this view, his charisma is none the less compelling. His tone is clear and focused, a fine ribbon of sound infinitely preferable to the mushy, wide vibrato so often mistaken for 'feeling'. A glance through press cuttings spanning almost 30 years in the USA shows that critics are well able to assess his qualities, and strangely enough the emphasis throughout is far more on warmth of expression than on cold technical facility.

Disturbingly frank in his opinions, Starker has not gone out of his way to endear himself to some of the world's great conductors, and has had differences with many of them. For this reason his début with the New York Philharmonic was delayed until 1972. It was in 1985, when he was sixty, that Starker first appeared with the Philadelphia Orchestra under the baton of Klaus Tennstedt. Characteristically, he chose the Hindemith Concerto, a work that represented a challenge. The review by Daniel Webster in the *Philadelphia Inquirer* epitomizes everything that Starker stands for:

The performance had tensions that heightened every phrase. Starker maintained his proportions masterfully. . . . His ability to articulate rapid passages clarified writing that is often blurred in performance. The cadenza in the first movement, instead of launching him on a soaring self-congratulatary flight, showed him controlling all the dimensions of the showy writing and placing them all in relation to the music that had gone before.[13]

CHAPTER XXVIII

From Russia—with Talent

TWO OF THE most outstanding women cellists to achieve success in the USA during the first half of the twentieth century are Raya Garbousova and Zara Nelsova, both of whom are Russian in origin.

Raya Garbousova was born in Tiflis in Russia in 1909, where her father was principal trumpeter in the Tiflis Symphony Orchestra and professor at the Tiflis Conservatory. She was reared 'with little food but plenty of music' and began taking lessons on the piano at four. But when she heard her father's friend, Koussevitsky, playing the double-bass she decided that she would like to play the cello. 'Women don't play cello', was her father's reaction. Undeterred, the cunning little Raya deliberately kept herself from progressing on the piano in the hope that her father would eventually buy her a cello. Meanwhile, she consulted the principal cellist in the orchestra, Leopold Rostropovich, who told her that she might be given a cello when her hands grew bigger. So every day she stretched her hands; her persistence won the day and at six she was the proud owner of a small cello.

A year later she entered the local conservatory to study with Konstantin Miniar, a pupil of Davidov, and within a short time made her début in Tiflis. The critics stressed the fact that she was not a 'drilled' child prodigy and praised her performance commenting on her 'truly exceptional intuition for a musical phrase'. In subsequent appearances critics remarked repeatedly on her 'inexpressibly beautiful tone' and 'outstanding musicality'.

In 1924 Raya left with her mother for Moscow and Leningrad and, after a concert in the latter city, when she played the *Rococo Variations*, a critic compared her playing with that of the mature artist, Emanuel Feuermann, opting in favour of Garbousova's 'talent and depth of emotion'. Garbousova recalls that at this same time she played chamber music with two young musicians, famous then only in Russia, Nathan Milstein and Vladimir Horowitz.

In 1925 she went to Leipzig with the intention of studying with

Klengel. Through an interpreter she obeyed his every command to play the Third Caprice by Piatti, studies by Grützmacher and Popper, and sections of the Davidov Concertos. 'After three hours, when he realized I knew all the pieces, including all four Davidov Concertos, he told me that he couldn't teach me anything because I knew everything. This was not true but I couldn't argue with him.'

Undismayed, Garbousova proceeded to Berlin where she studied one summer with Hugo Becker. Again the results were disappointing. 'He was so dogmatic and based everything on logic, not on the individual requirements of each pupil. Ironically, he was obsessed with anatomy but never took into consideration the fact that no two people have the same anatomy.' However, there were compensations. 'He had a fantastic class. Mainardi, Eva Heinitz and many others who later became well known were there and we all helped each other.'[1]

Garbousova made her recital début in Berlin in 1926 at the Singakademie with the pianist Michael Taube, who was also a well known conductor. Critics raved about her 'colossal talent' and called her 'an exceptional musical phenomenon'. It was Taube who introduced her to the scientist Albert Einstein, who had a passion for the violin. 'I played chamber music with him and I'm sorry to say he was not very good. His vibrato was very odd and he was always a little bit out of tune. He also held the fiddle downwards pointing to the ground. But he was a wonderful old man. He always came to my concerts in Berlin and afterwards he would put a box of chocolates on the stage instead of flowers.'

From Germany, she went on to Paris where she enjoyed a success similar to that she had experienced in Berlin. It was here that she met and played for Casals, who gave her lessons and was most encouraging. He also invited her to play both the Haydn D Major Concerto and the *Rococo Variations* with the orchestra he conducted in Barcelona.

It was Casals who suggested she should study with Alexanian. Garbousova is certain that what she learnt from this very controversial teacher remains today her musical capital.

What I learnt from that man is quite amazing. He altered my whole approach to the techniques of the instrument. His influence remains one of the most important periods of development in my life. And I do not necessarily mean study on the instrument. We would sit together just talking and this led to the most important revelations regarding the music and the technique of the cello. He

influenced a great many eminent musicians and we were all
desperate when he died. He was such a knowledgeable man. His
playing itself was not attractive but this is quite unimportant
compared with what he did for music as a whole.[2]

The course of Garbousova's life was considerably influenced by
her contacts in Paris. The pianist, Ossip Gabrilovitch, first heard her
in that city and invited her to play the Haydn D Major Concerto
with the Detroit Symphony Orchestra of which he was conductor.
Afterwards Garbousova learned that he had sent telegrams to all the
leading conductors in the US. Koussevitsky, then the conductor of
the Boston Symphony Orchestra, was delighted to renew acquaintance with his old friend's daughter, and even more impressed with
her talent. He engaged her immediately for a concert with his
orchestra.

In December 1934 she made her recital début at the Town Hall in
New York and had Olin Downes from the *New York Times* waxing
lyrical, 'She has a wonderful wrist and bow arm, and a left hand of
the most exceptional fleetness and virtuosity. Miss Garbousova's
technique is the vehicle of a contagious temperament, musicianship
and taste. The crowning fact is the distinction of her style.'[3]

From this time onwards she appeared in concerts all over the
world, but made her home in Paris. Her first husband died fighting
in the French Resistance Movement in 1943, and in 1946 she became
a citizen of the USA where she met and married the cardiologist, Dr
Kurt Biss.

Garbousova plays all the romantic and classical repertoire but also
favours music by contemporary composers. She has been responsible for many first performances of modern works. It was she who
premièred the Martinů Third Sonata in the USA and she also
introduced the Prokofiev Sonata to that country. She recalls that
when she first had the score from Prokofiev she complained that the
metronome markings were too slow. She told him that they were
not in rhythm with her own pulse. Prokofiev's answer was unequivocal, 'Use your pulse. Players should have freedom.' And again, in
1946, before she gave the first performance of the Samuel Barber
Concerto with Koussevitsky and the Boston Symphony Orchestra—which was commissioned and written for her—the composer
consulted Garbousova frequently on the instrumental possibilities
related to the cello. It was published with the cello part edited by
Garbousova, and she also made a recording.

Koussevitsky, who had put her name forward as soloist for the

Barber, played a most important role in the promotion of contemporary music in general. He would say to the artists, 'In the eighteenth century there were the Esterhazys and the Rasoumovskys, but today we don't have such patrons, so you have to take their place. You, the artists—who are making good money—should commission works from the young composers. If you don't, music will die, because they will starve to death.' This dictum was carried to some lengths by Koussevitsky who positively threatened the more successful artists that, unless they commissioned works from some of the gifted young composers, he would not re-engage them. It usually had the desired effect, to the mutual benefit of all concerned.

Garbousova remains sprightly and alert and, although she no longer performs, is fully occupied with her teaching at the University of Northern Illinois.

Teaching is very important to me. It has become my second profession. I have no special method but I do place an emphasis on the physical approach to the instrument and on the absolute need for exposure—by which I mean performance. With my own students it is a two-way process. I learn from them and I hope they learn from me. It is certainly very satisfying to see my students in positions with great orchestras and as successful professors.

When it comes to master classes, which Garbousova takes all over the USA, she is very conscious of the ethics involved.

When you are telling students what they should do, it could be in direct contradiction to the advice of their own professors. So you must be careful. If it is possible I try not to know whose student I am dealing with. I don't like the advice to be a reflection on the teacher concerned. I have seen some very great teachers make *faux pas* because they went a little too far.[4]

There is another important residual from her teaching and communication with students. Through this very active little lady with an elephantine memory, students can have privileged glimpses of some of the great musicians of the past, for in her time she has been partnered at the piano in recitals by Harold Craxton, Horowitz, Solomon, Artur Balsam, Gabrilovitch and Harold Bauer. She has played chamber music privately with Prokofiev, Piatigorsky,

Rachmaninov, Milstein, Huberman, Szigeti, Szell, Erica Morini
and many times with her very close friend, Emanuel Feuermann.
She relates a wonderful story about a chamber-music interlude
with Heifetz and Feuermann, the latter playing second violin
holding the instrument upside down.

Garbousova's sense of fun permeates everything she does. At a
party, many years ago, she once took on a five-dollar bet to kiss
Toscanini who was sitting at the next table. The maestro was
delighted to be approached by such a beautiful young girl and
offered his cheek. Encouraged by his enthusiasm she kissed him on
both cheeks with the excuse that she could now claim ten dollars!

On a more serious memory, she reflects that even though Feuermann has been dead for so many years, she still feels the loss.

> We first met in Leningrad when I was eighteen. What was so
> amusing was that I, a mere nobody, was playing in the large hall,
> and he, then unknown in Russia, was playing in the small hall. I
> could not speak German and he had no Russian, but somehow we
> communicated. We loved each other from the minute we met.
> After the recitals we got together in our room in the hotel and my
> mother collected all the food she could find and we ate and we
> played together—everything in unison—halfway through the
> night. Feuermann had an enormous sense of humour, and was
> inclined to make rather sarcastic jokes at the expense of others
> but, much later when I got to know him better, I realized that he
> was really a very modest man and terribly self-conscious both
> about his music and himself.[5]

In a lifetime of performing and teaching, perhaps the summary
that most reflects the extent of her musical integrity and technical
ability, is by Lev Ginsburg, 'What is so good about Garbousova is
her fine sense of style, graphic interpretation, variable moods, and
of course, her virtuoso technique, which is always perfectly adjusted
to the power of the music.'[6]

Zara Nelsova was born in Winnipeg in Canada, the youngest
daughter of Gregor Nelsov, a flautist and graduate from the St
Petersburg Conservatory who had emigrated to Canada in 1910.

She showed interest in the cello when she was only four and a
half, and her father gave her her first lessons on a converted viola.
'He was a great teacher and much of what I acquired technically in

my early years, I attribute to him. He not only taught me discipline but also how to practise.'[7]

Her first public appearance at the age of five was in what was known as the 'Canadian Trio' with her two sisters on piano and violin. A year later she went to study with the émigré Hungarian, Dezso Mahalek, an ex-pupil of Popper.

It was on the advice of Sir Hugh Roberton, who had heard Zara play when he was adjudicating in Canada, that the family came to London in 1930 to complete their daughters' musical education.

It was hoped that Zara would be able to enter the Royal Academy of Music but she was far too young. Instead she was immediately accepted as a pupil of Herbert Walenn at the London Violoncello School, where for six years he took care of the technical side of her training and concentrated on building a repertoire. Milly Stanfield, also a Walenn student, remembers the impact the young girl had on the others in the class who were all much older. 'During a lesson, one of the students, who had been on the same boat from Canada, rushed in and said "She's a genius!" As Zara was so young, we thought Walenn would send her to one of his assistants, but he insisted upon teaching her himself.'[8]

That same year, the Canadian Trio played at the Wigmore Hall, and Zara made her orchestral début at a Patrons' Fund Concert at the Royal College of Music. Meanwhile, the twelve-year-old Zara Nelson—the family had anglicized the name—was engaged as soloist under Malcolm Sargent and the London Symphony Orchestra, to play the Lalo Concerto. Sargent was known to be somewhat sceptical over child prodigies, but the mature playing of this young Canadian won him over. Nelsova says, 'It was my first professional orchestral appearance and the memory is still vivid. I can still recall the excitement I felt at hearing the introduction of the Lalo. Sargent was wonderfully kind and inspired me with his great confidence. It was an unforgettable experience.'[9]

Her London recital début, at the Wigmore Hall in 1936, brought unusually enthusiastic comment from the press. The *Daily Telegraph* critic was in no doubt, 'There seem to be few problems which this player cannot solve with engaging ease and brilliance of effect.'

John Barbirolli—also a Walenn student—was greatly impressed with her talent. She played for him often and respected his advice. 'I learnt a great deal from him, and in particular I attribute my *sound* to my work with Barbirolli.' It was he who took her to play for Casals, who was most complimentary about her playing and predicted a successful future. For the small girl it was a memorable occasion, and from the first moment, it was her ambition one day to study with *le maître*. It was not until 1948 that she achieved her ambition, when she went to study with Casals for two summers in Prades. She feels that she benefited enormously from his influence. They met on many occasions afterwards and, as a fully-fledged artist in her own right, she was invited to appear as soloist at several of the Casals festivals in Mexico.

Two other great cellists who had considerable impact on her development were Feuermann and Piatigorsky.

My studies with Feuermann were of short duration because of his untimely death, but what I learnt has been of the greatest value. When I went to him my technical equipment was already well-established but I was greatly influenced by his superb yet simple way of playing. The economic use of the left hand—the ever-perfect co-ordination and the simplicity of his interpretations was a profound influence which has never left me.[10]

At the outbreak of the 1939–45 War, the family moved to the USA, and it was not until Nelsova's début recital in the New York Town Hall in 1942, when critics acclaimed her 'impeccable performance', that she felt she was truly launched. From this time onwards she steadily built up a reputation as a distinguished artist fulfilling the demands of an international career meeting with continuing success. She has appeared with almost every major orchestra and under most leading conductors. In 1966 she was the first American cellist to tour the Soviet Union, and when she played the Rachmaninov Sonata and the Kodály Solo Sonata in Moscow, the audience went wild with enthusiasm. Lev Ginsburg wrote: 'Never to be forgotten are the nobility and temperament of her interpretation, the beautiful and expressive sound, her artistry and skill, and the extraordinary precise rhythm.'[11]

Nelsova has premièred a number of modern works. In 1949 she gave the first British performances of sonatas by Shostakovich and Hindemith, and in 1951 the European première of the Barber Concerto at a BBC studio performance with the BBC Symphony Orchestra conducted by Sir Adrian Boult. She has vivid memories of this performance, since because of other commitments she learned and memorized the concerto in less than three weeks. It was an unqualified success and, as a result, she was invited to record the concerto with Samuel Barber conducting. At the end of the recording session a cellist from the orchestra leapt to his feet and rushed to where Nelsova was sitting and screamed that he could never again play the cello after hearing her. He then proceeded to smash his cello against the wall to the accompaniment of loud applause from his colleagues. Nelsova realized that they had obviously picked up a cheap cello to make the symbolic gesture, but it was a unique way of demonstrating their regard for her artistry.

In 1949 she met the composer, Ernest Bloch, and was asked to participate in the Bloch Festival in London. She played *Schelomo* with the composer conducting and also recorded it with him. She also recorded the *Prayer, Supplication and Jewish Song* with Bloch at the piano. After this, the composer would often say 'Nelsova *is* my music'—she has a photograph of Bloch which is dedicated 'To Madame Schelomo'.

Teaching is a passion—at present she teaches at the Juilliard School in New York and the University of Cincinnati. In addition, she fulfils a busy concert schedule and regularly gives master-classes. The pianist, Julian Dawson-Lyell, her accompanist on one occasion, commented, 'I was immensely impressed by her unfailing patience with every problem, even when these problems were repeated in student after student [she instructed some twenty] as is inevitable in master classes; by her intense powers of concentration, so that every cellist was made to feel he was getting her full attention; and above all by her undying love for music which she must have performed thousands of times.' With Nelsova it seems it is not a question of dishing out fingerings and bowings plus a few musical points, but, 'rather the student was led to experience the work at a much deeper level of emotional and intellectual involvement, and to regard technique as inseparable from expression'.[12]

On the concert platform, Zara Nelsova compels attention, not only for her good looks but also for her impeccable taste in billowing full-length gowns, cunningly designed to give the impression that her cello is floating in space. She is that rarity today, the artist who is dramatic in character with a style and personality that attracts the audience like a magnet. But she is also one of the finest cellists of her generation. When she played the Saint-Saëns Concerto in A minor in Los Angeles in 1984—a work she must have played hundreds of times, the critic from the *Los Angeles Times* wrote, 'It emerged sounding fresher and more compelling than it has for a long time. It embodied an appropriate conception of the French style, polished but never bloodless, lyrical without license and continuously communicative.'[13]

The kind of situation that Nelsova's breadth of style can meet is exemplified in a story dating from the middle fifties. She arrived late for her first appearance of the winter in West Germany, her plane having been grounded in Ireland. There was no time for rehearsal and she reached the hall only minutes before the concert was due to begin. During the first item she began to practise the Dvořák Concerto, and was surprised when the librarian—who had come to welcome her—asked if she were playing that at her next concert. When she was seated on the platform she realized the significance of the question. Instead of the vigorous opening tutti of the Dvořák, she heard the introduction to the Tchaikovsky *Rococo Variations* which she had not played since the previous year. Without batting an eyelid she rose to the challenge and played magnificently. The letter advising her of the change of programme had missed her while she was travelling.

Nelsova plays on a magnificent Stradivari, dated 1726, known as the 'Marquis de Corberon' which has been loaned to her for life by the late Mrs Audrey Melville of London. She is so devoted to this instrument that, since it came into her possession, she has never seen fit to use any other.

CHAPTER XXIX

The Japanese Phenomenon

ONE OF THE most remarkable developments in the last twenty years has been the increasing number of fine string players emerging from the Orient. Not only are they making a definitive mark upon the great orchestras of the world, but also as first class soloists in their own right. Japan has contributed greatly to this influx and it is now an accepted fact that many students from that country display an advanced degree of technical skill, often comparing favourably with that of the West which has the advantage of tradition. It is nothing short of miraculous considering that, in a truly professional sense, 'Western' string playing has, in Japan, been taught at an institution only since 1948.

The pioneer in this movement was Hideo Saito (1902–74), a man whose European associations, allied to an extraordinary vision and integrity of character, changed the face of music in Japan.

Born in Tokyo into a wealthy academic family, Hideo was originally destined for an academic career. His father, a distinguished scholar, was an expert in studies of the English Language, and the first person to make a complete English-Japanese dictionary. His interest in Western literature coloured Hideo's approach to music, which, initially, was on the piano. Each of his eight brothers and sisters played a musical instrument but only for private pleasure.

At fourteen he had progressed sufficiently well to be allowed to conduct a local mandolin orchestra which, though not outstanding, provided him with valuable experience. It was this that prompted him, at sixteen, to learn the cello, much against his family's wishes. His father made it clear that he thought it preferable to be a bad teacher of English than any kind of a cellist!

At eighteen Saito entered Sophia University to study Modern Languages specializing in German. Nonetheless, his longing to continue his studies on the cello never diminished. During this time he had become associated with Prince Konoe, a member of the royal family, professor and conductor of the university orchestra, who later became one of the most important conductors in Japan. In 1923, when Konoe went to Leipzig, he took young Saito with him.

The difference between performing standards in Germany and Japan came as a shock and Saito decided he must stay in Leipzig to improve his own knowledge. For four years he studied with Klengel at the Conservatoire where two of his fellow students were Feuermann and Piatigorsky. Saito used to tell a story about the time when he secretly copied down Klengel's fingering of one of the Bach Suites. When he played it to his master, Klengel said, 'Oh no! Don't use *my* fingering. There's a newcomer on the scene called Casals who plays extremely well. Much better to see what he does.'

When he returned to Japan in 1927, Saito became principal cellist in the New Symphony Orchestra, conducted by Konoe. At the same time he appeared as a soloist in recitals and started teaching. He was also the first to organize chamber music in Japan. It was when his ideas were put into practice that he realized he still had much to learn. In 1930 he returned to Germany to study for two further years, this time with Feuermann at the Hochschule in Berlin.

Feuermann made the deepest impression on Saito, every one of whose students confirms that there was never a lesson without at least one mention of his mentor's name. However, Feuermann's strictness and insistence on students getting things right presented problems. Saito recalls that for him—coming from the East where there is a completely different set of manners—it was extremely difficult to understand Feuermann's sarcasm. For someone from an oriental background, and only just beginning to understand what cello playing was about, it was hard to readjust. He felt constantly threatened, especially when Feuermann said he would disown him as a pupil if he did not practise. Even in a bus or a train, Saito was practising mentally. By all accounts it was of benefit, for when he returned to Japan, he recognized the marked improvement in both his left and right hand technique. He went back to the NHK Symphony Orchestra (formerly the New SO) and at the same time continued his other musical activities.

The following year Joseph Rosenstock came from Germany to be principal conductor of the orchestra, and Saito seized the opportunity to have lessons with him. He regarded this as a very important development in his musical training. He valued the strict and precise methods adopted by Rosenstock and it was from him that Saito learnt the clear beat that later became the hallmark of his own conducting.

At the end of the 1939–45 war Saito again became active in

organizing the teaching of music. His first important venture was to open a school for conducting, and many musicians came to him for instruction. In order to establish continuity between what he had learned in Europe and what he was doing in Japan, he promoted chamber-music concerts. These were immensely popular and proved to him that if he could only graft Western music on to Japanese culture it would take root, and eventually send out its own shoots.

Saito recognized that in order to establish any lasting influence upon the musical life of Japan he would need to start with the children. He knew from his European experiences that, with string playing in particular, it was necessary to start very early. So it was on the children that he pinned his hopes.

In 1948 he founded the first children's music school, renting classrooms in a building attached to Tokyo Kasei Gakuen, a finishing school for girls, and worked tirelessly to develop this centre where children could begin their studies in the right way. Japanese schools demand a full daily attendance and a half day on Saturday. So, with about twenty children—their mothers in attendance—he started Saturday afternoon classes for lessons on the violin, cello and piano. As they advanced he provided chamber-music classes. Two years later he formed a children's orchestra, the first of its kind in Japan.

Saito's logical mind and obsession with continuity told him that it was no use training young children if they had no place for further education. So he persuaded the board members of Toho Gakuen to allow him to set up a music high school for his students in the fifteen to eighteen range. In 1952, the Toho Gakuen High School of Music was founded. Shortly after, it became the Toho Gakuen College of Music, where students from eighteen to twenty-two could, for the first time in Japan, be awarded a diploma or a degree in music. Practically every prominent Japanese musician who was trained at this time was a pupil of Saito.

Meanwhile the Toho Children's Orchestra was developing fast. The standards improved to such an extent that in 1964 Saito took them on an American tour, where their audiences were wildly enthusiastic. The same orchestra also went on an extensive tour of the USSR and Eastern and Western Europe, with similar success.

From this time he worked incessantly to promote and develop Western music in Japan, and although he was successful in persuading many wealthy firms and families to sponsor his projects, the increasing need for funds made a considerable hole in his own pocket. But, devoted to his students to the end, he always had time for them whatever they needed from him.

Saito had a lively interest in many subjects outside music. He knew about everything that was going on in the world and could converse equally well on art, literature or recent scientific discoveries. An excellent linguist, he was fluent in German, French and English and also spoke some Chinese—a very rare accomplishment at that time.

In 1974 he prepared his orchestra for a second American tour. He knew that his health would not stand up to the strain but worked with the children regardless. He died on the eve of its departure. Despite the tragedy, the tour went ahead—which would have been his wish.

On that occasion the orchestra was conducted by the young Seiji Osawa. Whatever his commitments, Osawa returns regularly to teach at the Toho School, because he and every other Japanese musician of his generation know how much they owe to 'Old Saito'.

No musician who has emerged from Japan in the last 30 years is without Saito's influence. The cellists, Yoritoyo Inoue, Takeichiro Hirai, Tsuyoshi Tsutsumi, Ko Iwasaki, Kenichiro Yasuda, Hirofumi Kanno, Mari Fujiwara and Nobuko Yamazaki all studied at some time with this incredible man.

Yoritoyo Inoue, born in Tokyo in 1912, did not start on the cello until he was seventeen. A pupil of Saito for ten years, he also had a few lessons with Feuermann when he visited Japan. In 1937 he became a member of the NHK Symphony Orchestra.

From 1945–48 he was a prisoner of war in Russia and on his return to Japan helped Saito to organize the music school for children. Subsequently he was appointed professor at Toho Gakuen College of Music, but at the same time continued his performing career. Inoue also took part in the first performances in Japan of the Debussy String Quartet, the late Beethoven Quartets, the Schubert String Quintet, and many works by Prokofiev, Bartók and Shostakovich.

Inoue is active in every field of music and has served on a number of international juries. In 1974 and 1978 he was the Japanese representative on the Jury of the Fifth and Sixth International Tchaikovsky Competition in Moscow.

Takeichiro Hirai, born in Tokyo in 1937, had his first music lessons on the piano and in composition from his father, Kozaburo Hirai, a well-known composer. Takechiro had composed over one hundred compositions before he took up the study of the cello at thirteen with Saito. At fifteen he made his first concert appearance and two years later graduated from the Toho School with the Mainichi Prize.

In 1957 Hirai was awarded a special prize in the First Casals Cello Competition in Paris and, on the recommendation of Piatigorsky, studied with Casals at Puerto Rico from 1957–61.

Hirai made his New York début in 1961 and since then has followed a busy international career as soloist, composer, editor and teacher at the Toho School.

A Saito pupil who has achieved an international reputation is Tsuyoshi Tsutsumi, born in Tokyo in 1942 into a family of professional musicians. His father had studied the cello with Uhichi Ohmura, a pupil of Feuermann, who was principal cellist in the NHK Symphony Orchestra. He also played the double-bass and taught all the stringed instruments at a school in Tokyo.

At the age of six, Tsuyoshi began learning the violin in a Suzuki school. When he was eight, a violin dealer and friend of his father showed him a half-size cello. The boy was so enchanted with its sound that he immediately wanted to study it.

Tsuyoshi's father was his instructor for the first year, and at nine he went to study with Hideo Saito at his Children's Music School. The young boy developed quickly, but was not happy when he was put to learning the Bach Suites.

Mr Saito was insistent upon the suites being learnt from memory, and made me write in almost everything that was concerned with the music, phrasing, harmonic structure and so on. Most of his approach was direct from Feuermann. We went through the suites three times, and eventually I began to have my own ideas and felt better about them. I owe him a tremendous amount for his teaching of those suites.

Although I had weekly lessons with him for ten years, I was never ever bored. Every time I learnt something new. Even if we were going over the same material he was able to explain things from a completely different point of view so that you never felt he was repeating anything.

Saito had a very special gift for teaching children. He could explain in terms that children could understand but he never talked down to them. He used images quite a lot and it was nothing unusual to have something explained by way of talking about cream cakes or the way a periscope popped its head out of the water with the submarine underneath.

All the leading cellists of today attended Saito's class, but none of them play in the same way. He allowed them to develop their individual style—in my opinion, the mark of a good teacher. [Clearly a legacy from Klengel.]

Saito also saw to it that his students became all-round musicians. 'He was very keen on small chamber-music groups and was himself very active in piano trio and string quartet playing, so I think I learned from him in these three areas, solo, chamber music and orchestral playing.'[1]

Tsutsumi made his first solo appearance at the age of twelve, playing the Saint-Saëns Concerto with the Tokyo Philharmonic Orchestra conducted by Saito. There followed engagements with all the leading Japanese orchestras. After his graduation in 1961, a Fulbright scholarship made it possible for Tsutsumi to go to Indiana University to study with Janos Starker.

Tsutsumi compared his two teachers, whom he claims were both very strict.

Saito solved the problems more on a human basis. If someone did not practise, he was not too upset. But he minded very much if you did not put enough effort into the study in hand. He considered that was laziness and he could become very angry. Starker would be furious if I didn't practise but it was more from the professional aspect. He maintained that if one did not practise, the playing was sloppy and scratchy and he couldn't bear it. I never perfected my technique but I tried very hard. Starker admired Saito's teaching and appreciated what I had done with him, and tried to build upon that foundation. He didn't really change anything basic, but gave me the professional background. I had to start all over again with scales—I think I must be the only pupil who had to do so. But he insisted that I work at scales and at bowing. He wouldn't allow me to leave a single piece until I'd improved my bowing. Then I was given a Vivaldi concerto. Mr Starker has a beautiful bow arm and his playing is so clean. This is what he aimed for, so I tried to tidy up my own playing.

Starker's gift for 'bringing out' his students if they are too reserved, was invaluable to Tsutsumi.

He is very keen that musicians should be able to express themselves verbally as well as musically. Basically, I'm rather a quiet person so he worked hard to make me more extrovert. He would say it was no use being like an oriental Buddha, so that nobody knows what one is thinking. He also liked his students to speak out in class, especially if we had to give an opinion about someone else's playing. For me this was very difficult because I not only lacked the confidence to express an opinion, I was afraid that if I used the wrong grammar I could be misunderstood.

Lessons with Starker consisted of 45 minutes' discussion on cello technique and the music, and fifteen minutes' playing the cello. With Saito there had been much more playing. Starker has such a broad view of everything artistic. We often talked about art and he would illustrate a point by referring to a certain painting or artist. It was a very influential and rich period in my life. I was so lucky that I first had Saito and then Starker both with an all-embracing view of their respective cultures. In my case the East and the West came together very well.[2]

Less than two years later, Tsutsumi became Starker's assistant, and stayed at Indiana for six years. In his last year, he was appointed Artist-in-Residence.

During this time he won several competitions and in 1964 gave début recitals in New York and London. The critics praised his luscious tone and his 'impeccable' fingerwork. He subsequently made successful solo appearances in the USA and Europe.

Tsutsumi's recording of the Dvořák Concerto, with the Czech Philharmonic Orchestra under Zdenek Kosler, is a fine example of his very sensitive playing, and belies the assumption that the Japanese are wonderful technicians but lack emotion. Tsutsumi believes that this is a shortcoming that Saito went a long way to solve.

I think that he recognized this problem himself when he saw the contrast between what he heard in Japan and in Europe. I feel sure that this was the reason he made me learn the Bach Suites at such an early age. He realized that it is no use just copying, but that it is essential for musicians to know what the composer is saying and must try to express this by way of their own interpretation. Saito used to say that one day some sort of style in Japanese string playing will emerge. Not in my generation but perhaps in the next. He always had this kind of vision and we who learned so much from him are grateful that he is finally being recognized as the great pioneer that he was. He had a very hard time getting his ideas across to people and they were unwilling to accept them.

There is little doubt that the Japanese are now acknowledging Saito's tremendous contribution to the development of all music and especially cello playing in his own country. In 1984, on the tenth anniversary of his death, a Memorial Concert was held in Tokyo in which a selected symphony orchestra was conducted by Seiji Osawa. The programme included Strauss's *Don Quixote* with Tsutsumi, the violist, Nobuko Imai and the violinist, Toru Yasunaga, now concertmaster of the Berlin Philharmonic Orchestra. 'It was an incredible occasion. The entire orchestra were graduates of the Toho Gakuen School and former students of Saito. It was only then that I saw and heard for myself how widely his influence has spread.'

Tsutsumi's repertoire includes most of the standard works but he is also a firm advocate of modern music. Like Rostropovich he is convinced that the future of the cello lies in the music that is now being written for it. Tsutsumi is fascinated by the phenomenal upsurge of contemporary Japanese composers.

The diversity of styles among our composers is quite remarkable. There are some interesting attempts to put together the Western and Japanese idiom with a synthesiser and the results are most interesting. *Musique concrète* and twelve tone techniques are all explored in interesting ways. But there are also composers who write music which is individual in style and owe nothing to these kind of experiments or to Western composers. They seem to have found something that is individual and modern and yet is still Japanese. I do not know why or how this has happened. It is also encouraging that young people in Japan are so enthusiastic about contemporary music.[3]

Kenichiro Yasuda, born in Tokyo in 1944, began his studies with Saito at the Toho Gakuen School and later studied with Cassadó and Fournier. It was winning third prize in the Tchaikovsky International Competition in Moscow in 1966 that launched him on an international career. A Russian critic remarked that despite his slight stature he possessed the ability to conquer by his will power and 'nobly virile performance'. It is interesting that the observer considered him 'an audacious disturber of traditions' and that his performance of the *Rococo Variations* differed from the accepted interpretation.

Yasuda lived for some time in Geneva, taking part in solo and chamber-music playing in the Lucerne Festival. He returned to Japan in 1974 and continues to enjoy a busy performing career. He also teaches at the Toho Gakuen School.

Another student of Saito's, and prizewinner in the Tchaikovsky Competition in 1970, is Ko Iwasaki, born in 1944 in Taiwan. Ko studied with Saito at the Toho Gakuen School at the age of eleven and later received a Fulbright Scholarship which enabled him to join Leonard Rose's class at the Juilliard School in New York. He also studied for a time with Harvey Shapiro and, finally (aided by a Rockefeller Scholarship), with Casals in Puerto Rico.

In an article about the 1970 Tchaikovsky Competition, a Soviet critic praised his magnificent command of the instrument and remarked upon his creative maturity and devotion to his art. The Adagio in Beethoven's Fifth Sonata, was 'worthy of a great artist'. Daniel Shafran, a member of the jury, commented on his 'bright originality, self-absorption, inner artistry'.[4]

Since 1974 Iwasaki has been teaching at Illinois State University but still continues a busy concert career, sometimes a little more ubiquitous than he bargains for. Once, when the soloist engaged to play with the Hong Kong Philharmonic Orchestra was taken ill, Iwasaki was the last-minute substitute. It took him 24 hours to fly to Hong Kong, arriving at 8 a.m. on the day of the concert. Neither at rehearsal nor performance did his playing show any sign of strain. Next day, a critic wrote, 'This was eminently stylish playing, with Mr Iwasaki's flawless technique and perfect intonation making it possible for him to express the most intense emotions. He was able to sustain his line through the welter of decoration that Tchaikovsky built around the theme in the *Rococo* variations.'[5]

Hirofumi Kanno, born in Tokyo in 1947, began lessons with Saito at the age of seven and continued with him at the Toho Gakuen School. On his graduation in 1970, he went to study with Fournier in Switzerland and two years later with Janos Starker at Indiana University. In 1975 Kanno became Starker's assistant.

During this time Kanno continued to follow his solo career and in 1974 was awarded third prize in the Tchaikovsky Competition in Moscow. Daniel Shafran wrote that he 'attracted everybody's attention in the second round by his individual playing style and his special ability to penetrate the music. . . . His playing is marked by a flight of imagination, a clear understanding of what the composer intended, and a subtle comprehension of the music texture. All these qualities were highlighted in his performance of the Rondo by Kabalevsky [for which he received a special prize] and *Bunraku* for cello solo by his compatriot Mayuzumi.' Shafran goes on to point out that Kanno was one of the few whose playing progressively improved in each round and that his playing of the Dvořák Concerto in the final round was excellent.

Kanno himself has no doubts as to his approach.

A musician should first of all be honest and sincere in his music and should be able to look inside himself. I do not accept the idea of catering to the public's taste and ceasing to be your own self. In music, like in life, you have to have your own face, your unique creative individuality. Only then, provided that one has virtuoso technique and a consistent objective, can a musician become a true artist.[6]

Mari Fujiwara, born in Osaka in 1949, was the first Japanese woman to succeed in following a professional career as a solo cellist. Her first cello lessons at the age of seven were with Saito and she continued to study with him at the Toho Gakuen School. She graduated in 1972 and began a successful solo and chamber-music career which has attracted critical attention, not only in her own country but in the USSR, Finland and Holland. She won second prize at the Moscow Competition in 1978.

Fujiwara's recording of the Bach Suites was recommended by several reviewers, and the comment by David Vernier in *Digital Audio*, June 1986, is interesting: 'Fujiwara has discovered and revealed the more subtle shadings of Bach's almost endless solo lines. She's able to combine sensitivity and power almost at the same moment, caressing and shaping each phrase with a confidence that makes her playing seem effortless.'

Another young woman now following a busy solo career, Nobuko Yamazaki, born in 1953, was Saito's last pupil at the Toho Gakuen School. She also had some instruction from Mari Fujiwara, Yasuda, Tsutsumi and the visiting French professor Reine Flachot. The French influence continued when she received a scholarship from the Japanese government to study for two years with Pièrre Fournier in Geneva.

The Japanese string player in general is now an accepted part of the international musical scene. It would seem also that first-class solo cellists are as plentiful as they are in the West. That they are to be reckoned with in international competitions proves itself time and time again.

It is now more than a decade since Daniel Shafran, summing up the Fifth Tchaikovsky Competition in Moscow, remarked upon the fact that Hirofumi Kanno had won a prize that year and that Yasuda and Iwasaki had been prizewinners in previous years. 'One can maintain that the success of all three is not a chance phenomenon, it shows the undoubted achievements of the Japanese performing school as a whole.'[7]

CHAPTER XXX

The British Heritage

FROM A SLOW start in the eighteenth century, British cellists have progressed considerably in 200 years: a number of excellent cellists have either made international careers or achieved distinction as teachers.

Herbert Walenn and Ivor James, two of the best known teachers born in the nineteenth century, have clearly influenced the training of most of the better known cellists born in the first half of the twentieth. Added to this is the influence of Klengel, Becker and Feuermann—often through a second generation. Finally, there is the indisputable impact of Casals—both direct and indirect—which has had a profound effect on the development of a British tradition. In all, a rich heritage which continues to provide a firm and healthy line that presages well for the future.

In the period just before the war, and for a decade after, the name of Thelma Reiss was known internationally as one of the most outstanding British cellists. Born in Plymouth in 1906, her father was a sailor in the Royal Navy who died in the 1914–18 war. Her mother sang and played the violin and, in order to supplement her meagre pension, she gave singing lessons.

Thelma's musical gifts showed at a very early age and she could play the piano by ear before she had even set eyes on the cello. Her mother picked up a small cello for £3 in a junk shop, and when it was handed to her, she at once played all the tunes she knew, running through the entire compass of the instrument. She then received weekly lessons from a cellist in the Royal Marines Band at Plymouth. At the age of seven, after only nine months' tuition, she played the Goltermann Concerto in public. Subsequently, in order to pay for her cello lessons, she toured the west country as a prodigy, working as a child entertainer, singing, dancing, playing both piano and cello. At eleven, Thelma was holding down her first professional job as the cellist in a trio in a Swiss restaurant in Plymouth.

Fortunately, her mother knew that if the child was to survive the prodigy years she would need some serious musical training. The opportunity came when, at thirteen, she won a scholarship to the Royal College of Music in London to study with Ivor James. She has always been grateful to him for recognizing her particular talent, even though she was so young, and never once tampering with her interpretations.

On leaving the College, the next years were hard going. Sandwiched in between her serious concerts there was an inevitable return to the round of jobs in cafés, night clubs and theatres. On one occasion she even appeared in a variety act on a pier.

In 1930, Reiss gave her first London recital at the Wigmore Hall with the pianist, Joan Black, a fellow student at the College. An enthusiastic press brought her an immediate engagement to play the Elgar Concerto under Sir Henry Wood at a Prom at the Queen's Hall. She also played chamber music with Harriet Cohen, John Ireland, Albert Sammons, John Hunt, and many times with Myra Hess, whom she admired greatly and came to know quite well.

From this point Reiss's career prospered. She was a frequent broadcaster and played regularly in the Proms and other concerts. She also travelled the world and was hailed as the 'great English cellist'. Her attractive appearance and warm platform personality endeared her to audiences everywhere. After a performance in Madrid, a Spanish critic compared her playing to that of Casals.

In 1939 in Ludwigshafen, Germany, with the State Orchestra under Ernst Boehe, Reiss played the Haydn D Major Concerto to audiences of 5,000 on two days in succession. She recalls that in the artists' room there hung a number of photos of famous artists. When she returned from the platform she was told that hers was to be placed next to that of Brahms. But after the war she heard that she and Brahms and all that famous company had been blown sky-high by a British bomber. In February of that same year, she performed the Brahms Double Concerto with Arthur Catterall under Weingartner at a Royal Philharmonic Society Concert at the Queen's Hall. She often shared recitals with great singers, and once remarked wryly that she started her performing life playing alongside amateurs who sometimes made the most excruciating noises, and ended up on the same platform with glorious singers like Elisabeth Schwarzkopf and Paul Robeson.

Despite her success on the concert platform, Thelma Reiss's early life had been fraught with problems. As a child, due to extreme privation, she contracted tuberculosis, which was fortunately cured, and at twenty-two she was dangerously ill wtih typhoid fever. After that she was blessed with splendid health and was able to sustain a long and successful career. But in 1955 she suffered a serious loss of strength and had to retire from the concert platform, though her naturally ebullient and optimistic nature enabled her to present a confident image to the outside world. She now lives in retirement in Suffolk, and has become a keen gardener.

She looks back with much gratitude for her 'wonderful life of music' and recalls the struggles of her early days with an all-pervading sense of humour. Those who heard her say that her playing was distinguished by a beautiful tone that was never forced. Perhaps the most telling description comes from the *Hamburger Anzeiger*, after her first appearance in Germany, in 1937. Following a headline, 'We simply could not leave the hall!' the critic wrote:

> After the first bars of the Sammartini Sonata . . . we knew what kind of artist we had with us last night. A cellist of outstanding ability whose marvellous technique constrains devout admiration, and whose playing moves the audience from beginning to end, whether it is Bach, Haydn, Debussy or Granados. Here we had a human being with the power of creation given only to a genius by the grace of God. One was thankful for the wonderful gift of the evening. No wonder that her success was sensational![1]

Antonia Butler, best known today as a teacher, was born in London in 1909 into a family steeped in music. Her father was an amateur violinist, and one of her earliest childhood memories is of Joachim's great nieces, the d'Aranyi sisters, coming to the house to play chamber music and rehearse their concertos with her mother, an amateur pianist.

Antonia first learnt the cello at the age of ten and later, through her parents' association with the d'Aranyis, spent four years with Klengel at the Leipzig Conservatoire and went on for a further period of study with Alexanian at the Ecole Normale in Paris. She is convinced that these three years were of the greatest importance, mainly because she stayed the course with Alexanian.

In the early 1930s, although she had given a successful Wigmore Hall début, and was getting a number of engagements, Butler began to have some doubts about her bowing. The solution was provided by a fellow artist, the French cellist, Juliette Alvin, 'who had a beautiful bow arm and seemingly without effort achieved the most

clear and carrying sound'. The remarkable result of this extra period
of study was that, by working with Alvin on open strings and one
of the Kreutzer violin studies, Butler was able to overcome the
difficulty while continuing her performances.

A few months later, when Butler was asked at short notice to
replace Thelma Reiss playing the Haydn D Major Concerto in the
Proms, the new approach proved its worth. 'I shall always be
grateful to Juliette for opening a door when I most needed it.'

It was also the Haydn D Major Concerto that Butler was due to
play at the Three Choirs Festival in 1939, but the outbreak of war
called a halt to all concert performances. 'It was disappointing. I had
had my first rehearsal for the concerto that morning when it was
announced that the festival would not be taking place. I was also
going to play trios with Jelly d'Aranyi and Myra Hess and I much
regretted that it never materialized.'

Butler's first performance of the Brahms Double Concerto was at
a Prom at the Queen's Hall in August 1940 with the violinist, Arthur
Catterall. She remembers this occasion very well because the air-
raid warning sounded half-way through the evening. The concert
continued, since regulations forbade people to go into the streets
during a raid, and nobody could leave the hall. The musicians
banded together to provide an extended programme. Antonia Butler
and Harvey Phillips played a two-cello arrangement of the two-
violin sonata of Handel, followed by the Schumann Piano Quintet,
and so on throughout the night. In the early hours of the morning
the All Clear signal was given and audience and musicians departed
tired but happy. 'To me it was the most exciting and inspiring
experience and symbolic of good triumphing over evil.'

Antonia Butler later played the Brahms Double Concerto with
leading violinists and conductors of the period. She feels that her
interpretation was greatly influenced by her studies with Klengel. 'I
was very privileged to have studied this work with him and to have
performed it twice with the Conservatoire Orchestra in Leipzig. He
had heard Joachim and Hausmann play it many times and [they]
passed on much good advice especially on *tempi*.'[2]

Following the initial uncertainties of the war, concerts were
resumed. Of particular importance were the lunchtime series given
at the National Gallery, organized by Myra Hess and a devoted band
of musicians who were determined that, despite the air-raids,
Londoners should still have their music. Many people had their first
taste of classical music at those concerts and became a substantial

part of the post-war audiences on a regular basis. Butler took part many times both as soloist and in chamber music.

In the sixties she appeared frequently with her husband, the pianist, Norman Greenwood, whom she had married in 1941. They became known for their innately musical interpretations, especially of the work of contemporary British composers. After her husband died in 1962, she gave a number of recitals with the pianist, Angus Morrison, and others. At this time she also added teaching to her musical activities, including the Junior and later Senior departments of the Royal College of Music. She has also taught at the Birmingham School of Music and at the Menuhin School.

Florence Hooton is a busy teacher who divides her time between the Royal Academy of Music in London and private teaching in Suffolk and Sheffield. Formerly, with her husband, the violinist David Martin (1911–82), she had had a busy career as soloist and chamber-music player. Today she directs all her energies to her students.

Born in Scarborough in 1912, she was the daughter of a professional cellist who had studied with Warwick Evans, founder member of the London String Quartet. Her first lessons on the cello, at nine years of age, were with him. At fourteen she entered the London Cello School as a pupil of Douglas Cameron, continuing her studies with him when she won a scholarship to the Royal Academy of Music.

A memorable year for Hooton was 1934. She gave her first solo recital at the Wigmore Hall with the pianist, Dorothy Manley, and played her first Prom with the BBC Symphony Orchestra conducted by Sir Henry Wood, in the Beethoven Triple Concerto with Frederick Grinke and Dorothy Manley, with whom she had also formed a trio. She gave first performances of Gordon Jacob's *Divertimento for Unaccompanied Cello*, and Arnold Bax's *Legend Sonata*, the latter with the pianist, Harriet Cohen.

Despite this encouragement, Hooton went for a further period of study with Feuermann in Zurich.

He was an incredible cellist. There was nothing he could not do either technically or musically on the instrument. He once played the Mendelssohn violin concerto for me on the cello in the *right* register. Not transposed! He taught me how to sharpen one's technique in a way that I have never been shown by anyone else. He had a wonderful bow arm and he had that knack of putting

the bow on the string at exactly the right angle so that it started
to vibrate immediately. This is what I try to instil in my students
and when I say 'Ping!' they know just what I mean.[3]

In 1936, Hooton gave the first performance of *Oration*, the cello
concerto by Frank Bridge, at a public concert at Broadcasting House
with the BBC Symphony Orchestra and Bridge conducting. Felix
Salmond and Suggia had both declined to perform the work because
they considered it uncellistic. The composer had refused to make the
necessary modifications and the work had been put aside.

Hooton's involvement had begun two years prior to the première
through a quirk of fate. She was playing a solo in a concert of
modern music in the Duke's Hall at the Academy where, unbe-
known to her, Frank Bridge was sitting in the gallery with Benjamin
Britten. It seems that hers was a very difficult cello part with an
inordinate number of top notes. At one point Bridge turned to
Britten and said, 'If that girl gets one more of those top notes spot-
on I'm going round to ask if she'd like to give the first performance
of my cello concerto.'

Two years later Hooton, who had studied the score very carefully
and after much experimentation discovered fingerings that worked,
gave the first performance. Bridge was delighted. A few days later
Hooton received a letter of congratulations from the composer
thanking her for taking on the hard work, of which others had
fought shy, and praising 'the way you got above the technical
considerations and found what I think is in the work'.[4] Curiously
enough, it remained in manuscript and was mislaid for some time
during the war. It was finally published in 1986.

From this point Florence Hooton's career as soloist and chamber-
music player flourished. She was the first cellist to appear on
television at Alexandra Palace, where she played the Haydn D Major
Concerto, sharing the programme with two dancers, then relatively
unknown—Margot Fonteyn and Robert Helpmann. She has given
many first performances, including John Ireland's Trio No. 3 in E
Minor (with Grinke and Ireland), and cello concertos by Gordon
Jacob, Alan Bush and Kenneth Leighton, all of which were written
for her. She remembers sadly that the Leighton received its première
at the Cheltenham Festival with the Hallé Orchestra conducted by
Barbirolli, who walked on to the podium with the aid of a stick. It
was one of the last concerts he ever conducted.

From 1950 until 1976 Florence Hooton and David Martin were
joined by the pianist, Iris Loveridge, in founding the Loveridge–

Martin–Hooton Trio which became one of the most sought after in the country.

Teaching and performing have always been parallel activities in her career, and in 1964 she was appointed professor of cello at the Royal Academy of Music in London. At the time, she and her husband were both fulfilling a packed schedule of concert engagements. Nonetheless, on reflection, they decided that whereas excellent players abounded, there was a dearth of good teachers; therefore they would best serve their profession by concentrating their skills in directing the young. 'The concert platform is a great draw and you have no idea how much you miss it. Communication between you and your audience is something that feeds you as a musician. But once you can redirect that energy into teaching and begin to see results then you have all the compensation you need.'[5]

The name of William Pleeth as a teacher has an international ring. His students come from every corner of the globe, and he in turn gives master classes all over Europe. He is also one of that special breed of teachers who inspire long-term affection from his pupils.

Pleeth was born in London in 1916 into a Polish émigré family, several generations of whom had been professional musicians. At the age of seven he first heard the cello played by a café musician who gave him a few lessons. After some months his progress made it clear that he needed serious tuition and he attended the London Academy. At ten he entered the London Cello School as a pupil of Herbert Walenn.

At thirteen, William won a scholarship to study for two years with Klengel at Leipzig and was the youngest student ever admitted. Despite his youth he managed to keep pace with the demands made upon him, and in two years learnt all the Bach Suites, all the Piatti Caprices and 32 concertos, 24 of which he knew from memory.

It was at Leipzig that Pleeth met Feuermann for the first time. Here he had the daunting experience of playing with him in a quartet for four cellos written by Klengel. The two other parts were taken by the composer and Fritz Schertel.

At fifteen, Pleeth took part in his first public concert at the Conservatoire playing the Dvořák Concerto, and shortly after made his début at the Gewandhaus under the baton of Walter Davison, playing the Haydn D Major Concerto. He recalls the awe-inspiring atmosphere of the Conservatoire at the time. 'As you entered you saw all the names of past professors on the board—Schumann, Mendelssohn and Reger and so on. The director at that time was the great pianist, Max Pauer. There were fewer students than we have today, so everybody had more attention. It was wonderful to work in such an environment.'[6]

Enthusiastic quotes from the German press had little effect on the agents when Pleeth returned to London. Music was at a low ebb and foreign artists were much preferred to British. In order to overcome the prejudice, many musicians added a -vitch or a -ski to their names. Pleeth, whose family had become British and anglicized their name, refused to revert to the Polish form simply to comply with the demands of inverted snobbery.

In 1933 when he was seventeen, Pleeth gave some broadcasts and a first recital at the old Aeolian Hall in Bond Street. For the magnificent fee of two guineas, his first important orchestral engagement was playing the Dvořák Concerto with the City of Birmingham Orchestra under Leslie Heward. His career then gained momentum and in 1940 he was engaged for his first solo orchestral broadcast playing the Schumann Concerto with Sir Adrian Boult and the BBC Symphony Orchestra.

From this time onwards the war of 1939–45 occupied most of his energies with five years' army service. During this time he met the composer, Edmund Rubbra, who became a lifelong friend. Rubbra dedicated his Sonata for Cello and Piano to Pleeth and his wife, the pianist, Margaret Good, whom he married in 1942. Rubbra's *Soliloquy for Cello* was also written for him.

In the early fifties Pleeth formed the original Allegri String Quartet with Eli Goren and James Barton, violins, and Patrick Ireland, viola, and discovered his great love.

Chamber music has always been a passion with me, and I return to it more and more. Not only is the concert itself an exciting experience but it is the satisfaction of working out a piece of music with three other human beings for whom you have affection. In many ways, a solo career is, for me, unsatisfying. I don't care for the solitary travelling, and like even less the isolation of being confronted with a large orchestra and an 'eminent' conductor.

His complaint—shared by many distinguished musicians—is that the soloist works at home on his concerto and formulates it in his mind and is ready to give his interpretation of what it should be. 'What happens? You arrive. You play it with a so-called "great" conductor—who may be miscast in his role anyway. All you have is a *bash* through.'[7] Pleeth stresses that this judgement does not apply to all conductors, he always enjoyed working with Sir Adrian Boult and Pierre Monteux and has very special memories of the French conductor, Albert Wolff.

The famous partnership between Pleeth and his wife started in 1938, and flourished for 40 years. Today, teaching occupies most of his time and he puts into practice with his own students what he learned with Klengel so long ago.

> I am a more personal player than Klengel, so I have to hitch them on to me, but one must have an understanding of that other person. Of course you discuss the differences between good music and musical rubbish and try to help them develop taste, but I do not believe in always pointing out how bad everything is. Nobody ever thinks of pointing out how good things are. It doesn't matter whether they do it from musical knowledge or instinct. When you can point out the good things you can work surreptitiously on the bad things with the result that your students gain confidence.[8]

Pleeth has had associations as a visiting teacher at the Menuhin School since 1977. Of his many British pupils, his son, Anthony (who has achieved considerable success in the Baroque field), Robert Cohen and Jacqueline du Pré are outstanding examples of his wise teaching. He also has high hopes of the young Canadian, Sophie Rolland, who is at present studying with him.

Pleeth's philosophy is based on optimism and balance. He believes in encouraging his students so that they work better and, as a result, play better. He is totally opposed to over-practice, because he knows the danger of practising mistakes.

> I like to leave a lot of leeway for them to develop along the lines of their own personality. I don't want them to be a reproduction of me. They are harnessed to me in a way, but they are *attached* not *bound*. . . . There are so many ways of being expressive. We discuss the drama and the lyrical quality together, but somehow the individual personality must come through. It is also my job to help that particular personality to bloom. . . . One has to be a psychologist to understand one's students.[9]

CHAPTER XXXI

The Continuing Line

THERE ARE A number of British cellists who, although they started their careers as soloists, have subsequently found teaching as much, if not more rewarding. A few have managed to enjoy parallel fulfilment in both fields but this is not easy to achieve. Total commitment is necessary if teachers are to be available for their students all the year round.

Anna Shuttleworth, Eileen Croxford and Olga Hegedus are three first-class ensemble players, who have also been responsible for teaching many of the fine young cellists of our present time. Joan Dickson, from Scotland, is one who opted for teaching as her main occupation. A professor at the Royal College of Music since 1967, she feels she has a special affinity with the young.

Born in Edinburgh in 1921, Joan Dickson was brought up surrounded by music. Her father was a lawyer with a passion for the violin and played second fiddle in an otherwise professional string quartet. Accustomed to hearing her father practising, she grew up knowing the Bach Partitas by heart. She also recalls that the D'Aranyi sisters were frequent guests at their house, as was Adrian Boult, who had been at school with her father.

At the age of five she started lessons on the piano and at nine, studied the cello; her progress must have been encouraging, for at twelve she played a Mozart trio at her home with Donald Tovey, a close friend of her father. Dickson remembers him as 'an *enormous* man who made dreadful puns'. It seems that Tovey dominated musical life in Edinburgh, and anyone who came within his orbit was profoundly influenced—including Joan Dickson.

During the war she taught the piano and gave concerts under the auspices of CEMA and ENSA, and on her free days drove a mobile canteen. In 1945 she was given a scholarship to the Royal College of Music where she studied with Ivor James.

One year after leaving College, she studied for a while with Pièrre Fournier. Although she found him very inspiring, he was not able to give her the basic technical help of which she was then so much in need. When she later went to Mainardi she realized the situation should have been *vice versa*. During this time she was fulfilling many solo and chamber-music engagements, including her first foreign tour with the Will Smit Trio.

When she was twenty-seven, she met Mainardi and, after three rewarding years studying with him, she made her Wigmore Hall début and the same year was appointed a professor at the Royal Scottish Academy of Music, where she taught for 27 years. She formed the Edinburgh String Quartet in 1953, but left after five years to join the Scottish Trio. She took part in her first Prom in 1957, playing Rubbra's *Soliloquy*.

Although she is probably one of the best known teachers in the country, Dickson has not gained her reputation by taking on only gifted pupils.

I have always been very interested in trying to help people to express themselves, because you see the happiness you bring when they are liberated. Often people have something inside that they cannot express due to a lack of technique. You can't teach them to be musical if they are not, but you can help to give them a technique so they can express what is locked up inside them. This has given me more joy than anything else.[1]

In addition to her work at the College, she has a number of younger pupils under her care, and has recently taken on an eight-year-old beginner, because she believes that the most vital lessons are those given in the first year.

Fewer students arriving at colleges of music would need so much remedial teaching if the instruction of beginners was generally better. I have spent most of my time doing remedial teaching and, although I love solving people's technical problems and helping them to play with ease, it oughtn't to be necessary if they were taught better from the beginning.

The students I like teaching best are cellists in their early teens. At that age they are ready to learn how to study really seriously; to analyse and think about what they are doing, and not just to play by intuition. Unfortunately, many of the students arriving at our conservatories are still in need of this basic training.

Dickson is emphatic about the need for pupils to become independent of the teacher as soon as possible, and she has strong views about holding on to them too long. Once she has taught them the basics of how to study music in depth and freed them from bad tensions, she sends them elsewhere. If they are talented, she recommends the great artist type of teacher.

It is this common-sense understanding of the basic principles of teaching that is the inspiration behind her tireless work for ESTA. Since its inception it has been a very important part of her musical life—she was the Scottish Secretary until 1979. Long before ESTA was founded she had given weekly teaching classes for her pupils at the RSAM. Her lectures on 'The Art of Teaching' are a firm part of the curriculum at the College.

I learnt teaching the hard way myself and I now know that there is a great deal of information that can benefit people if they have it *before* they start teaching. I think we have a long way to go at the moment, because I don't think that anyone is training teachers properly yet. String teaching is a very complicated business. Teaching bowing *and* left hand *and* intonation at the same time is very complicated.

One of Dickson's firmest convictions is her condemnation of the way we make distinctions between players and teachers. 'If our pupils are to go on developing after they stop having lessons, they need precisely the same kind of knowledge and understanding that a teacher needs, for they are going to have to teach themselves for the rest of their lives, or stand still.'[2] She believes that we can all continue developing until an advanced age provided we want to improve and that we work and think hard. But we must also have the necessary knowledge and understanding upon which to base our work.

A fellow professor at the RCM, whose pupils are known for their good technical grounding whilst retaining their individuality as performers, is Christopher Bunting.

Born in 1924 into a family where amateur music had flourished for several generations, Bunting's father, a distinguished civil engineer, was an amateur pianist and his mother sang and played both the piano and the cello. Improvisation on two pianos was the order of the day in the Bunting household.

Christopher's musical education began with piano lessons at the age of five and at six he started on the cello, continuing his studies with Ivor James. Unlike many string players who abandoned the keyboard in childhood, Bunting has kept up practice on both instruments and is today a very able pianist. He once made a broadcast of the Brahms E minor Sonata playing both parts himself.

Between terms at Cambridge Bunting went to the USA for a month to study intensively with Maurice Eisenberg whom he considered an outstanding teacher from both technical and interpretative standpoints. In 1952 he went to study with Casals in Prades, and was invited to play in the festival. His personal approach to performing and teaching would seem to have evolved from the fact that he was not overwhelmed by either Casals or Eisenberg, but rather took gratefully from them.

In September 1952, just before leaving for Prades, he gave his first Wigmore Hall recital with the pianist Gerald Moore and was hailed by the press as a 'great cellist'. In 1964, after another Wigmore recital, this time with Ernest Lush, a critic wrote that it provided London's outstanding cellistic event of the month, commenting on his 'lyrical tone', 'great technical facility' and the 'presentation of a musician's programme that was obviously both to his own taste and that of his audience.'³

A turning point came in his career when he was chosen by Gerald Finzi to give the première of his cello concerto at the Cheltenham Festival with the Hallé Orchestra under Sir John Barbirolli. This was followed by solo appearances with all the main orchestras and at the Proms. His recording of Bruch's *Kol Nidrei* with Sir Adrian Boult and the London Philharmonic Orchestra, made at this time, was widely praised.

Always a strong supporter of the work of contemporary composers, Bunting admits that in his early days, he would agree to play almost any new work because he felt that everything deserved a hearing. He has since modified that view and has reservations about a great deal of contemporary music, a certain amount of which he feels is spurious. Although he has found some atonal music interesting in performance from a purely exploratory angle, he becomes more and more convinced that it is not suitable for the cello as an instrument. 'I do think one has a right to expect a good tune from a composer, but one does occasionally come across a musical mind of quality that can express itself atonally.'⁴ Francis Routh is one of the composers whom he feels lies within this category. Routh wrote a double concerto for violin and cello which Bunting performed with Maria Lidka and he also wrote a cello concerto for him which was performed and broadcast in 1974 with the Belgian Chamber Orchestra. Other first performances include the Rawsthorne Concerto with Malcolm Sargent and the Philharmonia Orchestra, and the first British performance of Hans Werner Henze's *Ode to the West Wind* with the BBC Symphony Orchestra.

Collaboration between composer and performer in the early stages of composition is what Bunting finds rewarding, and he regrets that few composers are willing to co-operate in this way. 'It was never beneath the dignity of the great composers who, when they were writing for an instrument that they did not themselves play, would approach a player and make slight modifications to make the music lie well on the instrument.'[5] In his opinion the test of any piece is whether it still has a life of its own *after* its first performance. In order to achieve this 'life' the music must lie comfortably under the hand. Although music can have its hazardous passages, and may require playing of a high order, it must still be approachable by a competent musician. He points out that Bach, Beethoven, Mozart—and Hindemith and Britten in our own time—all played the viola and understood string writing, consequently they would never ask for notes that were impossible to play. He complains that many composers who write for strings have no knowledge of any other instrument but the piano and tend to write in note groups that demand five fingers instead of four. 'They do not understand that occasionally melodies which incorporate the interval of a fifth often go wrong. Such composers should confine themselves to electronic music where they can compose straight on to the tape, and not ask some long-suffering cellist to make nonsense of his art.'[6]

Christopher Bunting has a very personal approach to technique. Once, when questioned about this, he said: 'In my mind cello technique must be based upon an understanding of the mechanics of the human body and of the total dynamic system involved. With an instrument as difficult as the cello it is vital to bring everything to the simplest, in order that nothing may impede the expression of emotion. Actually there are two instruments to be studied—the cello and the cellist.'[7] His theories are all set down in his two-volume *Essay on the Craft of Cello Playing*, published in 1982. It has been described by an American reviewer as 'one of the finest manuals ever written on *any* craft or skill'.

In addition to solo and chamber-music performances, Bunting's musical activities extend to both composition and teaching. Among his works are a *Fugue for Six Cellos (on themes of Beethoven)* and a cello concerto which was recorded by the BBC in 1986. When that severe critic, Hans Keller, first heard the work, he wrote: 'What an achievement!' His many pupils include both adult professionals and children; he frequently coaches youth orchestras, has given master classes all over the world, and, having studied with Sir Adrian Boult, is also increasingly in demand as a conductor.

Another cellist who combined a successful solo career with chamber music and teaching is Amaryllis Fleming, born in 1925 into a family where the arts flourished. Her father was the famous painter, Augustus John, and her mother an amateur violinist who studied with Adila Fachiri. Two of her half-brothers, Peter and Ian Fleming were celebrated writers, and another, David John, was a professional oboist. She first learnt the piano at the age of three and at nine wanted to go on to the violin, but her mother thought one violinist in the family was enough and gave her a small sized cello.

By the time she was twelve, Amaryllis had decided she would be a professional cellist, and although she received little encouragement she never wavered in her purpose. At fifteen she made her first broadcast (on Children's Hour) and at seventeen won a scholarship to the RCM, where she studied for three years with Ivor James, and carried off every possible prize.

Hearing Pièrre Fournier play the *Rococo Variations* at the Royal Albert Hall in 1945 made a deep impression on her. 'I'd never heard playing like it. During the war we had no visits from international artists and it was a revelation.' She met Fournier afterwards, played to him, and as a result went to study with him in Paris.

'He opened my eyes to the immense possibilities of colour, nuance and phrasing, particularly in regard to bowing technique which enabled me to acquire a palette of far greater variety.'[8] Fleming's friendship with and admiration for Fournier remained until his death and she feels strongly that his musical influence is still with her.

There then followed a somewhat confusing period of study with Suggia in Oporto, during which time she also played for Cassadó who had some very contradictory ideas. He offered to take her into his international master-classes at the Accademia Chigiana at Siena and promised her professional engagements. But by this time Fleming considered she needed some self-assessment. This period was interrupted by the opportunity to study with Casals in Prades. They worked mainly on the Schumann Concerto, with every bowing, fingering and inflection dictated by Casals. After Prades, she put away the concerto for two years, in order to stand back from it. Having assimilated the various influences she could return to it and make it her own. She regards the opportunity to have been with Casals and to have heard him play was one that greatly enriched her musical experience.

In 1952 she won the Queen's Prize and, the same year, played for John Barbirolli—by a strange coincidence in the house where she now lives, then owned by the French violinist, André Mangeot. Barbirolli was so impressed that in 1953 he invited her to make her Prom début with the Elgar Concerto.

Fleming has always been her own severest critic and in the middle fifties, after winning the cello and piano duo competition at Munich with Lamar Crowson, she decided to go to Bologna to continue her self-assessment. Here she rented a room for two months with one prerequisite—a large mirror. Each day she sat in front of it to undergo muscular analysis. At the time it helped her considerably. Much later, in 1985, as the result of a broken ankle, she came into contact with Jean Gibson, whose teaching and healing, with regard to posture, breathing and movement, has profoundly influenced her.

In 1953, Fleming gave her first Wigmore Hall recital (with Gerald Moore) and attracted considerable attention from the press. She later appeared with Geoffrey Parsons, Peter Wallfisch and other leading pianists. On the platform she has a charismatic personality enhanced by an attractive physical appearance, captured in the well-known portrait by Augustus John. She has remained in the public eye, admired and respected by both colleagues and audiences for her elegant and stylish playing and always musical interpretations.

Although she has played concertos with many orchestras and under renowned conductors, it is the chamber-music repertoire that appeals most to her. She has also built a reputation for the interpretation of Bach Suites, which she plays from the Anna Magdalena MSS. Describing a performance of the Suite in G, a *Daily Telegraph* critic wrote, 'This virtuoso cellist captured the inner fire which is the life of all Bach's music.' Indeed, Bach Suites occupy a large part of her thinking: 'I would be quite happy to spend the rest of my life living and re-living them. The music of Bach is a link with eternity and as such has become a part of me.' She plays the Sixth Suite, 'à cinque cordes', on a five-stringed Amati cello.

Throughout her career Fleming has joined in small chamber-music groups with many distinguished artists. She now plays in a trio with violinist, Manoug Parikian and pianist, Hamish Milne. It was originally formed in 1977 at the instigation of the Arts Council in their 75th birthday series at the Wigmore Hall (then with pianist Bernard Roberts), and today enjoys international recognition.

A successful trio must consist of three personalities—three solo-ists. The difficulty is to find a pianist who has the sensitivity of sonority to blend with strings but has a soloist's technique to cope with the very demanding piano parts. The two string players need to share the same mental approach, by which I include style of bowing and anticipation of nuance. I think we have realized the answer to these problems. Our rehearsals are a joy because we aim for the highest standards and we have a sense of humour.

In the last ten years Amaryllis Fleming has gained a reputation as a first class teacher, both privately and as a professor at the RCM. 'I think that playing and teaching should go hand in hand and that one should try to pass on to others what one has learned. . . .This is a demanding discipline which can bring its own rewards to the teacher who aims to help each student to reach his or her potential.'[9]

CHAPTER XXXII

Russia—Home and Away

THE RUSSIAN BASS voice has a characteristic timbre that is easily recognizable and could be related to the richness of tone which is the hallmark of the great Russian cellists. Piatigorsky certainly possessed a sonority that gave us a clue to his origins.

Edmund Kurtz, a contemporary of Piatigorsky, from the old régime, was born in St Petersburg in 1908, and is now an Australian citizen. He had some early lessons on the piano but made little progress. At eight he was taken to a concert where a cellist played the *Rococo Variations*. He recalls making his choice of instrument there and then. 'I saw this box draped in red cloth with the soloist sitting down on it which impressed me very much.'

This was in 1917, the year of the Revolution, after which the family left for Germany where Edmund had his first cello lessons. At thirteen he studied with Klengel in Leipzig. Kurtz cannot praise his old professor enough. 'He would allow you to develop in your own way. You could do what you wanted—faults included. He would simply guide you, not put you in a straitjacket. If you were good, then the good was allowed to flourish. If you were not, you stayed where you were.'[1]

Kurtz treasures, to this day, a letter of recommendation written by Klengel in 1924:

> In spite of his young years, Edmund Kurtz is already one of the most outstanding violoncellists of today. In a very short time he will be one of our most celebrated soloists.
>
> During many years of my activities as a teacher, only rarely have I found a pupil who has developed so rapidly.

At sixteen, when Kurtz was about to make his début recital in Berlin, he began to have doubts as to the wisdom of doing so. Klengel's advice was, 'Try. Next time, it will be better. You'll have given your first recital and nothing can ever be so frightening again.'² The encouragement worked, for a critic from the *Berliner Zeitung Am Mittag*, Adolf Weissmann, wrote 'Cellists who truly make music are rare. Edmund Kurtz is one.'³ Soon Kurtz was performing in other European cities with similar response from the press.

In Paris, he came under the influence of Casals who advised him to have a period of study with Alexanian. Although in complete contrast to the teaching habits of Klengel, Kurtz considers he learnt a great deal in his time with this controversial teacher. He also went for a short period to Budapest to study with that great creative musician, Leo Weiner.

The next years were spent in a varied and active performing life in the main European countries. For a time, he toured with Anna Pavlova, playing the Saint-Saëns 'Le Cygne' for her famous Dying Swan dance.

Kurtz was principal cellist with the Bremen Opera Orchestra and later with the Prague German Opera under Georg Szell. In the thirties he toured the world in a trio with the two Spivakovsky brothers. In 1936 he was appointed principal cellist of the Chicago Symphony Orchestra and stayed for eight years. In 1944 he resigned in order to devote himself to his fast developing solo career. He first appeared before the American public as a soloist in January 1945, playing the Dvořák concerto with the NBC orchestra under Toscanini.

Kurtz made recordings for Polydor, dating from 1927. Recording in those days (on a wax master) was sometimes traumatic. 'There were no retakes or tape-splicing that we rely upon today. I do not claim to be the only person who made such recordings, but I'm probably one of the few who are still alive to tell the tale. You had only a few discs to get it right. It was terrifying!'⁴

There followed many years of solo playing all over the world with warm response from the critics. After a recital at Carnegie Hall in February 1950, Harriett Johnson wrote in the *New York Post*, 'He made his instrument sound expressive, agile and musicianly throughout the evening.' After remarking on the rarity of Kurtz's playing seemingly without effort, she continued, 'Combined with this, he possesses a tone which is so full it almost sounds like a choir of instruments instead of just one.'⁵

Kurtz has always included a number of contemporary works in his repertoire. He commissioned Ernest Křenek to write his Suite for Unaccompanied Cello Op.84, and he was the dedicatee of Ginastera's *Pampeana* No. 2., Darius Milhaud's *Elègie* and his

Concerto No. 2. The first performance of the Milhaud concerto under Artur Rodzinski with the New York Philharmonic Orchestra took place in November 1946. He also gave the first American performance of the Khachaturian concerto in Boston in March 1948 under Koussevitsky with the Boston Symphony Orchestra, and edited the American edition of that work.

A connoisseur of fine bows, Kurtz has a collection of five Tourtes, and he owns the 'Hausmann' Stradivari cello, dated 1724, which he bought in 1943. It is one of the finest examples of the master's work and is the instrument that was first heard in Great Britain on 25 April 1900 when the Joachim String Quartet made their début at the St James's Hall in London.

Edmund Kurtz's greatest contribution to the development of the art of the cello is his facsimile edition of the Bach Suites:[6] one of the most valuable in a long series of editions dating from H. A. Probst in 1825. As there is no manuscript in Bach's handwriting, the nearest to the original is the copy made by Anna Magdalena Bach, now in the State Library in Berlin. It is this manuscript he used and attached to his edition.

Kurtz has played the Bach Suites since his earliest youth, but throughout his performing life he admits having struggled to comply with all the directions in the various editions. He knew instinctively that for him the bowings and fingerings were not right, but was then unable to make any constructive changes. In 1978, at the age of seventy, he decided to make a new edition based strictly on the Anna Magdalena manuscript. It took almost four years to complete and was published in 1983 with the facsimile of the Berlin manuscript facing every page. Kurtz says that if someone discovers the manuscript in Bach's own hand, he is prepared to start again.

Clearly, he is well qualified to undertake the task of producing an edition specifically with the performer in mind. After a recital in which he played one of the Bach Suites at the Carnegie Hall in January 1952, Olin Downes, never a man to dole out praise to the unworthy, wrote in the *New York Times*, 'Mr Kurtz gave breadth and nobility to every melodic line. . . .In point of richness and variety of tone colour, sensitiveness of shading and treatment of Bach's arabesque [*sic*] this was not only an achievement, it was an intimate and eloquent discoursing of Bach.'[7]

During the first half of the present century a few cellists have contributed greatly to the development of cello playing in the USSR, although we seldom hear about them in the West. Sergei Shrinsky was professor of quartet playing at the Moscow Conservatoire and, with his violinist brother Vasily, Dimitri Tziganov (leader) and Vadim Borisovsky (viola), formed the Beethoven String Quartet, to which most of Shostakovich's quartets are dedicated.

Victor Kubatsky was solo cellist at the Bolshoi Theatre when he was only nineteen. Also professor at the Moscow Conservatoire, he later taught at the Gnessin Institute. The violinist Daniel Fradkin was a student in his quartet class and describes him as a great raconteur and a colourful figure whose lessons could go on for three hours. His communication was such that his students lost count of the time. He always used a metronome while teaching and, as a result, his students were known for their highly developed sense of rhythm.

In the early twenties Kubatsky was responsible for assembling the priceless State Collection of Stringed Instruments in Moscow. They are numbered in hundreds, many of which were abandoned when aristocrats fled from the Revolution. The most outstanding examples are in what were the private collections of the Counts Sheremetev and Youssopov, the latter includes the beautiful 'Youssopov' Stradivari violin.

By far the most important professor of cello during the first half of this century was Simeon Kosolupov (1884–1961). He studied at the St Petersburg Conservatoire with Wierzbilovich, a pupil of Davidov, and first taught at Kiev. From 1921–61 he was professor at the Moscow Conservatory, and many of his pupils have reached the top of the profession. A few names from a long list show the extent of his influence: Sergei Azlamazyan (Komitas Quartet), V. Berlinsky (Borodin Quartet), S. Knushevitzky (professor at Moscow Conservatory and cellist of the trio formed by Oistrakh and Oborin), Mstislav Rostropovich and Kosolupov's daughter, Galina who is one of the most sought after teachers of cello in the USSR today.

Several of the Russians who studied with Rostropovich at the Conservatory in Moscow have since achieved success in the West. David Geringer, winner of the 1970 Tchaikovsky Competition, was principal cellist in the Norddeutsche Rundfunk Orchestra for many years and now lives in Hamburg where he is professor at the Hochschule. He also manages to fit in a busy solo schedule appearing all over the world. Boris Pergamenschikov was born in Leningrad in 1948 and won the Tchaikovsky Competition in 1974. Three years later he emigrated to Germany where he now combines a solo career with a professorship at the Hochschule in Cologne. His playing is admired for its beauty of tone and impeccable musicianship, and when he played all six of the Bach Suites at the Israel Festival in 1984 he caused a sensation. He owns a magnificent Montagnana cello dated 1735 which belonged to the family of the Czar Nicholas III.

Following the standards set down by Kosolupov and others, musical training and performance in the USSR today has probably reached the highest peak in its history. Consequently the success rate in international competitions is similarly high. One of the most respected cellists, Daniel Shafran, was, in his earlier days, esteemed as a soloist. He is not only in demand as a teacher, but frequently appears on the juries of international competitions. The Fifth and Sixth Cello Competitions in Moscow were both chaired by Shafran. Unfortunately, he was seldom heard in the West.

Danial Shafran was born in Leningrad in 1923 into a family of professional musicians. His father was principal cellist of the Leningrad Philharmonic Orchestra and his mother, a pianist. When he was six, he had his first cello lessons from his father—a hard taskmaster. Even at this early age, his son was instilled with the need for diligent and regular practice and the importance of striving for the highest goals. So firmly were these dicta imprinted, that, in adult life, he puts on tails to simulate concert conditions when rehearsing.

At eight, when Daniel began studies with Aleksander Shtrimer at the Special Music School for Children, he had already decided to make music his career. Two years later he was one of ten talented children chosen to attend the Leningrad Conservatory, fortunately with the same professor. That year also marked his first appearance in public at one of the Conservatory concerts when he played two Popper pieces of considerable difficulty, 'Spinning Song' and 'Elfentanz'. He made his orchestral début the following year playing the *Rococo Variations* with the Leningrad Philharmonic Orchestra under the visiting British conductor, Albert Coates.

Shafran acknowledges the debt he owes to Shtrimer, whom he describes as a striking personality and a broad-minded man who had a profound understanding of law, literature and art, although he never intimidated his students with encyclopaedic knowledge. Each one was treated as an individual, and lessons embraced all art in relation to music.

In 1937, Shafran achieved national prominence when he entered the Soviet Union's National Cello Competition as an unofficial contestant and carried off the first prize. Part of the award was a magnificent Antonio Amati cello made in 1630, on which he has been playing ever since.

At both the World Democratic Youth Festival in Budapest in 1949, and at the Hanus Wihan Contest in Prague in 1950—the year of his graduation from the Leningrad Conservatory—he shared first prize with Rostropovich.

Shafran's removal to Moscow later that year caused an artistic crisis brought about by his final separation from the teacher on whom he had depended for so long. His wife, Nina Musinian, a pianist and his partner in recitals, helped by insisting that he forget all about having been a prodigy, and encouraged him to try to find his own way to becoming a mature artist.

In 1977 Shafran played in a concert at the Carnegie Hall in New York with the New Jersey Symphony Orchestra, an occasion somewhat marred by circumstances beyond his control. Milly Stanfield, who attended the concert, tells us that on the retirement of Henry Lewis, who had conducted the orchestra for several seasons, it was decided to engage a different conductor for each concert. Unfortunately on this occasion the conductor appeared to have little control over the orchestral sound. Shafran's tone was frequently submerged by the orchestra, and it was only when he played a movement from a Bach Suite as an encore that he could properly be heard—he was given no real opportunity to reveal his true stature.

During the remaining part of the tour the orchestra was under Thomas Michalak, an experienced and sensitive musician who gave Shafran the chance to show his playing in a more representative light. Stanfield writes:

> His bowing is splendid, free and always under complete control, his style commendably devoid of mannerisms and he never allows his technical prowess to lead to a display of pure skill at the expense of his conception of the musical expression. He has a delightful personality, seems deeply involved with the interpretation he is projecting and any hint of monotone in his use of dynamics and tone colour may well have been due to a transitory distrust of unfamiliar acoustics.

However, she does question whether 'any Amati, no matter how fine, is sufficiently powerful for a solo cellist at the summit of his career.'[8]

In his recordings, the Amati gives no hint of any lack of power.

He has a luscious tone and is a formidable interpreter of the romantic repertoire. He no longer plays the short pieces by Popper and Klengel himself but recommends them to those who aspire to a brilliant technique. He recalls Oistrakh's advice, 'Danny—always include a virtuoso piece in your daily dozen. The audience likes them as a reward.'

Shafran was always greatly respected as a teacher although never on the staff of any music college. His lessons were given in his own home or at that of his pupils. It seems that his rather shy and reserved personality was not suited to the hazards of working in a large institution.

The young cellist, Alfia Nakipbekova, was a pupil of Shafran's when she was fifteen and feels that the time she spent with him gave her a special polish that she could not have obtained elsewhere. 'He is a real master of his instrument and his technique is brilliant. He goes into detail so that you really understand what he is doing. His staccato and spiccato are wonderful and he achieves this by a very light but absolutely precise attack—a split second judgement of when the bow touches the string.' Shafran also uses the bow at the tip far more than most cellists and likes the hair to be on the loose side. 'This is how he makes that beautiful, silvery sound.'

Nakipbekova summed up his philosophy: 'He could feel each pupil's potential long before they were aware of it themselves. He was able to make you find your own way through your own experience so you did not imitate him but you took from him and then shaped your own playing.'

Shafran is somewhat idiosyncratic about the chair he uses on the stage. 'It is very high and he sits right on the very edge. Even when he is giving a recital with a pianist he has his little raised platform. But he is also very interesting to watch. He plays rather like a violinist, very light and without effort, yet at the same time he is very intense. A strange mixture.'[9]

Two more prize-winning cellists, also pupils of Rostropovich, and unquestionably products of the Soviet school's pursuit of excellence, are Natalia Gutman and Mischa Maisky. Both are building reputations in the West, Gutman as an infrequent visitor, Maisky as an émigré.

Natalia Gutman was born in Kazan in the USSR in 1942 into a family with musical links extending over several generations. Her mother was a pianist and her grandfather, Anasim Berlin, was a violinist and a pupil of Auer. Her grandmother—also a violinist—

studied with both Auer and Joachim. Her stepfather, Roman Sapozhnikov, is a cellist and teacher well known in Russia for his published writings on the teaching literature for his instrument.

As a small girl Natalia recalls hearing her stepfather's cello pupils when they had lessons at their home. When she was five she was given a small-size instrument and took to it immediately. Her first few lessons were with her stepfather but her progress was such that despite her age she was accepted into the Gnessin Music School. Here she studied at first with Sergei Aslamazyan and, from her fourth year onwards, with Galina Kosolupova. Gutman acknowledges her good fortune in being chosen for Kosolupova's class. 'She is one of the most important teachers in Russia today and has trained many fine cellists who are now coming before the public. I was lucky also that I was able to stay with her when I went on to the Conservatory in Moscow for the five year course.' Gutman spent the next four years in a post-graduate course with Rostropovich at the Leningrad Conservatory.

A further influence on her musical education was her grandfather who worked with her between the ages of fourteen and eighteen. 'It was just when I was finishing school and he brought me something quite different both through his violin playing and his general understanding of music. It broadened my outlook on everything concerned with music.'[10]

From this time onwards Gutman made a series of successful appearances in concerts in and around Moscow and achieved many prizes in national and international competitions such as the Tchaikovsky in Moscow, the Vienna Student Festival, the Munich Chamber Music Competition and the Dvořák Competition in Prague.

She has since played all over the world and made her British début at the Edinburgh Festival in 1980 with the London Symphony Orchestra conducted by Yevgeny Svetlanov playing the Brahms Double Concerto with her husband, Oleg Kagan.

In July 1985 Gutman made one of her all too rare appearances in Great Britain, again with the London Symphony Orchestra, conducted by Claudio Abbado, playing the Sinfonia Concertante for cello and orchestra by Prokofiev. Robert Henderson wrote in the *Daily Telegraph*: 'Not even Rostropovich himself however could have excelled the sustained, all-encompassing brilliance of the performance given at the Barbican on Wednesday by his one-time pupil.'[11]

Even Gutman admits that the Prokofiev is 'perhaps the most

difficult concerto in the repertoire. It is much more difficult than the Lutoslawski, which I also play.' In fact, she plays most of the modern concertos written for the instrument and is happy to play new works provided she likes them. When studying a work written especially for her, she likes to get the feeling of the piece *in toto* before she tackles the cello part. 'If I can play it myself I do, but if not then I get the composer to do so.'

Critics constantly draw attention to her brilliant technique and the ease of her execution. Much of this is due to her belief in practice. She stresses that, in Russia, from the earliest years onwards, scales are a very important part of every musician's daily routine. She feels that this is the correct way to achieve a good technique. 'We make it very complicated in that we practise not only plain scales but also in double and triple stopping, and lots of arpeggios. When you have perfected such studies your technique must improve. I notice that you do not insist upon this in the West.' As a mature artist she still likes to practise scales, but she admits that, with three small children, she does not have as much time as she would wish. 'For this reason I tend to be very quick so as not to waste time and I find the best thing is to focus attention on what you need at that moment and use all your concentration. It is also a good idea to practise everything in a slow tempo.' Gutman's overall advice is that the most important aspect in all playing is to know the *kind* of sound for which you are aiming.

Gutman plays a great deal of chamber music with Sviatoslav Richter and with her husband. 'It is very important for artists to play chamber music, whether they intend to be a soloist or not. It is an essential part of a musician's growth and I feel very privileged that I am able to play so much with my husband. I think if you enjoy playing chamber music it comes through in one's solo playing as well. After all, the solo field is very narrow. In chamber music there is so much more give and take and, for me, this is where music is at its most rewarding.'[12]

Mischa Maisky was born in Riga in 1948 into a musical family. Since his brother and sister played violin and piano respectively, he was given a cello. At the age of eight he had his first lessons and was soon playing in the family trio.

Mischa's studies progressed from the Children's Music School to the Riga Conservatory where he was bored by over-regimentation. At seventeen he moved to Leningrad where he found more opportunities for improvement and the added excitement of taking part in

the National Cello Competition in which he came first. Winning a
prize in the International Tchaikovsky Competition in Moscow the
following year changed his life. Rostropovich was a member of the
jury and invited Maisky to Moscow to study with him. He was a
regular visitor to Rostropovich's Dacha just outside Moscow and
was treated like a son. 'Rostropovich was a wonderful teacher, and
I owe him an immense amount. For every piece of music he had a
story, sought out comparisons, and knew the connections.'

As Maisky's career developed, Rostropovich advised him against
making records too soon. 'He told me not to rush into a studio. I
would become embarrassed later in life by the interpretations I was
then so proud of, and the records would be available for years
without my being able to do anything about it.'[13]

Then came a series of events which started with his sister's
emigration to Israel, made worse by his efforts to buy a tape
recorder on the black market, and culminated in his arrest. As a
result he spent eighteen months imprisoned in a Gorky labour camp.

After his release Maisky went to a mental hospital to avoid
military service and was later granted permission to leave the Soviet
Union provided he reimbursed the state for the cost of his education.
The then Mayor of Jerusalem, Teddy Kollek, approached a rich
American who offered to meet the debt which Maisky would repay
when the money was available. In November 1972 Maisky left for
Israel where he has made his home. He also has a house just outside
Paris which serves as a European base.

A year later Maisky went to New York where he was engaged by
Daniel Barenboim and Zubin Mehta for a tour with the Israel
Philharmonic Orchestra. He followed this with a successful Carnegie
Hall début with the Pittsburgh Symphony Orchestra conducted by
Steinberg. After the concert a young man came backstage asking
him if he would come to play for his uncle who was confined to a
wheel-chair. The old man was so moved that he made the young
Maisky a gift of his own cello, a beautiful Montagnana, saying that
perhaps Fate had wanted it that way. Maisky plays that instrument
at all his concerts and is still incredulous at the way it came into his
possession.

Since Rostropovich was still in the Soviet Union, Maisky was
obliged to look elsewhere for a suitable teacher with whom to take
his finishing studies. An introduction to Piatigorsky resulted in
Maisky going to California to become his last student. Maisky is the
only cellist to have studied with both of the great Russians. 'My
time in California was much shorter than that in Moscow, but I was

more mature and more able to assimilate Piatigorsky's suggestions. He gave my playing the final polish it needed.'[14]

Maisky made his London début in 1976 with the Royal Philharmonic Orchestra, followed by appearances with most of the leading British orchestras. He made his British recital début at the Queen Elizabeth Hall in September 1977 with Radu Lupu, with whom he had performed a complete Beethoven cycle in Moscow in 1969. In the *Daily Telegraph*, Robert Henderson wrote about 'the perfect unanimity and balance between the two instruments . . . without compromising their individual personalities, they maintained from the start a splendidly mature, richly satisfying corporate identity. So finely tempered and mutually responsive was their phrasing, articulation and tonal shading that to concentrate on one instrument at the expense of the other would be to distort the very nature of their performances.'[15]

Maisky now plays throughout Europe with his more recent partner, the pianist Martha Argerich. Their recordings of the Bach Cello Sonatas (Viola da Gamba) and Maisky's of the Bach Suites were awarded the Grand Prix du Disque and the Record Academy Prize of Tokyo. Maisky is the first cellist to have been given an exclusive contract with Deutsche Grammophon.

Fast gaining an international reputation, Maisky has made some memorable appearances with other distinguished artists. His playing of the Brahms Double Concerto with violinist Gidon Kremer under Ashkenazy with the BBC Symphony Orchestra was praised for the colourful contrasts he was able to draw and his ability to distil into 'unity of purpose all the excitement too often found only in conflict'.[16]

At a recital of Bach Suites at the Wigmore Hall in London in October 1985, a critic bemoaned the fact that his visit was so brief 'for Maisky plays Bach with marvellous poetry, eloquence and conviction. . . .Enough to say broadly that every movement of each suite had its distinctive character; textures were magically varied; everything was underpinned by a powerful rhythmic sense.'[17]

That playing was captured on disc when Maisky's recording of the six was issued by Deutsche Grammophon in 1984. The critics praised his clear creative vision and his consistency. Lawrence B. Johnson in *Ovation* wrote about his playing 'edged with a luminous Romantic quality . . . and a persuasive legato style foreign to the new esthetic of eighteenth-century performance practice.'[18]

Maisky has himself been described as a figure of extremes. His wild uncontrollable hair, the searching eyes and mercurial movements are merely outward indications of the inner conflicts that make for his sensitivity when he becomes an interpreter of the great composers. He sums it up himself in a sentence, 'Life has only dealt me two cards—utter contentment and utter catastrophe!'[19]

CHAPTER XXXIII

The Russian Dynamo

OF ALL THE Russians who have made their home in the West, the best known must be the ubiquitous Mstislav Rostropovich, who is likely to be as easily identified in a tiny Pacific Island as in any of the world's capital cities. However, he was not the first in his family to win a place in the top echelons of the performing arts.

Leopold Rostropovich (1892–1942), father of Mstislav, a highly gifted cellist and leading light in his day, came from a family where there had been many generations of musicians, but he was the first professional. Beginning with early lessons on the piano, he soon showed a preference for the cello, and by the age of twelve was playing in public. He continued his studies with Wierzbilowicz at the St Petersburg Conservatory and at fifteen was also teaching in a private school.

There are amusing descriptions of his over-exuberant temperament. Apparently he was in the habit of entering the classroom like a tornado and would throw his arms around his professor's neck. Wierzbilowicz was not impressed. He often expressed pity that although the boy was 'full of talent', he feared he would accomplish nothing because of his irregular attendance at classes. Glazounov, the then Director of the Conservatory, was less pessimistic. Impressed by his beautiful tone, and 'a flawless natural technique', he called him 'a great virtuoso and musical talent'. Glazounov also remarked that his hands were ideal for playing the cello.

Leopold Rostropovich made his début in Warsaw in 1911 and was warmly received by the critics. He then went on to Paris where he took lessons with the young Casals. From this time onwards his concert career gained momentum and he made numerous tours both in Europe and in his own country. In accounts of his playing the predominant qualities appear to be facility of technique and a powerful singing tone.

Also important as a teacher, he held, over the years, a number of appointments at conservatories in Russia. Doubtless he would have enjoyed an international career had he not suffered from ill health and died young. At his last concert, in April 1942, he introduced a cello concerto written by his son, Mstislav, who accompanied him on the piano.

Leopold's most important pupil, Mstislav, was born in 1927 in Baku in the state of Azerbaijan. He had lessons on the piano with his mother when he was four, and his first attempts at composition also date from this time; Rostropovich has a tattered manuscript to prove it. Another discovery made during this period was that the boy had perfect pitch.

When, at six, he took a broom and a stick and tried to play them cello fashion, it was obvious that, like his father before him, he preferred the cello. 'My first music on that instrument was therefore silence.'[1] For six years, he had lessons with his father. 'He was not necessarily the best teacher for me because he never worried much about the positions of the hands and other things which are normally dealt with very thoroughly by the best pedagogues. But his rare musicianship inspired me into a love of music—much the most important quality in a teacher.'

The family moved to Oranienburg during the 1939–45 war and it was here that Rostropovich had his formal education and attended the local Children's Music School. His performing career dates from the age of eight when he played duos with his sister at concerts, and at thirteen he made his orchestral début performing the Saint-Saëns Concerto in A minor with the orchestra of Slaviansk in the Ukraine. During the war the government had moved Leningrad's Small Opera Theatre to Oranienburg. This gave the young cellist an opportunity to join a small touring group taking concerts to a number of outlying towns in the area: at fourteen he was already an experienced traveller.

From 1943 to 1948 he studied the cello with Simeon Kosolupov and composition with Shostakovich at the Moscow Conservatory. Rostropovich is grateful to Kosolupov because he made 'a master of me with perfect command of the cello'. Rostropovich's learning process is interesting—from the outset he never experienced any technical difficulties. 'All my teachers were angry with my position when playing either piano or cello. It was the same with my father from the beginning. He would say "Make elbow higher", I make it for him but it is very uncomfortable. After lesson, elbow is coming down. But I have always played with low elbow because that is how it suits me. How it is comfortable.'

For this reason Rostropovich is flexible towards his students, and only makes rules that he considers strictly necessary, such as keeping the bow parallel to the bridge, or not throwing themselves about so that they make a figure eight when playing. 'When I tell them they ask "Where must I make this straight?" or "How?" I tell them not to worry because everyone has different length of arm. I insist only on bow parallel to bridge and perpendicular to strings. Otherwise be comfortable.'[2]

In 1955, Rostropovich married Galina Vishnevskaya, the leading soprano at the Bolshoi Opera. His ability as a pianist enabled them later to give joint recitals all over the world and their names are now linked as one of the world's most celebrated musical partnerships. But in 1956, when they were unknown, Rostropovich gave his first cello recital in New York to an almost empty Carnegie Hall.

From his first appearance in London in 1956 when he played the Dvořák concerto with Hugo Rignold at the Royal Festival Hall, the British took the ebullient Russian to their hearts. His charisma, his incredible handling of the instrument and innate musicality appealed immensely. Even the critics find it hard to disapprove of some outrageous interpretation which, in a lesser artist, would have received a sharp reprimand. The defending phrase encountered again and again is, 'Rostropovich is Rostropovich'. On the performance of the First Shostakovich Concerto, in 1961, *The Strad* writes, 'In his hands, the music was revealed with all its humour, fire, colour, intimacy and brilliance. His rhythm carried everything before it in the quick movements and he phrased them and the more lyrical middle sections of the work with an affectionate authority that will not soon be forgotten.'[3]

One of the musicians with whom Rostropovich formed a close friendship and professional association was Benjamin Britten, who first heard him in 1960 and, two years later, commented, 'It is difficult to write in a few words a description of my friendship and admiration for Slava Rostropovich. I was taken completely by his genius and personality when I heard him perform in London in September 1960 and, although I was never previously attracted by the cello as a solo instrument, I was determined immediately after this occasion to write something specially for him.' Subsequently, Britten composed for him his Cello Symphony, three suites for unaccompanied cello and the Sonata for cello and piano.

Thus began an association that saw Rostropovich frequently appearing at the Aldeburgh Festival; and, after Britten's death, the foundation of the first Rostropovich Festival at Aldeburgh in 1983, in memory of the composer.

When Rostropovich's second New York recital was announced for January 1972, it was sold out within a few hours—a strikingly different reaction to the first time. An interesting description of his playing by Milly Stanfield appeared in *The Strad* of February 1972:

> His bow sweeps over the strings so that unless one watches it constantly the changes of stroke and string are quite unnoticeable. It seems as natural as breathing—what should be the aim of all cellists from the elementary to the greatest. . . .The percussive articulation of the fingers of the left hand coupled with their powers of vocalization is perhaps the most outstanding single element in Mr Rostropovich's technique. It enables him to make the cello sing and carry, whether playing loudly or softly, fast or slow. It permits him to achieve his fine intonation and, with the backing of his flexible bowing, helps him to phrase as he would wish.

Rostropovich had been a professor at the Conservatory in Moscow since 1956 and was greatly respected as a teacher. One of his pupils, who regards him with much admiration, is Alfia Nakipbekova: 'He has such a wonderful sense of humour and he is so versatile. He could see through people immediately. He knew if they were playing sincerely or not the minute they began, and he had a sixth sense in recognizing potential.' He was also very direct in his criticism which was delivered at his master classes for all to hear. Nakipbekova never forgot his assessment of her own talent. 'You have everything. You have a big fire inside—but the walls around it are very thick!' From this time she is convinced that she was able to open up much more and Rostropovich became extremely encouraging as her playing developed.

The young Scottish cellist, Moray Welsh, also studied for two years with Rostropovich at the Moscow Conservatoire in 1969.

> All the students played regularly to Rostropovich's assistant, Stefan Kalianov, who dealt with technical preparation, thus leaving the lessons with the maestro for playing music. But occasionally he would pounce on one and demand a study or technical exercises transposed on the spot—just to test your responses. Those were terrifying moments.
>
> All the lessons were open classes so it was normal for people to

drop in on lessons on any instrument. The more flamboyant teachers attracted bigger 'audiences' so it was not unusual to find that in the middle of your lesson the eavesdroppers might include Richter or Oistrakh—a nerve-racking prospect.

Welsh confirms Nakipbekova's view: 'Rostropovich's teaching centred mainly on enlarging the imagination of the student, so that greater possibilities of characterization and sound could be opened up. He very rarely touched the cello, usually demonstrating on a second piano. It is true to say that he was highly critical of technical expertise without some more searching quality coming from a student.'[4]

Since Rostropovich's concerts abroad attracted such enthusiastic audiences, he gained a reputation in the West that could only be compared with that of the violinist, David Oistrakh. But in 1970, his relations with the Soviet authorities became strained. His friend, the dissident writer, Alexander Solzhenitzyn, was known to be living at his dacha on the Baltic coast. The situation worsened when permission to perform in the West became restricted. Perhaps the most unfortunate outcome was the refusal for him and his wife to appear in the première of Britten's *War Requiem* composed for the rededication of Coventry Cathedral. Finally, at their own request, Rostropovich and his family left the Soviet Union and were stripped of their Russian citizenship. Today, they have homes in London, New York and Paris and have been granted temporary Swiss nationality.

In 1975 Rostropovich made his conducting début with the Washington Symphony Orchestra, and has been their official conductor since 1977. He has also conducted many orchestras throughout the rest of the world. However, versatility of such dimensions must occasionally have its hazards. One instance was the performance on May 11 at the Royal Festival Hall when Rostropovich conducted the London Philharmonic Orchestra with Pierre Fournier playing the solo in *Don Quixote*. A critic remarked that the clash between two powerful musical personalities was not always constructive. What the public received were really two different performances of the masterpiece, though fortunately with much in common, notably exhilarating spontaneity.

Many composers have written works for Rostropovich, and composers are generally happy with his interpretation. Nonetheless, his approach to a new work is very personal.

First I must know some other work written by that composer. Of course not Britten or Shostakovich whose work I know well. But sometimes if it is less well known composer I have to find something—not necessarily for cello—to see how he works. After this, I not touch my cello. I read music so that it sounds in my head. If I try to play music first then technical difficulties come in the way. First I must understand what the music is about—which ideas there are and what feelings are there. It is much easier to read without sound. I then discover at which point music is brighter, or pathetic and of course, most important point—climax. As soon as I understand where climax is, I already begin understanding. Then I take my cello and play it with many faults and without proper fingering or bowing. It is very bad for people to hear me when I am doing this. After that I make fingerings and bowings. Fingerings are the most important thing for the expression of the music. I play it first very fast in tempo as for concert—then I make precise fingerings. I also must find out where are weak points. Weak points for interpretation and weak points for technique. These must both be worked out separately.

Rostropovich never works with the composer prior to his own preparation.

Sometimes I find composer is abstract. He does not always know what he wants, and if I play before he is ready we are *both* unsure. We therefore spend too much time on our research. After I receive score then I will not have contact with composer until I am ready. Then we can discuss tempi or dynamics, but the work now has a life whereas before it was only notes on a page.[5]

Over seventy new works have received first performances by Rostropovich. In general, he appears to have understood Lutoslawski, Dutilleux and Penderecki, but occasionally there were alterations after he had learned the work. Prokofiev wrote his very difficult Second Cello Concerto which Rostropovich performed for the first time in Moscow in 1951, and the composer told him that after hearing it he would like to make some modifications. It is the amended work that is performed today as Symphony Concerto.

Repertoire is something to which Rostropovich gives a great deal of attention. He considers that even though the cello has probably reached a peak in standards of performance and that more people play the instrument than ever in its history, there is a danger of it dying if the repertoire is not continually replenished.

> The standard cello repertoire is small. It is beautiful and we must play it, but the techniques are already known. I do not speak about interpretation, but *technique*. Composers such as we have been discussing and others like Berg and Stravinsky, all offer something different in technique. A challenge. Britten's Cello Suites, for instance, pose other technical questions for us. It is only these composers who will push the cello forward and make it exciting and progressive. If we are limited in repertoire we cannot progress. I am always delighted when I hear about new generation of cellists—and there are so many fine young players today, Yo Yo Ma, Lynn Harrell and Halvorssen from Sweden, and many others. Jackie du Pré did a wonderful service for the advancement of the cello. She had such a great talent and made wonderful propaganda for cello because she played everything and inspired composers to write for her.

He also cited Pierre Fournier and Maurice Maréchal, two cellists of the older generation who greatly supported the work of young composers by performing their works.

The Stradivarius cello that is now his prized possession is the famous 'Duport', once the property of Jean Louis Duport, who had to live for the rest of his life with the mark of Napoleon's spurs on the ribs of his precious instrument.

> This is the greatest instrument I see in my life. Not so much in power, but in quality of sound. It is like silver. I love the sound, but I also think that some instruments are better for different kinds of music than for others, therefore the cello must have a wide range of colours in its voice. Sometimes you need a baritone voice, and at other times a dramatic or lyrical tenor. Sometimes it must be a big bass with a deep baritone sound. I have a Gofriller that I like to use when I need the bass sound to be emphasized. I like to change instruments when I require a different quality of sound. I doubt if my Duport is so good for Bach Suites. I think for Bach you need a lower frequency of tone. I have not yet found the instrument for Bach, and for this reason I have not yet made recording of Bach Suites. All the ones you hear are pirates. I am waiting for right instrument.[6]

At various times he has owned a Storioni and another Stradivarius, the 'Visconti'. It was this instrument on which he made his recording of the Dvořák Concerto with Karajan and the Berlin Philharmonic Orchestra in 1969.

Although he is so in love with his Duport Strad, he is fully aware of the need to use modern instruments. He has a Peresson cello which he finds excellent for when he needs a powerful carrying tone, and another new instrument is one by Etienne Vatelot, made for the cellist's fiftieth birthday. Indeed, Rostropovich is one of the few top cellists who recognize that there is a place for instruments which are built to meet conditions in the modern concert hall and the size of the orchestra today. He gave an instance of the very difficult first cello concerto by Shostakovich. 'When I play in ending of finale I take my bow with my whole fist because the fingers are not strong enough to hold it in the normal way. I think perhaps there are new developments to be made with the cello to meet these demands. A good modern instrument sometimes is more capable of giving the sound you need.' However, he thinks that there is room for more development in both instrument and bow if the performer is to project the necessary power, undreamt of in the eighteenth century when these instruments were made. 'How can one reach an audience of 5,000 or 6,000 if you cannot project? I change my dynamic in a big hall but there are always limits. I would like a cello with a greater possibility and a bow which is more comfortable for my hand.' He cited the occasion when Shostakovich was conducting a rehearsal of his Horn Concerto. The player was having difficulty with the cadenza, and the composer said, '"Slava, perhaps I die before people construct instrument that can play much more perfect." I think it is the same for cello. The music dictates the instrument.'[7]

Whichever cello he plays, Rostropovich is recognized everywhere. However, there was once an embarrassing occasion when he was not. President Kennedy had invited him to play at a special charity concert at the Lincoln Center and, as the inverval drew to a close, a short bald-headed musician carrying a cello case was seen trying to enter the backstage area. Security guards pounced and told him he could not proceed without a ticket. Did he have a ticket? 'I am Rostropovich but I have no ticket.' Since the man obviously did not speak good English, the guard explained again, slowly. The plea was the same, 'I am Rostropovich, and I must go on.' After some tedious repetition, various security guards and officials were summoned from the higher echelons, but the question about the ticket always arose, and the answer still provided no reason for allowing him in. After a while they informed him rather angrily that the President and his guests were waiting for the next artist and he was holding up the concert. Finally, in a state of acute embarrassment, Kennedy's personal secretary arrived. He waived aside the army of security guards and, apologizing profusely, led the artist away. One of the guards scratched his head and said to the others, 'Say, who is this guy, Rostropovich?'

CHAPTER XXXIV

The Art of the Necessary

ALTHOUGH PRESENT-DAY performances of early music on authentic instruments can boast some excellent players on viols and violin, professional exponents of the baroque cello are rare. The first person to introduce the unmodified instrument, in modern times, was Rudolph Dolmetsch (1906–42), who played the solo cello part in the Sixth Brandenburg Concerto at the 1926 Haslemere Festival. The following year Rudolph played Bach's Sixth Suite on a five-stringed cello by Barak Norman. This had been the suggestion of F. T. Arnold, that great authority on the art of thorough-bass. Rudolph was given only three months to master it.

August Wenzinger, born in Basel in 1905, a pupil of Paul Grümmer in Cologne and Feuermann in Berlin, took up the viola da gamba in the 1920s and had some lessons on that instrument from Mabel Dolmetsch. He later also played the baroque cello and today performs on all three instruments. When asked if it was difficult to adapt to each, he replied, 'The only difficulty is that you have to find time to practise each instrument every day so you can switch whenever the need arises.'[1]

Wenzinger has in addition contributed greatly to the development of the performance of music on authentic instruments in the USA. Since its foundation in 1972, he has been Musical Director of the Baroque Performance Institute which is held every summer at the Conservatory of Music in Oberlin, Ohio.

Dimitry Markevitch, born in Switzerland in 1923, into a Russian family, plays both baroque and modern cello and teaches at the Ecole Normale and the Rachmaninov Conservatoire in Paris. He has also written a book on the cello.

The Austrian, Niklaus Harnoncourt, born in 1929, started his professional life as an orchestral cellist and later formed his Concentus Musicus of Vienna in which authentic instruments, including the baroque cello, were used.

Other performers on the baroque cello are Anthony Pleeth, the first to give the instrument prominence in Britain, Christophe Coin, the first in France, and John Hsu and Catharina Meints who were pioneers in the USA.

The Dutchman Anner Bylsma has been described as the 'greatest baroque cellist of his time'. Clearly supreme in that field his re-interpretation of the earlier cello repertoire is probably his most notable and lasting achievement. Nevertheless, he is in every way a complete musician, restricted neither in his repertoire, skills nor inclinations. What Bylsma has done is to bring to life some of the fundamental and neglected elements of the cello's identity by apply-ing his keen historical awareness to the changes in stylistic and technical perspectives. This same approach is directed with equal knowledge and enthusiasm towards the music of the romantic period and the twentieth century.

Bylsma was born in The Hague in 1934, the son of a professional violinist, trombonist, composer and conductor. When the family string quartet needed a cellist, Anner's father bought the eight-year-old a small cello and gave him some lessons. Anner's swift progress was no doubt influenced by learning so much of the chamber-music literature at an impressionable age.

In 1950, when he was sixteen, Anner entered the Royal Conserv-atory at The Hague where he studied for five years with Carel van Leeuwen Boomkamp, principal cellist of the Concertgebouw Orchestra and cellist of the Netherlands String Quartet. He found him an excellent teacher with a great interest in the history of cello playing. Boomkamp also had a fine collection of old instruments and it was here that Bylsma first saw and played the baroque cello.

Bylsma's first important professional appointment was in 1958 when he spent a year as principal cellist with the Netherlands Opera in Amsterdam—of course on the modern cello. The following year he won first prize in the Casals Competition in Mexico, where André Navarra happened to be a member of the jury. Impressed with the young man's playing, Navarra noted that his bow arm needed attention and invited Bylsma to come to his house in Paris where he would teach him free of charge. 'He was very kind to me and gave me three very good lessons. He must have been much busier than I am at present, yet he took time off to do this. He knew a great deal about bowing in general and particularly about the position of the fingers on the stick. It was most helpful and I shall never forget his generosity.'

Bylsma was subsequently engaged as principal cellist of the

Concertgebouw Orchestra where he stayed from 1962–68. Although he looks back on that period as one of personal enjoyment, in what he describes as 'a splendid cello section', he has reservations about orchestral playing. 'I agree that it provides valuable experience for an artist but on the whole, the trouble is that "beautiful and ugly" have more or less been traded in for "right and wrong".'[2]

When Bylsma gave a recital at the Wigmore Hall on 7 March 1963, there were obvious signs of his developing musicality although as yet no baroque leanings in a programme ranging from Beethoven, Weber and Tchaikovsky to Fauré and a modern Dutch composer, Henk Badings. *The Strad* critic wrote, 'He is genuinely musical and gives great pleasure because his readings are so convincing. His technique is always adequate to his demands and his intonation is excellent.'[3]

Since then Bylsma has gained an international reputation as a performer who plays both modern and baroque music on the instrument best suited to the period. He has a beautiful baroque cello by Gofriller, dated 1695, on which he uses two gut and two silver-plated strings. His modern cello is a Pressenda dated 1835, and here he favours an all gut A string, aluminium D, and silver-wound gut for the lower strings. He also has a violoncello piccolo thought to be Tyrolean *c.*1700, which he uses for the sixth of the Bach Suites.

He plays regularly in the USA, Australia and all over Europe and, in March 1986, made one of his rare appearances in Britain when he played the entire cycle of the Bach Suites at two London concerts, both to full houses. Proof of the esteem in which he is held by his colleagues was the abundance of well-known solo cellists in the audience, who afterwards flocked to express their admiration.

Unstinting praise came from William Pleeth:

When he plays a Bach suite he doesn't play it like Rachmaninov, which most people do. I've heard him on many occasions playing all kinds of repertoire. He is very rare, because he can speak so many languages in his music—not this narrow language of so called specialization. I've heard him play the Chopin Sonata—a big work—and he does it magnificently, and also the Beethoven Clarinet Trio. Superb! That's what I call a musician on the cello, not a cellist.[4]

Perhaps the best description of his playing comes from a close friend and pupil, Armand d'Angour:

He has steered a course between purism and pedantry. He is above all an artist, not an antiquarian; and he speaks with an individual and supremely musical voice. He plays on period instruments, strung with gut: when appropriate, he uses the shorter, arched baroque bow, held by the stick rather than at the frog, and supports the cello on his legs without an end-pin. For him, these are a means and a pointer to a wider variety of expression, not an excuse for less. He rejects the idea that these techniques need produce the weak or scratchy tone, faulty intonation and total absence of legato that some have mistaken for 'authentic' baroque sound. From his gut strings he can produce a lyrical tone of surpassing sweetness and purity. The distinctive qualities of gut are fully exploited: the variety of attack possible allows a speech-like quality, with a range of consonants and vowels at the player's disposal. Steel strings are well-suited to producing long singing lines, but gut demands the more subtle inflections that bring baroque music to life. In a recent interview on Swedish radio he remarked with a wry humour that is typical. 'Steel strings are old-fashioned!'[5]

Bylsma gave a series of master classes in spring 1986 in which he dealt with music from Boccherini and Bach to the Beethoven Sonatas, the Ravel Duo and the Hindemith Solo Sonata. Here again he had most of the best known cellists—of several generations—as spectators and often at a standing-room-only option. It is not only his own brilliant technical powers and natural musicianship that attracts his colleagues, but also his deep understanding of the history and development of his instrument and of its performers through the centuries. His gloriously lilting Schubert and his dancing Boccherini each have a life of their own.

His infectious delight in performing is not confined to the concert platform, it is also part of his success with students in his master classes. He is in complete contrast to the musical showman who projects a larger-than-life personality, but he is every bit as compelling. He has a dry humour, endless patience and sympathy with every possible problem, and the ability to will a student to play better at each step regardless of a distinguished and overtly inquisitive audience. He uses images such as, 'Try to think of someone you don't like and you'll get plenty of drama in that pizzicato!' or, 'A note is like smoke that you blow out of your mouth; it doesn't stop there.' In inventing a certain bowing or fingering, his advice is, 'If you can play as well as you do and can't master it in three days, change it. For some reason it is apparently not a good fingering.' He adds dryly, 'The reason might be interesting.'

Whatever the technique or interpretation he is trying to put across, he incorporates it all with a sense of fun. 'This intensely-concentrated yet self-concealing entertainer, makes the strongest of impressions,' wrote Nicholas Selo in *The Strad* when reporting on the master classes. One suspects that this gift for serious teaching delivered so positively and with such humour is inherited. He tells of his own youth when his father warned him against using too much arm in strong crossing. He compared it to 'a cow scratching its ear with its hind leg—virtuosic but unnecessary.'⁶ Bylsma is a past master of the Art of the Necessary.

He believes that the sillier the image the more likely one is to remember the serious underlying meaning.

> The fun that I imply in my teaching has two ideas behind it. First of all everybody takes everything too seriously, so they have a weight on their heads and are not free to move. When they sit down in front of others they are scared stiff. It is very important to make them laugh a little and relax. Also when I explain something I try to do it with an image that is childish. When they come home they remember it, and decide whether they like it or not.

Having proved in the master classes that he can interpret music from any given period with equal insight, Bylsma brushes aside any idea of specialization. 'You cannot separate modern and baroque because they both influence each other. You have only one music! I would certainly not wish to specialize personally. If people talk about style in baroque and say they did not like this or that style, what they mean is that the first time they heard a piece it was not played well, because if it had style it would not be so noticeable.' Nevertheless, Bylsma will concede that it is quite difficult to play both instruments to a good standard. 'A main problem is to play *pianissimo* on modern instruments and *fortissimo* on early ones.'

Anner Bylsma has a wide interest in many subjects outside music which embraces history, art, literature and politics, and he is an eloquent conversationalist (he is fluent in at least four languages) with a fund of experience and humour. His sharp and unconventional mind can cut through so much of the traditional but inaccurate thinking that surrounds musical history. Typically, when asked about the abundance of cello methods, he said, 'All early methods are French or Frenchified Italian. The Dutch and the French are the least talented people of Europe, therefore they had to invent "good taste" to spoil the pleasure of the more gifted Belgians, Germans and Italians.'[7]

One of the younger generation who has researched and performed much eighteenth-century music on original instruments is Anthony Pleeth (b. 1948) son of William Pleeth who gave him his first lessons on the cello.

Although Anthony Pleeth has stimulated interest in the playing of the baroque cello in Britain, he has also realized that the authentic movement has gone through many stages of development since the fifties when all early music had to be played on period instruments, regardless of their playing condition. He points out that eighteenth-century musicians would have been horrified at the idea of playing either instruments or music that was 200 years old. Therefore the argument for using facsimile rather than original instruments is more acceptable.

When I was at college we suffered the effects of the fifties movement which was a reaction against Victorian playing of baroque music which meant making it sound like Brahms. We were taught terraced dynamics, echos, sudden forte-piano, separate bowing and altogether clean detached style with very little expression. We were reacting against that movement and by developing our own ideas based on eighteenth century research we found that we were playing far more expressively.

One very interesting discovery I made was that when I once put in all the marks of expression on a perfectly clean copy, it ended up looking like the Victorian edition! It was quite obvious that we were ready for a much more overtly expressive approach which was still stylistically correct.

He deplores the way the various factions of early music have scoffed at each other in the past and would like to bring them together. 'My original idea was to try to do something different. Now that the early music movement has become part of the establishment and there are so many people to take care of it I feel that my interests are going elsewhere.'

He echoes Anner Bylsma's broad view: 'When people come to play to me, we first discuss where we are in terms of the relative cultures which are all strands of the one thing—*music*. We are trying to breed a generation of musicians who are less prejudiced and whose excellence transcends stylistic considerations although they can encompass them at the same time.'[8]

CHAPTER XXXV

Scandinavia and Europe

ERLING BLÖNDAL BENGTSSON, Denmark's leading cellist, has commissioned and given first performances of eleven concertos from composers living in Denmark, Norway, Sweden and Iceland. He has also had a firm hand in the training of many of the young cellists in these countries. For twenty years he taught at the Music School of the Swedish Radio at Edsberg Castle in Stockholm, and has been on the faculty of the Royal Danish Conservatory since 1953, where the proliferation of talented students would seem to follow the general pattern.

Born in Copenhagen in 1932 into a musical family, his father was a violinist and his mother a pianist. At the age of three he was given a violin which he flatly refused to place under his chin and, since he would only play it cello fashion, his father fitted an end-pin to a viola and gave him some lessons. A year later an old violin maker made him a real mini-cello which he imagines must be the smallest ever made. At the age of four-and-a-half, Bengtsson made his first public appearance playing 'The Swan', and a year later had extended his recital programme to Popper, Beethoven and Nolck. Bengtsson later had lessons from Fritz Dietzmann, principal cellist of the Royal Danish Opera Orchestra, and appeared as a soloist with the Tivoli Symphony Orchestra when he was ten.

Throughout the German occupation in the 1939–45 war, Denmark was completely isolated and it was impossible to follow a course of study either at home or abroad. Bengtsson's only musical contact at this time was through gramophone records.

Immediately after the war Bengtsson began giving concerts in Iceland—his mother's native country—and it was through financial assistance from what he calls his 'motherland' that the sixteen-year-old was able to go to the USA to enter the Curtis Institute in Philadelphia. Here he studied with Piatigorsky for two years, after which he became his assistant. When Piatigorsky moved to California in 1950, Bengtsson joined the teaching staff at the Curtis and stayed for three years. The summer of 1951 was spent as a guest at Piatigorsky's home in Los Angeles working in a very concentrated way.

Bengtsson's relationship with his master was much more than that of teacher and pupil.

> I remember his first words to me when I arrived: 'Now we are colleagues. We play for each other and exchange ideas.' What a reception for a boy of sixteen! He was the friend, the inspiration itself. He always got to the point of what was wrong and could see exactly how to help. He wanted his students to find their own personality. Never to imitate but to find out what was actually written in the music. He would show how even in the most familiar works there are new discoveries. In Piatigorsky one had a wise teacher and a warm friend.[1]

In 1957 Bengtsson made one of his rare appearances in Britain, playing the Walton Concerto with Sir Malcolm Sargent at a Prom, after which *The Times* wrote, 'He will be welcome at any time in any music from now on.'[2] He also performed the Walton on three other occasions conducted by the composer with the BBC Symphony and Hallé orchestras. A Canadian critic described his playing of the same concerto in glowing terms: 'He has warmth, security and a supreme elegance about his playing that captivated all who heard it . . . lovely cadenzas in the final movement were most elegant; and the final adagio was an epilogue that drew all the musical threads together in a peroration of Olympian calm.'[3]

There was one occasion when Bengtsson's calm stood him in good stead. He was playing the Lutoslawski Concerto in Copenhagen with the Danish Radio Orchestra conducted by Blomstedt, and had just started the opening solo which is an open D repeated at the rate of one note per second, 21 times. After the eighth or ninth D an elderly gentleman sitting in the front row stood up and said 'No! No! No! that couldn't possibly be in the score!' After a few more Ds the man gave up the unequal struggle and left. Order was soon restored but Bengtsson admits that his concentration was decidedly threatened.

Besides a busy concert schedule, his teaching commitments at colleges and in master classes have a high priority. He tries to be as individual as possible with all students—something he learnt from Piatigorsky—and tries also to create self-confidence, and make them listen to themselves. He feels that with the advent of the tape-recorder we tend to rely on it as a substitute for the ear. 'It is not enough afterwards to listen to what you *have* been doing. You must know it *while* you are actually playing.'

Bengtsson has recorded all the Beethoven works for cello and the Bach Suites. He recognizes that Bach represents a special challenge.

I think it is important to be practical and realistic when playing the suites, and one should find and choose the character of each movement. Bach wrote seven different movements because he wanted as many different characteristics. They are dance movements and one should try to imagine how a fine chamber orchestra would sound. Many of the liberties one hears would be impossible if orchestrated. And I see no justification for taking these liberties for the reason that only one instrument is playing.

Do not feel as if you are standing in front of a cathedral that overawes you. By this I do not mean disrespect—on the contrary—be happy, grateful and feel privileged to work on the most profound, healthy, genuine and straightforward music that was ever written.[4]

Bengtsson's cello is an able partner in his performances. It is a beautiful Nicholas Lupot made in Paris in 1823, still in immaculate condition with its original neck. He feels that a musician's instrument is almost like a living companion, and tells an amusing story of an occasion when his Lupot nearly assumed that role. His travel agent had booked two air tickets and accommodation at the Los Angeles Hilton. On arrival the receptionist told him she had a fine double room for the two of them. He often wonders if his Lupot felt slighted that he moved to a single room.

Bengtsson's main ideas on playing the cello are 'play with character, culture, temperament, conviction, beauty, imagination and variety. Sing, speak, cry, laugh on the cello. Think first of the music, then of the cello. Be faithful to the composer. He depends on you and is at your mercy. Enjoy playing. Be humble and grateful that you are a musician.'[5]

The German cellist Siegfried Palm has gained a reputation for the interpretation of avant garde music. He is said to have remarked, 'Strictly speaking, I have never yet seen an unperformable cello part.'[6]

Born in Barmen in 1927, Siegfried took his first lessons from his father who was principal cellist of the local orchestra. At eighteen he was appointed soloist of the municipal orchestra in Lübeck and subsequently held the same position with the North-West Radio Orchestra in Hamburg.

For some time he played with the Hamann String Quartet, famous for performances of the twentieth-century repertoire. They included all the quartets of Schoenberg, Berg and Webern. For three years from 1950, he attended Enrico Mainardi's master classes in Salzburg and Lucerne. As his interest in contemporary music increased, he found that Mainardi's analytical approach was of the greatest benefit.

As a soloist Palm has since travelled widely all over the world and has also gained a reputation as a teacher. From 1972–76 he was principal of the Hochschule in Cologne. Here he became closely associated with the professor of composition, Karlheinz Stockhausen, and derived considerable inspiration from the composer whose music was so close to his own heart. Since 1977 he has been professor at the Hochschule in Berlin, but continues to follow a solo career in which contemporary music plays the larger part.

Johannes Goritsky, born in Tübingen in Southern Germany in 1942, was a pupil of Cassadó in Cologne. He had previously studied with the Swiss, Rudolf van Tobel, who had also been greatly influenced by Casals. He then won a scholarship to study with André Navarra in Paris, and recollects the difference between him and Cassadó. 'Cassadó never talked about technique. Navarra never talked about anything else!' Later, Goritsky was grateful for this dual influence because he realized that he had been reared with musical ideas coming first. 'It is much easier to build technique upon a musical structure than vice versa.'

Goritsky's meeting with the Hungarian violinist, Sándor Végh, changed his attitude to musical performance. 'He has a unique way of showing how technique must be directly related to the musical meaning. He demonstrates that the accent in the music is also a physical act. He prepares his body for the accent by combining the right physical, mental and artistic approach. Immediately after the action—with its appropriate tension—comes relaxation. It is simply following the most natural way to do things.'[7]

Non-specialization is Goritsky's credo. He finds it necessary to have variety because he needs many influences for his own fulfilment. At present he plays solos with orchestra and participates in a number of small chamber groups as well as being Professor at the Robert Schumann Institute in Düsseldorf.

★

A writer once described Heinrich Schiff as 'broad, of middling height, he has the perfect build for a cellist: he fits snugly round his instrument as though they belonged together, like some composite organic form—no protuberant elbows or overlong limbs to disturb the simple unity of the shape.'[8]

Schiff was born in Gmunden in Austria in 1951 into a family where, although both parents were composers, theatre and sport were his home background. He learnt the piano at the age of six and turned to the cello at nine, under the tutelage of Tobias Kühne. Later he attended the Linz Music School where lessons were planned with Rostropovich but never materialized. At twenty he went on to study with André Navarra.

Schiff's playing today has been described as a 'cultured sound and expression, strength emerging from them as much through intellect as through emotional response', and therefore very different from the more personal and earthy style of Navarra. But Schiff explains that, although they are different, there were 'big influences—his honesty, his artistic *normality*. You'll never find him asking how he can make a special piece more special. That's an attitude regrettably common among cellists, though it's partly in the nature of people's attitude towards the instrument.' Schiff is particularly grateful for Navarra's 'freedom from artistic pride'. He says that Navarra's approach to bowing technique was 'allowing the right hand fingers to *listen*'. He explains that the fingertips were the last link in the chain between body and sound. They are the refiners—'the last point before the control passes from the body into the instrument.'[9]

Schiff has now carved out an international career as a soloist and as a teacher. In 1982 when he gave a series of master-classes at Dartington Hall the students were overwhelmed not only with his 'mastery, musical, intellectual and technical' but also his 'warmth and generosity of spirit',[10] qualities to be felt in both his playing and his teaching.

CHAPTER XXXVI

'Excellent is Enough'

PIATIGORSKY DIED IN 1976, but through his students he generates a powerful influence wherever the cello is played. Although all his pupils have inherited something of his Russian expressiveness, they are by no means copies of the master. Each has his or her individual style of playing, and their interpretations vary considerably. What they all have in common is that technique and musicianship are welded together making performance into an organic whole.

Leslie Parnas was born in St Louis Missouri in 1931 and began his piano studies at the age of five. Soon after he turned to the cello and at fourteen made his début as a soloist with the local symphony orchestra. He went on to study with Piatigorsky at the Curtis Institute.

Parnas distinguished himself by winning the Prix Pablo Casals in the International Cello Competition in Paris, in 1957, and there is a welcome sequel to that event in a comment from Sir John Barbirolli in America:

> A really superb principal cello here [Leslie Parnas] who turns out to be the boy to whom I helped to award the Casals prize in Paris two years or so ago. He was very keen to find out something about the Elgar Concerto which he did not know, curiously enough. Although played all over Europe it is practically unknown here. He got a copy and I took him right through it for tempo and interpretation. Would you believe that he *read* it and played it, including all the difficult passages, better than many I have heard who have studied it for years. As my dear old friend Adolf Busch used to say 'It is not to believe.'[1]

Parnas gave a recital début in New York in 1959 and went on to win Second Prize in the International Tchaikovsky Competition in Moscow in 1962. His playing elicited praise from Daniel Shafran, one of the jury members: '. . . great artistic charm, and courageous interpretation, unexpected and sometimes controversial.'[2]

As a winner in the Tchaikovsky Competition, Parnas quickly achieved world-wide recognition: soon he was appearing as soloist with leading orchestras all over the USA, South America, Europe and the USSR. He also played for Casals at the festivals at Prades and in Puerto Rico. Casals thought him 'one of the most outstanding and accomplished cellists of our time'.[3] When he played the Schumann Concerto in New York, the *New York Times* wrote, 'A fiery and romantic cellist . . . Mr Parnas did not play so much as he sang the work. And in his secure control of the notes, the daring way he dug into those high position passages added a gambler's excitement.'[4]

Parnas is at present Professor of Cello at Boston University and a founder member of the Lincoln Center Chamber Music Society whose series at the Alice Tully Hall are regularly sell-outs.

When he undertook an extended tour of the USSR in 1976, the Russian audiences warmed to him and critics wrote about his mature, accomplished playing remarking especially on his unique and inspired approach. Parnas feels a special affinity with his Russian audiences and tries incessantly to build some kind of musical bridge between the east and west. He recalls an incident when, immediately following an encore, a missile came flying from the audience. 'I was used to the audience throwing flowers but this was a little unusual.' The airborne object was a screwed up piece of paper, which, when opened, read, 'We love your beautiful music, and we hope it will bridge the gap between peoples of good will.' Parnas greatly treasures this anonymous plea. It so inspired Parnas that he and his wife started to learn Russian, and together they work on fostering good relations between artists from East and West. He does not consider it is possible to change or influence political movements but he believes that we can no longer separate political convictions from art. 'When I play music, it is not only an example of *emotional* freedom, but it is also a message for peace and for the right of each individual to express himself.'[5]

One of Piatigorsky's most devoted pupils, Stephen Kates, has a virile, compelling style, and is an especially fine interpreter of the romantic repertoire.

He was born in 1943 into a family in which music, especially the cello, had dominated for several generations. His maternal grandfather was born in Hungary and had studied with David Popper in

Budapest. His father, a professional violist, played in the New York Philharmonic Orchestra for 43 years.

Kates studied with Marie Roemaet-Rosanoff, and it was at Rosanoff's Summer School in Connecticut that he played the Dvořák Concerto for the first time in public. He was only fifteen but it was the moment when he decided to become a professional cellist.

Casals-worship was a way of life in the Kates family, particularly as various members had had personal contact. However, when Kates heard Rostropovich in a Carnegie Hall recital in 1959, his former idol was superseded. He was so stunned by the dynamic Russian that he knew he would be striving for the rest of his life to equal what he had heard that night. There was no opportunity to study with Rostropovich at that time—it was during the cold war, Rostropovich was virtually inaccessible, and there was no exchange between Russian and American students.

Two years at the Juilliard, with Leonard Rose, exposed Kates to yet another kind of teaching. 'Perhaps because of my youth, Rosanoff was not overtly analytical nor definitive in telling me what to do, whereas Rose clamped down on me getting me to understand technique, and stopped me running wild in my adoration of the cello. He made me think about what I was doing by insisting upon scales and études so that I practised more sensibly.'

Kates received honorable mention when, as one of the youngest competitors, he entered the Budapest Cello Competition in 1963. As a result, he appeared in a Young People's Concert on television. For this performance he was loaned the 'Pawle' Stradivarius cello by his former teacher, Marie Rosanoff.

There then followed another three years of study with Piatigorsky at the University of Southern California, a most fruitful period that came at just the right time in his musical development. 'It was a wonderful balance: first Rosanoff giving me confidence and then Rose showing me how things worked, with the Rostropovich explosion right in the middle. And then Piatigorsky, sitting back as a semi-retired artist with all the wisdom of the performer and nothing but time for his students. It was an unbelievable experience for a young person.' Kates also had the good fortune to be at the institution when Heifetz and Primrose were resident professors. Occasionally Heifetz would need a cellist for his chamber-music class and Piatigorsky would despatch one of his students to fill the need. 'You got the call. You went. No question.' Kates thinks that Piatigorsky's most important asset was that teaching and performing had been parallel throughout his career.

Master-classes twice a week in four hour sessions with no lunch break were the norm. Students discreetly ate a sandwich when they could. But it seems that if a student had a problem then Piatigorsky would give him a private lesson at his home.

That often meant arriving at 10 a.m. And leaving at 7.30 p.m. You would spend the morning playing, have lunch, go for a swim in the pool, then back to the cello. If you played your cards right you ended up staying for supper. All the time he was talking to you, planning for you, rationalizing for you, giving 'advices' as he called it.

He treated everyone as an individual. You didn't have to do everything as well as the other person, but you had to do it as well as *you* could manage. He was always aiming for something more than you were capable of. I cannot recall him saying more than two or three times that something was played perfectly.

In 1963 Kates was given a personal introduction by Lev Ginsburg to Rostropovich. After dining at the Kates' home, Rostropovich heard the young cellist play and gave him a most detailed lesson on numerous aspects of cello playing—conducted entirely in Russian with the aid of many Russian friends who spoke the language. The main piece of advice that Kates has always remembered was 'Get yourself the best teacher available. Make sure you have guidance from the person who can give you what you most need.'[6]

In 1966 Kates achieved a reputation overnight by winning the Silver Medal (Second Prize) at the Third International Tchaikovsky Competition. He was invited again to play with the New York Philharmonic and to give a Command Performance at the White House for President Lyndon Johnson. He also appeared as soloist in a performance of the Shostakovich Concerto No. 1 with Erich Leinsdorf and the Boston Symphony at Tanglewood.

Nevertheless he returned to the Juilliard where he worked for a further two years with Claus Adam to complete his degree studies.

Today, Kates enjoys an international solo career and has been on the faculty of the Peabody Institute in Baltimore since 1974. He is a regular guest lecturer at many other universities and was guest artist at the Gregor Piatigorsky Cello Seminar at the University of Southern California in 1977 and 1985. In 1986 he was invited to be a member of the jury of the Tchaikovsky Competition in Moscow.

He owns one of the most beautiful Montagnana cellos dated 1739, the 'Hancock', which he acquired from the late Captain Hancock, a distinguished collector of instruments and bows. Kates also possesses a Peccatte and two Tourte bows which were given to him by Hancock's widow.

Ralph Kirshbaum is a second generation Piatigorsky pupil with an international reputation both as a soloist and as the cellist of the Frankl–Pauk–Kirshbaum Trio. Born in Denton in Texas in 1946, he is the son of a professional violinist and conductor. His mother played the harp, two older brothers played violin and viola, and his sister the piano. At the age of six, Ralph had his first cello lessons from his father, and at eleven spent three years of study with Roberta Guastafeste—a pupil of Joseph Schuster—before going on to study with Lev Aronson, a Piatigorsky student and principal cellist of the Dallas Symphony.

When Kirshbaum was eighteen, Aronson advised him to study with Piatigorsky. But at the time he felt he wanted also to further his academic pursuits. Aronson was disappointed because he was convinced that it was not the right course for a great performing talent. Nevertheless, Kirshbaum won a scholarship to Yale, where he spent the next four years with Aldo Parisot, a brilliant soloist, chamber musician and teacher who based his ideas on the playing of Feuermann. Here he considers he had the best of both worlds.

> Aronson had the most beautiful sound production and his right hand technique and profound musicianship were of the greatest value, whereas Parisot had a virtuoso left hand technique and concentrated on developing my left hand significantly. It was a perfect counterbalance between two great teachers. Parisot also furthered the use of my musical imagination in a technical sense.

When Kirshbaum returned to Dallas and won a National Competition, Aronson was flexible enough to say he was pleased with his development. By this time he had decided to take up music as a profession, but found there was a distinction between loving his instrument and earning his living as a professional—a conflict always present in his family.

As a first practical step towards achieving a professional career, Kirshbaum followed Parisot's suggestion that he should go to Europe. His family all came from Central Europe originally, so it seemed the obvious course. The award of a Fulbright scholarship, to begin in September 1968, was also a help. But it was the period of the Vietnam War and Kirshbaum was due to take his physical examination in August, and the award came too late to inform the authorities, so Kirshbaum suggested they give it to someone else, which they did.

Kirshbaum saw nine doctors, none of whom found any defect in his physical condition. The tenth doctor happened to be English and a music enthusiast. After examining him he announced, 'I hope you are not counting on a military career as you won't pass. You have flat feet!'

After a year of study in Paris, on a grant from the French Government, Kirshbaum won a prize in the Tchaikovsky Competition in Moscow in 1970, and, as a result, his sponsors extended his grant for a further year. 'Being away from home enabled me to review everything I had been doing from the beginning. It was two years of a period of consolidation which gave me a new perspective.'[7]

In the autumn of 1970, there followed a Wigmore Hall recital in London with Ernest Lush. Two years later he made his orchestral début playing the *Rococo Variations* with the New Philharmonia Orchestra conducted by Eliahu Inbal. The *Daily Telegraph* critic was in no doubts about the talents of this newcomer. 'His performance was characterized by fire and elegance, and a rhythmical vitality quite as remarkable in slow-moving cantabile as in fast passage-work.'[8] On this occasion Kirshbaum played on the 'Davidov' Stradivari lent to him by Jacqueline du Pré. (Today he plays on a Montagnana of 1729 once owned by Piatti.)

Then came the first meeting with the pianist Peter Frankl and the violinist Gyorgy Pauk, brought together by Eleanor Warren, a cellist and producer at the BBC. The two had been playing together for ten years and were still looking for a cellist. 'At first I wondered what would happen. They were both ten years older than me and I was "the boy who had just arrived on the boat from the USA". But as soon as we started to play together we seemed to share that sensitivity that makes for musical understanding and leads to musical growth. It is rare that you feel that way so soon.' In the following eighteen months they broadcast some 30 trios for the BBC. In fact their first public performance was a live broadcast from the Edinburgh Festival. In the interim, the group is numbered among the great trios now appearing before the public, and despite their individual busy solo careers they give together some fifteen concerts a year.

The important thing about playing chamber music is that you must be listening all the time, both sonically and musically and must be open and flexible within the structure of the music. The amount of time we spend practising together is less than we imagined originally, but we do have this wonderful rapport so we can make progress at a faster rate than people who understand each other less well.[9]

In 1976 Kirshbaum made a sensational début recital in New York at the Metropolitan Museum, and although he has now made his home in Britain, returns to his native country every year for extensive solo tours. He has appeared as a soloist with almost every major orchestra in Europe and the USA. Two outstanding examples of his recordings are those of the Elgar and Walton concertos for Chandos, and the Tippett Triple Concerto with Gyorgy Pauk and Nobuko Imai for Phonogram, which was 'Record of the Year' for 1983. In addition he fits in master-classes, and regular teaching at the Royal Northern College of Music.

Occasionally travelling has its embarrassments. Once when about to take an Air India plane from New York to Heathrow, he was greeted with unusual friendliness and ushered into the VIP lounge. The supervisor, having examined his ticket, returned regularly to administer to his every comfort, repeating how nice it was to see him again. Since he had never met the man before he felt nonplussed. When he finally boarded the plane, the supervisor shook his hand once more, saying, 'We are delighted to have you with us after such a long time, Mr Barenboim!'

In 1978, Nathaniel Rosen was the first American instrumentalist to win the gold medal in the Tchaikovsky Competition in Moscow since Van Cliburn in 1958.

Rosen was born in Pasadena California in 1948 into a family where amateur music-making thrived: his father is a violist and his brother plays the violin. At the age of six he had his first lessons on the cello with Eleanore Schoenfeld and was soon participating in the family Friday-night chamber-music sessions. There was never any discussion about a career in music. 'My family enjoyed music for cultural reasons; professionalism was not something they thought about at all and I was thirteen before I decided that I wanted to follow music as a career.'

At eleven Nathaniel made his first public appearance at a State Music Festival and went on to win many local competitions. Two years later he entered one in which Piatigorsky was a juror, and was invited to become the master's youngest pupil. He continued to attend Piatigorsky's master classes at the University of Southern California until he was twenty-one.

Rosen was astonished at Piatigorsky's teaching.

> What mattered most were his own feelings and attitudes towards the music and the expression of the emotional content. He would talk about 'tasting the blood' when we played. It was rather an intense image but we all knew what he meant. . . . He would say that technical analysis alone would not help us to become masters of the instrument. His main concern was that we should make the music come alive, regardless of its intrinsic merit as music.[10]

During his first year of study Rosen spent the entire time on two pieces: the Piatti Caprice No. 8 in A minor and the Goltermann Concerto in A minor. Piatigorsky encouraged him to enter the 1966 Moscow Tchaikovsky Competition and at seventeen he was the youngest contestant among 42 cellists, and one of three Americans who won cash prizes.

Although taking part in a number of concerts and giving recitals in and around Los Angeles, Rosen—still in his teens—became Piatigorsky's assistant at USC, a position he held until the latter's death in 1976.

By this time, Rosen decided that life in Los Angeles was becoming too comfortable and predictable, and that he ought to leave the nest. He chose to spend a year in London where he was more or less unemployed. He gave a Wigmore Hall recital and a few other concerts but made no impression on the British press and returned to New York where he entered on what he calls his 'late competition career'.

He auditioned and was accepted for principal cellist of the Pittsburgh Symphony, but before he took up residence in Pittsburgh he managed to win the prestigious Naumburg Competition. This resulted in some New York concerts, a New York manager and very little else.

During his time in Pittsburgh, Rosen thought he would try and continue his winning streak and went to Moscow in 1978 to enter the Tchaikovsky Competition once more, this time to win first prize. He returned triumphant and appeared as soloist in a specially organized concert with the Pittsburgh Symphony which was taking part in the Temple University Music Festival at Ambler under its director, Sergiu Commissiona. The theatre was sold out in six days and Rosen's performances of the Moscow programme, Tchaikovsky's *Rococo*

Variations and the Dvořák Concerto, brought him a deafening ovation. Daniel Webster, from *Musical America*, writes of the Tchaikovsky: 'Everything about the performance indicated that he had won the gold medal by the sheer force of his talent. He played with a sound that was clearly focused and shaded into eloquence. It was not a lush, rich tone, but one which insured a prominent solo line and distinct impact even at pianissimo.' He continues, saying that the Dvořák was played with the same intensity. 'He had the chamber musician's gift for matching orchestral lines, but the soloist's gift for making even the subsidiary notes sound crucial. His concept of the music had large dimensions, and his choice of tempos, while they did not hesitate to show lefthand speed, were aimed at pacing which let the cello sing.'[11]

The popular demand for Rosen resulted in him leaving the orchestra and he has followed a career as a soloist ever since. However, whether he is playing or teaching, he feels very definite about the character he presents. He explained that there are, in his opinion, two kinds of artists: those who consciously wear a different mask for each composition they play and those who show their true face so that the essence of the music is filtered through their own characters, so that each composer is treated with integrity.

> I like to think of myself as one of those performers. I do not wish totally to lose my own character and my own sound to satisfy an abstract and sometimes false idea of stylistic differences between periods. I hope that my instincts as a musician come out in every piece and in every style. I want my confidence as a person to bring to bear on the musical problems. That confidence is necessary if you are to believe what you are doing is good.

These ideas stem directly from the influence of Piatigorsky. He considered that it was much easier to criticize than to praise oneself. He maintained it was only through realizing the positive aspects that one could gain the power to build and improve. A favourite expression was: 'How are you supposed to get any better if you don't build yourself up?'[12] Rosen realizes that this depends very largely upon individual character, but is still inclined to think that a healthy image of oneself is the most important motivating force.

Christine Walewska was born in Los Angeles in 1948. Her mother was a violinist and her father an expert and dealer in rare stringed instruments. She began lessons on the cello with her father when she was eight on a small-size Bernadel cello. At thirteen she began a year of study with Piatigorsky. She played in her first public concert that same year, appearing with the National Symphony Orchestra in Washington, D.C. At sixteen she won a scholarship to the Paris Conservatoire where she was taken into the class of Maurice Maréchal. She was the first American to win first prize in both cello and chamber music at that institution.

After a succesful début in Germany in 1963, her concert career blossomed spontaneously. She subsequently played all over Europe, Poland, Japan, North, South and Central America. However, it was when she was eighteen, and on her first tour of South America, that she felt drawn irresistibly to Argentina, its culture and its people.

Her first concert in that country was at the enormous Teatro Colon in Buenos Aires. She appeared three times there in one week, performing as soloist in the Brahms Double Concerto and at a recital. Her success paved the way for further appearances all over the South American continent and Walewska subsequently married and settled in Buenos Aires, where she is still active as a soloist.

Walewska was the first American artist to be invited to Castro's Cuba, and her concerts in Havana and in its provinces were enthusiastically received. As she toured the country she became deeply affected by all she had seen, and on her return made strong comment on the lack of class distinction and the absence of poverty. She stressed that all concerts are subsidised and tickets available to everyone. Another astounding piece of information is that there are 59 music schools and nineteen conservatories on that small island. Castro could not attend the concert himself, but he visited her at midnight to convey his thanks.

From this handful of the many Piatigorsky pupils, the all-encompassing breadth of his influence can clearly be seen. Once, when discussing his fears that the musical world was becoming like sport, where one has to be the biggest or the best in order to win, he turned to the paintings on his wall, naming each masterpiece in turn. He questioned: 'Would you ask me, who is the best of these? Wouldn't you say, to be excellent is enough?'[13]

CHAPTER XXXVII

The Rose Line

LEONARD ROSE'S UNTIMELY death was a sad loss, particularly as
a teacher, for which he had a special gift. His own playing,
distinguished by a most elegant bow arm, was passed on to his
pupils, and in their earlier years they tended to imitate him. Many
of his students have made highly successful careers. Two who have
achieved international reputations are Lynn Harrell and Yo Yo Ma.
A third, Lawrence Foster, would no doubt have joined this distinguished trio had he not been murdered by a car thief at the age of
twenty-six.

Lynn Harrell, born in New York in 1944, is the son of two
professional musicians, Mack Harrell, the celebrated bass-baritone
singer from the Metropolitan Opera, and violinist, Marjorie Fulton.
At the age of six he had some unsuccessful lessons on the piano, and
at eight, without any prompting from his parents, decided to learn
the cello on a full-size instrument. In adult life he stands six feet
three, and as a child was always a head taller than his classmates.

His first lessons were with Heinrich Joachim, a cellist in the New
York Philharmonic Orchestra but, when the family moved to
Dallas, he began studying with Lev Aronson, one of the great cello
teachers of his day. 'He was the true discoverer of my talent. No
one believed him when he said I would make a musician. I was
eleven when I went to study with him. He showed me passion, for
the instrument, for music and for life.' The next period of study was
with Leonard Rose at the Juilliard School.

The beauty and expressiveness of his playing made a lasting
impression on me. I was fifteen when I first went to study with
him at the Meadowmount School of Music [Galamian's summer
string camp], and sixteen when I went to live in New York and
study with him at the Juilliard. I had learned straight fingers, the
Russian school of right hand playing, from Lev. Rose showed me

a new flexibility of low wrist and very active fingers—it opened a whole new world of technique.

Within two years Harrell lost both parents and he moved to Philadelphia to continue his training with Orlando Cole at the Curtis Institute. On leaving, he asked Rose for advice on his future, telling him of his ambition to become a soloist. Rose suggested that he could either begin trying to win competitions or go into an orchestra. He reminded him that most of the great cellists had received their training in orchestras.

It was a visit to Robert Shaw, Harrell's godfather, and choral conductor of the Cleveland Orchestra, that forced a decision. Harrell played for Georg Szell who shortly after offered him a place in the orchestra. After two years he became principal cellist and held that position for seven years.

Harrell is one of the very few members of the younger generation who have created a solo career after serving an apprenticeship in an orchestra. He is convinced that it has helped tremendously in his musical development. 'At the time, I was attracted, not by the challenge of being in a great orchestra, but by the certainty of a weekly pay-cheque.' He recognizes that, to the average student today, the idea of orchestral work represents death of individuality and a decaying of instrumental skill. 'All that started to happen to me. My protection was a growing awareness of my ignorance.' When he walked into his first rehearsal, priding himself on his Boccherini Concerto and fast-fingered scales, he suddenly realized he'd never heard Beethoven's Fifth Symphony all the way through.

Georg Szell, a hard taskmaster but a fine musician and a great conductor, had considerable influence on the young Harrell. 'He showed me that all the encyclopaedic learning in the world is only a starting point—but an essential one. He was an educator in the finest, even if most dogmatic sense. He was a link with the past, with the birthplace of the music we played, with its cultural foundation. To work on *Don Quixote* with a pupil of Strauss was quite extraordinary.'

It was also in Cleveland that Harrell met James Levine, then associate conductor of the orchestra. They became firm friends and have remained so. 'Jimmy was my musical mentor, teacher, friend, guide, partner—unlimited in imagination and energy. My chrono-logical contemporary, but a generation ahead in thought, work and experience, he showed me the musical horizon and helped me find the tools to set off towards it.'

Around this time Harrell suddenly felt it necessary to examine his own playing under a microscope.

I ripped it apart and built it back together again. Being in an orchestra I could do this. You learn how to follow conductors, to be aware of the changes in tempo and dynamics. As a soloist it is so important to know how the score works—all the way through. It is then much easier to understand the smaller details of what the composer wants at certain places.

Harrell has little sympathy for those who consider that playing in an orchestra is settling for second best. 'The orchestral musician has to be able to do everything well. He must sight-read well. He must be able to play in any number of different styles and adjust to all kinds of colleagues and conductors. I think it essential that a string player should spend some time in an orchestra or in playing chamber music.'[1]

When Szell died, Harrell was twenty-seven and ready for a solo career. He spent all his savings on a New York recital given to an almost empty hall and managed only a few concerts for the next year. It was an invitation to be guest soloist with the Chamber Music Society of Lincoln Center in 1972 that prompted Harold Schonberg, critic of the *New York Times*, to write, 'This young man has everything.'[2]

Things started to improve, but it was winning the first Avery Fisher Prize in 1975 that was the turning point in Harrell's career. What appealed to him about that particular award is that it is not run on the normal competition lines: competitors do not play against others to be eliminated or retained. The competition exists but the outcome takes into account an assessment of the previous five or six years' work. Testimonials are taken from other musicians and the result based on the findings.

Since winning this award, Lynn Harrell has become known throughout the world as a leading soloist and also finds time for teaching. In September 1986 he was appointed the first holder of the Piatigorsky Chair for Cello at the University of Southern California. He also teaches at the RAM in London.

Harrell has made many recordings both of concertos and chamber music, which appeals to him particularly. One of his most successful enterprises is the series of piano trios he made with Perlman and Ashkenazy. For Harrell this has been what he calls:

. . .the most wonderful give and take and some of the most beautiful music-making that I've experienced. It is a fascinating combination because Itzhak is such an instinctive player—perhaps the most musical and instinctive violinist I've ever played with. What is so miraculous is that he hears something and it goes in and gets sorted out by this miraculous machine inside and he plays in the most profound way. He won't pass anything until it is absolutely perfect. Ashkenazy is very diligent and has to work everything out. When Itzhak says 'I play it this way because I feel it this way', Ashkenazy retorts, 'You can't play it by just *feeling* it! You have to see that the phrase structure works!' I was the American in the middle saying, 'Come on guys, let's play it again.'

Harrell feels that of all the recordings, the Tchaikovsky Trio in particular represents the kind of energy that he felt permeating the entire project. 'I think the energy and excitement is audible on the recording.' He suggests that part of this is probably due to the fact that they had only two days to record. 'The first day was spent trying things over and getting a good sound. Ashkenazy wanted another piano because the one we had was bad. He then said that if we didn't record it then, he couldn't work it up again. So we had a kind of stress to get the performance on tape. We were almost in a fever when it actually happened.'[3]

Lawrence Foster (1954–80), described by Leonard Bernstein as 'an authentic genius', was born in Oak Park, Illinois, a suburb of Chicago. He was to be cruelly murdered by a car thief. As a small boy, as soon as he heard the cello he was captivated and begged to be allowed to play it. At seven he began lessons with Karl Fruh of the Chicago Musical College of Roosevelt University. A year later he appeared at his first public concert and at eleven was soloist with the NBC Symphony on a television programme, 'Artists Showcase' and was also soloist with the Grant Park Symphony.

That same year, aged eleven, his phenomenal progress won him a scholarship to study for five years at the Juilliard in New York, while continuing to appear in public. At twelve he made débuts with the Philadelphia Orchestra and the Chicago Symphony as soloist, each time receiving rave reviews from the press. He also won several awards and appeared on national television with Leonard Bernstein for one of his Young People's Concerts with the New York Philharmonic. As a result, two leading agents offered him contracts, and requests for appearances with major symphony orchestras all over the country poured in. Most significant was the *New York Times* critic who agreed that Bernstein was probably not exaggerating when he called the fourteen-year-old a genius. He maintained that the youngster 'plays the cello as though he were an adult virtuoso . . . There was nothing to suggest that the interpretation was not that of a mature artist.'[4]

On leaving the Juilliard at sixteen, Lawrence could easily have launched himself on his career and become a household name. Engagements were offered in profusion and invitations for appearances on television—greatly enhanced by his tall stature and blond good looks—came in thick and fast. After a performance with the Omaha Symphony Orchestra under Yuri Krasnapolsky, a critic wrote, 'It seemed as natural for him to play the cello as it does for a fish to swim or a horse to gallop. He displayed a sonority even in *pianissimo*, an unforced *fortissimo*, a sustained legato and an unhurried vibrato.'[5]

However, young Foster and his parents were intent that his talent should be given time to mature naturally: under the unforeseen circumstances, a cruel irony. At sixteen he finished his studies with William Pleeth at the Guildhall School of Music in London. At the same time he enrolled for a degree course in English Literature in London. When asked why he had taken this step, he replied, 'I really want a university degree. In case something happens, like I lose a finger, I want something to fall back on. And since I like to read, literature seemed the best study. It makes you more creative and teaches another way to express yourself.'[6]

After graduating he continued to study with Pleeth until he was twenty-three, regularly crossing the Atlantic to play in concerts. Pleeth is still of the opinion that he was one of the most outstanding cellists of his generation. In 1974 he wrote, 'This is, without doubt, only the beginning of a great career.' Apart from Foster's great gifts, Pleeth admired his personality. 'He was such a happy boy, and very gentle. He loved life and did every imaginable kind of sport.'[7]

The impact that Foster had had in his own country was soon repeated in the UK. In November 1974, at nineteen, he was the only cellist selected from over 80 contestants up to thirty years of age, as winner of the Leeds International Musician's Platform—as it was then known. It later became the Leeds International Piano Competition. After Foster's death, Gerald Moore, who had been on the jury of the competition, wrote to Foster's mother, 'Listening to him at the competition in Leeds we were all struck by the spirit within him, the fire, the poetry and the love. He would have been proclaimed as a great master had he been spared.'⁸

As a result of the Leeds success, Foster gave concerts, made broadcasts and appeared on television for the BBC, and was invited by Benjamin Britten to play at the Aldeburgh Festival. On that occasion, the critic from the *Guardian* described his performance of the Schumann Concerto as rivalling that of Rostropovich.

Success did not turn his head. In 1975 he was interviewed about his future career and was quite emphatic that it was his duty to go beyond the 'boy wonder' stage, 'I feel I have passed out of that, actually—the whole child prodigy bit . . . A lot of young artists don't make it through this seventeen to twenty-one period. They forget their responsibility as an artist in growing and maturing. They're just thinking of the glamour life.'⁹

Yo Yo Ma travels more than 150,000 miles a year, averaging some 100 concerts *en route*. His performances nearly always attract full houses and are characterized by spontaneity, passion and individuality. The conductor, Benjamin Zander, who has worked with Ma and the Boston Symphony Orchestra on numerous occasions, says: 'Ma represents a great fusion between the two performing traditions of our century: the intellectual and analytical approach, as epitomized by Artur Schnabel, and the romantic and instinctual approach of, say, Arthur Rubinstein. What I love about Yo Yo's playing is that it satisfies everyone, from the most rigorous intellectual to the romantic matinée-idol worshippers.'¹⁰

Yo Yo Ma was born in Paris in 1955 into an émigré Chinese family of musicians. His mother was a singer from Hong Kong and his father, a conductor, composer and teacher. At four, he had his first lessons on the cello with his father, and even at that age he was made to memorize two bars from the Bach Suites every day. There is little doubt that this early exposure to composition and musical structure laid the foundation for the musical integrity so apparent in his adult performances.

Yo Yo gave his first recital at the University of Paris when he was four and a year later the family moved to New York where he became a pupil of Janos Scholz. At eight he appeared on American Television in 'The American Pageant of the Arts' conducted by Leonard Bernstein.

Next came his enrolment in the junior department of the Juilliard School as a pupil of Leonard Rose, but during the latter period Yo Yo found it difficult to reconcile his strict upbringing and traditional family life with the freedom of the American college system. He admits to being somewhat rebellious and did not spend as much time practising as he should have done. At that time he still had to come to terms with a reputation as an outstanding cellist. When he left the Juilliard in 1971, he had no idea if he even wanted to take up music as a career.

However, four years at Harvard and a meeting with Casals proved to be the influence he needed. It was at the Marlboro Festival, when he first saw the mighty little Catalan and other dedicated people in action, that he began to reassess his future. 'I met Casals at a moment when it was crucial. Here was this ninety-year-old man who was practically non-functional. But the second he got on to the podium, he was singing, screaming, and yelling. That strength was inspiring. By normal standards he couldn't play the cello [the way he had in earlier years], but the commitment behind each note, the belief he had, was a wonderful example.'[11]

There were also other important musical influences at university. 'My teachers at Harvard—Leon Kirchner, Earl Kim, Patricia Zander, Luise Vosgerohian—gave me the confidence to look at music and ask questions about myself and answer them. I had been playing since I was four, about twelve or thirteen years. But the question is: how can a young, talented musician grow: How make instinct and knowledge work together?' He decided that the answer was to develop a willingness to study scores conscientiously and to open himself to a variety of opinions and viewpoints.

Despite this precocity and its inherent problems, Ma considers himself lucky that as a child he was never exploited. 'I was always doing lots of chamber music and different sorts of things, but never pushed as a sort of child prodigy. . . . if you're pushed too soon you can get locked into habits, whereas I could draw on to a greater field of experience.'[12]

Ma made his British début at the Brighton Festival in 1977 and later that year appeared with the Royal Philharmonic Orchestra at the Royal Festival Hall.

He subsequently appeared with all the major American orchestras under the baton of conductors such as Maazel, Mehta, Ozawa, Previn and Rostropovich, but it was winning the Avery Fisher Prize in 1978 that opened the gateway to world-wide recognition. Today, there is scarcely a leading orchestra or conductor with whom he has not appeared. A very special occasion was in 1982 when he was invited to take part in the opening concert at the Barbican Centre in London in the presence of H.M. Queen Elizabeth.

The freshness he brings to the staple diet of the cello repertoire is admired by his fellow musicians. His reading of the Dvořák Concerto owes nothing to any previous great exponents of the work. By the same token, no two performances are ever the same because he refuses to imitate himself. He says:

A work like the Dvořák, or any great piece, stands many different interpretations, many different viewpoints . . . You try to relive a piece each time you play it, to reproduce the experience you had the first time you heard it. You have to rediscover the music night after night, to create an organic whole, to realize an inner logic. The danger comes when you try to *repeat* last night's good performance. As soon as you try that, you're going to fall flat on your face.[13]

Another remarkable compartment of this extraordinary young artist's life is the one devoted to playing chamber music. He plays regularly with friends of long standing, the violinist Lynn Chang and pianist Richard Kogan, and says, 'Making chamber music is the basis of all music making. You are responsible for every art that is there.'[14] As a cellist he realizes that he is the root of the harmonic structure and that he must deal with the other two elements to achieve a balance.

The duo that Ma formed with the pianist, Emanuel Ax, is recognized as one of the great partnerships among the younger generation of American musicians. They play at least fifteen concerts each season and have made some memorable recordings, of which their Brahms Sonatas won them a Grammy Award. Ma also gives recitals with another trio—comprising Ax and the violinist Young Uck Kim. They had all known each other since their first meeting at Marlboro, therefore the ensemble was built on friendship as well as good musical partnership. Ma explains that this friendship 'allows us to discuss things freely without ever feeling that anyone's being personal. And there's also an empathy which, however long we spend working independently, returns immediately the moment we meet again to work. It's the same with all old friends. You meet up again and find you have all the more to say.'[15] Ma has also played in a string quartet with the violinists, Gidon Kremer and Daniel Phillips, and Kim Kashkashian on viola.

As a person he is completely unspoiled. Friends who have known him since childhood claim that he has never lost the unassuming fun-loving traits in his personality that make him such a rewarding person to know and be with. Benjamin Zander says:

> His modesty is almost uncanny for someone at the level he is. It is very rare to find someone of that calibre who has maintained the inquiring mind of a student. And he's always interested in others' opinions. In the receiving line after a concert, he will always ask people what they are doing and thinking—whether it has to do with music or not. He is so down-to-earth and real. And he has this modesty and sweetness and caring about other people that is a wonderful protection against superstardom.[16]

Ma was discussing the differences between the arts and the sciences with an eminent theoretical physicist. The latter claimed that whilst both fields prize imagination and creativity, in science the most elegant theory has to be tested against truth, and that artistic work must rely upon imagination only. Ma disagreed, pointing out that whereas the scientific theory is tested through repeatable experiments, musical truth—which sets up its own internal laws—is revealed through the ritual of the concert. Ma explains, 'It is with a feeling of sharing this awe and wonderment of life that I approach the ritual of giving a concert. The ritual begins when there is a composer, performer and listener, and it develops meaning when there is a shared attempt at describing a kind of truth. One hopes, for moments, that truth can be captured in time and live on in the memories of all the participants.'[17]

Until about four years ago, Ma played a Matteo Gofriller dated 1722 which previously belonged to Pierre Fournier. He then bought a Montagnana which he plays alternately with the 'Davidov' Stradivari loaned to him by Jacqueline du Pré.

CHAPTER XXXVIII

The Sunset Touch:
Jacqueline du Pré

'SHE IS THE most outstanding cellistic and musical talent I have met so far, to which she adds incredible maturity of mind. I am of the opinion that she will have a great career and deserves every help to this end.'[1] This was written by William Pleeth in a letter of recommendation for the Suggia Award when Jacqueline du Pré was ten years old. His prophecy was certainly right. But what could not be envisaged was that this great career would be cut short by incurable illness at the age of twenty-six.

Jacqueline du Pré was born in Oxford in 1945 into a family where music was always present. Her mother had been a professional pianist, her father was a keen amateur on the piano accordion and her sister played the violin. Jacqueline could sing in tune before she could talk and at three she heard the cello on a Children's Hour programme on the BBC and announced that she wanted 'one of those'. On her fourth birthday she was given a full-size instrument and managed to play it without difficulty. She showed such obvious talent that when she was only five she was sent to the London Violoncello School as a pupil of Alison Dalrymple. She was not at all pleased when she was allocated a half-size cello, and gave her teacher no peace until allowed a full-size instrument.

At the age of seven she appeared in her first public concert and three years later was awarded the Suggia Gift. On this occasion the board of adjudicators included Sir John Barbirolli. Lady Barbirolli recalls that particular day very clearly. 'It was the first time John had ever heard Jackie. I had come to fetch my husband and sat in to listen. I remember that she had some difficulty in tuning her cello so John did it for her. I cannot recall what she played but I only know that I was absolutely fascinated by what I heard. She was so gifted and immediately compelled one's attention. A phenomenal talent.'[2]

The violist, Lionel Tertis—also a member of the board—remembered that as soon as Jackie played, Barbirolli turned to him and said 'This is it!'[3] From this time a very close friendship grew between

Barbirolli and the young cellist. He would occasionally advise her about her playing, and Lady Barbirolli remembers that he would tell her not to press too much with her bow. 'She was so exuberant with this talent which simply poured out of her that she needed to restrain herself a little. I think John was able to calm her down, and she would take it from him.'⁴

It was through the Suggia award that Jackie went to study with William Pleeth at the Guildhall School of Music. Pleeth recalled the very first lesson.

> She played a simple piece very well but there was nothing flashy about her. At the time she was not an outstanding genius, but there was something that came through and you knew that there was a vast talent that could flower at a tremendous speed once it was awakened. My first impression was of a simple nice child playing with a very nice sound. No fireworks. It was something you detected, and possibly because of the deep sincerity, she was probably not aware of it at the time. When you first hear these gifted youngsters you either get something that is innocent and bland or something which is pregnant. With Jackie it was pregnant. It was just a case of opening a few doors.

By the time she was thirteen, those doors were beginning to open fast. Pleeth recalls that he announced that the following week they would begin on the Elgar Concerto and one of the Piatti Caprices. She turned up four days later having memorized the first movement of the concerto and the first, very difficult caprice. Furthermore, she performed them almost impeccably. 'She was always a joy to teach. She had such a quick understanding, and even if she didn't understand at that moment, she did eventually. It was a kind of animal magic. As one talked to her you could see the understanding and the physical coming together. It was quite remarkable.'

Nonetheless, lessons were not always smooth. 'Jackie went through a bad patch of tears around the age of fourteen. We had vast struggles and needed to make some readjustments. It wasn't just a matter of getting on with the cello.'⁵ However, there were no signs of her struggles when, the following year, she carried off the Queen's Prize at the Guildhall, an award open to young musicians under the age of thirty. She was just fifteen.

Jackie also had had advice from Casals, who spotted her talent very early on. A few months with Tortelier in Paris and some time with Rostropovich in Moscow widened her horizons, but she always regarded Pleeth as her real teacher and her loyalty to him never diminished.

Her recital début at the Wigmore Hall took place on 1 March 1961, and there were 'house full' notices outside well before the day of the concert. A Wigmore début is enough of an ordeal in itself, but when the world has its eyes on an outstanding teenager, the stress is even greater. Jackie's experience was one that might have unnerved the most seasoned artist. All went well until she suddenly realized that her A string was beginning to unwind. She compensated until it was no longer possible to rescue it. So all she could do was apologize and leave the platform to replace it. She returned smiling and continued as if nothing had happened. The critics had a field day, everyone voted her playing outstanding, and a bright future was predicted. Colin Mason in the *Guardian* described her playing as 'rather impassive in its quiet mastery. The pleasure it gives is purely and "classically" musical, and the beauty of her phrasing is in its poise, its perfect control of rhythm and tone, its purity of sound, rather than in any extra-musical or supra-musical expressiveness.' He goes on to say that the dexterity of her fingers had her audience gasping. This 16-year-old had pleased one of the toughest and most critical audiences in the world and her future seemed assured.

From this point there followed a success that can only be paralleled with that of the youthful Menuhin. She played all over Europe and the UK, appearing with all the leading British orchestras and most celebrated conductors. The response she received from her audiences was overwhelming.

On 14 May 1965 du Pré made her New York début at the Carnegie Hall playing the Elgar Concerto with the BBC Symphony Orchestra conducted by Antal Dorati, and took the Americans by storm. Raymond Ericson, writing in the *New York Times* next day, gives an evocative picture:

A tall, slim blonde, Miss du Pré looked like a cross between Lewis Carroll's Alice and one of those angelic instrumentalists in Renaissance paintings. And, in truth, she played like an angel, one with extraordinary warmth and sensitivity . . .
Miss du Pré and the concerto seemed made for each other, because her playing was so completely imbued with the romantic spirit. Her tone was sizeable and beautifully burnished. Her technique was virtually flawless, whether she was playing the sweeping chords that open the concerto, sustaining a ravishing

pianissimo tone, or keeping the fast-repeated note figures in the
scherzo going at an even pace.

From this point du Pré could do no wrong. She was the greatest
young British musical talent in living memory, and became increasingly in demand for concerts all over the world. Her marriage to the
young Israeli pianist, Daniel Barenboim, now more famous as a
conductor, took place in Jerusalem in 1967 immediately following
the Six Day War. Their sonata recitals were given to packed
audiences and the critics were never more eloquent or lavish in their
praise. When joined by their close friend and colleague, the violinist,
Pinchas Zukerman, the critics ran out of superlatives.

Du Pré played on three magnificent cellos. Her two Stradivaris,
one dated 1672 and the other 1712, the 'Davidov', were both given
to her by an anonymous donor. In 1971 Barenboim presented her
with a cello made by the Philadelphia-based Sergio Peresson. Except
when playing chamber music in a small room, she used this
instrument for the rest of her performing life. She described it as
'very healthy and strong like a tank, with a wonderfully rich sound
that reaches the corners of the largest hall'.[6] This was the cello she
used for her last few sonata recordings and in the Elgar Concerto
with the Philadelphia Orchestra conducted by Barenboim, recorded
during a public concert.

It was difficult to find time to fit these recordings into an already
packed schedule. But, as always, she gave her full attention to this
as to every task in hand. Everyone who worked with her in the
recording studios 'adored' her. Suvi Raj Grubb, her recording
producer, writes:

She was the ideal recording artist, undemanding, understanding
of other people's problems and with no outbursts of what is called
'temperament'. . . .For the engineers she was the perfect artist
who never complained, however long it took to get the right
sound through the microphones. For me, the all-too-brief six
years in which we worked together are a golden memory of
spontaneous, unaffected, joyous music-making.[7]

Then came the gradual onset of the disease which was eventually
diagnosed as Multiple Sclerosis and which brought her splendid
career to an end. She was forced to cancel several concerts and in the
summer of 1971 she abandoned her cello for almost six months.
Suddenly, in December of that year, Barenboim telephoned Raj

Grubb to say they had been practising the Chopin and Franck sonatas and she was playing as well as ever. Should they not record them? The recordings were completed in two days. When they were finished du Pré suggested they might start on the Beethoven sonatas. Both Grubb and Barenboim noticed she looked tired, but agreed to make a start. They recorded the first movement of the Op. 5 No. 1. 'At the end of it she placed her cello back in its case with "That is that", and did not even want to listen to what we had taped. That was Jacqueline du Pré's last appearance in the recording studio.'⁸

Her final bow to London audiences took place in 1973, when she played the Elgar Concerto with the New Philharmonia Orchestra conducted by Zubin Mehta, another close personal friend. Sir Neville Cardus wrote in the *Guardian*, 'On this occasion Jacqueline went to the heart of the matter with a devotion remarkable in so young an artist, so that we did not appear so much to be hearing, as overhearing, music which has the sunset touch on it . . . telling of Elgar's acceptance of the end. The bright day is done, and he is for the dark.'⁹ Cardus must have thought many times on the poignancy of his prophetic phrase.

Du Pré went to America shortly afterwards to join her husband. It was here during a rehearsal that she finally realized she was fighting a losing battle. The rest of the story is one of a courageous young woman dealing with one of the cruellest fates a musician can face.

She always responded to her disability with cheerfulness and turned to various other artistic outlets. Her master classes on television were hugely successful and the limited amount of teaching she undertook has benefited many young cellists. Robert Cohen, also a pupil of Pleeth, talked about his lessons with du Pré: 'We both went to Pleeth at the same age so we often had long discussions on our own early training and how he coped with our individual problems. I learnt from just talking with her. But when one played, she would not allow a note to go by without discussing what that note demanded. She has a dedication to each note which is tremendously inspiring.'¹⁰

In being deprived of music as an expressive form, Jacqueline du Pré turned to words.

I find I adore words. Never having had to use them to any great extent, I am finding beautiful new things about speech I never knew existed. Recently I had to make a reading from the Old Testament for the Branch of the MS Society, of which I am a patron. I found that everything is the same as in a musical performance. The psychological emphasis, the structure and timing is all the same. I am also reading poetry for the first time in my life and I love it so much.[11]

In her short but brilliant performing life Jacqueline du Pré brought happiness to millions. She made fifteen recordings, the last of which was as narrator in Prokofiev's *Peter and the Wolf*. Since technical skills in recording are now so highly developed, her playing will remain a constant joy for posterity. There is also the delightful television film *Jackie*, made by Christopher Nupen which shows her uninhibited and exuberant nature and total commitment to her music and to life.

She was often accused of going at such a pace that she would burn herself out too quickly. An example is provided by Tortelier who tells of the time when he was teaching at Dartington Summer School and du Pré asked him to help her with Bloch's *Schelomo*. It was well past midnight, the day had been a very full one, and Tortelier suggested it might be too late. Du Pré insisted she knew a room where they would not be heard. Tortelier virtually gave her a lesson that went on until 2.30 in the morning.

Perhaps her guardian angel knew that she had a great deal to accomplish before the curtain came down. A quotation from her own notebook aptly sums up the situation. 'If the sunshine beckons you, accept its invitation and love the gold quality of it.'[12]

Jacqueline du Pré died on 19 October 1987.

CODA

CELLO PLAYING HAS come a long way since the seventeenth century, and much of that distance has been made in the last few decades. Now truly recognized as a virtuoso instrument in its own right, the cello has proved itself to be as romantic as the violin. Perhaps the most remarkable outcome is the ever-increasing interest of the young in playing the cello.

It is difficult to choose between some of the gifted young cellists who are steadily climbing to the top in Britain today; Rohan da Saram, Moray Welsh, Richard Markson, Julian Lloyd Webber, Raphael Wallfisch, Alexander Baillie, Colin Carr, Lowri Blake, Steven Isserlis, Marius May, Robert Cohen and Caroline Dale are among the most outstanding. The Hungarian-born Thomas Igloi, who died in 1976 at the age of 23, at the start of a brilliant career, would doubtless have been among this number had he lived. Marcy Rosen, Terry King, Paul Tobias, Carter Brey, Sharon Robinson, Timothy Eddy, Sophie Rolland, Shauna Rolston, Peter Rejto (son of the late Gabor Rejto), Charles Curtis and Matt Haimovitz form a similar pattern on the American continent.

To a great extent this extraordinary situation is probably due to the impact on the musical world of Jacqueline du Pré's phenomenal talent. Young people were immediately inspired to take up the instrument and ambitious parents began to nurse hopes of a similar flowering in their own offspring. However, there would appear to be deeper reasons for preferring an instrument that is bulky and difficult to transport, notwithstanding the hostility shown by the airline operators towards cellists who are afraid to allow their valuable instruments to travel as cargo.

What, then, are the main attractions of the cello? It can sing treble, alto, tenor or bass, and its pitch range is wider than that of any other stringed instrument. A composer can reckon on five octaves when he is writing for the cello, which gives him plenty of scope.

Could it be that, when reflecting upon some of the imponderables of our modern age, the more thoughtful of our young people find the deeper voice of the cello is more in accord with the temper of their thinking? Another aspect is the dichotomy that exists between performing alone and in a group. Young people enjoy collective pursuits, which is probably one of the reasons why chamber music is so popular with the young. Certainly some of the youthful string quartets are evidence of the high standards prevailing in this field.

Cello orchestras of from 50 to 200 players are being formed all over the world. The sound they produce is extraordinarily beautiful, and, because the carrying of harmony is natural to the cello, all orchestral structures are secure. This would not be possible on either violin or viola. These massed cello enterprises are in many ways a necessity, for, with the increasing number of excellent cellists everywhere, some provision must be made for them to play their instrument.

Which brings us to the vital question of what will happen to all the young cellists who daily add their talents to a pool that has been above flood level for a decade. As the talent multiplies, the competition will increase alongside the problems inherent in a surfeit of excellence. We are liable to find the cello sections in our orchestras becoming akin to the superb band at Mannheim which Charles Burney described as 'an army of generals'.

If there is not enough work for the performers, they will turn to teaching and thereby train even more cellists. In the USA the situation has reached immense proportions, made even more difficult by the fact that, at one time, universities regarded performers as inferior. Only by taking a doctorate in music could they compete with academics in other subjects. The violinist, Henri Temianka once recalled a situation when he was lecturing to about 50 musicians at a university and was the only one without a doctorate.

Whatever the prevailing circumstances and however abundant the talent, one thing is certain. The cream will always float to the top. As we have seen throughout the centuries, there are many fine cellists, but only half a dozen names will easily be remembered. This is because it takes more than talent, musicianship or a brilliant technique to earn a place for posterity. What is needed is a combination of all these qualities, set off by the personality of the performer and his or her ability to communicate with an audience. These are the true 'greats' and even with the abundance of talent we have today, they are still very few and far between.

NOTES

SELECTED BIBLIOGRAPHY

CHRONOLOGY

INDEX

NOTES

PRELUDE: *The Tools of the Trade*

1 Letter from Charles Beare to MC   2 Pleeth, p 261

I *The Birth of the Butterfly*

1 Van der Straeten, pp 371–2
2 Ibid., p 372
3 Pleeth, p 231
4 Burney, i, p 629
5 Ibid., ii, p 1005
6 Van der Straeten, p 154

II *Berteau and the Duports*

1 Van der Straeten, p 263
2 Grancino Editions: publishers of Early Cello Music
3 Quoted in Van der Straeten, p 278
4 Ibid., p 281

III *The French Influence*

1 Van der Straeten, p 293
2 Spiccato: A succession of notes (martelé) in one bow—the bow remaining on the string.
3 Staccato: A single note played by a single bow stroke (detached).
4 Hill, p 141

IV *The Forgotten Genius: Boccherini*

1 Rothschild, p 14
2 Ibid., p 14
3 Ibid., p 19
4 Mendelssohn, Felix, *Reisebriefe aus den Fahren 1830–1832*, quoted in Rothschild, p 89
5 Grove VI, ii, p 828
6 Interview, MC

V *Enter the English*

1 *The General Advertiser*, 6 February 1752
2 Burney, ii, p 1012
3 Crome, quoted in Cowling, pp 47–8
4 Van der Straeten, p 326

VI *Father of the German School: Romberg*

1 AmZ 1807 p 543
2 Ibid., 1833 p 394
3 Ibid., 1834 p 515
4 The last 'discantist' boy soprano of C. P. E. Bach
5 Becker and Rynar, *Mechanik und Asthetik des Violoncellspiels*, p 264, quoted in Ginsburg, p 27

VII *The Dresden School*

1 Wasielewski, p 123

VIII *The Dresden Influence*

1 Quoted in Ginsburg, pp 130–31   3 Ibid., p 122
2 Brown, p 121

IX *'Paganini of the Cello': Servais*

1 Quoted in Ginsburg, p 35   2 Ibid., p 34

X *Belgium and Holland*

1 Van der Straeten, p 555   3 Shaw, *The World*, 9 July 1890
2 Gavoty, p 10

XI *'Czar of Cellists': Davidov*

1 *The Strad*, January 1952, p 276   cellist of the Oldenburg Court
2 Ibid., p 278   Chapel.
3 The concerto was first performed on   4 *The Strad*, January 1952, p 278
  9 June 1860 in Leipzig on the   5 Letter from Fyodor Cherniavsky to
  composer's 50th birthday. The   MC
  soloist was Ludwig Ebert, principal

XII *The Bohemian Touch*

1 Burney, *The Present State of Music in*   2 Cowling, p 122
  Germany, the Netherlands and the   3 Ginsburg, p 101
  United Provinces, p 104   4 *The Strad*, December 1981, p 578

XIII *'Sarasate of the Cello': Popper*

1 *Musikinstrumenten-Zeitung*, quoted in   5 *The Musical Times and Singing Class*
  De'ak, p 170   *Circular*, 1 December 1891
2 Hanslick, *Geschichte des Konzertwesen*   6 Shaw, *The World*, 2 December 1891
  in Wien, quoted in De'ak, p 119   7 De'ak, p 222
3 Ibid., p 177   8 Ibid., p 241
4 *The Scotsman*, 3 November 1891

XIV *'Grand Master of the Cello': Piatti*

1 Ginsburg, p 87   3 Van der Straeten, p 584
2 Hanslick, *Aus dem Konsertsaal*, 1870, 4 Wasielewski, p 111
  pp 162–3

XV *The Twin Peaks: Klengel and Becker*

1 Grove, V, iv, p 781   5 Van der Straeten, p 483
2 *The Strad*, October 1978, p 523   6 Fuchs, p 48
3 Piatigorsky, pp 64–5   7 Ibid., p 42
4 Quoted from interview, MC   8 Quoted from interview, MC

XVI *The British Element*

1 Quoted from interview, MC   3 Quoted from interview, MC
2 *Royal College of Music Union*   4 BBC Radio 4, 1969
  Magazine, May 1963, LIX No.2   5 Kennedy, p 28

XVII *'Freedom with Order': Casals*

1 Kahn, p 30
2 With his father he wrote music for a pageant, *Els Pastorets* (Adoration of the Shepherds), in which Casals played the Devil
3 Kahn, p 35
4 Ibid., p 70
5 Ibid., p 76
6 Ibid., p 92
7 *The Strad*, January 1967, p 339
8 Kahn, p 116
9 Ibid., p 227
10 A wealthy patroness of the arts. She built an Italian-style palace in Boston and filled it with 14th and 15th century paintings and sculpture: now the Gardner Museum.
11 *The Strad*, December 1953, p 238
12 Quoted from interview, MC
13 *The Strad*, November 1975, p 483

XVIII *The European Vanguard*

1 Quoted from interview, MC
2 VS, NL, May 1968, p 6
3 Quoted from interview, MC
4 Ibid.
5 *Chicago Tribune*, c. early 1940's
6 *The Strad*, April 1946, p 268

XIX *Across the Atlantic: Salmond*

1 Cole, *An appreciation* (unpublished)
2 VS, NL, Winter 1972, p 4
3 *The Strad*, January 1970, p 411
4 Quoted from interview, MC
5 VS, NL, Winter 1972, p 2
6 Quoted from interview, MC
7 Letter from Lynn Harrell to MC

XX *'The Jewel in the Crown': Feuermann*

1 Itzkoff, p 43
2 *The Strad*, September 1972, p 249
3 Itzkoff, p 81
4 Ibid., p 112
5 *The Strad*, October 1938, p 276
6 Itzkoff, p 155
7 Ibid., p 157
8 *The Strad*, July 1938, p 136
9 Quoted from interview, MC
10 Ibid.
11 Itzkoff, pp 197–8
12 Ibid., p 198
13 VS, NL, Spring 1972, p 2
14 Quoted from interview, MC

XXI *The Last Great Romantic: Piatigorsky*

1 Piatigorsky, p 5
2 Ibid., p 10
3 VS, NL, September 1968, p 2
4 Quoted from interview, MC
5 Applebaum, i, p 309–10
6 Ginsburg, p 258
7 VS, NL, March 1977, p 3
8 *The Strad*, October 1976, p 445

XXII *The Unique View*

1 VS, NL, February 1980, p 7
2 Letter from William Vandenburg to MC
3 Quoted from interview, MC
4 Ibid.
5 Ibid.
6 VS, NL, May 1978, p 6
7 Ibid., June 1982, p 4
8 Ibid., February 1980, p 5
9 Letter from Joel Krosnick to MC
10 Gavoty, *Antonio Janigro*, p 8
11 Ibid., p 15

XXIII *Versatility par Excellence: Greenhouse and Rose*

1 Quoted from interview, MC
2 Ibid.
3 *The Strad*, November 1958, p 229
4 Quoted from interview, MC
5 Applebaum, i, p 320
6 Ibid., p 329
7 Cowling, p 176

XXIV *The Italian Quartet*

1 *The Strad*, February 1967, p 389
2 Grove V, ii, p 110
3 Ginsburg, p 235
4 Quoted from interview, MC
5 *Archi e Musica* (free translation), pp 69–71, undated
6 Letter from Radu Aldulescu to MC

XXV *Ladies on the Bass Line*

1 Cowling, pp 180–1
2 Van der Straeten, p 599
3 Quoted from interview, MC
4 *Daily Telegraph*, 23 October 1930
5 VS, NL, March 1975, p 5
6 Harrison, p 55
7 Ibid., pp 94–5
8 Ibid., p 96
9 Ibid., p 104
10 Ibid., p 28
11 Ibid., 120
12 Ibid., 127
13 *The Strad*, April 1965, p 461

XXVI *The French Tradition*

1 *Le Monde Musicale*, 1927, No. 2
2 Ginsburg, p 196
3 Ibid., pp 190–1
4 *The Strad*, November 1953, pp 200–2
5 Quoted from interview, MC
6 Szigeti, p 335
7 Ibid., p 358
8 Ginsburg, p 200
9 Quoted from interview, MC
10 Ibid.
11 *The Strad*, April 1984, p 838
12 Tortelier/Blum, p 37
13 Ibid., p 50
14 Ibid., p 101
15 Quoted from interview, MC
16 Ibid.
17 Ibid.
18 Quoted from interview, MC

XXVII *American by Choice*

1 VS, NL, December 1983, p 4
2 Ibid.
3 Ibid., pp 5–6
4 Ibid., April 1982, p 5
5 Quoted from interview, MC
6 Quoted from interview, MC
7 Ibid.
8 *Newsweek*, No. 29, 1973, p 75
9 Quoted from interview, MC
10 Ibid.
11 *New York Times*, 15 April 1960
12 Quoted from interview, MC
13 *Philadelphia Inquirer*, 11 January 1985

XXVIII *From Russia—with Talent*

1 Quoted from interview, MC
2 Ibid.
3 *New York Times*, 4 December 1934
4 Quoted from interview, MC
5 Ibid.
6 Ginsburg, p 264
7 Letter from Zara Nelsova to MC
8 Quoted from interview, MC
9 Letter from Zara Nelsova to MC
10 Ibid.
11 Ginsburg, p 266
12 *The Strad*, October 1978, p 517
13 *Los Angeles Times*, 4 December 1984

XXIX *The Japanese Phenomenon*

1 Quoted from interview, MC
2 Ibid.
3 Quoted from interview, MC
4 Ginsburg, p 284
5 *South China Morning Post*, 12 April 1985
6 Ginsburg, pp 285–6
7 Ibid., p 286

XXX *The British Heritage*

1 *Hamburger Anzeiger*, 19 March 1937
2 Quoted from interview, MC
3 Ibid.
4 Letter from Frank Bridge to Florence Hooton, 19 June 1936
5 Quoted from interview, MC
6 Ibid.
7 *The Strad*, May 1977, p 9
8 Quoted from interview, MC
9 Ibid.

XXXI *The Continuing Line*

1 Quoted from interview, MC
2 Ibid.
3 *The Strad*, July 1964, p 103
4 Ibid., October 1975, p 411
5 Ibid., p 411
6 Ibid., p 413
7 Quoted from interview, MC
8 Ibid.
9 Quoted from interview, MC

XXXII *Russia—Home and Away*

1 Quoted from interview, MC
2 Ibid.
3 *Berliner Zeitung am Mittag*, 28 October 1925
4 Quoted from interview, MC
5 *New York Post*, 23 February 1950
6 IMC/Kalmus, New York, 1983
7 *New York Times*, 10 January 1952
8 *The Strad*, May 1977, p 60
9 Quoted from interview, MC
10 Ibid.
11 *Daily Telegraph*, 2 August 1985
12 Quoted from interview, MC
13 Hanno Rinke, 'A Profile': DG Information
14 Ibid.
15 *Daily Telegraph*, 26 September 1977
16 *The Times*, Hilary Finch, 2 June 1983
17 *Financial Times*, Dominic Gill, 3 October 1985
18 *Ovation*, June 1986
19 Hanno Rinke, 'A Profile': DG Information

XXXIII *The Russian Dynamo*

1 Quoted from interview, MC
2 Ibid.
3 *The Strad*, August 1961, p 117
4 Letter from Moray Welsh to MC
5 Quoted from interview, MC
6 Ibid.
7 Ibid.

XXXIV *The Art of the Necessary*

1 Quoted from interview, MC
2 Ibid.
3 *The Strad*, April 1963, pp 437 and 439
4 Quoted from interview, MC
5 Letter from Armand d'Angour to MC
6 *The Strad*, June 1986, p 114
7 Quoted from interview, MC
8 Ibid.

xxxv *Scandinavia and Europe*

1 Letter from Erhling Bengtsson to MC
2 *The Times*, 22 August, 1957
3 *Winnipeg Free Press*, 10 February 1974
4 Letter from Erhling Bengtsson to MC
5 Ibid.
6 *Neue Zeitschrift fur Musik*, 1969, No. 9, p 423
7 Quoted from interview, MC
8 *The Strad*, November 1982, p 503
9 *The Gramophone*, August 1984
10 *The Strad*, November 1982, p 505

xxxvi *'Excellent is Enough'*

1 Kennedy, p 268, a letter to Audrey Napier-Smith, 26 January 1960.
2 Ginsburg, p 274
3 Ibid.
4 Quoted in *Columbia Artists Management*
5 Ibid., Linda Richardson, 2 July 1978
6 Quoted from interview, MC
7 Ibid.
8 *Daily Telegraph*, 9 October 1972
9 Quoted from interview, MC
10 Quoted from interview, MC
11 *Musical America*, December 1978, quoted in VS, NL February 1979, p 8
12 Quoted from interview, MC
13 VS, NL, March 1977, p 5

xxxvii *The Rose Line*

1 Quoted from interview, MC
2 *New York Times*
3 Quoted from interview, MC
4 *New York Times*, 28 January, 1968
5 *Omaha World-Herald*, 24 November 1970
6 *Sumpter Daily Item*, 22 November 1977
7 Quoted from interview, MC
8 Letter from Gerald Moore to Mrs Foster
9 *Green Bay Press Gazette*, 10 December 1975
10 ICM Artists
11 Ibid.
12 *Classical Music*, 19 September 1981, p 16
13 ICM Artists
14 Ibid., 21 December 1984
15 *The Gramophone*, June 1984, p 6
16 ICM Artists
17 *Keynote*, March 1985, p 30

xxxviii *The Sunset Touch: du Pré*

1 Wordsworth, p 52
2 Quoted from interview, MC
3 Ibid.
4 Ibid.
5 Ibid.
6 Ibid.
7 Wordsworth, p 99
8 Ibid., p 100
9 *Guardian*, 9 February 1973
10 Quoted from interview, MC
11 Ibid.
12 Wordsworth, p 136

SELECTED BIBLIOGRAPHY

Editions to which reference is made in the notes have been consulted in all cases.

APPLEBAUM, SAMUEL and SADA, *The Way They Play*, Paganiniana, Books I–XII (New Jersey 1973–83).
—— *With the Artists*, Markert (New York 1955).
BAINES, A., *Musical Instruments Through the Ages*, Pelican (London 1969).
BOYDEN, DAVID D., *The History of Violin Playing from its Origins to 1761*, O.U.P. (Oxford 1965).
BROWN, DAVID, *Tchaikovsky: A Biographical and Critical Study Vol II: The Crisis Years (1874–78)*, Gollancz (London 1982).
BUNTING, CHRISTOPHER, *Essay on the Craft of Cello Playing* Vols I and II, Cambridge University Press (Cambridge 1982).
BURNEY, CHARLES, *A General History of Music* Vols I and II, Foulis (London 1935).
——*The Present State of Music in Germany, the Netherlands, and the United Provinces*, (London 1773).
COWLING, ELIZABETH, *The Cello*, Batsford (London 1975).
DE'AK, STEVEN, *David Popper*, Paganiniana (New Jersey 1980).
ELKIN, ROBERT, *Queen's Hall (1893–1941)*, Rider (London 1944).
FUCHS, CARL, *Musical and Other Recollections*, Sherratt & Hughes (Manchester 1937).
GAVOTY, BERNARD, *Pierre Fournier*, Kister (Geneva 1956).
——*Antonio Janigro*, Kister (Geneva 1962).
GÉRARD, YVES, *Thematic, Bibliographical and Critical Catalogue of the Works of Luigi Boccherini*, OUP (London 1969).
GINSBURG, LEV, *History of the Violoncello*, Paganiniana (New Jersey 1983).
GROVE *Dictionary of Music and Musicians*, 5th and 6th eds, Macmillan; St Martin's Press (London 1954; New York 1980).
HARLEY, JOHN, *Music in Purcells's London*, Dobson (London 1968).
HARRISON, BEATRICE, *The Cello and the Nightingale* ed. Patricia Cleveland-Peck, Murray (London 1985).
HILL, RALPH, *Brahms*, Archer (London 1933).
HILL, W. HENRY, Arthur F. and Alfred E., *Antonio Stradivari: His Life and Work (1644–1737)*, Dover (New York 1963).
ITZKOFF, Seymour W., *Emanuel Feuermann, Virtuoso*, University of Alabama Press (Alabama 1979).
KAHN, ALBERT E., *Joys and Sorrows*, Eel Pie (Chichester 1970).
KENNEDY, MICHAEL, *Barbirolli*, McGibbon & Kee (London 1971).
LATHAM, PETER, *Brahms*, Dent (London 1962).

Markevitch, Dimitry, *Cello Story*, translated Florence W. Seder, Summy-Birchard Music (New Jersey 1984).

Moore, Gerald, *Am I Too Loud?*, Hamish Hamilton (London 1962).

The New Oxford History of Music: The Modern Age, Vol. X ed. Martin Cooper, O.U.P. (Oxford 1974).

Piatigorsky, G., *Cellist*, Da Capo (New York 1965).

Pincherle, M., *Vivaldi, Genius of the Baroque*, Norton; Gollancz (New York 1957; London 1958).

Pleeth, W., *The Cello,* ed. Nona Pyron, Macdonald (London 1982).

Racster, Olga, *Chats on Violoncellos*, Werner Laurie (London 1907).

Rothschild, Germaine de, *Luigi Boccherini: His Life and Work*, translated Andreas Mayor, O.U.P. (Oxford 1965).

Rubinstein, A., *My Young Years*, Cape (London 1973).

——*My Many Years*, Cape (London 1980).

Sandys & Forster, *History of the Violin*, Reeves (London 1864).

Shaw, George Bernard, *Music in London* Vols II and III, Constable (London 1932).

The Strad, Novello (London 1898–1986).

Szigeti, J., *With Strings Attached,* Knopf (New York 1967).

Temianka, H., *Facing the Music*, Alfred (California 1980).

Tortelier, P., *How I Play I Teach*, Chester (London 1975).

Tortelier, P. and Blum, D., *Paul Tortelier: A Self-Portrait*, Heinemann (London 1984).

Van der Straeten, A.E., *History of the Violoncello, the Viola da Gamba, their Precursors and Collateral Instruments*, Reeves (London 1914).

Violoncello Society *Newsletters* (New York 1968–1984).

Wasielewski, W.J.D., *The Violoncello and its History*, translated Isobella S.E. Stigand, Novello (London 1894).

Wordsworth, William (ed.), *Jacqueline du Pré: Impressions*, Granada (1983).

★

Unless quoted otherwise in the text, these are the main concertos indicated throughout:

Barber, Samuel, Cello Concerto Op. 22 (1946).

Boccherini, Luigi, Concerto in Bb arr. Grützmacher, Cat. No. 482 (Gérard).

Brahms, Johannes, Double Concerto in A minor, Op. 102 (1887).

Britten, Benjamin, *Cello Symphony*, Op. 68 (1963).

Davidov, Karl, Concerto No. 2 in A minor, Op. 14

Delius, Frederick, Cello Concerto (1921).

Dutilleux, Henri, *Tout un monde lointain*, (1970).

Elgar, Sir Edward, Concerto in E minor, Op. 85 (1919).

Finzi, Gerald, Concerto, Op. 40 (1951–5).

Haydn, Joseph, Concerto No. 2 in D major (1783).

Lalo, Edouard, Concerto in D minor (1876).

Lutoslawski, Witold, Concerto (1970).

PENDERECKI, KRZYZTOF, Sonata for Cello and Orchestra, No. 1 (1964).
PROKOFIEV, SERGEI, Cello Concerto No. 1, Op. 58 (1938).
——Sinfonia Concertante (Symphony-Concerto), Op. 125 (1952).
SAINT-SAËNS, CAMILLE, Concerto in A minor, Op. 33 (1873).
SCHUMANN, ROBERT, Concerto in A minor, Op. 129 (1854).
SHOSTAKOVICH, DIMITRI, Cello Concerto, Op. 107 (1959).
STRAUSS, RICHARD, *Don Quixote*, variations, Op. 35 (1897).
TCHAIKOVSKY, PIOTR ILYICH, *Variations on a Rococo Theme*, Op. 33 (1876).
——*Pezzo capriccioso*, Op. 62 (1887).
WALTON, WILLIAM, Cello Concerto (1957).

CHRONOLOGICAL LIST OF CELLISTS

Saunders c.1600–
Bononcini 1670–1755
Stuck 1680–1755
Cervetto 1682–1783
Marcello 1686–1739
Dall'Abaco, E. 1675–1742
Franciscello 1691–1739
Vandini c.1700–1773
Dall'Oglio 1700–
Berteau 1700–1771
Lanzetti 1710–80
Dall'Abaco, J. 1710–1805
Johnson 1710–1814
Neruda 1716–1780
Mara I, c.1721–1783
Petrik 1727–c.1798
Barrière c.1707–1747
Corrette kn 1741
Cupis b.1741–
Duport, J.P. 1741–1818
Boccherini 1743–1805
Janson 1742–1803
Hallet b.1743
Mara, J.B. 1744–1808
Reicha 1746–1795
Cervetto, J. 1747–1837
Duport, J.L. 1749–1819
Fiala 1751–1816
Kraft, A. 1752–1820
Rovelli 1753–1806
Crosdill 1755–1825
Bréval 1756–1825
Schlick 1759–c.1825
Cernak c.1760–
Casella, Pietro 1762–1844
Polliari kn 1763–
Levasseur 1765–1823
Romberg 1767–1841
Stiastny, B. 1760–1835
Lamarre 1772–1823
Baudiot 1773–1849
Stiastny, J. 1774–c.1826
Lindley 1776–1855

Platel 1777–1835
Kraft 1778–1853
Norblin 1781–1854
Dotzauer 1783–1860
Wielhorsky 1787–1863
Hüttner 1793–1840
Vaslin 1794–
Merighi 1795–1849
Kummer 1797–1879
Dreschler 1800–1873
Lee 1805–1887
Servais 1807–1866
Franchomme 1808–1884
Schmidt 1810–1862
Schuberth 1811–1863
Chevillard 1811–1877
De Munck, F. 1815–1854
Franco-Mendes 1816–1860
Batta 1816–1902
Hegenbarth 1818–1887
Casella, Cesare G. 1819–1886
Piatti 1822–1901
Cossmann 1822–1910
Goltermann 1824–1898
Cristiani 1827–1853
Grützmacher 1832–1903
Appy 1834–
Diem 1836–1894
Davidov 1838–1889
De Munck, E. 1840–1915
Libotton 1842–1891
Hegar 1843–1921
Neruda, F. 1843–
De Swert 1843–1891
Popper 1843–1913
Delsart 1844–1900
Howell 1846–1898
Casella, Cesare 1849–
Fitzenhagen 1848–1890
Van Biene c.1850–
Wierzbilowicz 1850–1911
Jacobs 1851–1925
Hausmann 1852–1909
Klingenberg 1852–1905

Hollman 1852–1927
Platteau c.1855–1875
Wihan 1855–1920
Herbert 1859–1924
Brandoukov 1859–1930
Klengel 1859–1933
Whitehouse 1859–1935
Stern 1862–1904
Becker 1864–1941
Fuchs 1865–1951
Hekking, A. 1866–1925
Mossel 1870–1923
Walenn 1870–1953
Squire 1871–1963
Lebell 1872–
Neruda, A. c.1872–
Casals 1876–1973
Ballio 1879–
Hekking, G. 1879–1942
d'Archambeau 1879–1956
Grümmer 1879–1965
Willeke 1880–1950
Mukle 1880–1963
Britt 1881–1971
Zelenka 1881–1957
Alexanian 1881–1954
James 1882–1963
Casella, Alfredo 1883–1947
Kubatsky c.1920
Hambourg 1884–1954
Kosolupov 1884–1961
Van der Straeten 1885–1934
Rosanoff 1885–1974
Suggia 1888–1950
Salmond 1888–1952
Gauntlett 1889–1978
Rostropovich, L. 1892–1942
Maréchal 1892–1964
Harrison 1892–1965
Bolognini 1893–1979
Cherniavsky 1893–1982
Roemaet-Rosanoff 1896–1967
Cassadò 1897–1966
Mainardi 1897–1976
Barbirolli 1899–1971
Maas 1901–1948
Matz 1901–
Cameron 1902–1972
Eisenberg 1902–1973
Feuermann 1902–1942
Saito 1902–1974
Pini 1902–

Van den Burg 1902–
Silva 1903–1961
Piatigorsky 1903–1976
Scholz 1903–
Wenzinger 1905–
Fournier 1906–1986
Saidenberg 1906–
Reiss 1906–
Kilbey 1907–1982
Clark 1908–1976
Kurtz 1908–
Cole 1908–
Butler 1909–
Garbousova 1909–
Maas 1910–1948
Navarra 1911–
Whitehead 1912–1979
de Machula 1912–1982
Miller 1912–1986
Hooton 1912–
Aronson 1912–
Inoue 1912–
Rickelman 1912–
Magg 1914–
Tortelier 1914–
Shulman, Alan 1915–
Pleeth 1916–
Baldovino 1916–
Greenhouse 1916–
Rejto 1916–1987
Aller 1917–
Rose 1918–1984
Janigro 1918–
Nelsova 1918–
Gendron 1920–
Dickson 1921–
Aldulescu 1922–
Shafran 1923–
Markevitch 1923–
Bunting 1924–
Starker 1924–
Fleming 1925–
Cristiani 1927–1953
Lovett 1927–
Rostropovich, M. 1927–
Palm 1927–
Simpson 1928–
Harnoncourt 1929–
Parnas 1931–
Bengtsson 1932–
Bylsma 1934–
Hirai 1937–
Harvey 1938–
de Saram 1939–
Tsutsumi 1942–

Goritsky 1942–
Gutman 1942–
Kates 1943–
Yasuda 1944–
Harrell 1944–
Iwasaki 1944–
du Pré 1945–1987
Kirshbaum 1946–
Welsh 1947–
Kanno 1947–
Walewska 1948–
Rosen 1948–
Maisky 1948–
Pleeth, A. 1948–
Markson 1949–

Fujiwara 1949–
Lloyd Webber 1951–
Schiff 1951–
Igloi 1953–1976
Wallfisch 1953–
Yamazaki 1953–
Foster 1954–1980
Ma 1955–
Baillie 1956–
Carr 1957–
Blake 1957–
Isserlis 1958–
May 1958–
Cohen 1959–
Shulman, Andrew 1960–

INDEX

Abbado, Claudio, 276
Abel, Karl Friedrich, 57
Accardo, Salvatore, 199
Adam, Claus, 305
Adamowksi, Joseph, 77
Alard, Delphin, 46
Albani, Dame Emma, 126
Albéniz, Isaac, 127, 134
Albert, Eugene d', 206
Alborea, Francesco ('Franciscello'), 31, 32, 34
Aldulescu, Radu, 192, 198, 199
Alexanian, Diran, 151, 175–8, 183, 185, 186, 254, 270
Alvin, Juliette, 141, 254, 255
Amati, Andrea, 23, 25
Amati, Nicolò, 24, 25, 87, 111, 191, 267, 274
Anda, Géza, 227
Anderson, Marian, 165
Angour, Armand d', 292, 335n
Anhalt-Dessau, Duke of, 68
Applebaum, Samuel, 333n, 334n
Appy, Charles Ernest, 83
Ara, Ugo, 88
Aranyi, d' (sisters), 156, 192, 254, 255, 261
Archambeau, Iwan d', 87, 88
Archambeau, Jean Michel d', 88
Archambeau, Pierre d', 88
Argerich, Martha, 279
Arico, Fortunato, 159
Ariosti, Attilio, 113
Arnold, F.T., 290
Aronson, Lev, 306, 312
Ashkenazy, Vladimir, 279, 314, 315
Auer, Leopold, 85, 92, 93, 106, 117, 161, 275, 276
Ax, Emanuel, 319
Azlamazyan, Sergei, 272, 276

Bach, Anna Magdalena, 267, 271
Bach, C.P.E., 23, 331n
Bach, J.S. 31, 66, 73, 85, 88–9, 113, 118, 119, 121, 133–4, 140, 156, 177, 180, 187, 194, 195, 215, 216, 217, 221, 245, 247, 250, 254, 258, 261, 265, 267, 271, 273, 274, 279, 287, 290, 292, 293, 299, 317
Backhaus, Wilhelm, 120, 123, 194, 226
Bachrich, Sigismund, 105
Badings, Henk, 292

Badura-Skoda, Paul, 183
Bagge, Baron, 50, 61
Baillie, Alexander, 213, 327
Baillot, Pierre, 43, 45, 47
Bain, Wilfred, 229
Balakirev, Mily Alexeyevich, 92
Baldovino, Amedeo, 192, 196–8
Balsam, Artur, 235
Barber, Samuel, 157, 234, 235, 238
Barbirolli, Sir John, 128, 130, 131, 138–9, 154, 212, 237, 257, 264, 267, 302, 321, 322
Barbirolli, Lady, 321, 322
Barbirolli, Rosa, 130
Barenboim, Daniel, 278, 308, 324, 325
Barjansky, Serge, 207
Barrère, Georges, 146
Barrière, Jean, 35, 36
Barsham, Eve, 193
Bartók, Béla, 106, 108, 224, 225, 227, 244
Barton, James, 259
Batta, Alexander, 44, 83
Baudiot, Charles Nicolas, 40, 42, 43, 45, 47, 173
Bauer, Gertrud, 201
Bauer, Harold, 137, 146, 201, 235
Baumann, Pierre, 46
Baumgarten, Karl Friedrich, 58
Bax, Arnold, 209, 256
Bazelaire, Paul, 47, 214
Beare, Charles, 331n
Becker, Carl, Jnr., 25
Becker, Hugo, 63, 65, 72, 73, 88, 91, 95, 102, 112, 116, 118, 119, 120, 128, 151, 155, 170, 180, 194, 200, 206, 233, 252, 331n
Becker, Jean, 118
Beecham, Sir Thomas, 94, 123, 192
Beer, Sydney, 131
Beethoven, Ludwig van, 38, 47, 54, 62, 63, 68, 72, 76, 82, 92, 97–9, 117–19, 123, 133, 156, 162, 194, 215–17, 221, 224, 244, 249, 256, 265, 279, 292, 293, 297, 299, 313, 325
Bellman, Richard, 67
Benavente-Osuna, Countess, 52
Benda, Franz, 31, 97
Benedetti, René, 212
Bengtsson, Erling Blöndal, 297–9, 336n
Bennewitz, Anton, 100

Benvenuti, G., 212
Berg, Alban, 287, 300
Berger, Otakar, 101
Bergonzi, Carlo, 24, 121, 123
Bergson, Henri, 136, 141
Berlin, Anasim, 275
Berlinsky, V., 272
Berlioz, Hector, 79, 89, 104, 109
Bernac, Pierre, 220
Bernadel family, 25, 311
Bernstein, Jascha, 159
Bernstein, Leonard, 191, 315–7
Berrsche, Alexander, 194
Berteau, Martin, 34, 35, 37, 42
Berti, Giovanni, 183
Betti, Adolfo, 87
Bianchi, Luigi, 199
Biene, August Van, 85, 130
Biss, Kurt, 234
Bissolotti, Francesco, 25
Black, Joan, 253
Blake, Lowri, 327
Blanc, Hubert le, 34
Bloch, Ernest, 146, 191, 239, 326
Blomstedt, Herbert, 298
Bluhm, Béatrice, 200, 216
Boccherini, Leopoldo, 49
Boccherini, Luigi, 29, 30, 48–54, 61, 63, 64,
    72, 73, 110, 113, 151, 160, 173, 181, 193,
    214, 221, 293, 313
Böchmann, Ferdinand, 67, 69
Boehe, Ernst, 253
Böhm, Karl, 212
Böhme, Emil, 120
Bohrer, Max, 59
Boïto, Arrigo, 113
Bok, Mrs Mary Louise, 157
Bolognini, Egidio, 147
Bolognini, Ennio, 147–50
Bonaparte, Napoleon, 23, 39, 43, 49, 287
Bononcini, Giovanni, 31
Bonucci, Arturo, 180
Boomkamp, Carel van Leeuwen, 291
Borge, Victor, 150
Borisovsky, Vadim, 272
Boult, Sir Adrian, 131, 138, 204, 238,
    259–61, 264, 266
Bouette, Martin, 25
Boulanger, Nadia, 183
Brahms, Johannes, 70, 75, 107, 117, 120,
    133, 145, 152, 154, 156, 160, 162, 166,
    175, 188–9, 192–3, 197, 201, 206, 214,
    220, 253, 255, 264, 276, 279, 295, 311,
    319
Brandoukov, Anatoly, 76, 93, 169
Breton, Tomas, 134
Bréval, Jean Baptiste, 37
Brey, Carter, 327
Bridge, Frank, 129, 154, 257, 335n
Briggs, Rawdon, 123
Britt, Horace, 145–6
Britten, Benjamin, 220, 221, 257, 265, 283,
    285, 286, 287, 317
Brodsky, Adolf, 105, 122, 123
Brosa, Antonio, 162

Brown, David, 332n
Bruch, Max, 75, 86, 106, 156, 264
Brunetti, Gaetano, 52
Bülow, Hans von, 70, 100, 104, 105, 120
Bunting, Christopher, 141–2, 263–265
Burg, William Van den, 86, 175–6, 333n
Burney, Charles, 32, 55, 57, 96, 328, 331n,
    332n
Busch, Adolf, 121, 302
Bush, Alan, 257
Busoni, Ferruccio, 123
Butler, Antonia, 176, 177, 254, 255
Butler, Hugh, 117
Buxbaum, Friedrich, 160
Bylsma, Anner, 53, 54, 72, 291–5

Cambini, Giovanni Giuseppe, 49
Camden, Archie, 123
Cameron, Douglas, 128, 131, 132, 256
Caplet, André, 210
Caporali, Andrea, 32
Cardus, Sir Neville, 325
Carr, Colin, 327
Carrière, Eugene, 136
Caruso, Enrico, 148
Casadesus, Henri, 47
Casals, Pablo, 24, 91, 108, 111, 118, 128,
    130, 131, 133–142, 146, 147, 150, 151,
    155, 160, 163, 165, 173, 174, 175, 177,
    181, 183, 185–7, 192, 193, 202, 204, 212,
    213, 216, 217, 218, 221, 226, 230, 233,
    237, 238, 242, 245, 249, 252, 253, 264,
    266, 267, 270, 281, 291, 300, 302, 304,
    318, 322, 333n
Casella, Alfredo, 111
Casella, Carlo, 110
Casella, Cesare, 110
Casella, Cesare G., 110
Casella, Pietro, 110
Cassadó, Gaspar, 140, 174, 192, 193, 198,
    199, 248, 266, 300
Cassadó, Joaquin, 192
Cassidy, Claudia, 150
Castro, Fidel, 311
Castaldi, Alfonso, 178
Catalini, Angelica, 42
Catel, Charles-Simon, 43
Catterall, Arthur, 253, 255
Čermak, Johann, 96
Cervetto, Giacobo Basevi, 32, 33, 55, 57
Cervetto, James, 33, 38, 57, 58, 59
Chaliapin, Feodor, 173
Chang, Lynn, 319
Cherniavsky, Abraham, 94
Cherniavsky, Fyodor, 94, 332n
Cherniavsky, Mischel, 94, 128
Cherubini, Luigi, 42
Chevillard, Pierre Alexandre, 82
Chimay, Prince de, 44
Chopin, Frédéric, 46, 72, 292, 325
Chorchewski, 90
Chotzinoff, Samuel, 163, 164
Clapham, John, 101
Clarke, Rebecca, 201
Cleveland-Peck, Patricia, 208

Cliburn, Van, 308
Cluytens, André, 212
Coates, Albert, 154, 273
Cocteau, Jean, 220
Coëlho, 86
Cohen, Harriet, 198, 209, 253, 256
Cohen, Robert, 260, 325
Coin, Christophe, 291
Cole, Orlando, 153, 155, 157, 158, 313, 333n
Commissiona, Sergiu, 309
Conti, Prince de, 37
Coolidge, Elizabeth, 88, 145–6
Corelli, Arcangelo, 54, 59, 125
Corrette, Michel, 35, 40
Cortot, Alfred, 137, 183, 212, 216
Cossmann, Bernhard, 67, 69, 70, 71, 88, 105, 121, 124, 143
Costa, Sir Michael, 85
Costanzi, Giovanni Battista, 48
Couling, Vivian, 23
Cowen, F.H., 107
Cowling, Elizabeth, 175, 181, 203, 332n, 334n
Craxton, Harold, 235
Crepax, Gilberto, 183
Crickboom, Mathieu, 135
Cristiani, Lisa, 200
Crome, Robert, 58, 80
Crosdill, John, 39, 56–8, 99
Crowson, Lamar, 267
Croxford, Eileen, 261
Cummings, Douglas, 132
Cupis, Jean Baptiste, 34, 35, 37, 43
Curtis, Charles, 327

Dale, Caroline, 327
Dale, S.S., 117, 118, 154
Dall'Abaco, Evaristo, 32
Dall'Abaco, Joseph, 32
Dall'Oglio, Domenico, 32
Dall'Oglio, Giuseppe, 32
Dalrymple, Alison, 321
Damrosch, Walter, 147, 151
da Saram, Rohan, 327
Daubert, Hugo, 126
David, Ferdinand, 71, 91
Davidov, Karl, 61, 65, 70, 72, 80, 87, 91–3, 100, 102, 105, 116, 121, 122, 126, 146, 156, 160, 169, 210, 232, 233, 272
Davison, Walter, 258
Dawson-Lyell, Julian, 239
De'ak, Steven, 106–9, 156, 332n
Debussy, Claude, 170, 211, 215, 220, 225, 244, 254
Degas, Hilaire, 136
Delius, Frederick, 207–9
Del Mar, Norman, 131
Delsart, Jules, 47, 107, 126, 146, 216
Dempsey, Jack, 148, 150
Deutsch, 100
Dickson, Joan, 195, 261–3
Diem, Josef, 124
Dietzmann, Fritz, 297
Dinicu, Dimitrie, 178, 198

Dodd, Thomas, 25
Dohler, Theodore, 111
Dohnányi, Ernö, 106, 119, 166, 194, 227
Dolmetsch, Arnold, 59, 113
Dolmetsch, Hélène, 113
Dolmetsch, Mabel, 290
Dolmetsch, Rudolph, 290
Don Luis, Infante, 51–2
Dorati, Antal, 227–8, 323
Dotzauer, J.J.F., 65–9, 71, 74, 77, 99
Downes, Olin, 163, 164, 234, 271
Dragonetti, Domenico, 59, 125
Dreschler, Karl, 67–71
Dukas, Paul, 183
Duport, Jean Louis, 23, 24, 37–41, 43–4, 46, 56–8, 61–3, 66, 74, 99, 104, 179, 287, 288
Duport, Jean Pierre (l'ainé), 34, 37, 38, 39, 50, 61–2, 66
du Pré, Jacqueline, 25, 91, 260, 287, 307, 320–7
Dutilleux, Henri, 286
Dvořák, Antonin, 93, 100–1, 120, 126, 144, 171, 175, 198, 206, 216, 221, 228, 240, 247, 258–9, 270, 276, 283, 288, 304, 319

Eberle, Oscar, 87
Eddy, Timothy, 327
Edison, Thomas A., 144
Eisenberg, Maurice, 140, 150, 151, 175, 264
Elgar, Edward, 127, 131, 154, 155, 203, 208, 209, 212, 253, 267, 302, 308, 322–5
Enesco, Georges, 137, 146, 175, 183
Ericson, Raymond, 323
Ernst, Heinrich Wilhelm, 112
Espenhahn, Fritz, 69
Esterhazy, Prince, 98, 235
Evans, Warwick, 126, 256
Eveline, Beatrice, 126, 200

Fabbri, Umberto, 178
Fachiri, Adila, 266
Faes, Gustav, 146
Falla, Manuel de, 192
Fauré, Gabriel, 127, 211, 220, 292
Feder, Edgard, 177, 178
Feder, Jean, 178
Fer, Jambe de, 30
Fesch, William de, 78
Fétis, François, 44, 78
Feuermann, Emanuel, 24, 91, 118, 132, 140, 149, 150, 157, 160–8, 170, 175, 176, 181, 185, 186, 212, 220, 221, 226, 230, 232, 236, 238, 242, 244, 245, 252, 256, 258, 290, 306
Feuermann, Sophie, 165
Feuermann, Zigmund, 160, 161
Feuillard, Louis, 216
Fiala, Joseph, 96–8
Finch, Hilary, 335n
Finzi, Gerald, 264
Firpo, Luis, 148
Fischer, Edwin, 194
Fitzenhagen, Wilhelm, 72, 75, 76, 77, 93
Flachot, Reine, 250

Fleming, Amaryllis, 129, 141, 266–8
Fleming, Ian, 266
Fleming, Peter, 266
Flesch, Carl, 119, 162, 170, 175, 212–3
Földesy, Arnold, 109, 119
Fonteyn, Margot, 257
Font family, 51
Forster, Thérèse, 144
Forster, William, 25
Foster, Lawrence, 312, 315–7
Fournier, Pierre, 86, 140, 159, 175, 178, 214–6, 248–50, 261, 266, 285, 287, 320
Fradkin, Daniel, 272
Françaix, Jean, 220
Francheschini, Petronio, 30
Franchomme, Auguste, 40, 45–7, 124, 156
Franciscello *see* Alborea, Francesco
Franck, César, 47, 156, 325
Franco, General, 134, 138, 140
Franco-Mendes, Jacques, 82–3
Franco-Mendes, Joseph, 82
Frankl, Peter, 306–7
Frederick the Great, 31, 38, 52, 90
Friedrich, Wilhelm (Frederick William II), 38, 52
Friedrichs, 120
Fruh, Karl, 315
Fuchs, Carl, 71, 93, 121–4, 332n
Fuchs, Harry, 159
Fujiwara, Mari, 244, 250
Fulton, Marjorie, 312
Fürstenberg, Prince, 98
Furtwängler, Wilhelm, 116, 170, 192, 216, 226

Gabrielli, Domenico, 30
Gabrilovitch, Ossip, 234–5
Gagliano, Alexander, 87
Galamian, Ivan, 312
Galitzin, Prince Nikolay, 63
Galley, Jules, 47
Gallon, Jean, 217
Galvez, 135
Gand, Charles-François, 25, 47, 141
Garbousova, Raya, 140, 167, 176, 177, 232–6
García, José, 133–5, 147
Gardner, Mrs Jack, 141
Garrick, David, 32, 33, 56
Gasparo, 90
Gaviniès, Pierre, 50
Gavoty, Bernard, 332n, 333n
Geminiani, Francesco, 32
Gendron, Maurice, 72, 87, 141, 219–22
George IV, 57
Geringer, David, 272
Gevaert, François, 107, 134
Ginastera, Alberto, 270
Gingold, Josef, 230
Ginsburg, Lev, 101, 193, 204, 211, 215, 236, 238, 305, 332n–335n
Giuranna, Bruno, 197
Glazounov, Alexander, 148–9, 281
Glehn, Alfred von, 169

Gofriller, Matteo, 24, 124, 141, 287, 292, 320
Goldberg, Szymon, 162
Goltermann, Georg, 71, 118, 130, 172, 173, 252, 309
Goltermann, Julius, 67, 104, 105
Good, Margaret, 259
Goodwin, Amina, 126
Goossens, Eugene, 201, 207
Goren, Eli, 259
Goritsky, Johannes, 300
Gossec, François, 50
Grainger, Percy, 123
Granados, Enrique, 135, 254
Grancino, Giovanni, 24
Grassalkowitz, Prince, 98
Graupner, Gottlieb, 143
Greenhouse, Bernard, 110, 140, 156, 176, 185–8
Griesbach, Adolphus, 126
Griesbach, Henry, 57
Grieg, Edvard, 72, 145
Grinke, Frederick, 256, 257
Grossman, Walter, 189
Grubb, Suvi Raj, 324–5
Gruenberg, Erich, 131
Grümmer, Paul, 118–21, 290
Grünfeld, Heinrich, 100
Grützmacher, Friedrich, 69, 71–4, 76, 77, 91, 105, 113, 116, 118, 134, 161, 173, 175, 233
Grützmacher, Leopold, 72
Guadagnini, Giovanni Battista, 24
Guarneri del Gesù, Joseph, 25, 124
Guastafeste, Roberta, 306
Gubariov, 169
Guilet, Daniel, 188
Gulli, Franco, 197
Gutman, Natalia, 275–7

Habeneck, François, 46
Haimovitz, Matt, 327
Halíř, Karol, 106
Hallé, Charles (Karl) 46, 121–3
Hallet, Benjamin, 56
Halvorssen, 287
Hambourg, Boris, 95, 119, 128
Hambourg, Jan, 95
Hambourg, Mark, 95
Hambourg, Michael, 95
Hamme, Van, 86
Hancock, Captain, 305
Hancock, Mrs, 306
Handel, G.F., 143, 255
Hanslick, Eduard, 75, 105, 112, 332n
Hara, Chieko, 193
Harnoncourt, Niklaus, 290
Harrell, Lynn, 153, 158, 190, 287, 313–5, 333n
Harrell, Mack, 312
Harrison, Annie, 205–7
Harrison, Beatrice, 119, 126, 132, 203, 205–9, 334n
Harrison, May, 205–7
Harty, Hamilton, 127
Harvey, Keith, 132

Hauptmann, Moritz, 70, 91
Hausmann, Robert, 59, 74, 75, 152, 255
Haydn, Josef, 41, 48, 68, 73, 88, 98, 99, 107,
    109, 112, 117, 139, 143, 145, 160, 163,
    206, 211, 215, 219, 221, 233, 234, 253,
    254, 255, 257-8
Haydn, Michael, 98
Hayward, Marjorie, 201
Heberlein, Hermann, 77
Heermann, Hugo, 119
Hegar, Emil, 72, 77, 116
Hegar, Johannes, 119
Hegedus, Olga, 261
Hegenbarth, Frantisek, 100
Hegyesi, Louis, 124
Heifetz, Jascha, 148-50, 166, 226, 236, 304
Heinitz, Eva, 233
Hekking, André, 87, 157
Hekking, Anton, 214
Hekking, Charles, 87
Hekking, Gérard, 87, 211, 216, 217, 220
Hellmesberger, Joseph, 105
Henderson, Robert, 276, 279
Henze, Hans Werner, 265
Herbert, Victor, 143, 144, 148
Hermann, Friedrich, 86, 106
Herold, Jiří, 102
Herrmann, Emil, 89
Hess, Myra, 129, 146, 156, 253, 255
Heward, Leslie, 259
Hill, W. Henry, 47, 65, 80, 84, 91, 147, 198,
    202, 204, 331n
Hindemith, Paul, 88, 162, 171, 215, 231,
    238, 265, 293
Hirai, Kozaburo, 244
Hirai, Takeichiro, 244
Hirsch, Albert, 165
Hoecke, Johannes, 124
Hoffmann, Karl, 101
Hofmann, Josef, 157
Hollmann, Joseph, 81, 86, 225
Holst, Gustav, 202
Honegger, Arthur, 212
Hooton, Florence, 132, 256-8, 335n
Horowitz, Vladimir, 148, 170, 232, 235
Horszowski, Mieczyslaw, 229
Howell, Arthur, 125
Howell, Edward, 47, 107, 125-8
Hřimaly, Jan, 100
Hsu, John, 291
Hubay, Jenö, 106, 107, 227
Huberman, Bronislav, 120, 165, 192, 226,
    236
Huml, Václav, 178
Hunt, John, 253
Hüttner, Jan Nepomuk, 100

Ibert, Jacques, 212
Ideler, Pearl Sutherland, 203
Igloi, Thomas, 132, 327
Imai, Nobuko, 248, 308
Inbal, Eliahu, 307
Indy, Vincent d', 137, 146
Inoue, Yoritoyo, 244
Ippolitov-Ivanov, Mikhail, 204

Ireland, John, 202, 209, 253, 257
Ireland, Patrick, 259
Isserlis, Steven, 327
Istomin, Eugene, 140, 185, 191
Itzkoff, Seymour W., 166, 333n
Iwasaki, Ko, 244, 249, 251

Jacchini, Giuseppe, 30
Jacob, Gordon, 256-7
Jacobs, Edouard, 85, 88, 134, 153
Jacquard, Leon, 86
James, Ivor, 126, 128, 129, 252, 261, 264,
    266
Janigro, Antonio, 175, 179, 180, 183-4
Janson, Jean Baptiste, 34, 42
Joachim, Heinrich, 312
Joachim, Joseph, 70, 74, 75, 95, 112, 117,
    120, 126, 145, 152, 175, 254, 255, 276
John, Augustus, 204, 266-7
John, David, 266
Johnson, Bartholomew, 55-6
Johnson, Harriett, 270
Johnson, Lawrence B., 279
Jourdan-Morhange, Hélène, 210
Jullien, Louis Antoine, 84
Just, Helen, 129

Kabalevsky, Dimitry, 249
Kagan, Oleg, 276
Kahn, Albert E., 333n
Kahn, Eric Itor, 186
Kalbeck, Max, 75, 201
Kalianov, Stefan, 284
Kampen, Christopher van, 132
Kanno, Hirofumi, 244, 249, 250
Kapucinsky, Richard, 156
Karajan, Herbert von, 216, 288
Kashkashian, Kim, 319
Kates, Stephen, 147, 149, 150, 189, 190,
    303-6
Keller, Hans, 266
Kempf, Wilhelm, 216
Kennedy, Michael, 332n, 336n
Kenneson, Claude, 146
Kerpély, Jenö, 109
Kerrison, Jan, 123
Khachaturian, Aram, 139, 271
Kim, Earl, 318
Kim, Young Uck, 319
King, Terry, 327
Kinsky, Prince, 100
Kirchner, Leon, 318
Kirshbaum, Ralph, 306-8
Kitzinger, Fritz, 163, 165
Kleiber, Erich, 194
Klemperer, Otto, 226
Klengel, Julius, 77, 92, 116-8, 120, 122, 126,
    151, 155, 157, 160, 161, 167, 169, 170,
    177, 180, 204, 233, 242, 246, 252, 254,
    255, 258, 260, 269, 270, 275
Klingenberg, Johann, 72, 74
Klingler, Karl, 152
Knushevitzky, Sviatoslav, 77, 272
Kochanski, Paul, 201
Kodály, Zoltán, 106, 202, 209, 227, 229, 238

Kogan, Richard, 319
Kohler, Louis, 87
Konoe, Prince, 241–2
Kosler, Zdenek, 247
Kosolupova, Galina, 272, 276
Kosolupov, Simeon, 272, 273, 282
Koussevitzky, Serge, 171, 234, 235, 271
Kraft, Anton, 98, 99
Kraft, Nicolaus, 99, 105
Krasnapolsky, Yuri, 316
Kreisler, Fritz, 150, 165, 189, 207
Kreisler, Harriet, 207
Kremer, Gidon, 279, 319
Křenek, Ernst, 270
Kreutzer, Rudolphe, 182, 255
Kriegk, J.J., 66
Krips, Josef, 189
Krosnick, Joel, 182, 333n
Kubatsky, Victor, 77
Kubelik, Jan, 120
Kubelik, Rafael, 216
Kuhlenkampff, Georg, 194
Kühne, Tobias, 301
Kuijken, Wieland, 23
Kummer, Friedrich, 65, 67, 68, 70, 77, 101,
    104, 111, 124
Kummer, Ernst, 67
Kummer, Max, 67
Kündinger, Kanut, 118
Kurtz, Edmund, 65, 75, 118, 177, 204, 269,
    270, 271

Lachner, Ferdinand, 101
Lahoussaye, Pierre, 37
Lalo, Edouard, 122, 136, 189, 204, 215, 217,
    237
Lamarre, Jacques, 43–4, 59
Lamoureux, Charles, 136
Lana, Libero, 197
Landowska, Wanda, 121
Lanzetti, Salvatore, 32
Laub, Ferdinand, 70
Lebell, Ludwig, 77, 109
Lee, Sebastian, 69
Lehnsen, Eva, 166, 167
Leighton, Kenneth, 257
Leinsdorf, Erich, 305
Léonard, Hubert, 79
Leopold-Loeb, Jules, 210, 212
Levasseur, Jean Henri, 37, 43, 45, 46
Levine, James, 313
Lewis, Henry, 274
Liberace, 150
Libotton, Gustav, 85, 124–5
Lichnowski, Prince, 98
Lidka, Maria, 264
Lindley, Robert, 57, 59, 60, 99, 125, 130
Lindner, August, 69
Linigke, Johann, 31
Lipatti, Dinu, 183, 220
Lipinsky, Karol, 68
Liszt, Franz, 70, 76, 84, 100, 109, 111
Litolff, Henry, 74
Lloyd Webber, Julian, 132, 327
Lobkowitz, Prince, 99

Locatelli, Pietro, 88, 113
Long, Kathleen, 201
Lott, John, F., 25
Loveridge, Iris, 257–8
Lovett, Martin, 47, 129
Lucas, Charles, 125
Lucca, Pauline, 70
Lukács, Mici, 109
Lully, Jean-Baptiste, 30, 97
Lupot, Nicolas, 25, 299
Lupu, Radu, 279
Lush, Ernest, 264, 307
Lutoslawski, Witold, 277, 286, 298

Ma, Yo Yo, 153, 190. 287, 312, 317–20
Maas, Robert, 88–9
Maazel, Lorin, 318
Machula, Tibor de, 156
Maes, 46
Maggini, Giovanni, 23, 24
Mahalek, Dezso, 237
Mahler, Gustav, 146, 175
Mainardi, Enrico, 119, 192–6, 198, 233, 262,
    300
Maisky, Mischa, 275, 277–80
Maletić, Ana, 178
Manfredi, Filippo, 50–1
Mangeot, André, 267
Mangot, Jean, 220
Manley, Dorothy, 256
Manns, August, 136
Mara, Ignaz, 96
Mara, John Baptist, 97
Marcello, Benedetto, 31, 113
March, Dionisio, 192
Maréchal, Maurice, 210–1, 297, 311
Marguerie, Lyndon de L., 202
Markevitch, Dimitry, 290
Maria Christina, Queen, 136
Markson, Richard, 215, 218, 327
Marteau, Franz, 61
Marteau, Henri, 119
Martin, Frank, 215
Martin, David, 256, 258
Martinon, Jean, 215
Martinů, Bohuslav, 183, 215, 234
Mas, 82
Mason, Colin, 323
Massau, Alfred, 88
Mattei, 99
Matz, Rudolf, 178–180, 183
Maurin, Jean Pierre, 82, 84
May, Marius, 327
Mayes, Samuel, 156
Mayuzumi, Toshiró, 249
Max Emanuel, Elector, 32
Max Joseph, Elector, 98
McArdell, James, 56
Mehta, Zubin, 278, 318, 325
Meints, Catharina, 291
Melville, Audrey, 240
Mendelssohn, Felix, 53, 70, 72, 91, 111, 116,
    134, 256, 258
Mendelssohn, Giulietta von, 192
Mendelssohn, Robert von, 114

Mengelberg, Willem, 87, 171
Menter, Sophie, 106
Menuhin, Hepzibah, 221
Menuhin, Yehudi, 221–2, 256, 260, 323
Merighi, Vincenzo, 110, 111
Merk, Joseph, 82, 105
Merlen, 83
Michalak, Thomas, 274
Milhaud, Darius, 171, 270–1
Miller, Frank, 156, 159, 189
Milne, Hamish, 267
Milstein, Nathan, 170, 232, 236
Miniar, Konstantin, 232
Miremont, Claude-Augustin, 25
Mitropoulos, Dimitri, 159
Monasterio, Jesus de, 134
Moncrieff, Margaret, 215
Montagnana, Domenico, 24, 158, 202, 204, 278, 305, 307, 320
Montañez, Martita, 140, 147
Monteux, Pierre, 201, 260
Montigny, Charles, 83
Moór, Emanuel, 204
Moore, Gerald, 151, 207, 264, 267, 316, 336n
Moreau, Léon, 137
Morini, Erica, 236
Morrison, Angus, 256
Morphy, Count de, 134, 136
Moscheles, Ignaz, 91, 111
Mossel, Isaac, 87
Mozart, W.A., 38, 47, 54, 62, 68, 98, 217, 221, 261, 265
Mukle, May, 201–3
Müller, Hippolyt, 124
Müller, Theodore, 70, 74, 76
Müller, Wilhelm, 74
Munch, Charles, 171, 212
Munck, Camille De, 84
Munck, François De, 83–4
Munck, Joseph Ernest De, 44, 81, 84
Musinian, Nina, 274

Nakipbekova, Alfia, 275, 284
Napier-Smith, Audrey, 336n
Nardini, Pietro, 50
Navarra, André, 212–3, 291, 300–1
Nedbal, Oskar, 101
Nejedlý Zedeněk, 101
Nelsov, Gregor, 236
Nelsova, Zara, 128, 232, 236–40, 334n
Neruda, Franz, 96
Neruda, Johann, 96
Neruda, Wilhelmina (Lady Hallé), 96, 106, 128
Nevada, Emma, 137
Neveu, Ginette, 183, 220
Neveu, Jean, 220
Newman, Ernest, 154
Nicolini, 32
Nikisch, Artur, 118, 175, 204, 210
Noé, Heinrich, 206
Nolck, 297
Norblin, Louis, Pierre, 42–3, 45–6, 65, 69, 82

Norman, Barak, 290
North, Lord Francis, 55
Nupen, Christopher, 326

Oblach, Camillo, 196
Oborin, Lev, 272
Odero, Stephane, 220
Offenbach, Jacques, 47
Ohmura, Uhichi, 245
Oistrakh, David, 193, 272, 275, 285
Onnou, Alphonse, 88, 89
Orleans, Duke of, 31
Ormandy, Eugene, 140, 166, 191, 227
Osborn, Franz, 162
Ould, Kate, 126
Osawa, Seiji, 244, 248, 318

Paderewski, Jan, 102
Paganini, Niccolò, 25, 64, 79, 89, 110, 182, 189, 213
Palm, Siegfried, 299–300
Paquin, 206
Parikian, Manoug, 267
Parisot, Aldo, 306
Parnas, Leslie, 302
Parry, Hubert, 127
Parsons, Geoffrey, 267
Pasqualini, 32
Patti, Carlotta, 84, 126
Pauer, Max, 259
Pauk, Gyorgy, 227, 306–8
Pavlova, Anna, 131, 270
Pawle, Mr, 147
Pears, Peter, 220–21
Peccatte, Dominique, 306
Pelicho, Clementina, 51
Penderecki, Krzyztof, 286
Peresson, Sergio, 25, 288, 324
Pergamenschikov, Boris, 272
Perkins, Louise, 210
Perlman, Itzhak, 314–5
Persinger, Louis, 146
Peters, C.F., 43
Petrik, E. Viceslaus, 96
Pettit, Walter, 126
Pezze, Alexander, 110, 126, 201
Philidor, François, 61
Phillips, Daniel, 319
Phillips, Harvey, 129, 255
Phillips, Lilly, 132
Piatigorsky, Gregor, 24, 118, 150, 152, 158, 169, 170–5, 181, 199, 226, 235, 238, 242, 245, 269, 278, 279, 297–8, 302–5, 308–11, 332n, 333n
Piatti, Alfredo, 24, 31, 74, 96, 105, 110–15, 119, 125–7, 134, 153, 156, 173, 233, 258, 309, 322
Piatti, Antonio, 111
Piatti-Lochis, Rosa, 114
Pierné, Gabriel, 212
Pincherle, Marc, 211
Planken, van der, 78
Platel, Nicolas Joseph, 44, 45, 78, 80, 82–4
Platteau, Gabrielle, 200
Playford, John, 59
Pleeth, Anthony, 260, 290, 295

Pleeth, William, 118, 258–60, 292, 295, 316, 321–23, 325, 331n
Pleyel, Ignaz, 52, 53
Pochon, Alfred, 87
Polliari, Cicio, 90
Pons, Lily, 149
Popper, David, 47, 71, 77, 94, 104–9, 126, 156, 160, 182, 223, 233, 273, 275, 297, 303
Porpora, Nicola, 113
Porreti, Domingo, 52
Porreti, Maria, 52
Poulenc, Francis, 215, 220
Powell, Maud, 201
Prell, August, 65, 69, 71
Press, Adolf, 65
Pressenda, Francesco, 24–5, 292
Pressler, Menahem, 188
Previn, André, 318
Prihóda, Vasá, 120
Primrose, William, 166, 214, 304
Probst, H.A., 271
Prochaska, Josepha, 98
Prokofiev, Sergei, 139, 171, 215, 221, 234, 235, 244, 276, 286, 326
Puccini, Giacomo, 148
Pyron, Nona, 26

Quantz, Johann, 31
Quarenghi, Guglielmo, 110
Quast, Daniel, 119
Queipo de Llano, General, 138

Rachmaninov, Sergei, 235, 238
Raff, Joachim, 105
Rambeaux, Claude-Victor, 47
Rasoumovsky, Count, 62, 235
Ravel, Maurice, 137, 146, 148, 192, 202, 210, 293
Rebner, Wolfgang, 165
Reger, Max, 117, 120–1, 258
Reicha, Anton, 97
Reicha, Joseph, 62, 97
Reifenberg, Eva, 164
Reiner, Fritz, 106, 228–9
Reiss, Thelma, 129, 252–3, 255
Rejto, Gabor, 223, 225
Rejto, Peter, 327
Rensberg, J., 77
Respighi, Ottorino, 194
Ricci, George, 176
Richardson, Linda, 336n
Richter, Hans, 122
Richter, Sviatoslav, 277, 285
Rickelman, Boris, 128
Riedel, 31, 90
Riedel, Robert, 121
Ries, Franz, 62
Rimsky-Korsakov, Nikolay, 208–9
Rinke, Hanno, 335n
Robbins, Channing, 153
Roberton, Sir Hugh, 237
Roberts, Bernard, 267
Robeson, Paul, 253
Robinson, Sharon, 327

Rocca, Giuseppe Antonio, 24, 25, 148
Rochlitz, Johann, 62
Rode, Pierre, 44
Rodin, François, 219
Rodzinski, Artur, 189, 271
Roemaet-Rosanoff, Marie, 145–7, 304
Rogeri, Pietro Giacomo, 24, 114
Rolland, Romain, 137
Rolland, Sophie, 260, 327
Rolston, Shauna, 327
Romberg, Andreas, 61–2, 65
Romberg, Cyprian, 65
Romberg, Bernhard, 45, 59, 61–7, 69, 93, 104, 121, 126, 156
Rosanoff, Lieff, 147
Rose, Leonard, 153, 159, 185, 189–91, 249, 304, 312–3, 317
Rosen, Marcy, 158, 327
Rosen, Nathaniel, 172–3, 308–10
Rosenstock, Joseph, 242
Rossini, Gioacchino, 182
Rostropovich, Leopold, 232, 281
Rostropovich, Mstislav, 40, 141, 171, 221, 248, 272, 275–6, 278, 281–9, 301, 304–5, 317–8, 322
Rothschild, Germaine de, 52–3, 331n
Routh, Francis, 264
Rovatti, Luigi, 148, 150
Rovelli, Giuseppe, 110
Rubbra, Edmund, 259, 262
Rubini, Giovanni, 83
Rubinstein, Anton, 117
Rubinstein, Arthur, 148, 166, 201, 317
Rubio, Augustin, 201
Ruggieri family, 24, 141
Rupp, Franz, 165
Ruttinger, 66
Rynar, Dr Dago, 120, 331n

Sabbatier, 82
Safonov, Vassilij, 92, 117
Saidenberg, Daniel, 156–7
Saint-Saëns, Camille, 84, 86, 127, 131, 136–7, 148, 194, 204–5, 239, 246, 270, 282
Saito, Hideo, 241–50
Salmon, Joseph, 136, 183
Salmond, Felix, 126, 153–8, 185–6, 189, 201, 208, 257
Salmond, Norman, 153
Salò, Gasparo da (Bertolotti), 23
Salzedo, Carlos, 146
Sammartini, Giovanni, 254
Sammons, Albert, 154, 201, 253
Sapozhnikov, Roman, 276
Sarasate, Pablo, 107, 146
Sargent, Sir Malcolm, 237, 265, 298, 151, 197
Saunders, William, 55
Sauret, Emil, 106, 109
Scarlatti, Alessandro, 32
Schertel, Fritz, 258
Schiff, Heinrich, 301
Schiffer, Adolf, 109, 223, 225, 227
Schmeling, Gertrude Elisabeth, 97

Schlick, Johann, 61
Schmidt, Heinrich, 91
Schmidt, Jindřich, 100
Schmitt, Florent, 212
Schnabel, Artur, 119, 146, 162, 170, 214, 216, 317
Schneider, Alexander, 140, 176
Schneider, Friedrich, 68
Schneider, Mischa, 159, 176
Schneiderhan, Wolfgang, 194
Schoenberg, Arnold, 137, 300
Schoenfeld, Alice, 152
Schoenfeld, Eleanore, 151-2, 308
Scholz, Janos, 174, 223-5, 317
Schonberg, Harold C., 229, 314
Schubert, Franz, 137, 156, 166, 214, 224, 231, 244, 293
Schuberth, Gottlob, 69
Schuberth, Karl, 67, 69-70, 91
Schumann, Clara, 83, 85, 121-2, 153
Schumann, Robert, 92, 109-10, 120, 134, 139-40, 145, 191, 215, 255, 258-9, 266, 317
Schuppanzigh, Ignaz, 98
Schuster, Joseph, 306
Schwarz, Rudolf, 131
Schwarzkopf, Elisabeth, 253
Scott, Cyril, 206
Segovia, Andrés, 148
Seidl, Anton, 144
Seidler, Karl August, 99
Seifriz, Max, 144
Selo, Nicholas, 294
Serato, Francesco, 196
Serkin, Rudolf, 140
Serov, Alexander, 92
Servais, Adrien François, 40, 44, 59, 61, 65, 78-86, 90, 96, 124, 135, 200
Servais, Joseph, 40, 81
Ševčik, Otakar, 175, 178, 213, 215
Shafran, Daniel, 249-50, 273, 275, 302
Shapiro, Harvey, 249
Shaw, George Bernard, 86, 107, 332n
Shaw, Robert, 313
Sheremetev, Count, 272
Shostakovich, Dimitri, 139, 238, 244, 272, 282-3, 286, 288, 305
Shrinsky, Sergei, 271
Shrinsky, Vasily, 272
Shtrimer, Aleksander, 273
Shulman, Alan, 156, 158, 159
Shumsky, Oscar, 158, 188
Shuttleworth, Anna, 261
Siloti, Alexander, 123, 137
Silva, Luigi, 178, 180-3
Silvestre, Pierre, 25
Simpson, Christopher, 29
Simpson, Derek, 132
Simonetti, Achille, 126
Singer, Edmund, 70
Siprutini, 57
Sirmen, Maddalena Lombardini, 37
Smetana, Bedřich, 100
Solomon, 235
Solti, Georg, 227

Sons, Maurice, 154
Soyer, David, 176
Speelman, 123
Spohr, Ludwig, 44, 53, 62, 64, 66, 200
Squire, W.H., 127
Stainer, Jacob, 25
Stanfield, Milly, 128, 130, 174, 204, 237, 274, 284
Stanlein, Count, 110
Starcke, Herman, 105
Starker, Janos, 109, 223, 227-31, 246-7, 249
Steinberg, William, 278
Stern, Isaac, 140, 150, 158, 185, 189, 190-1
Stern, Leo, 93, 101, 112, 126, 127
Stiastny, Bernard, 97, 99-100
Stiastny, Jan, 97, 99
Stockhausen, Karlheinz, 300
Stokowski, Leopold, 151, 171, 211, 224
Storioni, Lorenzo, 288
Stradivari, Antonio, 24, 25, 39, 46, 47, 65, 75, 110, 114, 120, 141, 147, 157, 173, 193, 198, 200, 204, 240, 271, 272, 287, 288, 304, 307, 320, 324
Straeten, Edmund Van der, 59, 64, 68, 85, 100, 109, 112-3, 118, 124, 200, 331-2, 334n
Strange, David, 132
Stransky, Josef, 207
Straus, Ludwig, 112
Strauss, Richard, 72, 100, 120, 122, 124, 145, 148, 175, 210, 217, 219, 248, 313
Stravinsky, Igor, 183, 287
Stuck, Johann Baptist, 31
Stutschewsky, Joachim, 118
Suggia, Guilhermina, 118, 140, 155, 203-5, 257, 266
Suk, Josef, 101-2
Sulzer, Herbert, 94
Susskind, Walter, 221
Svendsen, Johann, 77
Svetlanov, Yevgeny, 276
Svilokos, Pablo, 180
Swert, Jules De, 81, 84
Szaboky, Marta, 225
Szell, Georg, 236, 270, 313, 314
Szigeti, Josef, 140, 150, 192, 214, 224, 236, 334n

Tartini, Giuseppe, 31, 37-8, 48, 54, 213
Taube, Michael, 233
Tchaikovsky, Peter Ilyich, 76-7, 92-4, 122, 206, 232-3, 240, 244, 248, 250, 272-3, 276, 278, 292, 302, 309-10
Tcherepnin, Alexander, 121
Tecchler, David, 25
Teller, Frederick, 225
Temianka, Henri, 89, 172, 328
Tennstedt, Klaus, 231
Tertis, Lionel, 130, 201, 209, 322
Thibaud, Jacques, 137, 183, 201, 212, 216
Thibout, Jacques-Pierre, 83
Tillière, Joseph, 34-5
Tippett, Sir Michael, 308
Tkalčić, Juro, 178
Tobel, Rudolf Van, 300

Tobias, Paul, 327
Tononi, Carlo-Antonio, 141, 198
Tortelier, Paul, 128, 132, 140, 200, 214,
216–7, 322, 326, 334n
Toscanini, Arturo, 147–9, 156, 159, 164,
189, 217, 226, 236, 270
Touche, Francis, 216
Tourte, François, 26–7, 65, 271, 306
Tovey, Donald, 261
Tsutsumi, Tsuyoshi, 244–5, 247–8
Tziganov, Dimitri, 272

Uhlenfeld, Count, 32
Uhlmann, Bernard, 105

Valentini, Giuseppe, 119, 163
Vandini, Antonio, 31
Vanucci, Abbé, 48
Vaslin, 42, 47, 82
Vatelot, Etienne, 288
Vaughan Williams, Ralph, 202
Vecsey, Franz von, 120
Végh, Sándor, 300
Veracini, Antonio, 113
Verdi, Giuseppe, 113
Vernier, David, 250
Vertova, Count of Bergamo, 111
Vidal, Louis, 59
Vieuxtemps, Henri, 79, 84, 107
Viotti, Giovanni Battista, 39, 45, 61, 64, 213
Vishnevskaya, Galina, 283
Vitali, Giovanni Battista, 30
Vito, Gioconda de, 197
Vivaldi, Antonio, 31
Vočadlo, Bernard, 102–3
Voigt, Karl Ludwig, 67
Volkmann, Robert, 104
Vosgerohian, Luise, 318
Vuillaume, Jean-Baptiste, 25, 80, 110, 114

Wagner, Richard, 70, 85, 100, 104, 109
Walenn, Herbert, 94–5, 119, 126, 128,
130–1, 140, 237, 252, 258
Walewska, Christine, 150, 211, 310–1
Wallenstein, Alfred, 157
Wallfisch, Peter, 267
Wallfisch, Raphael, 77, 327
Walter, Anton, 160
Walter, Bruno, 163, 217, 224
Walton, William, 171, 298, 308

Warlock, Peter, 207
Warren, Eleanor, 307
Wasielewski, Joseph, 55, 69–70, 115, 331n,
332n
Webern, Anton, 300
Weber, Carl Maria von, 292
Webster, Daniel, 231, 310
Weigl, Josef, 105
Weiner, Leo, 227, 270
Weingartner, Felix, 160, 192, 210, 253
Weiss, Franz, 98
Weissman, Adolf, 270
Welsh, Moray, 284, 327, 335n
Wenzinger, August, 290
Werner, Joseph, 97–8
Whitehead, James, 129
Whitehouse, William, 113–4, 126, 128–9,
153, 156, 201
Wielhorsky, Count Mathieu, 63, 65, 90–1
Wieniawski, Henryk, 79, 92, 112, 163
Wierzbilowicz, Alexander, 93–4, 272, 281
Wihan, Hanus, 93, 100–1, 126–7
Willeke, Willem, 145–6
Withers, Herbert, 119, 126
Wolf-Ferrari, Ermanno, 121
Wolf, Albert, 260
Wolfstahl, Joseph, 162
Wood, Sir Henry, 131, 162, 192, 194,
205–6, 253, 256
Woolhouse, Edmund, 130
Wordsworth, William, 336n

Yamazaki, Nobuko, 244, 250
Yampolsky, 169
Yasuda, Kenichiro, 244, 248, 250–1
Yasunaga, Toru, 248
Young, Phyllis, 146
Youssopov, Count, 272
Youssopova, Princess, 80
Ysaÿe, Eugene, 95, 137

Zambelli, Vanna, 25
Zander, Benjamin, 317, 320
Zander, Patricia, 317
Zanetti, Gaetano, 111
Zecchi, Carlo, 194, 199
Zelenka, Ladislav, 102–3
Zerbini, 112
Zerrahn, Carl, 143
Zimbalist, Efrem, 171
Zukerman, Pinchas, 324